TROLLEYS AND SQUIBS

A GOLFER'S GUIDE TO IRISH LINKS

LOUISE AND RICK MIRACLE

Pomegranate

SAN FRANCISCO

To Sis and Stan, who sparked our journey; to Debbie, George, and Tova,
who have launched their own; and to wane Connor.

Published by Pomegranate Communications, Inc.
Box 6099, Rohnert Park, California 94927
800-227-1428; www.pomegranate.com

Pomegranate Europe Ltd.
Fullbridge House, Fullbridge
Maldon, Essex CM9 4LE, England

Caveat: All materials offered within this book are presented
as accurately and fairly as possible. Because prices and conditions are subject to change, the authors and publisher
encourage readers to consult up-to-date information
sources regarding airlines, golf courses, lodging accommodations, and rental and travel agencies prior to arranging
their trip. Any perceived personal or organizational affront
is unintentional. Neither the authors nor the publisher
accept responsibility for any inconsistencies, omissions, or
errors that may result in inconvenience, injury, or loss by
users of the information or advice in this book.

Library of Congress Cataloging-in-Publication Data

Miracle, Louise, 1947–
    Trolleys and squibs : a golfer's guide to Irish links /
Louise and Rick Miracle.
        p. cm.
    Includes index.
    ISBN 0-7649-1336-0 (pbk.)
    1. Golf—Ireland. 2. Golf courses—Ireland—Directories.
3. Golf courses—Ireland—Guidebooks. 4. Ireland—
Guidebooks. I. Miracle, Rick, 1948– II. Title.

GV985.I7 M57 2000
796.352'06'8415—dc21
                                                00-028291

Pomegranate Catalog No. A545

Cover and interior design by Lynn Bell,
    Monroe Street Studios, Santa Rosa, California
Golf course illustrations by Gene Harrawood

Printed in China

09 08 07 06 05 04 03 02 01 00
10 9 8 7 6 5 4 3 2 1

Table of Contents

Map of Ireland

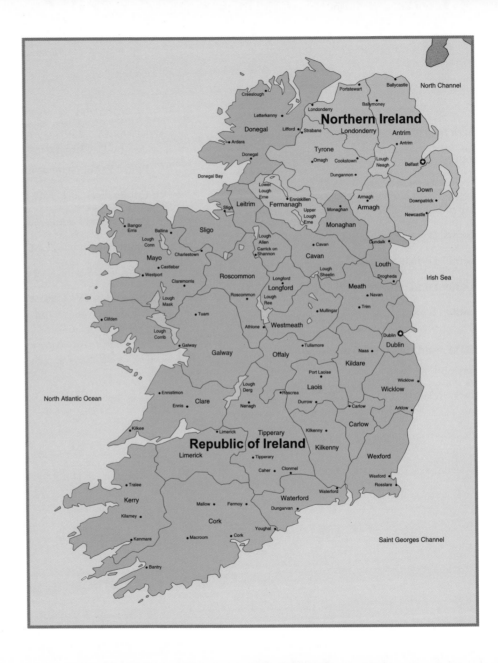

Acknowledgments

We have completed our book with a great deal of help from friends, from others who have become friends, and from strangers whom we fondly remember. Before we left for Ireland, a stranger came into our lives and showed us the full generosity of the human spirit. Marlene Emory shared with us a love of all things Irish and contributed more to the development of this book than can ever be told. We will forever remember her enthusiasm for our project and her sincere generosity.

While in Ireland, we were often privileged to see the Irish spirit at work through the friendliness and helpfulness of its people. We found, almost without exception, the staff at all of the courses we visited to be gracious ambassadors for their clubs and the Irish culture. In particular, the staff at Lahinch Golf Club—including Mike, Robert, John, Paul, and, of course, Alan—was a fantastic group of people. John Byrne, Irish-American owner of Emerald Isle Golf Tours, was another incredibly helpful stranger who became a fast friend.

And Pat Ruddy, who only knows friends, invited us into his world of golf and has been an inspiration henceforth.

Upon our return to the States, we continued to receive abundant help from a host of people. These included Mr. Peter Rolph of the Royal County Down Golf Club and Professor George Sevastopulo of Trinity College, Dublin. Both of these kind and professional gentlemen pulled through for us in a pinch. We also thank Dr. Gary Lane of Indiana University. Barbara Brown, Louise's mother, read, edited, and offered sage comments. Tova Miracle, Rick's daughter, helped with some of the tedious proofing. Gene Harrawood provided his expertise and creative suggestions for the graphic layouts and other questions that cropped up.

To Jill, Molly, and Leslie we owe great thanks, and to Dave King, our fond appreciation. And final thanks go to a group of Shark men who have befriended and continue to counsel Rick. Indeed, a project like this lets us know how truly good life is and what a treat it is to be here.

Welcome to Irish Golf

BY JOE B. CARR

In the annals of Irish and European golf, few names are more renowned or beloved than that of Mr. Joe B. Carr. The son of Portmarnock Golf Club's steward, Joe won four Irish Amateur Open titles (1946, 1950, 1954, 1956), three British Amateur titles (1953, 1958, 1960), and six Irish Amateur Close titles (1954, 1957, 1963, 1964, 1965, 1967). He also represented Ireland in ten Walker Cup matches and was captain of the Royal and Ancient Golf Club of St. Andrews. More recently, Mr. Carr has been intimately involved in the design of one of Ireland's newest premier golf clubs, Old Head Golf Links at Kinsale.

Throughout these many years, I have been to many countries, playing in Walker Cup matches and in Eisenhower, Irish, and European International events. In fact; I have begun to feel as though I have two passports. One gives me entrance into another country itself, and the other gives me the privilege of entering the homes and hearts of the many people who play this great game of golf. Golf has many wonderful qualities, but the thing that makes it most special to me is the friendships made while playing and competing. In my experience, these friendships tend to last a lifetime.

Some people are born with a "silver spoon" in their mouth. I can say I was born with a golf club in my hand. My mother and father were managers of Portmarnock Golf Club from 1922, the year I was born, to 1939, the year my father died. You can well imagine why golf is in my blood and the spirit of the game in my heart. I have been fortunate to receive many honors through playing this great game. These have included the Bob Jones Award, the Walter

Hagan Award, the Hall of Fame, the Golden Tee Award, the Golf Writers Trophy, and an honorary Doctorate of Law from Trinity College, Dublin. I would say the greatest honor both to Ireland and to me personally was the captaincy of the Royal and Ancient Golf Club of St. Andrews. This wonderful honor gave me the opportunity to travel the world and renew friendships with people I have played against.

It was during my captaincy that one of those funny incidents one has over a lifetime occurred. I was asked to be an observer for the leaders in the last pairing of the 1991 U.S. Open at Pebble Beach. Ian Woosnam and Gill Morgan were on the tee, along with what seemed to be ten thousand spectators. The players had been introduced with much fanfare, and eventually the introduction got around to me. Over the intercom, the announcer stated, "We have as an observer for this pairing Mr. J. B. Carr, Captain of the Royal and Ancient Golf Club of St. Andrews, Scotland. Mr. Carr is from Dublin, England." Peter Alliss, who was announcing for television coverage and who is always quick on the ball, immediately understood the announcer's gaffe and added, "Wars have been started for less!" Well, maybe not, but I along with a few others got quite a laugh to start that splendid day.

Ireland, like Scotland, is famous for its links golf courses. The definition for *links,* as I know it, is "a meeting of sea and sand." Indeed, we in Ireland are privileged to have some of the best links in the world. The introduction of golf to Ireland came about in 1606, when the sport was imported from Scotland by a Scottish adventurer who had come to Ulster. To the best of my knowledge, the first course in Ireland was laid out at the Curragh. At that time, the Curragh was an army base that housed some regiments from Scotland. Those Scottish lads must have grown homesick for the game and built a course right on the base. To this day, the course at the Curragh awaits the player hungry for a game.

During more recent times, golf has been growing at an extraordinary rate in my country. In 1985, for example, 247 golf clubs were affiliated with the Golfing Union of Ireland. In 1999, there were 384 affiliates. Over the past few years, I have been involved in the design of what must be one of the most spectacular pieces of real estate ever a golf course was built on, the Old Head at Kinsale. One of the loveliest remarks I ever heard was "If God were going to play golf, he would definitely pick the Old Head of Kinsale as his home course." I must say I tend to agree. Indeed, I invite each of you to pack your bags and come visit us at Old Head Golf Links. Rick and Louise, the authors of this fine guide to Irish golf, came to Old Head and told me it was one of the great highlights of their time here in Ireland. I have to believe them, because they are featuring a photograph of Old Head on the cover of this book.

In closing, I am delighted to share these few words and remembrances with you. As an Irish golfer, I welcome you to Ireland and hope you have many memorable rounds on my country's wonderful links.

Introduction

The mystery of golf and our reasons for playing it are as elusive as the mastery we seek. If you have picked up this book, chances are you are a golfer intrigued by the game and the passion it brings to your life, and you are thinking about taking your game to the cradling countries of its birth. You have played all the local clubs and may even have taken your game to some of the extraordinary courses on your home soil. Now you are looking for some big magic; you are looking to play some dreams. Every golfer fantasizes about St. Andrews, Troon, and Turnberry, to name a few. But there is a growing awareness that a whole wonderland of golf exists apart from the courses of Scotland—and that wonderland is Ireland.

The idea for *Trolleys and Squibs: A Golfer's Guide to Irish Links* came to us when we were planning for a 9-month sabbatical to Ireland. We thought we were fully prepared for the trip—we had a detailed road map, two guides to Irish golf courses, and a place to stay. As it turned out, no maps convey the reality of Irish roads, and the golf books offered anecdotal entertainment but no hard-core information for the serious golfer. We quickly realized the need for a clear, concise, truly helpful guide to finding and playing the golf courses of Ireland and to finding places to eat and sleep.

Mapping the Irish road system is beyond mere mortals, but a straightforward and easy-to-use golf guide is now a reality. *Trolleys and Squibs* is a practical and comprehensive guide to all the golf courses in Ireland, as compiled by a 3-handicap golfer and his caddy/psychologist wife.

Over the last decade or so, golf has started to boom in Ireland. Some of the island's courses, such as Lahinch, Ballybunion, Portmarnock, and the Royal County Down, rival the finest courses anywhere. The best players—including Greg Norman, Nick Faldo, Tom Watson, and Jack Nicklaus—have played these great venues. As the old courses, both links and parkland, continue to offer their timeless splendor, equally beautiful new courses are springing up all over Ireland. And while most of the fantasy courses in the United States are often unavailable to the public, all of the really great Irish courses are open to you and await your pleasure.

Playing golf in Ireland lets you touch the essence of your game. You will awaken to or rediscover some of the reasons why you started to play in the first place. Carts, for example, are practically nonexistent, as are those infernal cart paths that deface your ball and send it careening another 30 yards in the wrong direction. The Irish play in all sorts of weather, and they play quickly, the way golf was meant to be played. You will, too, and you might remember when you played that way as a kid. Golf in Ireland is magical, and what you will find within these pages is meant to help you unlock your dreams.

We wrote *Trolleys and Squibs* to be your guide, your personal travel planner as you put together that Perfect Golfing Trip to Ireland. We organized it to be as clear and readable as possible, so that you can literally sit in your living room and plan a logical itinerary and sequence of courses, along with places to stay and eat. In case you would like an already-planned itinerary, we include several recommendations. You will find, for example, itineraries for 1- to 3-week trips, trips in selected geographical areas, and "theme" trips. The latter include such themes as links courses, fancy 4-star accommodations, and "Irish Experiences." Contact information is included for each course, hotel, guesthouse, and bed-and-breakfast, so that you can book your tee times and make lodging reservations before you leave home. Using our guide, you can plan where you will play during the day and stay for the night, from the time you land in Ireland until you depart. Or, if you are the more spontaneous type,

you can just arrive and put your trip together with *Trolleys and Squibs* and a good road atlas at hand.

Ireland is blessed with more than 350 links and parkland golf courses. It is interesting to note that about 3 percent of the world's courses are links courses, and of those, roughly two-thirds are in Ireland and the British Isles. This probably explains why most visitors head directly for the links courses upon arrival, and there is little fault to be found in that strategy. Visitors who limit themselves to these courses, though, will miss some extraordinary parkland golf.

In this guide, we include courses throughout both the Republic of Ireland and Northern Ireland. You may already be aware that these are two different countries (or were at the time of writing). In some instances, we refer directly to either one. If we refer just to "Ireland," we are talking about some feature that is characteristic of the whole of Ireland, regardless of state. You will need to find good road maps of Ireland (both the Republic and Northern Ireland) to locate the courses reviewed in this guide. As further explained in chapter 1, distances are deceptive in Ireland. Considerably more travel time is needed than you would expect between destinations because of the rural nature of the road system.

To help you make the tough decisions about which courses to visit, we break the 291 courses reviewed in this book into two lists: the Trolleys List of 153 featured courses and the Squibs List of 138 additional courses. The Trolleys List includes detailed descriptions of the courses featured in the main text. We indicate whether the courses are true classic links, parkland, a combination of links and parkland, moorland, or seaside. Each of the featured courses also has a small map of Ireland with the course's general location indicated. These maps are not drawn to scale and are not meant to give precise locations of the courses; they are intended simply to help you find the general area of Ireland in which the course is located. A larger map of Ireland shows some of the country's larger towns and cities (see page 6). You will need some good road maps to find the exact locations for each of the courses.

We have reviewed the 153 courses on the Trolleys List in terms of our experiences while visiting and playing each venue. We have limited our guide primarily to courses of 18 holes or more but do include some 9-hole venues that are exceptionally fun to play. Each course description comprises a page of important details to assist you in deciding whether to play that course while planning your trip and, once on Irish soil, to use as a reference prior to your round. We include directions for getting to the course, often a challenge in the Irish countryside. This list is organized by country (Republic of Ireland first, then Northern Ireland). Within each country, counties and their respective courses are listed alphabetically.

Because this guide is written specifically for the golfer, a course layout graphic and scorecard chart identifying each hole's yardage and par are included for each of the featured courses. One advantage to using the scorecard charts in this guide is that we have transposed the hole distances from the commonly used meters into yards. In fact, you may find it helpful to copy the yardage charts for courses you will be playing so that you don't have to do the arithmetic on the course. On each course's page, you will also see that club's crest. Many of the golf clubs throughout Ireland have venerable histories and take pride in their crest or shield. Finally, we rate each course according to its quality and playability. Chapter 2 gives a more complete discussion of the criteria we use.

The Squibs List is an alphabetized compilation of 138 additional courses throughout the whole of Ireland; we give our rationale for inclusion of these selected courses in the introduction to this list. The Squibs List includes each club's address and telephone number, its founding date and architect (when known), some unique feature of the course, and a recommended hotel or guesthouse with telephone number. We collected much of this information by contacting the courses.

Between the Trolleys List and the Squibs List, then, this guide offers a comprehensive review of the golf courses of both the Republic of Ireland and Northern Ireland. At the end of the guide is an alphabetized Master List of all 291 courses. Finally, in the back of the guide is a handy glossary of terms. We highly recommend that you peruse it, as there is nothing more disconcerting than asking for a pull cart and having the vendor stare back at you without a glimmer of recognition.

Other special features of this guide are a preface and seven "mini chapters" on selected topics; we believe they add breadth and depth. It was our good fortune to enlist the aid of five Irishmen who share their passion for golf and Ireland. Each has written a personal article that expresses his feel for the land and unique elements of golf in Ireland. Their firsthand accounts add a quality to this guide that, we hope, will take you one level deeper in terms of your appreciation for Irish golf. We have a preface written by the world-renowned Mr. Joe Carr about some of his golfing experiences through the years. Mr. Brian Coburn, covenor of the Royal County Down Golf Club and editor of the Irish golf magazine *Greenside,* has written an article about his club's famous bunkers. Mr. John Rouine, course superintendent of Lahinch Golf Club, writes about the unique maintenance of links courses. Mr. Pat Ruddy, one of Ireland's premier golf course designers, writers, and club owners, writes about the unique factors of Irish golf links. Professor George Sevastopulo, an Irish geologist with Trinity College, Dublin, writes on the Irish climate.

We, the authors, wrote the three remaining "mini chapters." The first includes biographies of some of the old masters in golf course architecture who plied their trade on Irish soil. The second sets forth characteristics and clears up some of the confusion surrounding true "links" courses. The last delves into Irish geology and how this island's unique geological features affect many of its golf courses.

Golf mastery is indeed an elusive goal, but it is no mystery at all that we love it and love to play it. Ireland, like few other places in the world, will quickly put you in touch with your reasons for playing the game. It only takes one day—one time with the wind blowing so hard that the sand is blowing up and out of a fairway bunker—for you to know that you are experiencing some big magic. You need only to witness the sea crashing against the distant cliffs at Lahinch to know that you have put yourself into an original experience and that Ireland has brought you one step closer to understanding the power of your passion. It is therefore our most sincere hope, from golfers to golfers, that *Trolleys and Squibs: A Golfer's Guide to Irish Links* in some way helps you through your journey. Good luck, and may the wind be forever at your back.

CHAPTER ONE

Planning Your Trip to Ireland

INTRODUCTION TO THE ISLAND

Ireland is an island roughly the size of the state of Indiana. This is an amazing fact given the incredible array of scenic beauty and variety of terrain found within its shores. While you won't find deserts per se, you will find lush forests, snow-capped mountain peaks, lunarlike barren landscapes, gardens and naturally occurring tracts of riotous flowers, rugged and jagged cliffs, sandy beaches with palm trees, peat bogs and foggy moorlands—all among the jewellike splendor of the Irish green. Ireland is an island made lush by frequent rain showers followed by bright sunshine; expect to see vibrant rainbows almost daily and shades of green found only on the Emerald Isle.

While Ireland has several large cities, such as Dublin, Belfast, Cork, and Galway, it is predominantly a rural island characterized by quaint villages connected by narrow roads often lined with hedges of native fuchsia, blackberries, and hydrangea. In some areas of Ireland, the countryside is flat, with farmsteads consisting of 200-year-old stone houses and barns separated by stone walls and hedgerows. Occasionally you will see cottages that have thatched roofs and are heated by peat turf. It's not unusual to see houses without electricity on nearby hills. Cattle and sheep are allowed to roam on open range. It is common to round a bend on a narrow country road and be confronted by the soft and gen-tle eyes of a Hereford being directed by a farmer dressed in cap, tweed jacket, and "Wellies," with a walking stick and trusted dog. Other times you may have to dodge a woolly-coated sheep asleep on the side of the road.

This is a fascinating island; parts of Ireland appear to belong on another planet. On the western coast are rugged mountains sending steep slopes onto cliffs overlooking the Atlantic Ocean, made an azure blue by deep waters just off the sea cliff. Hundreds of miles of roads travel through areas with sparse populations, villages with four to five houses and roads often barely wide enough for one car, let alone two passing. One area of the Republic of Ireland in County Clare, called the Burren, offers incredible sights to the eye. This extraordinary region has a lunarlike landscape and encompasses thousands of acres of treeless desolation on top of bare basalt and limestone. The Burren is actually an ancient, gigantic seabed exposed by the last ice age and sub-sequently stripped bare of trees. A little further north, in the Connemara region, you will encounter peat bogs still being harvested, majestic mountains sweeping down to the sea, and a coast dotted by chains of rugged and remote small islands connected by human-made bridges. Gaelic (aka "Irish") is the language of choice in this region. Another mind-boggling tract of land is found in Northern Ireland at the Giant's Causeway. On this northern coast, the causeway consists of thousands of multisided volcanic basalt columns over which you can climb. Incredible as it sounds, these basalt columns extend underwater all the way to Scotland.

All across Ireland are remnants and evidence of ancient peoples. In certain areas, huge Stonehenge-type burial spots of Neolithic inhabitants reach back to at least 3000 B.C. Expect to see throughout the countryside ghostly stone abbeys and cathedrals, often with just the walls remaining, dating to the 1100s. Castles and fortifications left by the Norman Invasion in the 12th century will somehow make their way into many of your photographs for the folks back home.

One of the truly poignant aspects of Ireland's history is the potato famine of 1845 through 1850, during which roughly 1.5 million of Ireland's 8 million residents starved to death. Estimates are that another 3 to 4 million of the more fortunate were able to emigrate to the United States and other parts of the world. This is an astounding figure, given that the current population of Ireland is about 4 million. The legacy of the famine is everywhere, with small stone cottages and farmsteads left standing after their inhabitants either died or left the country, giving stark testimony to this portion of Ireland's history.

And so it is that, nestled among these incredible historical, geographical, and geological events and sights, you are going to be playing golf on extraordinarily beautiful seaside links with their rugged moguls of dunegrass, or on unbelievably lush and verdant parkland courses. Many courses have as features old dry-stone fences with sheep grazing the fairways or perhaps the leftover wall of a castle built in 1450 directing you to the next tee box. You may also encounter 200-year-old cottages now used as sheds for lawnmowers and other greenkeeper's tools, and ancient orchards and farmlands dotting fairways and separating greens.

THE IRISH EXPERIENCE

Let's talk about what we call "the Irish Experience." It may help to keep in mind that your golf holiday to Ireland is not so much a chance to make personal bests in your scores and drastically improve your game as it is a chance to experience a rich essence of the game. Such a holiday is made even more spectacular by Irish courses unlike courses you have played anywhere else. You will see sheep-bedding grounds on adjacent fields, the prototypes for today's sand bunkers, and you may have to pick your way through rabbit "scrapes" in the rough, the antecedents of today's cup. These features, part of the untamed and unchanged natural surroundings that remind us of the ancient and original aspects of the game, form the Irish Experience. Whether you play with a low or a higher handicap, you will be rewarded by courses of unparalleled beauty as well as by challenging fairways and greens. So relax and enjoy your golfing in Ireland; you'll be able to work seriously on your game back home. Go for the Irish Experience every chance you get: in the long run, your memories will be less about particular shots than about spectacular ocean views, quaint fishing villages, and the experience of playing amid sheep and castles.

IRELAND: THE REPUBLIC OF IRELAND AND NORTHERN IRELAND

Before we go further, let's define a couple of terms. First, this guide describes 291 courses throughout both the Republic of Ireland (an independent state) and Northern Ireland, part of the United Kingdom. Thus, two distinct countries occupy the island we call Ireland. In this guide, we are specific to a given country when necessary. But if we refer to something simply "in Ireland," we are talking about the island in general and not a specific country.

Second, one unique aspect of golf in Ireland has been its unifying effect on the island as a whole. Thus, the Golfing Union of Ireland (GUI) takes pride in crossing political and religious lines. Throughout the years, the GUI has divided Ireland into four separate provinces, each with specific counties. One of the provinces, Ulster, has counties that overlap both countries. Many golfing circles refer to these provinces. We decided not to organize this guide in terms of province because we suspect the average golfing tourist is inundated with enough new information without trying to figure out which province includes the county of a course of interest. For those who are interested, we have listed the provinces with their respective counties in the glossary.

WHEN TO GO

Many of Ireland's courses can be played on a year-round basis. The season of highest use, however, is May through September, during which time you will compete for tee times with other tourists and with the clubs' members-only ("society") competitions. These competitions usually occur on weekends, and Ladies Days (also members only) are often on Thursdays. You might want to find out if the competitions or members-only days are for part or the whole day. Another handy piece of information is that weekdays between 11:30 and 1:30 p.m. are often more amenable for arranging tee times, because many Irish golfers are home having lunch with their families during that time.

The term *squibs,* used throughout this guide, refers to a weather phenomenon you will encounter often in Ireland. A squib is a short spurt of rain shower encountered on Ireland's coasts, sometimes lasting just a few minutes and often accompanied by a whipping wind. A squib can appear suddenly amid a sunny sky, treating you to a richly hued rainbow, or can sweep by on an overcast day. Along the coasts, squibs can happen any time, making the toting of rain gear a must. In fact, Irish weather can be unpredictable any time of year. You may encounter rain showers lasting 15 minutes, followed by dazzling sunshine and double rainbows, with winds gusting up to 50 miles per hour on the links courses; or you may find absolute calm, with even the flags on the greens limp.

Generally, however, you can expect temperate weather suitable for shirtsleeves during the summer, between May and September, and colder, rainier, windier weather during the winter months (see fig. 1). Rarely does it get down to the freezing mark in the winter, however, and if you dress warmly enough, the advantages to playing off-season include easier arrangements for tee times and less press on the courses by other tourists or Irish golfers. Playing off-season also means less competition for guesthouses and hotels, not to mention less traffic on the narrow roads.

There are three main factors to keep in mind when playing off-season. First, especially on inland parkland courses, you are likely to run into more rain, which makes the courses soggy and muddy. At times, they are even closed.

Second, during the winter months, some of the larger courses are closed for a few weeks so that the greens and fairways may be tended after their heavy summer use. Also, if you are picky about green conditions, you may want to ask as you book a course when the greens are more likely to be aerated or if "winter" (temporary) greens or tees are used.

Third, many of the smaller country bed-and-breakfasts close between November and April or May. If you plan to make lodging arrangements on a spontaneous basis when in Ireland, it's often helpful to stop at a town's Tourist Information Centre (denoted by the letter i on maps). The local townspeople who work in these offices are always very helpful and can suggest reasonable options, give you directions, and even make phone calls to book a lodging for you.

Wind is a significant factor in Ireland and can play quite a role in your game. Wind can be nearly gale-force on any of the links courses, whether you're on the more rugged western side of the island or on the eastern side, also with its share of seaside cliffs. Both

	F°	C°		F°	C°		F°	C°
JAN	45	7	**MAY**	59	15	**SEP**	64	17
	35	2		44	6		49	9
FEB	46	8	**JUN**	66	18	**OCT**	57	14
	37	2		49	9		44	7
MAR	50	10	**JUL**	67	19	**NOV**	51	10
	39	3		53	11		40	4
APR	55	13	**AUG**	66	19	**DEC**	46	8
	45	4		53	11		38	3

Figure 1. Average Monthly Temperatures throughout Ireland

Fahrenheit and Celsius readings for each month's high and low temperatures.

sides offer rocky, jagged, rugged, cliff-type topography, along with some areas of wider, more sandy beaches. Because the links courses are indigenous to the seaside, whether you're on the west or east, north or south coast, expect prevailing winds to be at times strong and gusty. Wind can also be a factor further inland. Remember, Ireland is an island with no western buffer to the winds. In fact, it offers some protection to England (to the east), thus making Ireland more susceptible to wind than England or Wales.

Finally, see chapter 2, "Playing Golf in Ireland," for suggested clothing and other essentials.

GETTING TO IRELAND

We assume that you will work with a travel agent who can find you the best deal for flying to Ireland. Following are some tips that your agent may or may not know.

First, be sure to always carry your passport with you in some safe place, preferably not in your luggage. Most importantly, make photocopies of each person's passport in the event you lose your passports. If this happens to you, go to the nearest Guardai Station (see the glossary), and they will assist you in obtaining replacements.

A second hint has to do with any medicines you may be taking to Ireland. Be sure to leave all over-the-counter or prescription medicines in their original packages. In the case of a thorough search at Customs, this will alleviate any suspicion of illegal drugs. Also, take with you any medicines that you take for granted, such as laxatives, antidiarrheals, or pain relievers. You may not be able to find their exact equivalents in Ireland.

Unless your destination is Dublin or Belfast, have the agent book your flight into the Shannon Airport. We can't emphasize this point strongly enough; doing so will spare you the incredibly difficult time you would most certainly have struggling to read confusing maps while trying to make your way through the labyrinth of streets and congested traffic in Dublin or Belfast. The traffic problems in these two cities make even the most gridlocked big-city American traffic pale by comparison.

By the same token, avoid taking the ferry from Holyhead, Wales, to Dun Laoghaire, Ireland. This is a consideration if you've booked yourself into, say, Heathrow Airport in England so that you can play some golf in Great Britain prior to going to Ireland. You might think you can avoid Dublin's traffic because Dun Laoghaire appears to be far enough south and out of the city limits, but that is definitely not the case. (Another city to avoid during rush-hour traffic is Cork. It's a lovely town, with great hotels and restaurants, but if you arrive there at peak traffic times, you're in for hours of traffic jams amid confusing or nonexistent signage.)

If you do visit Great Britain first, consider taking a car ferry to either the Republic or Northern Ireland. One trip that we have made a couple of times, and that seems to be less confusing than landing in Dublin or Dun Laoghaire, is by ferry from Stranraer, Scotland, to Larne, Northern Ireland. Larne is on the eastern coast just north of Belfast and is easy to negotiate. Its close proximity to the great courses up north, such as Royal Portrush, Portstewart, and Portsalon, makes it a good jumping-off place.

Furthermore, be sure to consider the effects of jet lag. You might try flying by night to help yourself deal with this travelers' lament. Remember that there's a 5-hour time difference from the east coast of the States, a 6-hour difference from the States' intermountain area, and a 7-hour difference from the West Coast. If it's noon in Chicago, for example, it's 5:00 p.m. in Ireland. That can add up to a pretty heavy adjustment for your circadian rhythms.

To deal with jet lag, some people find it works best to get to Ireland, find the nearest hotel or bed-and-breakfast, hole up, and go to sleep (if they can) for 8 to10 hours—and then reestablish themselves to the local time zone. Others do not go to sleep but rather make themselves stay up on that first day until their normal bedtime. You might ask around to see if anyone you know has found a way to deal with the problem. We find it helpful to immediately reset our watches for local time once we land in our host country and then begin the psychological adjustment. In any event, try to get plenty of sleep for the couple of days before your trip. Under the best of circumstances, you're going to arrive in Ireland tired, with a lot of luggage and your clubs in cumbersome cases to haul around. You'll still have to find the rental car, figure out the maps, and learn how to drive on the "wrong side" of the road (see tips in "Traveling in Ireland," page 28). Keep in mind, this is the adventure you've been looking forward to all these months!

CAR RENTAL

Another thing to keep in mind is that you will want to rent a car once you land on Irish soil. Generally, your travel agent can book a car for you much less expensively than you can if you wait until you get to the airport in Ireland. (Kemwell Holiday Autos, for example, works through travel agencies stateside and offers good value.) You will want to be sure that you have unlimited mileage and ask that you not be charged beforehand for a full tank of "petrol." Gasoline is incredibly expensive in Ireland, and prices vary widely throughout the different regions. You will want to pay for as little gas as possible. (It's not unusual to pay £25–30, or roughly $45, for a fill-up.)

When your travel agent books the car, be sure he or she secures a make and model that will accommodate your suitcases and golf gear. Owing to narrow roads, the kinds of cars you will find in Ireland are tiny compared to the average American family car. What might be ample for the typical tourist could be unsuitable for the golfing party. You'll also want to be sure that your automobile insurance covers travel in Ireland (the same is true for your health insurance!). Some credit cards offer overseas coverage. You won't need an international license to drive in Ireland unless you plan to stay longer than 6 months—but be sure your state driver's license won't expire during your stay.

CURRENCY IN THE REPUBLIC OF IRELAND AND NORTHERN IRELAND

The subject of money is important to consider before you leave for Ireland. The Republic of Ireland has its own forms of coins and bills that differ from those of the United Kingdom (which includes, confusingly, Northern Ireland). Thus, the Republic of Ireland uses the Irish *pound* (paper money), called a *punt* if you're referring to the silver coin (similar to our silver dollar). Both 1 pound (written as £1) and 1 punt have an American dollar value that changes on a daily basis. There are also paper bills for £5, £10, £20, and £50, along with an array of coinage from 1 pence (also referred to as 1 P) to 50 pence (50 P). The exchange rate can get confusing. Northern Ireland, as part of the United Kingdom, also uses the pound, but it is referred to as British pound sterling, also written as £1. Its value differs from that

of the Irish pound and consequently from that of the American dollar.

For the most part, prices, rates, and fees mentioned in this guide are in Irish or British pounds. The reason for this is simple: although the actual price in dollars will fluctuate according to the daily exchange rates, the price in pounds will remain relatively stable. Call your bank for today's currency rates.

Because the Republic of Ireland has joined the European Community in its change over to the Euro (written as *E*), the Irish money system will become obsolete (according to current plans), some say by the year 2003. In any event, whether you're faced with using the Irish pound system (£) or the Euro, you may want to invest in a small handheld calculator that can make the adjustment—or devise your own system for converting pounds/Euros to dollars. (At the time of writing, for example, we multiplied the Irish price in pounds/punts by 1.5, a close enough approximation into dollars.)

Here are a few more points regarding money. You may or may not decide to purchase traveler's checks made out in the Irish pound or British pound sterling. If you do, small denominations will be more convenient, especially if you plan to travel to more remote areas, where bed-and-breakfast hosts may not have a ready supply of cash for change. Also, always carry at least £50 in cash, because, surprising as it might seem, shopkeepers (and sometimes even golf clubs for green fees) in many communities honor neither traveler's checks nor credit cards. It can be quite a shock when you roll into a club, restaurant, or hotel and find that only cash is accepted. Fortunately, most communities in the Republic have a Bank of Ireland or in Northern Ireland a Bank of England where you can readily exchange traveler's checks for cash. Another word to the wise: don't expect to conduct business anywhere in Ireland between 1:00 and 2:00 p.m., because most banks and shops are closed then for lunch. Typical commercial hours, along with times when you can reach personnel at golf clubs for reserving tee times, are from 9:00 a.m. to 5:00 p.m.

A final word to the travel-wise: we have found exchanging traveler's checks to be inconvenient and would recommend instead that you just carry your credit or debit cards. Even in the smallest town, you'll see the ubiquitous automatic teller machine. When possible, use your credit cards for lodging, meals, or purchases. In these situations, credit cards have the advantage over debit cards in that they offer a recourse if you encounter a problem. However, debit cards are more prudent than credit cards at ATMs in obtaining local currency, since they offer the better exchange rate. Regardless of whether you use credit or debit cards, plan on always having at least £50 in local currency per person.

MAKING TELEPHONE CALLS

This may seem like a fairly innocuous process, but there's nothing more frustrating than not being able to figure out how to do something as simple as placing a telephone call! So, here are a few guidelines. You should know that the Republic of Ireland is undergoing significant changes in its telephone numbering system, and not all changes are consistent across the country. Although we are providing the most up-to-date instructions at the time of publication, you may need to consult the international operator regarding changes that have occurred since then. For Northern Ireland, we are listing numbers that took effect as of April 2000.

To call from the United States to the Republic of Ireland, dial 011 (international access code) 353 (country code for the Republic) XX (city code; two digits in this example, though it can have from one to three digits) YYYYY (local number; five digits in this example, though the total number of digits will vary) = 011 353 XX YYYYY. Numbers in County Dublin and some areas adjacent to Dublin use 1 as the city code, followed usually by a seven-digit number: 011 353 1 YYY YYYY.

To call from one county to another in the Republic, dial 0XX YYYYY (always add 0 to the city code).

To call within the same county in the Republic, drop the 0XX (city code) and dial just the YYYYY (local number).

To call Northern Ireland from the Republic, dial 00 44 28 ZZZZ ZZZZ.

To call from the United States to Northern Ireland, dial 011 (international access code) 44 (country code for the United Kingdom) 28 (new area code for Northern Ireland) ZZZZ ZZZZ (eight-digit local number) = 011 44 28 ZZZZ ZZZZ.

To call from one county to another in Northern Ireland, dial 028 ZZZZ ZZZZ (add 0 to the area code). After 16 September 2000, you should be able to dial just the eight-digit local number without the area code.

To call within the same county in Northern Ireland, dial ZZZZ ZZZZ (local number).

To call the Republic of Ireland from Northern Ireland, dial 00 353 XX YYYYY.

To call from either the Republic or Northern Ireland to the United States, dial 00 1 (area code) (telephone number).

LODGING ACCOMMODATIONS THROUGHOUT IRELAND

One of the charming and unique aspects of your golfing holiday in Ireland will be sampling the system of ubiquitous hotels, guesthouses, and bed-and-breakfasts (B&Bs)—a variety of choices not available in the States. Following is a little about each of these types of accommodations.

Hotels, usually singularly owned and nonfranchised, are primarily found in the larger towns and cities. They can be located in the town center around pubs and restaurants or on streets or roads leading into towns. Most hotels have seasonal rates and are priced on a per-person (not a per-room) basis. Most include breakfast, usually available from around 8:00 until 10:30 in the mornings. If you ask ahead and say that you have an early tee time, many will try to accommodate your schedule. Remember, however, that most Irish readily admit that they do not enjoy getting up early, so regardless of where you stay, if you're an early bird, you will want to confirm that with your hosts. Hotels most often have rooms *en suite*, which means the rooms have their own bathrooms. Many will give you the key to your room along with one to the main front door if you expect to return to the hotel from elsewhere after midnight.

One advantage of hotels is their anonymous nature, meaning that you'll have a sense of freedom in coming and going, which you may not have staying in a family home's bed-and-breakfast. Hotels in Ireland often have their own restaurant and pub, along with snooker rooms and lounge areas. One word to the wise: carry extra bars of soap and your own shampoo and deodorant, because Irish hotels do not always offer these amenities. Also, hotels located in towns may have their rooms above an area used as a restaurant or pub. In such cases, expect to hear music, laughing, and sometimes singing until quite late at night and to hear the sounds of the kitchen and smell the odors of food. These factors can be distracting, or you may view them as aspects of your Irish Adventure. We always carry earplugs, because it's not always convenient or pleasant to ask others to tone down their festivities just because you want to be in bed early. Also, keep in mind that many pubs with Irish music really don't "get going" until 11:30 p.m., and if you're in a room nearby, sleeping may be difficult without those earplugs.

Guesthouse is a specific term in Ireland designating a smaller, hotel-type establishment with a certain percentage of guest rooms *en suite*. Guesthouses often have the feel of a small hotel but provide a more friendly, homey atmosphere. For example, you can order a tray of tea and "biscuits" (cookies) after a day's journey and not expect to pay extra— it's considered part of the host atmosphere of the guesthouse. Many guesthouses also have their own dining facilities, often with excellent cuisine prepared by the hosts. If you enjoy socializing with both hosts and other guests, guesthouses are ideal in that they usually offer cozy lounges where you can casually mix and mingle. You will want to be sure to reserve a room *en suite*, unless you don't mind sharing a bathroom down the hall with other guests. Guesthouses are often run by individuals who really enjoy meeting people and making them feel at home and will give you their recommendations regarding local sights and attractions.

Bed-and-breakfasts (B&Bs) dot the Irish countryside all the way from the most remote regions to the town centers. Sometimes, particularly during the tourist season, it seems as though every other house has its B&B sign out. This type of accommodation usually consists of several rooms within a family home, some *en suite* and some not. Guests are given their own room key and a key to the house's front (or sometimes back) door, and you will have the sense of leaving and entering someone's home. Breakfast (and sometimes dinner) will be served in the host's dining room. Some B&B homes also have a parlor or living room for guest use. One of the obvious charming qualities of B&B lodging is that you can get more of the feel of living in another culture as you share stories and experiences with your host and other guests. Often you will find a fascinating array of other nationalities. As with guesthouses, you can order a tray of "biscuits" and tea, which will usually be brought to your room by your host with a lovely lace cloth and china teacups.

One important aspect of this accommodation, however, is the variety of standards: some houses have guestrooms just above the kitchen, which means you will hear typical family sounds as your host family goes about its everyday (and night) business. Bed-and-breakfast homes are often advertised with a prominent sign outside the home, making them quite easy to identify. Be sure to look for a B&B sign that displays the three-leafed shamrock of the Bord Fáilte (the Irish Tourist Board), indicating that it has met certain standards and inspections.

Whether you choose a hotel, guesthouse, or B&B, inquire if traveler's checks or credit cards are accepted when you book in advance or when you register at your destination. Keep in mind that lodging facilities in both towns and villages may not honor either of these forms of exchange. Also note that Irish lodging may or may not include a television, and you can't automatically assume that there will be a telephone in your room. You may find just a bathtub without shower, and be aware that Irish showerheads require some getting used to: types of water-heating arrangements and power units vary considerably. If you're not sure about your mechanical expertise, have the proprietor demonstrate the shower's usage when showing you the room.

When checking into a room, we have found it helpful to be shown the room before hauling luggage into it. You may want to keep in mind the following questions. If you encounter something that makes the room less than desirable to you, most proprietors are quite willing to assign you another room if available.

🍀 Is the room big enough for you? We have been pleasantly surprised to discover on several occasions, upon asking for a larger room, that there can be quite a difference in room size and convenience but not necessarily in cost. We especially like a room with a double bed along with a single bed on which to spread out our maps, books, hats, and so on.

🍀 Would you prefer a double bed or twins?

🍀 Is the room near some entry (such as a swinging door) that's likely to be noisy as other guests come and go?

🍀 Is it located directly over the kitchen, making it more susceptible to kitchen odors and noises?

🍀 Is it near or over a pub, thus promising a noise factor that could be frustrating if you're trying to get to sleep for an early tee time?

🍀 When does the heat get turned on and off? (See "Room Heat and Electrical Appliances," page 25.)

🍀 When is breakfast served? Do you need to arrange an earlier time so that you can get to the course first thing in the morning? Also, if you enjoy freshly brewed coffee, you may need to make prior arrangements.

For the purposes of this guide, we have included two types of lodging to fit your preference and budget. These suggestions are for those who would like to make all their arrangements before arriving on Irish soil. Others may prefer discovering on their own that quaint B&B in a small village or that great hotel with all the amenities. Don't forget that Ireland has a system of helpful Tourist Information Centres that, if you find one during its working hours, can often call ahead to book a room and give you much-needed directions for finding the hotel, guesthouse, or B&B.

We have generally not included B&B recommendations but rather have concentrated on hotels and guesthouses. The reason for this is that B&B's come and go and are often less enduring establishments than the longer-lasting hotels and guesthouses. Also, if you plan to visit Ireland in the off-season, B&B's might not be open, whereas hotels and guesthouses probably will be. A word of warning, however: even the latter are subject to closure, especially during the months of November through January.

We have stayed in many of the accommodations listed in this guide or at least driven by them or had them recommended to us. As with everything else, though, prices can change from season to season and year to year, along with management. Of the two types of lodging suggested for each featured course, we have designated the first as "standard." These establishments are usually more American in feel and often similar to a typical American hotel. The rooms will likely have televisions and telephones, there will be soap and shampoo samples in the bathrooms, and the prices will be higher.

The second type, which we have designated as "local," is generally lower priced (although not always) and often more European in feel. If you're looking for a truly Irish Experience, the local type will probably fit your needs—just don't expect American standards (that is, televisions, phones, or large showerheads). Some of the local accommodations include castle grounds, quaint gardens, and personable guesthouses with live-in hosts.

ROOM HEAT AND ELECTRICAL APPLIANCES

Another point that separates the seasoned from the unseasoned traveler is the knowledge that, on a whole, the Irish have less need of indoor heat than some others do, especially Americans. Those thick and comfy Irish-knit sweaters aren't just for show; they can make the difference between being truly cold and being comfortable in most restaurants and accommodations. You can almost count on the heat being turned completely off at night, winter or summer (generally from early evening until about 6:00 a.m.). Here's what you need to do if you are concerned about staying warm: as soon as you land on Irish soil and have picked up your rental car, head for the nearest hardware store and buy a small electric heater (usually for around £20, a real bargain). When you get to your lodging, plug it in, and you'll be set for whatever ambient room temperature your host supplies. This is especially important in the fall through spring. We know all too well the consequences of shivering under the comforters at 1:00 in the morning, praying for that heat to turn on!

If you plan to take things like hair dryers or electric shavers, be aware that the appliance converter used in the Republic of Ireland is three-pronged, unlike that used in the United Kingdom and the rest of Europe, which is two-pronged. Throughout Ireland, you will find 220 voltage with 50 cycles alternating current. Be sure not to use the plugs marked "For Shavers Only" for hair dryers, curling irons, or irons. One of the amenities you are likely to find in most hotels, guesthouses, and B&Bs is a pants press (rather than an iron). We were at first skeptical about these, but if you place trousers, blouses, or shirts neatly in them, you'll be surprised how great these devices work!

IRISH COOKING

Aside from the two lodging options offered for each club in this guide, we also include a pub or restaurant in case you want to make reservations ahead of time for a group. Keep in mind, too, that most golf clubs have very good meal options in their clubhouses, and you may just want to eat there and share a Guinness (see glossary) after your round. Also, most of the hotels that we have listed offer bar and dining facilities. Those with 3- and 4-star ratings have facilities that would be considered quite nice anywhere.

In the food category, you may want to know about the "full Irish breakfast" that accompanies every type of accommodation. This consists of tea and coffee (usually instant rather than brewed), orange juice, and possibly grapefruit juice. You usually have a choice of several types of dry cereals (go ahead and try the Wheatabix!), sometimes fruited yogurts, and canned fruits such as prunes or grapefruit slices. The pièce de résistance of this breakfast is the usually large and very hot plate of plain scrambled eggs, breakfast sausage similar to bratwurst, and "rashers," or what we would call thick pieces of sautéed (not crispy) bacon. To top it all off are pieces of "black-and-white pudding" (black blood sausages with pieces of potato in them) and often a piece of white bread fried in the sausage and rasher drippings. Somewhere on the plate you'll find half a warmed tomato and sometimes a couple of mushroom slices. There is always a basket of brown bread, called "soda bread" (similar to our whole-wheat bread), and white toast, along with marmalade. Clearly, this full breakfast will more than amply use up your weekly cholesterol allowance. We have tried to describe other breakfast alternatives such as pancakes and French toast and asked if they could be provided instead of this "full" breakfast, to no avail. We've been very happy with large, steaming bowls of porridge (oatmeal), which tastes great on an Irish morn. You may eventually decide to settle for two bowls of the cereal and toast, but whatever your choice, unbuckle your belt and enjoy!

If you are an inveterate coffee drinker, you may have to brew your own. Starbucks has not yet made Irish inroads, and you may be surprised at the number of wait-staff who do not know the difference between instant and freshly brewed coffee made from newly ground coffee beans. We learned to carry our own small drip coffeemaker, complete with filters, Melitta cone, and bags of ground coffee, which you can find in some of the larger grocery stores. Ask for a pot of boiling water (which can easily and happily be supplied, given that tea is so common), and you're all set.

A couple more words about Irish cooking may help you adjust any preconceived expectations you have about indulging in creative country cuisine. As much as the Irish countryside is breathtakingly beautiful, with lush shades of green that defy description, and as fascinating as the landscape is with its meandering stone walls, imposing castles, and quaint cottages, nothing can really prepare you for the straightforward simplicity of Irish cooking. This is not a country that has devoted recent generations of study to the creative use of herbs or whose methods of food preparation deviate from frying or boiling.

You've heard about Irish potatoes. Expect them with every meal, often in several guises. You may get a plate of lamb with mashed potatoes, an additional pile of French fries, and a couple of boiled potatoes on the side, for example (no kidding!). Soups tend to be delicately thin or to be thick with cream, such as the ubiquitous "veg soup" consisting of pureed vegetables in a cream broth. Green vegetables are often well cooked and are served in very large portions. "Salads" find their way onto most menus, but not salad dressings. If you order salad, you will likely get a large plate of several types of mayonnaise-based salads. If you ask for a "seasonal salad," you will probably get a small bowl of greens with a few tomatoes and sliced onions but without dressing.

Sandwiches may be advertised as having cheese, but don't be surprised if you get white bread with a piece or two of American-style processed cheese. A favorite and common type of Irish sandwich is the "toasty," any combination of grilled ham or chicken, tomato, onion, and cheese, with or without "chips" (French fries). "Irish stew" consists of boiled lamb with pieces of potato and carrot, often in a thin broth and served with brown bread. Dinner menus always feature some form of lamb or salmon, along with Irish-style pasta (lasagne without pasta noodles, for example) and baked chicken. If you are fortunate enough to have the option of a plate of "bacon and cabbage," go for it! You will be well rewarded with a tasty meal of thick ham slices (not corned beef), well-cooked shredded cabbage, and boiled turnips on the side. Favorite desserts include the "trifle," pieces of cake and fruit cocktail soaked in unflavored gelatin; melon with a berry sauce; and a Bailey's cheesecake, which is often quite good.

While a good part of provincial Irish cooking presents simple yet hearty fare, there are pockets of excellent cuisine. Dublin is quickly gearing up for nouvelle-style cuisine that is creative, innovative, and sure to please most tastes. Kinsale in County Cork is traditionally known as the gourmet capital of Ireland and surely deserves that title. Stop in any pub or restaurant in or around Kinsale and you won't be disappointed. You will find abundant types of fish that are fresh, creatively prepared, and elegantly presented; vegetables are crisp and thoughtfully prepared; desserts are outstanding. And you'll think you're in California with the fresh, crisp salads tossed with grated pepper and delicious herbed salad dressings.

One potentially confusing aspect of the Irish food scene is its standards of food service. Inattentive or even rude food service is not a personal affront. You might have to seat yourself, and you may not be given water or a menu for 10 minutes. When you finally do order, you may have to request, for example, that your drink accompany your meal or that tea or coffee be brought at the same time as your dessert. For breakfast, if you prefer your toast with whatever you order (such as porridge or scrambled eggs), you will need to make a special request; otherwise, the toast will more than likely be brought far ahead of your main entrée. Even at the end of your meal, you may need to get up and find your wait-staff, who may be nowhere in sight, to ask for the bill. If you go to a pub, expect to do all ordering at the bar, even though the food eventually will be brought to you by some staff person.

TRAVELING IN IRELAND

About the only thing we can say to prepare you for driving in Ireland is, "Expect the unexpected!" This experience will probably be like no other. If you keep an upbeat attitude, you will constantly remind yourself that this is all part of the Irish Adventure you have chosen. That is, you are experiencing golf in another culture. Try not to let yourself get flustered and frustrated as you compare Irish travel standards with your own—such a comparison is unfair. We've included this section in our guide because chances are you're going to be doing a lot of traveling as you make your way from course to course.

Maps. It is imperative that you buy good road maps of Ireland—one for the Republic and another for Northern Ireland, if necessary. We found it most helpful and convenient to have on hand two maps: a "big picture" map, which you can unfold to understand the larger territory, and a smaller map book with pages of specific locales, which you can consult while driving down the road.

Irish Roads. Although Ireland is relatively small, don't think that you can travel distances in the same time as in the United States (and consequently overschedule). Traveling from Lahinch to Ballybunion, a distance of only 45 miles, for example, took us 2 hours on a day unhindered by traffic, rainy weather, or sheep.

Irish roads can include relatively familiar "dual carriage-ways," designated as M50, M1, and so on. These have two lanes in each direction and a safe median between. You will also find the equivalent of two-lane highways that actually meander around, about, and through small streets and villages, usually designated by N, such as N24 or N11. Finally, smaller, rural "roads" are truly one-car-wide paths with no shoulders, lined by unwavering dry-stone fences or thick and dense hedgerows; these are usually designated with an R, such as R579 or R619.

It's not unusual to encounter farmers herding cattle or sheep down the "interstates" (N and R roads), and in some parts (such as the Connemara to the north), sheep actually nap on the roads. Dogs, pedestrians, and bicyclists share all these roads, making the driver's job at times tiring and stressful. So when you're driving from one town or golf course to another and expecting to get in a round when you pop out of the car, be sure to give yourself more than enough time to unwind from what may have been an intense drive through the countryside.

Asking Directions. In any event, expect to ask directions frequently, because the map system at times does not correspond to reality. Road signs may be changed, names may appear on your map but not in the town or village you're expecting to see them in, and, with all the road construction going on, you may encounter rerouting not yet recorded on road maps. Another common source of confusion for the tourist-traveler is that the typical Irish local person thinks not in terms of, say, N71 or R356, but rather in terms of villages or towns along the road. If you ask for directions to the N71, for example, the local person may or may not even know what the N71 is. Instead, you will be able to get directions to the nearest town (which happens to be on the N71) and then be on your way.

Driving on the Left-Hand Side. One unique feature of driving in Ireland is getting used to driving on the left-hand side of the road. As driver, you will be switched to the right-hand side of the car, and if you drive a stick shift, you'll be changing gears with your left hand. The brake and accelerator are in their same positions as in American cars. For the first couple of days, it may help to put a note to "DRIVE ON THE LEFT" next to the steering wheel.

Roundabouts. Irish roads have another unusual feature called a "roundabout." This may look and sound like a daunting obstacle, but actually, it is a handy device. The roundabout takes the place of street traffic lights; you just have to know a couple of rules. First, as you approach a roundabout, you encounter a stretch of about 50 feet of yellow, raised stripes and (you hope) a road sign showing the different exits of the upcoming roundabout and the nearest town off each exit. Watch for a sign announcing the town you're trying to get to so that you'll know which exit to take. As a street or road approaches a roundabout, you will be duly warned by arrows, and you'll have to come to a stop or near stop, yielding the right-of-way to those vehicles already in the roundabout. When the coast is clear, jump in and loop around until you see signage for the exit or road you want. The really great thing about roundabouts is that if you miss your sign or are lost or confused, you can just keep looping around until you figure out which exit to take.

Once in the roundabout, if you intend to take the most immediate left-hand exit, then get in the left-hand lane. If, however, you know that you need to go around the loop and bypass the first, say, two exits, then get in the right-hand lane; as you approach your exit, shift into the left-hand lane and exit the roundabout. This sounds confusing at first, but after a couple of tries, you'll quickly adjust.

Driver and Navigator. Another characteristic of driving in Ireland involves maps, road signage, and directions. Expect to get lost nearly every time you venture out onto Irish roads—it's just a matter of course, so give yourself plenty of time, and try to keep your sense of humor. The best bet is to have one person in your party operate just as the driver and another just as the navigator, because it is next to impossible to function as both. Go ahead: read that last sentence again; we can't stress it enough! The maps that you'll pick up with your rental car will make routes appear easy and well marked. Your attempt to get to your destination will often go fairly well for part of the time, but you will spend the rest of your time trying to fill in the gaps with small roads that don't appear on the maps.

We have found that it's easier for the designated driver to just stay in that role, and the same for the navigator. If you're the driver, you'll need to trust the navigator implicitly and avoid second-guessing. If you're the navigator, be patient with the driver, who may need to make copious U-turns for any number of machines, people, and animals that make immediate compliance with your directions impossible! In addition to these hazards, the driver faces the daunting task of keeping track of which side of the road to stay on and how to negotiate a turn. At the end of the day, you'll have plenty of laughs as you relive your traveling adventures. The folks back home will be amazed!

Road Signs. To add to your confusion, road signs are often small and positioned at the intersections themselves without any advanced warning. This means you will fly right past the turn you intended to take, requiring a hasty U-turn. Road signs are often misaligned, because Irish posts are round, versus square, which means that gusty winds can completely change their direction. Another common occurrence is that a road sign will tell you about, say, two upcoming towns. You'll go for a couple of miles, and then another sign will tell you about two completely new towns, and you'll wonder if you're still on the right road. You may also find yourself confused when you turn onto what you hope is the right road but can't find any verification of its name or number. There is, however, a kind of logic to the Irish road structure. This logic is the principle that you shouldn't make any turns off roads or change direction going through towns unless you definitely see a road sign.

Driving Customs. As previously described, most Irish roads (except for rare stretches of dual carriageways) go right through the smallest of Irish villages and hamlets. Consequently, this means that you can expect slow-moving

delivery trucks and private cars parked right in the middle of the street (there are often no parking spaces). A unique and charming feature of the Irish character is the population's apparent lack of frustration over having to wait for others. It's not unusual for two cars, or a car and a pedestrian, to stop traffic both ways while some sort of conversation or business is transacted. We grew to appreciate what we called "earnest conversation" in progress. People appear patient and respectful; you definitely will not find the noisy, impatient, gesturing traffic so characteristic of towns and cities elsewhere.

Although many of the roads are narrow and don't have shoulders or turnoffs, it's not unusual for people to pass one another even with what appears to be a dangerously close oncoming car. People just move over as far as they can, and things seem to work out. If you come to a herd of cattle or sheep, just wait for the farmer to signal you and be on your way. Pedestrians seem oddly unconcerned about sharing the roads with cars and trucks and often walk two across, taking up half the roadway. Because of all the possible unforeseen impediments, therefore, you as driver will need to keep your eyes on the road and leave your navigator to read the map and change the radio station.

Kilometers and Miles. Another potentially confusing aspect of the road system in the Republic of Ireland is that, while car odometers and speedometers give miles traveled and miles per hour, traffic and directional signage is based on the metric system. Thus you will deal with kilometers per hour for speed limits and kilometer distances on road signs. One easy, although not completely accurate, way to change kilometers into miles is to divide the number of kilometers by 3 and then multiply by 2. If the distance between two towns is 21 kilometers, then, you're talking about roughly 14 miles. All this changes, however, in Northern Ireland, where distances are measured in miles, as they are in all of the United Kingdom. In the final analysis, any attempt to compute travel time is just an intellectual exercise. Actual time will be dictated by weather conditions, number of sheep asleep on the roads or cattle herds encountered, and whether or not you get caught behind a farmer on his 1947 tractor as he unhurriedly carries a load of hay down the road. Keep your camera ready!

SHOPPING AND TIPPING IN IRELAND

Value-added tax. When shopping in Ireland, you will encounter an array of absolutely wonderful and gorgeous goods to buy, everything from hand-spun woven or knit sweaters and caps to stunning Belleek china, sparkling Waterford crystal, and delicate laces and linens. Lurking in the background, however, is the dreaded VAT, or value-added tax. To the unsuspecting traveler and buyer, it may come as a shock that a full 21 percent of what you buy (in certain categories) is added onto the value of the goods. If you are a non–European Community resident, you can claim back the VAT prior to your departure. There is no VAT on food, meals, children's clothing, accommodations, car rental, or personal services. But you can reclaim it on books, adult clothing, and items such as crystal, china, and fabrics. Some stores assist with this process by deducting the VAT at the time of purchase. It never hurts to ask about this, because sometimes, in the heat of the busy tourist season, you may not be informed. Others provide a cash-back form that you have to fill out and present to the duty and customs desk at airport departure, along with the goods themselves and proof-of-purchase. In any event, don't be afraid to ask any salesperson about the VAT; with luck, you can get it back.

Tipping. Surprising as it seems, tipping in restaurants is not always expected in Ireland. Some hotels and restaurants automatically add 10 percent to the bill, so ask before you leave a tip. The whole issue of tipping can be very confusing, so the best advice is to ask or just leave 10 percent and move on.

After having read this chapter, you should have the background information to plan your trip to Ireland. In the next chapter, we'll get down to the business of what to expect as you play golf there. You're on your way!

CHAPTER TWO

Playing Golf in Ireland

Congratulations! You've just made the leap to actually planning those wonderful rounds of golf in Ireland. In the Trolleys List, we provide you with detailed information on 153 featured courses. After studying that list, you will be able to put together a reasonable itinerary, depending on how much time you have. You should also consult the Squibs List of 138 additional clubs to see if you'd like to add other courses to your agenda. Or perhaps you would rather rely on the various itineraries we have set forth and choose one that suits your interests and needs.

This chapter will get you ready for whatever unique golfing experience in Ireland you are planning. Much of this information is based on our own firsthand experiences during our 9-month stint there; many of the hints are things we wished someone had told us beforehand. Our suggestions probably are not exhaustive, but we hope they prepare you for your Experience of a Lifetime.

GOLF COURSES

As you might expect, Ireland's golf courses offer scenic views, a variety of terrain, and unparalleled experiences. On the links courses, you will find breathtaking views of Ireland's azure blue ocean on some days, in contrast to its steely gray subtlety on others. Unusual seabirds fly over-head and stroll across the courses; notable is the red-legged black chough. You may also see the roosts of puffins in jagged cliffs. Perhaps among the most unique characteristics of Irish links courses are the sand dunes and native dune-grass (also known as marram grass, or, more scientifically, *Ammophila arenaria).* This dense grass can swallow a ball almost instantaneously.

In some contrast to the rugged links, Ireland also offers up parkland courses resplendent with lush green under-growth and, on many of the older estate courses, ancient trees and flowering bushes. On or adjacent to many of these courses are the fascinating ruins of pre-Norman Invasion castles, post-Invasion fortifications, and remnants of quaint stone cottages. On some of the parkland courses, Georgian mansions have been converted into clubhouses, complete with outbuildings, barns, and stables. You may have diffi-culty remembering that you've come to Ireland to play golf when there is so much beauty with each glance and glimpse!

GETTING READY PHYSICALLY

Irish golf courses have not yet, thankfully, been inundated with golf carts and cart paths to blight the otherwise natural settings. Just as it's common in Ireland to see people of all ages and generations riding their bicycles on country roads, shopping bags hanging from the handlebars, so too will you be aware of the priority for walking, not riding, on golf courses. In fact, most older courses require that a player produce a physician's proof, or "certification," attesting to some medical reason for not being able to walk if a cart is to be used. Many courses don't even have carts, and those that do have just a few. Note, though, that most of the newer "tourist" or "resort" courses do have "buggies" (as carts are called in Ireland), and these clubs encourage their use. You will not need a "cert" on these courses.

In general, though, if you plan to play golf in Ireland, be sure to engage in enough physical activity beforehand to build your strength and confidence such that you can haul yourself and your clubs around courses that can be long and strenuous—and at a fairly fast clip. If you plan to use a buggy, by all means have your family physician write a letter attesting to your medical condition and inability to walk a course. Be sure to let the persons who schedule your tee times know this.

BOOKING TEE TIMES

Here we'll talk a bit about getting onto Irish golf courses. In general, if you plan to play during the season from May through September, you will need to arrange a tee time ahead of schedule, rather than just showing up, especially if you are a member of a "fourball" (foursome). In fact, on some of the more well-known and prestigious courses—such as the Royal County Down, the Royal Dublin, and the Royal Belfast, along with the Druids Glen, Waterville, the K Club, Ballybunion, and Lahinch—you may need to book several months to a year in advance. If, however, you play as a single, are willing to play with strangers, and have flexibility for tee times, you may have some luck in just showing up. If you are a single or double and play during the off-season, you are much more likely to maintain a spontaneous schedule. Even this may not apply, though, at the previously mentioned prestigious clubs, where getting on without prior arrangement is difficult. If you do choose to just show up, be prepared to play immediately, without any warm-up. Conversely, you may have to wait awhile for an opening.

HANDICAP CARDS

You will need to have on hand your handicap card in case it's requested by the caddymaster, course manager, or secretary. It seems that Irish golf places more emphasis on this than you might encounter, for example, in the United States. In fact, if you end up playing with Irish partners, plan to be asked, "What do you play off?" meaning, "What's your handicap?" The Irish golfer is more interested in handicaps for a couple of simple but interesting reasons. First, golf just seems to be more competitive in Ireland, with each club's "society" having a competition at least every weekend. Second, and probably more important, a handicap is essential for the Stableford scoring method used in most competitions. This scoring system allows for a couple of really bad holes while still leaving you "in the game" and competitive. Stroke play competitions on Ireland's rugged links courses would be grueling for most amateurs and club players.

CADDIES

Many of Ireland's larger courses have caddies for hire, but you may need to reserve them well ahead of time. When you book your tee time, if you think you would like a caddy, be sure to ask that one be "organized" (arranged) for you and anyone else in your party. During the summer, some of the larger clubs have caddies "waiting in the wings," available on a spur-of-the-moment basis. But don't count on being able to secure a caddy without prior arrangement; you could be disappointed when all of them have been hired out. Caddies work on a per-person basis, although some are willing to tell others in the party (who don't have a caddy) where they saw a ball land. Fees vary, but you can generally expect to pay £20–30 per person, plus tip.

If you're just interested in some means of hauling around your clubs, an alternative is the pull cart, called a "trolley" in Ireland. These are available almost universally without reservations, and occasionally you can find a course with motorized trolleys. One thing to keep in mind, however, is that they are often not allowed onto tees.

This leads to the question of whether "to caddy or not to caddy." Many of the courses, notably the Old Course at Lahinch, both the Old Course and the Cashen Courses at Ballybunion, and Northern Ireland's Royal County Down (all classic links), offer strategic challenges to even the lowest-handicap golfer. These and other courses serve up blind drives, teacup-size greens requiring precision shots, and intelligently placed bunkers that demand knowledge of the course. Hiring a caddy for your first time through these courses can make all the difference. Without one, your once-in-a lifetime game on one of these spectacular courses might be reduced to just figuring out where the next hole is and trying to find your ball (innumerable times!) in deep marram grass. With a caddy, you'll have some confidence in hole sequence and demands, and the benefit of the at-times surreal ability of the caddy to ferret out your ball in deep rough. Add to these concerns the factor of wind, which could mean a formidable day on the course without a caddy.

Caddies are often local players, sometimes club members and even high school teenagers. They can be young or old, male or female. It's fairly safe to say that most of them have a love of golf, take a keen interest in your game, and have incredible knowledge of the course. They understand the effects of even minor changes in wind patterns and always provide first-rate advice regarding club choice and placement of shots.

Gone are the days, though, when you'll be matched with a timeworn, veteran caddy who has been on the course since boyhood, who is there just for the sport of it, who can entertain with witty anecdotes about old-time players for whom he has caddied through the ages, and who is happy with whatever money you squeeze into his gnarled hand at the end of the round. Instead, today's caddies are often local townspeople there for the extra money. One of the best caddies we encountered was a young woman who was going to law school and helped pay her way by caddying in the summer. In any event, when in doubt, get a caddy. You won't be disappointed.

CLOTHING ON AND OFF THE COURSE

Rain Gear. As you well might guess, the whole reason that Ireland is so incredibly green and beautiful is that it rains there *a lot* (see chapter 3, "Forty Shades of Green"). This is not altogether a bad thing for the golfer. Chances are, if you wait 15 minutes or so, an intensely hued rainbow and bright blue, sunny sky will follow the rain. But be prepared for rain showers, squibs, and at times gale-force winds, particularly on the coasts.

It's up to you, but you might want to leave the umbrella in your car—it will just get in the way of the winds and will be practically impossible to keep from getting sprung. If you decide to take one, leave the large one at home and settle for the single-person, smaller type, unless you have one with really strong spokes. The smaller the better for managing the wind. Do have an adequate club cover for your golf bag; it should be convenient to get on and off at a moment's notice. This cover is essential for Irish golf. Find a good one before you leave home.

For yourself, plan to take the best rain gear you can afford, and make sure the leg bottoms fit easily over your shoes. Even though Ireland doesn't get near-freezing temperatures, be prepared for the wind and rain by bringing along sweaters with water-repellent liners, gloves, and head-gear that covers your ears. In the warmer, summer months, you will still need some form of rain gear to keep dry, although not necessarily to keep warm. A good, water-repellent windbreaker is essential.

Clothing in General. One of the enjoyable things about visiting Ireland is that "smart but casual" wear is appropriate wherever you go. You should be aware, however, of clothing standards on most golf courses. Specifically, this may mean avoiding denim either on the course or in the clubhouse, taking off your hat in the clubhouse, and leaving your spikes outside the clubhouse. Most Irish golfers prefer wearing golfing attire separate from their street clothes, so you will see many players carrying duffel bags with their golf clothes. Shower facilities are available in the locker or changing rooms of most courses.

Clothing requirements are fairly person-specific, but following are some guidelines you may want to remember when packing. Be sure to take enough dry socks, because you'll probably get damp feet even with the best waterproof shoes. In the summer, take a couple of lightweight, short-sleeved shirts, as well as a turtleneck or two. For slacks, summer-weight khakis are great for most courses. And remember to have on hand the best water-repellent jacket you can afford, along with a hat or cap.

For winter wear, you can't have too many turtlenecks and flannel-lined slacks. We have even used long underwear and thick, wool socks. You'll want a hat that won't blow off in the wind. Knit ski hats are great, whereas baseball hats can be a bother. Warm, waterproof gloves are essential. One of the truly great amenities that most Irish hotels, guesthouses, and B&Bs have is a heating device in the bathroom over which you can spread some of your damp clothes. These devices are actually towel warmers and are turned on when the heat is on. So, for at least a couple of hours before you go to bed, you'll be able to get some of your dampened clothes dry.

Off the course, you will find that Ireland is fairly relaxed and casual when it comes to clothing. If you have lunch or dinner in an upscale hotel or restaurant, however, you will want to dress accordingly.

FOOD AND AMENITIES ON THE COURSE

Irish golf courses definitely don't have staff running about in hospitality golf carts offering food and drink—so put in your bag whatever snacks and liquids you'll need. Also, while some of the courses have their turn at the clubhouse (thus making restroom facilities available), many do not. Few have restroom accommodations on the course, so plan accordingly.

THE FAST PACE OF IRISH GOLF

One of the differences between golf in Ireland and golf in the United States and other countries is the pace at which it is played. In Ireland, a typical golfer, male or female, plays the game at a very fast clip between shots. You'll not find any slow walkers on the Irish links; in fact, some of the speediest players are the women. The electric, remote-controlled pull cart is starting to appear on Irish golf courses, speeding up play even more. The Irish player also respects other players who make quick exits off the green at the conclusion of their putts and who keep good lookout for where their ball lands on the drive. This is not always an easy feat, given the often high and untamed rough on most of the classic links. Furthermore, the Irish player will be out on the course in weather conditions you never thought possible for playing golf. What we might call "breezy winds" are nothing more than "fresh air" to the Irish player—probably another reason that golf in Ireland is definitely not played at a leisurely stroll.

LAYOUTS AND STROKESAVERS

For each of the 153 featured courses in this guide, you will notice a graphic depiction of the layout along with each hole's yardage and par. While most courses have an intuitive layout, studying them beforehand may be helpful. Many courses also have guides, called "strokesavers," which come in various shapes and sizes. Some are professionally executed, with glossy covers, in-depth hole analysis and descriptions, and local lore. Others, particularly for the smaller clubs, may be relatively simple, home-produced affairs. In either case, they are well worth the money (usually £3–5).

METERS TO YARDS

One important thing to keep in mind is that our guide describes hole distances in yards. Throughout Ireland, however, a curious blend of metric and yardage dimensions is used. In fact, it's not unusual to find the scorecard registered in yards but the distance markers in meters, or vice versa,

on a given course. You might want to check this out before playing a club's course.

If you're playing a course presented in meters, here's a quick way to convert the figures into yards: use the 10 percent rule. To do this, add 10 percent of the meter distance to the total meter distance to arrive at a fairly close approximation in yards. If a hole's distance is 360 meters, for example, add 36 (10 percent) to 360, equaling *about* 396 yards. To be more accurate, add 9 percent to the total. This will get you a more precise idea of yards from meters: 360 meters actually represents 392 yards.

CHAMPIONSHIP TEES

In Ireland, unless you are specifically invited to do so, you will not be playing off the championship tees. These are by convention reserved for members of the club, and for you to use them would be considered presumptuous and rude. You could be embarrassed, in fact, if you begin your swing and are summarily asked by the caddymaster (or even a member-player) to use the forward tees.

EQUIPMENT AND OTHER CONSIDERATIONS

Golf Balls. Be sure to have on hand enough golf balls, especially for the links courses. Check your bag before you leave your car; balls in your trunk won't do you any good after you've exhausted your supply by the 10th hole on a gusty day out on a rugged links course. The heather, heath, gorse, fescue, steep dunes, and generally hilly terrain can at times seem to eat up golf balls quicker than you can hit them.

Clubs. As a general rule, don't plan to buy clubs or balls in Ireland; they are quite expensive. Instead, use one of the great carrying cases available, sturdily built and on wheels, for transporting clubs on airplanes. The only drawback to these is that they are often rather long, so be sure to arrange for a car rental that will accommodate your golf carrier's length. (We pack a lightweight down comforter in the carrying case with our clubs—great for those chilly Irish mornings when we're waiting for the heat to be turned on!)

Miscellaneous. You may want to carry along an individual lightweight seat, since most Irish courses do not have benches for sitting on between holes. Because of the fast pace of the Irish game, however, you may not have time to sit between holes anyway! With respect to a camera, be aware that you're likely to encounter rain and mist on any course during any season, and blowing sand can be a factor on the links courses. You might also check to make sure that you have a pencil for marking your scorecard before beginning your game; smaller courses do not always supply these.

THE BUMP AND RUN

You have undoubtedly heard of the shot called the "bump and run" and may even have it in your repertoire. This type of shot involves using your 7 or 8 iron at 50 to 100 yards, rather than trying to lob the ball up into the air with, say, your wedge. The advantage to the bump-and-run shot is that the ball stays close to the ground, critical when a gale-force wind is blowing. In Ireland, this is a great shot to use, because wind can be a critical factor for most courses. To shoot the ball up into the air would spell disaster as the ball goes sailing into parts unknown, carried by the gusty Irish wind.

GREEN FEES

For each of the 153 courses featured in the Trolleys List, you will see a "Green Fees" line, followed by one of three remarks: low, moderate, or high. Green fees, like the weather, can change. Thus, instead of listing specific prices which may be outdated, we decided to give you a generic indication of the green fees, so that you will know what to expect when you call or arrive at a course. Roughly, then, a course rated "low" will cost less than £25, a "moderate" course will cost between £26 and £65, and a course rated "high" will cost more than £65. As always, we have tried to make these indicators as accurate as possible, but for the most recent and specific information, use the telephone numbers provided and call ahead.

THE SHAMROCK RATING SYSTEM

In addition to the Green Fees rating, each featured course will have one to four shamrocks in the colored bar at the outside edge of each page. This is our course rating system, based on the criteria listed below. The more shamrocks, the better our rating for that course. Rating a golf course is always undertaken upon the most slippery of slopes. We readily admit that regardless of how objective the criteria are, their application is subjective and thus potentially controversial. Nevertheless, after developing solid criteria, we made every effort to apply them as consistently as possible to all the courses we visited and played. We hope our shamrock rating system will help you make the difficult choices about which courses to play. Following are the questions we used in rating the courses, presented in the order of their importance.

- Did the course capture an essence of golf that is unique to Ireland, or what we refer to as the "Irish Experience"?
- To what extent did the course's design allow for a multiplicity of strategies depending on the skills of the golfer?
- Did the course provide a layout that was intuitive, with a logical sequence of holes?
- To what extent was there evidence of satisfactory course maintenance, such as the cultivation and health of greens and fairway turf and upkeep of rough, bunkers, and other course features?
- Did the course incorporate design features that demonstrate sensitivity to the existing terrain, natural wildlife, and indigenous plants?
- Did the course supply scorecards that were sufficiently informative and accurate?
- Were there accurate and consistent distance markers and signage at each of the tee boxes?
- Did the course employ staff who were helpful, friendly, and knowledgeable?
- Did the course provide adequate maintenance for such items as roadways, landscaping, and building facilities (e.g., bathrooms, locker rooms, showers, lounging facilities and, of course, the restaurant)?

So get out your suitcases, polish up your clubs, start making your phone calls, and get someone to take care of your dog, because you're going to Ireland to play some of the best golf in the world. Welcome to the land of Trolleys and Squibs; *Sláinte!* (Cheers!)

CHAPTER THREE

Forty Shades of Green

BY PROFESSOR GEORGE D. SEVASTOPULO

Have you been wondering why it rains so much in Ireland? The following piece was written by one of Ireland's top geologists, Professor George D. Sevastopulo, who is with the Department of Geology, Trinity College, Dublin. George is an international expert on foraminifera, a particular type of ancient marine protozoa whose fossilized remains he has tracked across the globe. As a result of his geological studies, he has become quite knowledgeable about the Irish climate. We first met George through Dr. Gary Lane of Indiana University's Department of Geology. What follows is probably all you will need to know about Irish weather patterns as you plan your trip.

The "Emerald Isle," "forty shades of green," and similar phrases refer indirectly to Ireland's benign climate, which allows golfers to enjoy their game all through the year. Because Dublin lies closer to the North Pole than does Calgary, Canada, the lack of temperature extremes in Ireland may at first seem surprising. Two factors are largely responsible.

First, Ireland is a relatively small island set amid the surrounding sea. The sea, as one might guess, has much less temperature variation throughout the year than does land. Thus, the sea has an ameliorating influence on Ireland's more temperate climate. Ireland's location in the sea does not completely explain its weather, though; Labrador, on the eastern coast of Canada, is an island at the same latitude as Ireland, yet Labrador is renowned for its fiercely cold winters.

The second crucial factor is the presence of the Gulf Stream, a current of warm surface water. It is interesting to note that the stream was first named and mapped by Benjamin Franklin. The Gulf Stream starts in the Caribbean and carries warm surface water northward obliquely across the Atlantic, warming Ireland and other coastal areas of the eastern Atlantic Ocean. Paradoxically, one of the outcomes of global warming may be a disturbance of the ocean current system, leading to cessation of the Gulf Stream. A consequence may be that Ireland's winters, far from becoming warmer, could change to be like those of Labrador. At the present time, however, palms grow in Dublin's suburban gardens, hedgerows of scarlet fuchsia flowers abound in the south, and some of the southwest's great gardens contain such tender plants as tree ferns.

As is typical of islands, the lowest winter and highest summer temperatures occur in the center of the country, away from the moderating influence of the sea, whereas the highest winter temperatures are along the coasts. In the center of the country, such as around Birr in County Offaly, January's mean daily air temperature is approximately 39°F (4°C), with sporadic nighttime frost. Temperatures can drop as low as 10°F (−12°C) from early October to mid-May. By contrast, at the extremities of County Cork's peninsulas in the country's southwest, the combination effect of the Gulf Stream and the proximity of the ocean results in almost no frost, with January's mean daily air temperature running about 46°F (8°C).

These variations in winter temperatures are reflected in differing start and end dates for the grass-growing season in different places, a matter of some importance to greenkeepers and farmers alike. Along the southwestern peninsulas, the grass-growing season lasts throughout the year. Throughout much of the country's central locales, however, it starts in early to mid-March and concludes in middle to late November. Summer temperatures seldom rise above 80°F (27°C) anywhere. Anything above 75°F (24°C) is usually reported in the press as a heat wave! Mean temperatures for July are typically 57–61°F (14–16°C).

If you play links courses on the west coast, one of the features you will come to appreciate is the wind. You will see relatively few trees along the coast, and those that do persist are bent over and lopsided, allowing you to estimate the dominant wind direction. These trees show almost no growth on their windward side, which is typically to the northwest and southwest. Periods of calm on the west coast are very short, perhaps accounting for less than 3 percent of the time. Winds of force 4 on the Beaufort scale (a moderate breeze, approximately 16 miles per hour) blow for more than 10 percent of the time, and gales (over 40 mph) for at least 1 percent of the time.[1] In the country's east, northwesterly to southwesterly winds are the norm. In the winter and summer months, large, stable, high-pressure systems over continental Europe generate easterly winds that may accompany very cold, dry weather.

Throughout Ireland, Meteorological Services, called Met Eireann, forecasts the weather. In former times, the forecasts were based on information from weather stations and ships in the North Atlantic. Although forecasters were able to put together sequences of events that were generally accurate, their timing of these events was less so. Nowadays, the forecasters have at their disposal a much greater range of information, including that acquired by satellites, and their forecasts are generally very accurate. Weather forecasts are given on the radio and television, usually before or after the national news.

An interesting sidelight is that in 1999, Radio Telefis Eireann (the National Television Service) replaced the weather reporters from Met Eireann, who used to present the forecasts, with professional television "presenters." But after great public outcry, the professional weathercasting personnel from Met Eireann were reinstated. So when you anxiously listen to the radio or television the evening

---

[1] Force 8 on the Beaufort scale is called a gale, with wind speeds of 39 to 46 miles per hour. Force 9 is designated as a strong gale, with winds of 47 to 54 mph. Force 10 is storm force, with winds of 55 to 63 mph.

before your next round, you will probably be listening to a weather professional who actually had a part in drawing up the forecast.

Let's turn to the specific topic of rain. The Atlantic Ocean is the major controlling factor of this aspect of Ireland's climate. A string of depressions moves across the Atlantic from west to east, between the latitudes of 50° and 65° north. Normally, these produce low pressure to the north and west of Ireland, so that rain-bearing clouds move in from the northwest, west, and southwest. Much of the rain falls on the west coast, where annual precipitation is typically 46 inches (1,200 mm), rising to as much as 126 inches (3,200 mm) in parts of northern Connemara. There is a gradual decrease eastward, so that in the Dublin area and along the east coast, there may be less than 31 inches (800 mm). Throughout the upland areas, such as the Wicklow Mountains, one can expect up to 92 inches (2,400

mm). Although rainfall can be expected in every month, total precipitation is statistically least in April, relatively low in May and June, and highest from November to January. Precipitation of more than 0.039 inches (1 mm) occurs on average less than 150 days in the eastern coastal region. In the upland areas of Donegal, north Connemara, and south of Killarney, however, one can expect more than 0.039 inches (1 mm) of rain at least 225 days of the year. Ireland's sunniest area is the southeast, such as around Wexford, with averages of more than 1,700 hours of sunshine each year. By contrast, the northwest receives less than 1,300 hours per year.

In a nutshell, the reason it rains so much in Ireland is that this island is the first land encountered by the westerly winds that bring in moisture-laden air from the Atlantic. And so it is that we can thank the rain for those dazzling forty shades of green on the Emerald Isle.

CHAPTER FOUR

Early Golf Architects

We hadn't been in Ireland very long before a number of golf course architects and designers began to capture our attention and fancy. We were impressed not only by the sheer number of courses designed by these men (no women in those early ranks), but also by the unparalleled natural beauty they were able to take advantage of as they laid down challenging courses. If you have a yen for history and would like to know a bit more about these early designers, you may find the following interesting and helpful as you play the courses they fashioned upon Irish soil.

Before embarking on these profiles, let's take a few moments to consider the early development of golf course design. Scotland's St. Andrews seems to be the home not only of golf but of golf course design and maintenance as well. Consensus is that some form of golf was played on St. Andrews as early as the 1400s. Until the mid-1700s, interested members and hired townspeople had pretty much made changes in its structure and dealt with its upkeep on an ad hoc basis. In the 1760s, rabbit scrapes were filled in and new holes cut by local laborers a day or two before the members' monthly meetings. One such enterprising soul, Charles Robertson, had the job for about 20 years, quitting around 1800 because the rabbit population was getting out of control. Hard as it is to believe, during that brief period,

the links at St. Andrews were owned by a businessman who actually encouraged the breeding of rabbits upon the hallowed ground!

A succession of other Robertsons and a Robert Morris followed, each "let go" by the first bona fide Links Committee for providing unsatisfactory work. Golf course architecture was in its very early infancy, to the extent that in 1832, a major decision was made to cut two holes (outward and inward) for each green. Another Robertson, Allan, was actually given the title "superintendent" in 1848, and he was the first true greenkeeper and designer. Allan Robertson widened the St. Andrews fairways, designed its huge double greens, and laid in place the now-famous 17th or Road Hole. During his tenure, he also straightened bunker walls, returfed putting greens, and instituted white (outward) and red (inward) flags.

After Allan Robertson died in 1859, it wasn't until 1865 that the committee appointed a new superintendent, Tom Morris. After having been at Prestwick for the previous 14 years, "Old" Tom Morris, at age 44, was ready and able to get St. Andrews' links in top-notch shape. He made several substantial changes to the links, including rolling the putting greens, which had formerly been allowed to go "natural"; employing two new machines, one for rolling and the other for mowing; and making separate tee boxes that protected the greens from serving as such. Tom also added a new 18th green (just across the street from his own club-making shop) and filled in some older bunkers and constructed new ones. As might be expected, his efforts were not met with universal enthusiasm. In 1878, the members of St. Andrews asked the Links Committee to submit any further proposals *before* implementing them.

So the stage was set for golf course management to graduate from mere custodial maintenance to full-blown architecture and design. All across Scotland, England, Ireland, and the United States, greens were carved into sand dunes, lakes and streams made their way onto formerly arid land, trees took root on timbered plots, and rabbit scrapes became the prototype for cups, as did sheep bedding grounds for bunkers. Golf course architecture had come into its own.

Let's take a look, now, at some other outstanding names you will encounter as you play the courses throughout Ireland.

James Braid (1870–1950). Most of you may be aware that Braid was part of the "Great Triumvirate," which also included John Henry Taylor and Harry Vardon. These three golfers dominated British golf for the 20 years preceding World War I. From 1894 until 1914, they won between them the British Open Championship sixteen times. Braid was the first player to win five Open Championships. After retiring from competition in 1912, he went on to design or remodel some two hundred golf courses throughout the British Isles and Ireland. He is somewhat unknown in U.S. golf architectural circles because his fear of flying kept him from plying his trade on U.S. soil. Scottish courses that bear his stamp include Carnoustie, Gleneagles, Royal Troon, Prestwick, Crieff, and Nairn. In Ireland, he designed courses at Howth, Mullingar, Tullamore, and Waterford and contributed some renovations to Ballybunion's Old Course.

Some of Braid's trademarks were a type of hole not seen on the links courses, but he found it useful on some of his inland courses; today we call it a dogleg. One of his aims was to include as many hazards as possible on his nonlinks courses, thus the advantage of trees and streams included in doglegs. He is also known for his potbunkers, crossbunkers, and variety of hazards. Strategy of the game was important to him, and he made sure his greens and their approach shots matched. Modern-day players appreciate his emphasis on large tee boxes, undulating greens, and carefully placed bunkers. In playing his courses throughout Ireland, we noticed that one of his features was a distinct, almost pronounced back-of-the-green contouring that helped prevent the ball from running through the green. This can be seen most easily at Mullingar Golf Club.

Harry S. Colt (1869–1951). One of Cambridge University's golf team members who went on to earn a degree in law was Harry Colt. He became an attorney but continued to play golf and even helped design a course, Rye, in England (1894). Hooked, he abandoned the law and took up professional golf course design. It is interesting to note that Colt was the first golf course designer who had not been a professional golfer. As might be expected, a certain competition existed among the burgeoning numbers of designers. Colt stands out in that he refrained from bidding when he found out other designers were also being solicited. Colt and Alister MacKenzie entered into an at-times stormy collaboration from 1913 to 1928. Colt then entered into business with C. Hugh Alison and John S. F. Morrison until his death in 1951. Scottish courses bearing his name include the Eden Course at St. Andrews, and Longniddry. In England, he designed Sunningdale and St. George's Hill. In the United States, his courses are found in the cities of Detroit and Milwaukee, Georgia's Sea Island, and Philadelphia's Pine Valley. In Ireland, he designed the courses at Royal Belfast, Royal Dublin, Royal Portrush, Rosapenna, and County Sligo.

Colt was known for walking the land and taking shots prior to actual design. He also advocated careful study of the lie of the land and its drainage; he would take soil and turf samples so that both soils and grasses were as similar as possible to indigenous forms. He was one of the first designers to include tree-planting programs that provided hazards and strategic interest to his inland courses. Contrary to some of the earlier designers, Colt was not fond of blind shots but instead favored holes that allowed for "placing" of tee shots with a clear line to the hole for the second shot. While he provides plenty of room for strategic shots, you may notice in playing his courses that they are not punitive.

Eddie Hackett (1910–1996). As you make your way through Ireland's golf courses, you are sure to notice that practically every other one is designed by a fellow probably obscure to you, Eddie Hackett. In stark contrast to many of the other designers reviewed herein, Eddie Hackett limited his courses to Irish soil and in fact never even visited American courses. We spoke with countless people as we tried to piece together an understanding of this prolific yet unpretentious man and came to realize a certain pride and reverence among Irish golfers and designers when his name is mentioned.

Eddie was born and raised in Dublin and experienced a childhood all too common to earlier generations in

Ireland—one with periods of poverty and want. At age 29, he landed a job as pro at the prestigious Portmarnock Golf Club, a venue he left at age 40 in 1950. Ironically, Eddie's illustrious career as a golf course designer came as a result of his not being able to play the game because of ill health. In 1936, he had a kidney removed, and later, in 1954, he suffered for a year after being hospitalized for meningitis. Legend has it that one of his most cherished memories was having lunch with James Braid, John Henry Taylor, and Harry Vardon in 1936.

Eddie was asked to lay out his first course around 1950, with no prior design training, and he went on to design hundreds of Irish courses over his lifetime. It is said that his mission was to help fledgling golf memberships put together as good a course as their pocketbooks would allow, with Eddie himself often accepting minuscule fees (around $300). As you play his courses, you may in some instances be able to tell when funds didn't allow for detailed contouring of mounds and other such features. Eddie's courses are usually straightforward, without blind shots or hidden bunkers, and he had the rare opportunity of designing ten of Ireland's classic links courses. These links courses include the clubs at Carne, Cheann Sibeal (with Christy O'Connor Jr.), Connemara, Donegal, Enniscrone, the Island (with Fred G. Hawtree), Ring of Kerry (a links-style course), St. Anne's, Strandhill, and Waterville. The many parkland courses that claim his name include clubs at Athenry, Bantry Bay (with Christy O'Connor Jr.), Kilkee, Killarney (Killeen Course), Macroom, County Meath, and Strabane.

Frederick George Hawtree (1883–1955).

Since the first Fred Hawtree laid out England's Croham Hurst in 1912, through the recent history of golf course design, the Hawtree family has been a dynasty. Frederick George was joined by his son Frederick William in 1938, who subsequently was joined by his son, Martin, in 1972. Fred G. joined forces with John Henry Taylor (see James Braid, page 45), who often played an exhibition match on the official opening of a course they had designed. Together, Hawtree and Taylor had a vision of providing excellent courses even at the municipal course level and founded England's National Association of Public Courses.

Fred G. Hawtree understood the technical and aesthetic differences between true links and what we now call parkland courses. For the latter, he recognized the necessity of artificial bunkering but firmly favored the imitation of nature rather than nonaesthetic, out-of-context course features. One of his pet peeves was the unimaginative and haphazard placing of bunkers; his preferred style was a system of bunkering based on the land's natural contours. He also favored courses designed with lots of variety in their holes, regardless of flat or uninteresting natural features. Another hallmark of the Hawtree course is lack of symmetry in hummocks, with instead natural-appearing irregularity. In Ireland, you can play Hawtree-designed courses at Arklow, Deer Park in Howth, the Island (with Eddie Hackett) in Donabate, and Westport.

Robert Trent Jones Sr. (1906–). Robert Trent Jones has been designing courses for 70 years. He is not to be confused with his son, Robert Trent Jones II, who has his own burgeoning golf course design company but has not yet laid out a course in Ireland. The elder Jones was born in 1906 on the Trent River in England; he came to New York in 1911. He studied at Cornell University and is purported to be the first person to fashion his own degree program in golf course design. He joined forces with Stanley Thompson, a Canadian architect; their collaboration lasted from 1930 to 1938. Despite some setbacks due to the Depression, Jones's reputation and abilities flourished after World War II. For example, he and the legendary Bobby Jones designed Atlanta's Peachtree (1948), and he made some critical changes on Augusta National. Over his career, he has designed nearly five hundred new courses and redesigned hundreds of existing courses.

In terms of his work, Jones is famous for fearlessly employing earth-moving equipment, transforming flat land into spectacular elevated greens, and fashioning huge lakes. Tales abound regarding his often iconoclastic approach: he has done such things as pulverizing on-site granite and converting it into topsoil (Sardinia, Italy) or crushing lava in Hawaii to make soil, defying others' advice to the contrary. He is also known for designing courses that are challenges even to low handicappers. His greens often demand shots flown into the air over sand and water, rather than the bump and run so favored in the United Kingdom and Ireland. Unwilling to provide courses where pros could break 70, he added length and water hazards to penalize better golfers for their errors. His style has sparked some controversy, with the creation of massive undulating bunkers and greens, smoothing out of the natural terrain of fairways, and creation of long, tough, unforgiving American courses. An interesting recent development is the Robert Trent Jones Trail in Alabama. Jones, together with his design partner, Roger Rulewich, designed this system of public courses supported by Alabama's public employee pension fund.

Some of Jones's courses include Spain's Sotogrande on the Costa del Sol, California's Spyglass Hill at Pebble Beach, and Mauna Kea in Hawaii. In Ireland, you will play Jones courses at Adare Manor Golf Club, Ballybunion's Cashen Course, and Dromoland Castle in County Clare.

Alister MacKenzie (1870–1934). One of the first things you will notice about playing Alister MacKenzie courses is that they demand the same heroic efforts he must have appreciated in the soldiers for whom he acted as field surgeon during the Boer War, and for whom he designed camouflage and protective bunkers and trenches. After World War I, he and the British Army had a parting of ways. His name was excised from official accounts of British camouflage, and, being ever the avid golfer, he channeled his resources and considerable talents into golf course architecture. In the United States alone, between 1918 and 1933, he designed some fabulous courses that only get better with time. Hallmarks of his courses include very few bunkers, minimal rough, massive undulating greens, and challenges to even the seasoned golfer. A truly international golf architect, he designed courses in Ireland, Scotland, Australia, New Zealand, Canada, and Uruguay, as well as many throughout the United States and his native England.

Prior to his career as golf architect, MacKenzie had obtained degrees in chemistry and medicine at Cambridge University. In his own medical practice, he touted the advantages of golf for health and fitness. While serving in the Boer War and World War I, he was especially impressed by the enemy's ability to hide within strategically concealed trenchworks. Part of the challenge of a MacKenzie course is in the deception of his greens. Expect to encounter greens cleverly tucked behind bunkers, with high arcs of sand rising upward; large valleys that must be straddled on a green's approach; and, of course, his well-known elevated greens.

His famous book, *Golf Architecture* (1920), outlines the essential features of a golf course. As you play his courses, you might want to watch for these characteristics. They include a good variety of holes requiring a plethora of shot-making skills, little walking between greens and tees, and two loops of 9 holes to accommodate different wind patterns. He also advocated that the course itself should be practically indistinguishable from nature and that links courses especially should have as little construction as possible, relying instead on existing natural features. Finally, regarding hazards, he recommended that they should be viewed not as punitive but rather as "interesting"; they should be positioned on the line of play toward the hole, and there shouldn't be too many of them.

Throughout his career, MacKenzie collaborated with other big names in golf, notably Bobby Jones, C. Hugh Alison, and Harry S. Colt. Some of his courses include Australia's Royal Melbourne, England's Moortown, California's Cypress Point and Pasatiempo, Georgia's Augusta National, the University of Michigan course, and Ohio State University-Scarlet course. In Ireland, MacKenzie courses include those at Cork Golf Club and Galway Golf Club and several holes at Lahinch Golf Club.

Old Tom Morris (1821–1908). Perhaps no other name in golf evokes such reverence and respect as that of Tom Morris Sr. He became known as Old Tom after his son, Tom Morris Jr., leaped to great heights as a golfer and club maker in his own right. Old Tom lived and spent most of his life in St. Andrews, Scotland. As pro there for more than 40 years, he even had his own club-making shop directly across the street from the 18th green (the shop is still there, catering to tourists buying sweatshirts and logo-embossed mugs). He won the British Open four times (1861, 1862, 1864, 1867) and made quite a name for himself as club and golf ball maker. Between 1860 and 1895, he designed and laid out some thirty classic links courses throughout Scotland and Ireland. Some of his Scottish courses are Carnoustie, Machrihanish, Muirfield, North Inch, Prestwick, Royal Dornock, and the New Course at St. Andrews. In Ireland, he designed Lahinch Old Course, Rosapenna, and Royal County Down.

Old Tom led quite an illustrious life. He and Allan Robertson (the first greenkeeper at St. Andrews) often played together, at least while the featherie ball was in vogue. After the newer Haskell (gutta percha) ball was introduced, the two parted ways, because Old Tom wanted to manufacture the Haskell, but Robertson saw it as a threat to his own thriving featherie ball–making enterprise. In terms of golf course design, Old Tom often redesigned and improved venerable links courses. He instituted top-dressing greens with sand for smoother surfaces, for example, and leaving old ruins and relics as part of these ancient courses. Other Morris hallmarks include standardizing course length to 18 holes and having outward and inward loops both ending at the clubhouse. When he was hired as pro and green-keeper for St. Andrews in 1864, he was paid a salary of £50 per year and given a shovel, wheelbarrow, and spade.

Old Tom and his son, Young Tom Morris (aka Tommy), were known as championship golfers. Back in their days, anyone who won the Open Championship three times in a row had automatic rights to keep the fancy red Moroccan leather belt trophy. Young Tom won the championship in 1868 (at the age of 17), 1869, and 1870, thus entitling him to keep the red belt. As a result, there was no trophy and therefore no competition in 1871. So the Royal and Ancient Golf Club and what was known as the Honourable Company of Edinburgh Golfers chipped in and bought a whole new trophy, the claret jug. This revered jug continues to be the present-day Open Championship trophy.

Tragedy struck both Old Tom and Young Tom. In September of 1875, after they had played together the last hole of an important match, Young Tom received word that his pregnant wife was gravely ill. He and his father found a boat to take them across the Firth of Forth. Sadly, en route, they received another telegram that Young Tom's wife had died in childbirth. Young Tom, then 25 years old, went to live with his parents. He died that same December, having never fully recovered from his grief over the loss of his wife. Old Tom went on to live until the age of 80, when he accidentally fell down the cellar stairs of the St. Andrews clubhouse and died.

Willie Park Jr. (1864–1925).

Willie was born and raised in Scotland. By the time he was 16, he had already lived a boyhood steeped in golf legend and lore. His father won four Open Championships, and his uncle (Mungo) won the Open in 1874. Willie and his boyhood friend, Young Willie Dunn, regularly spent their days caddying and golfing. By 1889, Park had won two Open Championships (1887, 1889), and by age 22, he had laid out his first golf course. Willie left Scotland in early 1900 and began a successful golf course design business in London. He went on to design more than 175 courses in Austria, Canada, France, Monaco, Switzerland, and the United States. He was well known for his ability to play in Open Championships and on Scottish international teams while at the same time having several courses in progress.

Some of Park's courses in the United States are New York's Maidstone, Olympia Fields in Chicago, and Tumble Brook in Connecticut. In Northern Ireland, Park designed the first 9 holes of the City of Derry Golf Club and gave advice in remodeling Larne Golf Club. In the Republic of Ireland, he was consulted on the bunkering at Killarney Golf Club and had a hand in revisions at Tramore and Waterford.

Park had his own ideas when it came to golf course architecture. He believed that in order to lay down a course, the designer had to be a player as well. He also preferred seashore land with its grasses over the expense of sowing a course. Park also advocated the classic links layout—that is, straight out for the first 9 holes and straight back for the back 9. One of his truly visionary opinions was that crisscrossing fairways should be at a minimum. This was not only to prevent accidents, but also to provide a more enjoyable game for the more timid player. Park recommended two or three long holes at the start, to prevent congestion of players and provide a warm-up to the game. His courses feature a variety of large greens with natural turf that, while level, are not flat. Finally, with regard to bunkers, Park was a firm believer in their intelligent and strategic placement. He felt that a good golfer should never "visit" them and that they should be within view at the tee. He also criticized the practice of placing hazards in front of every green, because doing so forced players to pitch all their approaches rather than exercise their judgment regarding lofting or running up.

Harry Vardon (1870–1937). Born in England, Vardon learned golf as a young boy while caddying at the Royal Jersey Golf Club. His rise to golfing acclaim did not come until he was about 26, when he beat John Henry Taylor in 1896. Later that same year, he won his first British Open, becoming the first Englishman to win that title. He went on to win six Open Championships, the last at age 44. Vardon was plagued throughout his life with poor health, beginning with a bout of severe faintness during the 1903 Open. Diagnosed with tuberculosis, he entered a sanatorium.

In terms of his playing, he was famous for the accuracy and power of his swing. An interesting side note is that, contrary to popular opinion, Vardon did not invent the "Vardon grip." In reality, another well-known golfer, J. E. Laidlay of Scotland, invented the then-unorthodox overlapping grip. Laidlay won two Amateur Championships, in 1889 and 1891, using his grip, well before Vardon went on to popularize it.

Vardon's professional life was centered for 34 years at South Hertfordshire Golf Club outside London. In January of 1900, he traveled to the United States, where he spent a year touring and promoting a new ball called the Vardon Flyer. You probably have not heard of it, because the Haskell rubber-cored ball overshadowed it. But Vardon played many exhibition matches while in the States, including the U.S. Open Championship, during which he beat John Henry Taylor by two strokes. Another great golfing story is that Vardon returned to the States in 1913 with the intention of winning the U.S. Open again. Odds were placed in favor of either Vardon or the current British Open Champion, Ted Ray. A dark-horse American amateur named Francis Ouimet decided to enter the match because it was being played in his hometown, however, and he ended up beating both of the illustrious British golfers. This was the point, at Vardon's expense, at which American golfers entered the golfing arena.

Vardon was not as prolific a writer on golf architecture as some of his peers, but his views are no less specific. His guidelines are readily apparent as his architectural "signature." Watch for them while playing one of his courses. For one thing, Vardon stressed the importance of having the necessary amount of land for a given course. Thus, he recommended at least 70 acres for an 18-hole course and 200 to 300 acres for a good links course. He also suggested that a good 9-hole course is better than a cramped 18-hole layout if land is in short supply. Another of his preferences was to have a short 4th hole, so that a player having a difficult day with drives could recover early in the round. He also had little patience for holes longer than 530 yards, because he felt that the serious golfer's skills were not really tested in length alone.

One of Vardon's iconoclastic views was that it was preferable to test the scratch player than to "water down" a course's difficulty for higher-handicap players, contrary to the preferences of club committees who tried to cater to their higher-handicap members. He favored bunkers that demanded a long carry from the tee so that all players could improve their games. Further, he recommended many bunkers made as difficult as the committees would allow. Other Vardon hallmarks were undulating greens and at least two tees per hole for variation of play. In Ireland, one can play Vardon-designed courses at Bundoran (County Donegal), Delgany (County Wicklow), Douglass (County Cork), and portions of Rosapenna (County Donegal).

This concludes our brief biography section for some of Ireland's time-honored golf architects. Many younger-generation Irishmen have made or are making considerable marks upon the landscape as well; these include Robert Browne, Eddie Connaughton, Tom Craddock, Maurice Fives, Peter McEvoy, Patrick Merrigan, Christy O'Connor Jr., Pat Ruddy, Des Smyth, Arthur Spring, and Philip Walton. We're sure that Old Tom Morris is watching their handiwork, wishing he could send a featherie across any of the courses of these men. That's the beauty of golf in Ireland—it just keeps getting better.

CHAPTER FIVE

What about Linksland?

There seems to be considerable confusion over the terms *links* and *linksland.* Some golf course architects, administrators, golf pros, and course members refer to their courses as "links" courses, while others loudly proclaim that the courses in question are "seaside" at best. Others merrily tell their living partners that they are "off to the links" when they are referring to the course down the road whether the road happens to be in Kansas or in County Derbyshire. Even the title of this book uses the word *links* in reference to all the courses in Ireland. Still others insist that *linksland* has a very specific definition and, further, that there is very little of it on the entire planet.

So what is the deal with *links* and *linksland,* and how are we to make any sense of the matter? Well, we are not so foolish as to pretend that we can completely resolve an issue that has been around for centuries and will no doubt continue through this century, but we will resolve it to the best of our knowledge and for the purposes of this book.

We have posed the question "What is linksland?" to many people, ranging from a Scottish greenkeeper to an Irish golf course architect. We have also poured over the writings of old masters in golf course design. Compiling these thoughts, opinions, and some facts, we have arrived at the following definition. Linksland is the transitional stretch of soil-covered sand that occurs between the sea and the ground structure of the landmass. This condition invariably occurs in areas referred to as dunes or where the sea has receded and the soil builds up a thin crust over the sand below. Thus, linksland can only occur where a thin layer of topsoil overlies substantial deposits of naturally occurring sand.

The fact that a course is situated by the sea does not by itself render it a links course, despite what the folks at Pebble Beach and a host of other courses throughout the world would like you to believe. The *link* in *linksland* is all about this notion of linking the sea to the prevailing soil structure of the main landmass. In some places, there is no buildup of sand layered with topsoil. Instead, there is simply prevailing landmass meeting the sea, such as where steep cliffs lead to higher ground covered with deep topsoil. There is no link of topsoil-covered sand between the cliffs and the sea, and without this link, there is no linksland. Such a course is simply and more accurately called *seaside,* Pebble Beach being an example. Seaside courses are often extremely beautiful and may be glorious to play, but they do not play in the same unique manner as true links courses.

Defining *linksland* and distinguishing a links course from other course types is important because of the unique playing characteristics of links golf courses. Most golfers who are not used to playing links courses assume that the main characteristics of linksland are sand dunes, heavy winds, ocean views, and some sort of nasty, wide-open rough, perhaps dotted with a few gorse shrubs but never with trees. While these characteristics are indeed on or near many links courses, they represent only part of the links picture. Equally important is how the course plays, and links courses play like no other courses in the world. Firm, well-drained fairways and greens are salient characteristics of linksland. Close-cut fairways, where you could use a putter from tee to greens, and greens so hard that you must sneak your ball onto them are also hallmarks of links golf. And then there is the wind: wind that blows from any direction, sometimes even circular; wind that gusts and wind that sustains at practically gale-force intensity. Wind in every conceivable manifestation is both the unseen terror and the fascinating aspect of linksland.

As if this linksland issue were not complicated enough, along come some really intense golf aficionados who talk about a course "playing like a links" and in fact call such courses *links-like.* Some of Ireland rests upon a porous limestone substructure, known as karst topography, that drains the soil above it very effectively. When a golf course is located on karst features and is exposed to strong winds and sun, the result is often fairways and greens that are hard and fast. Indeed, we find the curious reference of "links-like" to courses that in reality have no true links characteristics, except that they have similar playing conditions, and only at certain times of the year.

Linksland does not exist where seaside ground has had thousands of truckloads of sand dumped on it and spread to a uniform thickness, with a soil layer of varying thickness spread over that artificial sand base. This is sometimes done in Ireland to help the soil drain, enabling the course to remain open all year. Many of the parkland courses not located on karst topography become waterlogged in the winter by almost daily showers. When courses close, members get vocal, and revenues plummet. In recent times, a few courses have started using this type of course preparation primarily for the drainage benefits. As a perceived secondary benefit, however, these courses are being referred to as "links" or as "links-like." This practice, according to our way of thinking, stretches the definition beyond the bulwark of its credibility.

Finally, what about this usage of *links* in everyday language and in our book title? As most of you are aware, the home and origin of the modern game of golf is St. Andrews in Scotland. St. Andrews and many courses built for some period of time thereafter were on classic linksland and were called, correctly, links courses. Playing a round of golf was commonly referred to as "going to the links" or "playing a round on the links." In time, *golf* and *links* became synonymous. As golf course development expanded inland, onto land other than linksland, the reference of "going to the links" remained. Therefore, phrases in common usage, such as "I'm heading off for the links" when the reference is clearly to a parkland course, have become perfectly acceptable, although technically incorrect. Golfers are even called *linksmen*. Our language, then, has adopted the term *links* to refer in a general sense to all things golf, and it is in this vein that we use *links* in the title of our book.

So back to the question, What exactly is linksland, and how are we to make any sense of the matter? Obviously, most people take great liberties with the term *links*, and this ruffles the feathers of a few purists. In the final analysis, though, we do not think that the great masters and forefathers of golf were as concerned about precise terminology as they were about a good round of golf, wherever it might be located. Indeed, Old Tom Morris, as the father of golf course architecture, used both links and parkland ground to achieve the desired result at one of his classics, Rosapenna Golf Club. Our gift to you, then, is permission not to be too concerned with semantics. Rather, just go out and enjoy the course, wherever it may be located, in this great golfing mecca called Ireland.

CHAPTER SIX

The Evolution of the Links

BY PAT RUDDY

Mr. Pat Ruddy is one of Ireland's unique personalities when it comes to golf. Not only is he a golf writer and editor of his own golf magazine, Golfer's Companion, but he has also designed some of Ireland's premier courses, including Ballyliffin (Glashedy Links), St. Margaret's, Connemara Isles, and Druids Glen. Most notably, Pat has designed and operates the European Club, his own version of Ireland's cherished classic links. Players who visit his venue are given a card with his own philosophy ("local rules") as they leave the world behind to play this special course.

When asked to name the single thing that has most improved golf in the last century, few people can answer correctly, it seems to me. Better golf balls and better golf clubs spring to the minds of most. Thus, it may come as a surprise that advances in grass-cutting equipment have actually done the most for the growth of golf. This single improvement has made it possible for the game to be played in all seasons and in all terrains upon which grass grows. In the beginning, the game was played only on linksland. Even then, it was confined largely to winter and early spring, when the grasses were dormant and the golf ball could be found. It was a truth then and still is today that this very difficult game becomes impossible to play if you cannot find your golf ball!

Advances in golf-related machinery also play a part in the evolution of the game. Cross-over holes were a big feature of the early linksland game. For example, old sketches of the layout at Prestwick in Scotland show as many as 14 holes crisscrossing in a crazy tapestry of lines.

Two reasons come to mind for this arrangement of holes, aside from the fact that the game was in its infancy and in the beginning merely an adornment to an afternoon's stroll in the countryside. First, possibilities for moving earth were limited in the premachine age, and early golfers probably arranged the tees and fairways so that they could see where the ball went after the stroke was made. Large valleys in the dunes would have been visible from several sides; crisscrossing would allow players to revisit these valleys often. A second reason for revisiting the same spot via crisscrossing had to do with grass growth as a result of high traffic. In frequently traversed areas, the grass would be naturally sparse; the bare spots allowed for better golf, as the passage of many feet helped keep the grasses down. With so few people playing the game in those days, this was a feasible solution to the problem of "fairway quality" and links routing. Even the early British Open Championships attracted as few as eight competitors; it wasn't until the forty-first championship at Muirfield (1901) that 101 players took part!

Such a crisscross layout would lead to utter chaos and mammoth danger today, when the busier centers of the sport see two hundred plus players teeing up daily. Thankfully, the lawn mower has come to the rescue. Indeed, this machine has opened up the game to the millions of people who do not have easy access to linksland (the sandy deposits, whether on high dunes or in flatter systems, that link the beach to the inland soils). With the lawn mower, today the game can be played in pastures and meadows, reclaimed swamps, and mountains and, very important, even during grass-growing seasons.[1]

With the advent of new earth-moving and grass-mowing machinery, America awoke to golf, and that great landmass presented itself as a magnificent target for the propagation of the sport. Enterprising souls who set out to establish inland golf courses copied the shapes and forms, even the grasses, of the old links. They had nothing else on which to base their thinking. So all modern golf courses have, insofar as drainage and budgets allow, human-made mounds, swales, and bunkers that imitate what happened largely as a

gift of nature on the links. In the early 1890s, two Scots, "Young Willie" Dunn and Donald Ross, arrived in America to lay out golf courses. Shinnecock Hills, which started as a 12-hole course, was Young Willie's first big contribution, and Pinehurst was Ross's big calling card. It can hardly be coincidental that both of these creations are on sandy ground, whose free-draining properties allowed their creators to introduce the deep bunkering, dramatic greenside swales, and hollow features that are natural characteristics of links golf.

The trans-Atlantic influence in golf architecture continues to this day, with the great exponents of the art traveling to Britain and Ireland to immerse themselves in the feel and spirit of the original game: linksland golf. Charles Blair Macdonald unashamedly copied features from famous links when establishing the National Golf Links of America just over the fence from Shinnecock Hills. Many Pete Dye courses give British and Irish visitors quite a shock when the players recognize elements from their own links. The "younger" men, such as Tom Watson, Ben Crenshaw, and Johnny Miller, are open admirers of links golf and design. Courses associated with their names invariably carry a links-look or two. A procession of other worldwide designers patrols the British and Irish links in search of virtually endless inspiration. A month never goes by without visits by golf course designers from America,

---

[1] Recent promoters of seaside and cliff-top courses, led by Pebble Beach in America, seek to describe their golf courses as *links*. In point of fact, only a course set out upon linksland is a true "links" course. All others are, strictly speaking, golf courses. To allow confusion on this issue is to allow the corruption of the language and definitions of the sport. In turn, this leads to further confusion over the origins of golf architecture.

Australia, Japan, Africa, and, indeed, every place that the game is played.

So what do these people hope to find? *Ruggedness* springs to mind. Today seems to be an age of socialite golfers who play golf for business or social reasons more than for the love of the sport itself. Thus we see golf courses turned into flower-bestrewn botanical gardens with not a blade of grass tall enough to upset the progress of a lame grasshopper.

It's not surprising that there is a natural impulse for the game to remain true to its origins. Golf, like all sport in its essence, is meant to be a test of the human spirit and body. It is meant to be bruising to those who fail to meet their own targets and absolutely elating to the victor who reaches the personal pinnacle, whether that be a 70, 80, or 90, or even a first 99! What an extraordinary game it is that can engage both a great champion struggling with the demon of self-doubt and a local 24-handicapper exulting over the achievements of the day. Both restlessly and confidently await more triumphs on the morrow. The overcoming of the foe is the thing: the defeat of the cowardly foe within, or the skilled foe without, or the foe represented by Nature's elements, never more adversarial than on the true links. For it is on the links that one meets the primeval forces of the sea, the land, and the sky coming together in a convulsion of savage movement, with noise and rain in the morning and as a shadow-strewn seductress in the afternoon sun!

This factor of ruggedness cannot be copied and brought inland. When the gods of golf are at play in the seaside dunes, they are at their most vexatious and amusing best. The fairway wood of the morning becomes an afternoon short iron. The morning player declares a hole "Impossible!" and the afternoon player finds it an "Easy birdie!"

So a true links becomes several golf courses all in one. And the task of the designer becomes all the more complex. It becomes a task that could lead to dementia but for the fact that the moods of the links are at least matched by the lovely craziness and adventuresome nature of the true golfer who revels in golf, with all its cruel and lovely shapes and moods. The game proceeds no matter. In this situation, how can one define the best of essential elements of a links? How can one set about designing a golf links that will be a great challenge for the champion and a pleasure to the duffer?

The answer: rely on the spirit of the golfer to identify with his or her own instincts on each given piece of linksland. Let the land and the sky and the sea venture into one's soul, and let the art form emerge. By all means, use rulers and engineers' tools to measure playable golf shots, and try to present a collection of golf situations that relate to modern shot values. But when the winds blow and howl, it becomes much more a battle with Nature and with oneself than with anything a human designer could create. This is when the modern golfer has to really learn about golf as a form of self-expression rather than a set of mathematical equations. God help the American who has become dependent on the yardage book or sprinkler heads with distances. With the winds howling, that flag 150 yards away is now out of reach! Or how can a ball be stopped on a green the size of a tablecloth and as welcoming as concrete with a force 8 tailwind? What this translates to is that a modern links expecting to host major tournament golf needs the protection of yardage. The best exponents of the game can make low numbers on courses below 7,000 yards on a calm day. But tournament golf is only one element of the game, and thrills and tribulations aplenty await the average player in the dunes, even at 6,500 yards.

Finally, a word on beauty. Upmarket, inland golf has become something of a gardening contest. On the links, golf has more to do with raw Nature. This is a person's opportunity to step back into time, when humans first began to walk this planet. The best linksland holes are presented not just as great tests of physical skill and human spirit, but also as microlandscapes, with the player walking into one picture postcard after another, gasping at the splendor of it all, wondering how anything could be more perfect. On a links course, one looks back and sees the wonderland that one has just left. Time is suspended. A troubled world has vanished. Don't spoil it by resisting. Get out of that worrying, aching, snarling animal body that controls too much of your life. Forget dinner, forget the mobile phone, forget the stock market, forget the family.…Get into the links and let it get into you. That, my friend, is Golf.

CHAPTER SEVEN

The Unique Maintenance of Links Courses

BY JOHN ROUINE

Mr. John Rouine has been Lahinch Golf Club's superintendent of the course since 1988. John obtained his Diploma of Amenity Horticulture from Dublin's Botanical Gardens, along with a degree in Rural Science and certification in Sport Turf Management. He is also chief handler and keeper of Lahinch's famous wild goats.

If you're looking for a challenge as well as the best year-round conditions for playing golf in Ireland, then look no further than a golf course on duneland. In Ireland's spectacular duneland, you will play courses that take you over towering sand dunes, rolling terrain of marram grass, and undulating fescue-and-bent fairways. You will be met with breathtaking ocean views, rugged cliffs, and sand dunes flowing onto sandy shores—all forming the backdrop so unique to Ireland's links courses.

If playing a links is an exhilarating experience, course maintenance can be equally demanding and challenging. On a year-round basis, a links course is exposed to extreme weather conditions. The summer and autumn seasons bring warm, damp winds from the southwest, while winter calls forth the less common northern and eastern winds that can linger into spring and become a greenkeeper's nightmare. The northern and eastern winds are drier and colder, constituting a threat to freshly sown indigenous grasses such as fine bent and fescue. Experienced greenkeepers on seaside courses are aware of the problems of sowing indigenous grass seed into light, sandy soils but take the risks because these grasses remain the best grasses upon which to play.

The wind interferes with turf growth in a number of ways. First, the winds cause cooling that increases transpiration, along with salt deposition and displacement. Wind also sets in motion the transport of sand that results in abrasive action on plants and bunker edges. Whipping wind results in sand-shift in bunkers, giving poor lies for wind-stressed golfers. Second, deposition of windblown sand can smother the grass completely. However, while the wind wreaks havoc with most plants, accumulating sand among the marram grass near the shoreline actually helps this unique grass flourish, because the replenished sand is a rooting medium. A third effect of wind is that the abrasive, blasting action of gale-force winds frequently shears off turf plants at the soil surface. Only the tough indigenous dune-grasses are adapted to these conditions. These salt-tolerant grasses stand up to the constant action of the sea dashing against the rocks and shoreline, with onshore winds laden with salt.

Thus, we see that it is vital for the links greenkeeper to understand the basic conditions found so widely in nature in order to maximize growing conditions throughout the year. Further, the links greenkeeper must beware of overfeeding with nitrates and phosphates and of artificial watering—these processes favor the invasion of annual meadow grass at the expense of fescue and bents. Annual meadow grass is disease susceptible, shallow rooting, and not drought tolerant. Of more immediate concern to the golfer, meadow grass produces a slower putting surface and, because it seeds twice a year, can reduce a good green to a bad one in short order.

Most well-managed links courses have fescue-dominated greens with some bent and a little poa (preferably less than 5 percent). At Lahinch, the aim of our maintenance program is to produce firm, fast, true greens. In order to achieve this, we aerate regularly, using a variety of aeration tools. For example, we routinely use the coremaster and vertidrain, as well as drought-resistant and tolerant finer grasses, to encourage deeper rooting. We have found that this is the only way our climate can produce ecologically viable and manageable golf turf. This system ensures optimum greens, taking account of our climate and increasing levels of play.

Every links greenkeeper faces several serious challenges. One is to keep the playing surfaces aerated regularly and deeply. A second is to counteract the increasing compaction from machinery and feet as the amount of play increases. The greenkeeper also must strike a balance between feeding and aerating (to counteract wear) and overfeeding and overwatering, since the indigenous bents and fescues require well-structured, well-drained, uncompacted soils of low fertility.

A sound knowledge of greens and their formation, maintenance, and development is essential for the chair of the greens. The chair, ultimately, will be in a position to convincingly explain to the members the importance of aeration (why and when) and how aeration affects the greens on which they play. By and large, members are helpful if they know what is going on but, alternatively, very unforgiving if they do not.

It is not always possible to aerate the links as much as one would like. As soon as the weather begins to improve, out come the golfers, and it becomes impractical to aerate more frequently than once a month. The process of aeration causes delays to players who have paid fees and want to enjoy their game, preferably undisturbed by the machinery and manpower required. In order to strike the greenkeeper-golfer balance, one must compromise on frequency of aeration to avoid interference with the game that, after all, provides the links course's "bread and butter."

A bone of contention between greenkeeper and golfer arises when a decision is made to close the course because of frosty weather. This can often be the situation in the depths of winter, when temperatures drop below freezing. The greenkeeper must ensure that the course remains open, if at all possible. Professional judgment must also be utilized, however, in the care and protection of the course. It is often difficult to decide when to reopen a course that has been closed once the frost begins to thaw. A difficulty can arise if the secretary, captain, chair of greens, or even the professional overrules the greenkeeper and opens the course (as may be the case at any club). If that happens, the person opening the course must straight away take responsibility with the Greens Committee for any damage that may occur when a penetrating frost begins to thaw.

You might wonder why a frost is so potentially devastating for a links course. In a frost, a wet surface forms over deeper, frozen ground. Playing upon this surface causes shearing of roots, muddying around pin positions, and discoloration—all of which lead to thinning of the swards, a weakened root structure, and, come spring, delayed leaf and root growth. This further results in poor and slow growing conditions, thus delaying the availability of quality putting surfaces for the main competition season. This is particularly true of the slow-growing grasses on links courses, leading to tricky putting surfaces, where the pitch-and-run shot is part and parcel of the game. The greenkeeper is in the best position to decide if the course should be open or closed when thawing begins. It is this person, after all, who best understands the greens, their maintenance and treatment, and how vital work could be instantly undone by playing in adverse conditions. The greenkeeper's decision to close the course may not always be popular, but it will ultimately ensure that the player enjoys his or her game on better greens for longer periods of time.

In writing this article, I have tried to touch on basic, practical principles that in some way or another affect the maintenance of links courses and hence their playability. There are many more integral parts of links management, beyond the scope of this chapter. Some apply to golf courses in general, while others are unique to the links, such as the occurrence and treatment of particular diseases, pests of turf, and species of weeds, as well as divot repair and rough management. Revetting of bunkers, a method of hazard construction often found on links courses, is

another concern. The role of modern maintenance equipment and adequate maintenance sheds, along with an effi-
cient, dedicated, and knowledgeable staff, cannot be
overlooked. I hope that this discussion gives you a better
understanding and appreciation of the unique features of
links courses and the importance of careful attention and
maintenance to our spectacular Irish courses.

CHAPTER EIGHT

The Natural Bunkers of the Royal County Down

BY BRIAN COBURN

We had the wonderful good fortune of enlisting Mr. Brian Coburn to write the following article for our guide. Mr. Coburn is covenor (superintendent) of the Royal County Down Golf Club in Northern Ireland. He is also editor of the Irish golf magazine Greenside.

The most memorable feature for a visitor playing the links at the Royal County Down Golf Club in Northern Ireland is the backdrop of the Mourne Mountains. A close second is the natural bunkers found on this unique course.

Going back in time to the misty past of golf, it is hard to identify exactly how and when the game began. One thing is certain, however—this ancient sport was developed in Scotland on that country's seaside links, and it was the Scots who taught other nations how to play it. According to one theory, Scottish fishermen invented the game to amuse themselves on their way home as they returned from their boats to their village. As they made their way through the coastal paths of the sand dunes, they would sometimes hit a pebble with a piece of driftwood. At times the pebble would fall into a sandy hollow created by the scraping of animals; these hollows formed obstacles that were probably the birth of bunkers.

The famous Old Tom Morris was commissioned to design a links course at Newcastle in County Down for a fee not to exceed four guineas, and in time it became the Royal County Down Golf Club. The site was chosen because it was close to the railway connection between Belfast and Newcastle, convenient for Belfast businesspeople. In those days, the golf architect followed the natural pathways that snaked their way through the duneland; animals set down these paths as they foraged through the dunes. The greens were formed on the flat, lush areas closely grazed by sheep or other animals, where the natural fescue and bent grass flourished on their droppings.

With no earth-moving equipment of any kind available, the designer in earlier days had to make use of the natural terrain and weave the course through the sand hills and mounds created by wind. The only grasses available were the natural fescues and bent grasses of the area and other seaside grasses such as marram grass. Bunkers were dug out by hand from loose areas close to fairways or greens. When the popularity of the game increased and the extra traffic caused wear on these old links, turf science was gradually introduced to keep them maintained.

Although there have been many changes to the layout of the Royal County Down course, the construction and appearance of the bunkers have changed little over the years. These bunkers were constructed in such a way to generally gather a stray ball, or they were strategically placed beside a green to catch the shot that slipped across the wind. The natural dune sand of the area is used in the bunkers, and each one has a shield of marram grass, heather, wildflowers, and other natural grasses growing along the sides and edges. Members know this mixture of grasses and heather as "the features," often referred to as "the beardies." The maintenance staff take great care to avoid chemical spray drift into these areas, because chemicals could be harmful and damaging to the wild grasses and heather. The "run-in" area of the bunkers is left open to gladly accept a ball traveling off the fairway or green.

The British Isles is a particularly windy area, and Northern Ireland is certainly no exception. The prevailing wind generally blows from the southwest, but it can come from any direction. In the early part of the year, during the spring equinox, the County Down coast can be subject to a cold, biting east wind that makes course maintenance difficult for the superintendent. One practical use of the bunker "features" is that they provide some shelter and protection from the wind. During windy periods, sand loss from the bunkers is common, and sometimes the front is undermined by the swirling currents; the "features" help to keep this to a minimum.

These famous features are unpopular with some of the club's lower-handicap players, because a ball buried in the marram grass can be unplayable. Getting a proper stance to address the ball can be a problem. This is unusual, however; the ball is most likely to land or finish in the sand.

With advances in golf club and golf ball technology, a number of small modifications and minor remodeling projects have taken place in recent years. These changes have been in an effort to cope with the extra distance players are now achieving. A few new bunkers have been introduced in strategic positions, but they have been constructed in exactly the same format as the older ones. Despite modern golf techniques, most of the existing bunkers are still well in play.

When Sir Michael Bonallack, in his position as secretary of the Royal and Ancient Golf Club of St. Andrews, inspected the links at the Royal County Down prior to the Amateur Championship in early 1999, he was asked if the bunkers were acceptable. He said he was delighted with the bunkering; it reminded him of the time he won the Amateur at the Royal County Down back in 1970. As he emphasized, "If a player is off line, then he must pay the price." Since then, Sir Michael has taken up the honor of being elected captain of the Royal and Ancient.

The bunkering at the Royal County Down is unique and totally different from that at other links courses in the British Isles. All links in Scotland and England, and indeed most others in Ireland, have some revetted bunkers. This specialized type of bunker is characterized by numerous layers of sod forming a steep face, with the sand tapered back to allow the golfer to splash out. One well-known Scottish greenkeeper said, "A links course is not a links without revetted bunkers"—a statement that I totally reject.

The natural bunkers surrounded by marram grass and heather are part of the heritage of the Royal County Down Golf Club. They have caused grief to every member of the club at some time and indeed to many famous golfers over the years. They must be preserved, however. This message will be passed on to the next generation, and, I hope, the bunkering will remain a great feature of this world-famous golf course for a very long time.

CHAPTER NINE

Golf and Geology in Ireland

Unless you're a professional geologist or consummate rock hound, you probably don't know that Ireland is a mecca for anyone interested in geology in general and glaciers in particular. You might well ask, "What the heck do geology and glaciers have to do with golf, and why would I ever need to know anything about them when I go golfing in Ireland?"

The answer lies in many of Ireland's golf courses that include or are in close proximity to remarkable geological features that make these courses unique. One of our basic philosophies is that the more you know about something, the more you may appreciate it, and perhaps that extra knowledge and understanding will come in handy. Just think of your own game. If you know that a course uses bent grass on its greens and you know the properties of bent grass, you will probably adjust your putting to allow for faster play on a warm, dry day. You will play better if you know the differences between bent, fescue, Bermuda, and zoysia grasses. We're not implying that you'll have better golf in Ireland if you know the difference between certain glacial features, such as eskers and drumlins, but the knowledge may help you understand why some courses drain better than others, have different kinds of rough, and are more hilly, for example—and it may just help you appreciate their natural landscape more.

So let's start with a nutshell version of Ireland's geological history, and then we'll more closely relate it to geological features that characterize Irish golf courses and, in some cases, could affect your play.

Ireland as we know it today is a large island off the northwestern shore of mainland Europe. Scientists estimate Earth's age at about 4 billion years, and Ireland's oldest rocks date to 1.7 billion years. These are found on the smaller island of Inishtrahull, just off the northern coast of County Donegal. (You can get a glimpse of Inishtrahull from Ballyliffin Golf Club; head for Malin Head peninsula, from which the island is north about 5 miles out to sea.) These last 1.7 billion years have been characterized by huge changes on the Earth's crust, including massive mountain building and, in places such as Ireland, the shearing away by glaciers of land miles thick. Most of the erosion, however, is a consequence of mountain uplift during the following periods: Tertiary (1–63 million years ago), Permian (230–280 million years ago), Devonian (345–405 million years ago), and Silurian (405–600 million years ago). This means that, while glaciation wore down many of Ireland's mountains, it did not affect more lowland areas.

You may be surprised to learn that Ireland has not always been what we see today and has not always been in the same location. Geologists suggest that Earth passed through a hot, liquid stage as it was formed. As the liquid cooled, it formed a solid crust, called Pangaea. This is the name that Alfred Wegener gave in 1910 to the supercontinent that he believed existed from 300 to 200 million years ago. Pangaea was actually the first continent, huge in scope. It went through several phases of splitting and joining, such that the landmasses we know as our modern continents were finally separated by about 250 million years ago. Continents do not actually have "roots." They float across the Earth's crust in a process called continental drift. This drift continues even today, causing faults such as California's San Andreas Fault. Scientists describe continents as tips of huge chunks of the Earth's crust, or plates; the movement of these plates is called plate tectonics.

Test this notion for yourself on a map of the world. You will see that our modern continents seem to fit together like pieces of a gigantic jigsaw puzzle, reminiscent of the old Pangaea. Thus, South America could neatly fit against the western coast of Africa, and the eastern coast of North America, when added to Greenland, could fit together with the European plate and the western bulge of the African plate. We also know that the oceans of today were formed as the plates moved apart. An early ocean called the Iapetus

Ocean separated the North American and European plates and was the ancestor of our present-day Atlantic Ocean. Scientists have also documented several reversals of Earth's magnetic field, meaning that the North and South Poles have switched positions. All this activity—continents drifting, oceans widening, and magnetic poles reversing—continues today. In fact, geologists estimate that the North American and European plates continue to move apart at a rate of about 2 inches per year.

Although Ireland today appears to be one large, intact island, this has not always been the case. Scientists have put together a fossil record showing that Ireland was at one time two smaller pieces. The northern half was part of Greenland on the North American plate, and the southern half was part of the European plate, with the Iapetus Ocean separating them. It's amazing to think that Ireland began its journey about 500 million years ago, somewhere near the latitude of today's South Africa. By about 440 million years ago, these two halves slammed together (geologically speaking), with the "seam" in the area around Clogher Head in County Louth, a little north and inland from Drogheda. Scientists have found a mixture of fossils, some North American and others European, on this seam, showing that plants and animals from the two different continents mingled. You will be in this zone if you play County Louth Golf Club at Baltray or Seapoint Golf Club near Termonfeckin. By 250 million years ago, Ireland had a desert climate and was located somewhere near present-day Egypt.

Despite all these phenomenal geological changes, a fairly extensive fossil record suggests that life on Earth probably began sometime around 3.5 billion years ago. Early marine forms found in Ireland include small algae, trilobites (walnut- to fist-size animals with hard, jointed shells), bony-plated fish, and marine creatures called brachiopods, with shells formed of two valves. The earlier, more primitive forms of fish gave rise to amphibians and then reptiles, including dinosaurs by about 225 million years ago. Valencia Island in County Kerry has a 10-yard stretch of priceless footprints made by an amphibian some 385 million years ago. Scientists speculate that this creature was about a yard in length and had four legs well adapted to walking. It probably had a tail that did not leave imprints because the animal was wading in shallow, muddy waters with its tail buoyed by the water. It is a privilege to see this trail of fossil footprints on Valencia; only five other such sites exist on all of Earth, and the other four are in Australia and Brazil. Valencia Island is just off the Ring of Kerry, about midway between Dooks and Waterville Golf Clubs.

Just as there have been remarkable changes in Earth's fauna (animals), so too have there been shifts and changes as the flora (plants) have evolved and developed. Primitive plant life in the form of algae (550 million years ago) left behind beautiful trace fossils of fanlike impressions on Bray Head in County Wicklow, near Woodbrook Golf Club. The first land plants had evolved by 450 million years ago. A fascinating part of the fossil record shows that very primitive land plants were swept into the sea around 430 million years ago and preserved in submarine sediments in what are now the Slieve Bloom Mountains. (If you play the clubs at Roscrea, Tullamore, or Heath, you will be in the foothills of these gorgeous mountains.) Forms similar to today's horsetails are prevalent in the fossil record by 320 million years ago, with their debris accumulating in swamps and eventually being transformed into coal. Coal was formerly mined in limited areas in Counties Laois, Kilkenny, and Tipperary; around Lough Allen in County Leitrim and Coalisland near Dungannon (County Tyrone); and at Ballycastle in County Antrim.

As we have seen, Ireland has gone through several significant climatic changes, resulting in various rock layers, or strata, depending on the source of the sediment. For example, there have been many cycles in which the ocean has flooded the land, followed by mountain building and glaciers which soaked up seawater, causing the land to rise again above sea level. Thus, limestone (about 330 million years old) of the Burren in County Clare and chalk layers (about 85 million years old) seen in Northern Ireland around Ballycastle Golf Club were formed by marine creatures with skeletons or shells that died and formed deposits on the bottom of the oceans. Sandstone strata such as the Old Red layers around County Cork (clearly visible from the clubhouse at Youghal Golf Club, looking at the opposite shore of the River Blackwater) were formed by rivers transporting huge quantities of sand that eventually hardened. The layers of shale found along the southwestern coast were deposited in times of shallow, muddy estuaries. The granite seen in and around the Wicklow Mountains formed as molten rock oozed upward from the Earth's core to harden in the form of mountains some 400 million years ago. If you get to Rathsallagh Golf Club in Dunlavin, you will be able to see the looming, snow-capped form of Lugnaquilla Mountain, the highest point of the Wicklow Mountain range.

In Ireland, much of the bedrock is limestone that was laid down between 350 and 320 million years ago. Younger rocks—including sandstone and shale, readily seen in west County Clare (Lahinch, Kilkee), and chalk, now primarily confined to the northeast—have been removed by erosion over much of the country. Many of the limestone areas show evidence of solution of the rocks by rainwater. As you walk in the Burren area of County Clare (about 6 miles from Lahinch Golf Club), you will be directly on "pave-ment" that is a basal layer of limestone without its protective covering of soil and plants. This landform type, called karst topography, is similar to the rock underlying Indiana, with its limestone base cut through by caves, sinkholes, and underground channels.

As an interesting digression, Ireland's farming practices may not be amenable to karst topography. As you drive the country roads, you will notice pieces of plastic (usually black) everywhere. Farmers store their silage in large, black, plastic-coated rounds rather than in barns, and their fertilizers and feed are transported in large plastic sacks. You will see small shreds torn apart by the wind and stuck in tree-tops, with larger pieces impaled on fences and hedges and other pieces blowing across fields. The unsightliness of all this plastic is far less a problem than its effect on the Irish landmass. What happens is that the plastic finds its way from the treetops and fences down into ditches and across creeks and fields into larger rivers, finally getting lodged in a sinkhole or some other inaccessible place. The upshot is that the plastic clogs channels within the karst topography (caves and underground rivers) that once transported water and allowed for surface drainage. This has recently resulted in large- and small-scale floods and is sure to be a growing concern.

If you get up to Northern Ireland, be sure to check out the Giant's Causeway near Royal Portrush and Portstewart

Golf Clubs. This unique place was created about 65 million years ago when large-scale volcanic activity caused fissures in the ocean crust around Ireland, and molten lava was thrust upward as the North American and European plates moved apart. The lava came into contact with water and cooled, forming gigantic, multifaceted crystals of basalt over which you can climb and hike. Intrusion of granite resulted in massive mountain building, such as in the spectacular Mourne Mountains surrounding the Royal County Down Golf Club.

Ireland underwent a tremendous amount of volcanic activity from about 65 million years ago until about 50 million years ago. As this activity waned, it entered a period of warm weather. About 35 million years ago, Ireland was heavily forested and resembled today's Great Smoky Mountains. A huge lake, Lough Neagh in Northern Ireland's County Antrim, formed and was eventually surrounded by redwoods, palms, and swamp cypress. Scientists believe that by 25 million years ago, Ireland was still drifting away from North America and had reached its present-day latitude. By 13 million years ago, temperatures started falling as the Antarctic ice cap began to form.

The whole picture began to change by around 2 million years ago with the opening of the Ice Age, also known as the Pleistocene epoch. This period, which lasted until about 10,000 years ago, was a fascinating stage in geological history during which glaciers built up over Ireland and the entire British Isles, scouring and eroding many preceding layers and landforms. To be precise, this period comprised a succession of numerous stages of glaciation, each lasting around 10,000 to 40,000 years, interspersed with interglacial periods of warmer weather. The current "warm stage" in which we find ourselves is merely part of this overall pattern and will probably be followed by another period of glaciation.

We have now set the stage for you to understand the Irish countryside as you travel between golf courses. Most noticeable is the whole phenomenon of glaciers and their impact on the Irish landscape. Let's turn our attention now to examples of glacial processes and relate those features to some of Ireland's golf courses.

One of Ireland's great golfers and course designers is Christy O'Connor Jr. As it turns out, a course he recently designed, Esker Hills in Tullamore, County Offaly, has within its name a glacial feature. An esker is a long, vein-like ridge caused by glaciation. Scientists estimate that all of Ireland was once covered by a large mass of ice, possibly 1 to 1½ miles thick. As the meltwater on the surface of the glacier percolated down through fissures in the ice, it created discharge tunnels that ran along the surface of the land but underneath the glacial ice mass. Because glaciers are in a state of constant flux, water in some of the channels was diverted. This resulted in many ice tunnels being abandoned and filled up with sand and gravel. When the glacial ice finally melted away, the filled-in tunnels were left behind as long ridges, sometimes miles in length. The sand and gravel in the eskers is actually the material that was transported in the subglacial streams. The word *esker* is derived from a Gaelic word meaning "causeway," because eskers afforded natural roadways across the often boggy countryside. Eskers thus entered scientific geological jargon based on their presence in Ireland.

How do eskers affect golf in Ireland? Play Esker Hills Golf Club, and you will experience firsthand how these glacial features make for physically challenging play. You will be carrying your clubs and hiking up and down, across and around numerous ridges (the eskers), some of which are 10 to 15 feet high, several yards across, and hundreds of yards long. Other courses where you'll see eskers include Roscommon Golf Club in County Roscommon, County Longford Golf Club, and Mullingar Golf Club in County Westmeath.

A second glacial feature common to Ireland is the drumlin. This geological term originally meant "small hill." It is another example of a Gaelic word entering international scientific usage. Scientists are not certain how drumlins were formed but suggest that glacial ice molded mud, sand, and gravel at its base into ovoid masses as it moved across the landscape. When the ice finally melted, these masses were deposited onto the underlying land in clusters of drumlins, sometimes referred to as "egg-basket" formations. Today, fields of drumlins abound in Ireland and are large enough to be mistaken for ordinary small hills. As with eskers, drumlins make for hilly terrain and challenging golf.

Several areas in Ireland have heavy concentrations of drumlins. In Northern Ireland, these include the following counties: Antrim (Gracehill G.C.), Down (Clandeboye G.C.), Armagh, Fermanagh (Enniskillen G.C.), and parts of Tyrone (Dungannon G.C.). In the Republic, counties with drumlins dotting the landscape include Monaghan (Nuremore Country Club), Cavan (Slieve Russell G.C.), and parts of Roscommon and up into Donegal around Donegal Bay (Donegal G.C.). A second area of heavy concentration in the Republic is in Counties Mayo (Castlebar G.C.) and Clare (East Clare G.C.). A third, smaller area of drumlins is around the Slieve Miskish Mountains of County Cork (Bantry Bay G.C.).

A third glacial feature closely related to the drumlin is the erratic. Once you know what to look for, you'll be amazed at how common this phenomenon is as you traverse the Irish countryside. Erratics are often solitary boulders, sometimes the size of a small car, that have been dislodged from their original outcrop, caught up in a glacier, and transported, often hundreds of miles, finally to be dumped on some distant soil. To give you an idea of this remarkable process, consider Ailsa Craig, a huge conical peak in the Firth of Clyde, Scotland. If you play Turnberry Golf Club, you can see Ailsa Craig looming out at sea; the Ailsa Course is its namesake. It turns out that Ailsa Craig is composed of a unique type of very dense and easily recognizable granite. Chunks were broken off this cone by a passing glacier, and the erratics created from it have been found as far away as Cork Harbor in southeastern Ireland. While you probably won't see pieces of Ailsa, watch for large boulders dotting otherwise flat Irish farmlands. They are probably erratics.

A fourth glacial phenomenon quite prevalent in Ireland is the shape of many of its valleys. When a river cuts through high ground, it creates a V-shaped valley. The grinding action of the rocks embedded in the ice of glaciers, however, gouges out a U-shaped trench. If you drive through the Wicklow Mountains or play Mount Wolseley Golf Club in Tullow (County Carlow), Kilkea Castle in Castledermot, or the Curragh (County Kildare), you will see numerous U-shaped valleys.

Finally, a fifth glacial feature has to do with the soil itself. Glaciers move across and scour the underlying land; sand, rocks, gravel, and boulders are captured without any attention to size or mass. This unsorted mixture is carried along with the ice floe, actually causing the glacier to have "teeth" that in turn churn up even more rock material.

When glacial ice finally melts, this unsorted mixture is left behind; it is called glacial till, or diamict. This process differs from other geological processes, such as river flow, erosion, volcanic activity, or cycles of sea inundating land. In these nonglacial processes, the layers formed are distinct from each other and show internal organization such that older rock is generally found beneath younger forms—not the case with many glacial deposits. As you drive through Ireland, take a look at road cuts or other disturbances. You will often see that the soil is actually a jumble of pebbles, sand, gravel, and boulders—all evidence of glacial till.

So how does glacial till affect a golfer in Ireland? During particularly rainy months, golf courses located directly over glacial sand have naturally occurring drainage, because water can percolate through the deposit. As a result, they often remain playable even during heavy rainy seasons. These courses stand in contrast to those located on more homogeneous soil, such as parkland courses built on the alluvium of the Shannon River basin (e.g., Dromoland Castle G.C. in County Clare), and to moorland courses built over peat bogs (e.g., Ballinasloe G.C. in County Galway), both of which have difficulty staying playable during months of heavy rain because of problems with soil drainage.

Many golfing tourists seek out Ireland's classic links courses. The unique characteristics of these courses are described in another chapter, but let's take a moment here to consider their geological origins. Links courses are distinguished from the moorland, parkland, and seaside courses in that they are located on a thin topsoil over naturally occurring sand dunes in coastal areas. Where did this sand come from, and why is it limited to certain areas in coastal regions? Geologists speculate that coastal sand was deposited on the ocean floors after the glaciers finally melted (about 13,000 years ago) and was later transported back to land by wave action and then blown up onto the coast to form the spectacular dunes. Some examples of links courses are Ballybunion Golf Club in County Kerry, Lahinch Golf Club in County Clare, Rosapenna Golf Club in County Donegal, Royal Dublin Golf Club in County Dublin, and Cheann Sibeal Golf Club in County Kerry.

The other question related to the links courses is "Where did the topsoil come from?" This leads us to the topic of soil development. It's fairly remarkable that Ireland has any soil at all after glacial action scoured so many layers of its landmass. Geologists speculate that the Ireland of about 10,000 years ago did not have the soils that we see today. Many processes have contributed to the formation of today's soil, some natural and some artificial. Natural processes have included the formation of peat, as grasses called fens grew in and around the many lake basins left by the ice. The fens died and accumulated, eventually forming the fen peat that covers much of the Connemara and Ring of Kerry regions. If you have a chance to play Bearna Golf Club in County Galway, you will walk across an extensive tract of peat that in many places feels "bouncy" beneath your feet. Other natural processes of soil development have included the crushing of rock debris by freeze-thaw action; "sludging," during which subsoil has been brought to the surface; chemical changes brought about by water; the reduction of evaporation caused by high humidity; and the formation of humus by the decay of lush plant growth. For the links courses, soil development is a fragile and risky proposition, dependent on sparse grasses setting root, dying, and then contributing to the thin layer of humus that provides roots for successive generations of grass. So as you walk across the topsoil of links courses, think of the fragile soil clinging to the underlying sand, and fill in those divots.

As for human-made soil development, Irish farmers are responsible for much of the island's arable soil. They have been able to prevent a lot of soil erosion by erecting the netting of dry-stone fences, which can be seen everywhere; the fences "check" water runoff. Furthermore, farmers have, in effect, created soil. Within the stone fences along the coastal areas, farmers through the generations have dumped vast quantities of seaweed and sand, planted crops, and added crushed limestone, farmyard manure, or slurry to turn rocky terrain into arable soil.

One of Ireland's unique landscapes is that of its moorlands. These are areas covered by peat bogs, including blanket bogs and raised bogs. Bogs started to appear about 9,000 years ago and are buildups of fen grasses and sphagnum, often in the poorly drained land between drumlins. Today, these massive bogs practically envelop the terrain and are especially prominent in County Kerry and parts of Mayo. If you play Tralee Golf Club or Killarney Golf Club, you will see the surrounding countryside draped with dark, earthy peat bogs. One unusual aspect of these bogs is that they create a thick, but nonetheless delicate, covering that spreads over the land. If cuts are made into this mass so that additional rain can soak through, the whole mass becomes an unsteady water bog, sliding onto the surrounding countryside. This phenomenon is called bog-burst, and indeed, there are accounts of entire villages being overrun by a bog.

Ireland's parkland courses are characterized by lush vegetation and old-growth trees. This brings us to the controversial topic of the island's deforestation. Just as bogs began to appear alongside the forested areas around 9,000 years ago, the first appearance of humans in Ireland also dates to this time. These early inhabitants found most of Ireland covered with trees, and they subsisted by hunting small game and gathering seeds and nuts. The picture changed around 8,000 years ago, as Neolithic cultures perfected stone axes and other implements with which to start massive clearing of the woodlands. Between 6,000 and 4,000 years ago, these early farmers cleared huge forested areas for cultivation and living sites. Large-scale tree cutting, along with several outbreaks of elm disease and beetle infestations, resulted in the virtually treeless Irish landscape of today. Certainly by early Christian times, bogs and treeless pastures had overtaken many formerly forested areas across the whole of Ireland. But scientists speculate that substantial woodland areas existed into medieval times, and this is reflected in many place names that refer to woods and particular sorts of trees (e.g., Ashford, Holywood, Kellysgrove, Roundwood, Treehoo, Woodford, Woodstown, and Woodtown). The last important phase of deforestation was in the 16th and 17th centuries.

Many of the parkland golf courses are located on former estates that have passed through generations of owners. These lands were protected from the timber cutting that destroyed surrounding forests. This means that today, as you walk the fairways and enjoy the old-growth trees of these parkland courses, you are getting a rare glimpse of a bygone Ireland. That scene would have provided wide vistas of endless tracts of trees, interrupted only by rivers and lakes, even atop the karst topographies. One particular area in Ireland, the valley of the Lee River around Macroom Golf Club, County Cork, is notable for providing a look at the vanished Irish woodlands. Some of the parkland courses set amid estate grounds include Malone in Belfast, Slieve Russell in County Cavan, Dromoland in County Clare, Oughterard in County Galway, Mount Juliet in County Kilkenny, Adare Golf Club at Adare Manor in County Limerick, Tullamore in County Offaly, County Tipperary Golf Club, Waterford Castle in County Waterford, and Glasson in County Westmeath.

We have come to the end of our nutshell version of Irish geology as it relates to golf. There are other glacial features found throughout Ireland, such as corries, kames, kettle holes, moraines, pingos, and striae. These features are a little more difficult to spot, so they have not been included in this chapter. There is much to appreciate as you travel the Irish countryside, not the least of which is the stunning landscape and its origins. So have some great golf, and watch out for those eskers!

Trolleys List

FEATURED COURSES

This list includes detailed descriptions of the 153 featured courses. We compiled the Trolleys List, whimsically named after the Irish pull cart, with an eye toward balanced geographical representation and playing enjoyment. The list is organized by country, with the Republic of Ireland first, followed by Northern Ireland. Within each country are the various counties or districts and their alphabetically arranged courses.

Each page-long description provides the following information. First, basic data include address and contact numbers (telephone, fax, web page, and e-mail), map directions, green fees, availability of equipment rental, date founded, architect (when known), and type of course (classic links, parkland, a combination of links and parkland, moorland, or seaside). Also included are assessments of the course's facilities and maintenance. The next section, course description, is a concise summary of some of the course's unique features and aspects of playability, along with comments that may be helpful for first-time play at this venue. We also include a course layout and scorecard data that state each hole's yardage, par, and index. A small locator map (not drawn to scale), the club's crest, and a Shamrock Rating (see page 40) are also here. Finally, we suggest two accommodations and a restaurant, each followed by a telephone number.

The Republic of Ireland

COUNTY CARLOW

Carlow Golf Club
Mount Wolseley Golf Club

COUNTY CAVAN

County Cavan Golf Club
Slieve Russell Hotel, Golf and
　　Country Club

COUNTY CLARE

Dromoland Golf and Country Club
East Clare Golf Club
Kilkee Golf Club
Lahinch Golf Club (Castle Course)
Lahinch Golf Club (Old Course)
Shannon Golf Club
Spanish Point Golf and Sports Club

Woodstock House Golf and
　　Country Club

COUNTY CORK

Bantry Bay Golf Club
Cork Golf Club
Fota Island Golf Club
Kinsale Golf Club
Lee Valley Golf and Country Club

Macroom Golf Club

Mallow Golf Club

Old Head Golf Links

Skibbereen and West Carbery Golf Club

Youghal Golf Club

COUNTY DONEGAL

Ballyliffin Golf Club (Glashedy Links)

Ballyliffin Golf Club (Old Links)

Bundoran Golf Club

Donegal Golf Club

Narin and Portnoo Golf Club

Portsalon Golf Club

Rosapenna Golf Club

COUNTY DUBLIN

City West Hotel, Conference Centre
    and Golf Resort

Corballis Public Golf Course

Deer Park Hotel and Golf Courses

Forrest Little Golf Club

Howth Golf Club

The Island Golf Club

Luttrellstown Castle Golf and
    Country Club

Portmarnock Golf Club

Portmarnock Hotel and Golf Links

The Royal Dublin Golf Club

Rush Golf Club

St. Anne's Golf Club

St. Margaret's Golf and Country Club

COUNTY GALWAY

Athenry Golf Club

Ballinasloe Golf Club

Bearna Golf Club

Connemara Golf Club

Connemara Isles Golf Club

Galway Bay Golf and Country Club

Galway Golf Club

Gort Golf Club

Loughrea Golf Club

Oughterard Golf Club

Portumna Golf Club

Tuam Golf Club

COUNTY KERRY

Ballybunion Golf Club
    (Cashen Course)

Ballybunion Golf Club (Old Course)

Cheann Sibeal Golf Club

Dooks Golf Club

Kenmare Golf Club

Killarney Golf and Fishing Club
    (Killeen Course)

Killarney Golf and Fishing Club
    (Mahony's Point Course)

Ring of Kerry Golf and Country Club

Tralee Golf Club at Barrow

Waterville Golf Links

COUNTY KILDARE

The Curragh Golf Club

The K Club (Kildare Hotel and
    Country Club)

Kilkea Castle Hotel and Golf Club

COUNTY KILKENNY

Kilkenny Golf Club

Mount Juliet Golf Club

Waterford Golf Club

COUNTY LAOIS

Heath Golf Club

COUNTY LIMERICK

Adare Manor Golf Club

Adare Manor Hotel and Golf Club

Limerick County Golf and
   Country Club

Newcastle West Golf Club

COUNTY LONGFORD

County Longford Golf Club

COUNTY LOUTH

Ardee Golf Club

County Louth Golf Club

Dundalk Golf Club

Greenore Golf Club

Seapoint Golf Club

COUNTY MAYO

Ballinrobe Golf Club

Ballyhaunis Golf Club

Carne (Belmullet) Golf Links

Castlebar Golf Club

Mulranny Golf Club

Westport Golf Club

COUNTY MEATH

Black Bush Golf Club

County Meath Golf Club

Headfort Golf Club

Laytown and Bettystown Golf Club

Royal Tara Golf Club

COUNTY MONAGHAN

Nuremore Hotel and Country Club

Rossmore Golf Club

COUNTY OFFALY

Birr Golf Club

Edenderry Golf Club

Esker Hills Golf and Country Club

Tullamore Golf Club

COUNTY ROSCOMMON

Athlone Golf Club

Roscommon Golf Club

COUNTY SLIGO

County Sligo Golf Club

Enniscrone Golf Club

Strandhill Golf Club

COUNTY TIPPERARY

Ballykisteen Golf and Country Club

County Tipperary Golf Club

Roscrea Golf Club

Thurles Golf Club

COUNTY WATERFORD

Dungarvan Golf Club

Dunmore East Golf Club

Faithlegg Golf Club

Gold Coast Golf Club

Tramore Golf Club

Waterford Castle Golf and
   Country Club

West Waterford Golf and Country Club

COUNTY WESTMEATH

Glasson Golf and Country Club

Mount Temple Golf Club

Mullingar Golf Club

COUNTY WEXFORD

Enniscorthy Golf Club

Rosslare Golf Club

St. Helen's Bay Golf and Country Club

COUNTY WICKLOW

Arklow Golf Club

Blainroe Golf Club

Druids Glen Golf Club

The European Club

Old Conna Golf Club

Powerscourt Golf Club

Rathsallagh Golf Club

Wicklow Golf Club

Woodbrook Golf Club

Northern Ireland

COUNTY ANTRIM

Ballycastle Golf Club

Cairndhu Golf Club

Galgorm Castle Golf and Country Club

Gracehill Golf Club

Royal Portrush Golf Club (Dunluce
  Course)

Royal Portrush Golf Club (Valley
  Links)

COUNTY ARMAGH

Craigavon Golf and Ski Centre
  (Silverwood Course)

CITY OF BELFAST

Belvoir Park Golf Club

Malone Golf Club

COUNTY DOWN

Ardglass Golf Club

Blackwood Golf Centre (Hamilton
  Course)

Clandeboye Golf Club
  (Dufferin Course)

Downpatrick Golf Club

Kirkistown Castle Golf Club

The Royal Belfast Golf Club

The Royal County Down Golf Club

COUNTY FERMANAGH

Enniskillen Golf Club

COUNTY LONDONDERRY

Castlerock Golf Club

City of Derry Golf Club
  (Prehen Course)

Moyola Park Golf Club

Portstewart Golf Club (Strand Course)

COUNTY TYRONE

Dungannon Golf Club

Omagh Golf Club

Strabane Golf Club

Carlow Golf Club

ADDRESS:
Deerpark,
County Carlow,
Ireland

TELEPHONE:
353 503 31695

FAX:
353 503 40065

WEB PAGE: NA

E-MAIL: NA

DIRECTIONS TO COURSE: 2 miles north of Carlow town, on the N9 (Dublin Rd.).

SCORECARD

HOLE	YDG	PAR	INDEX
1	437	4	4
2	318	4	14
3	142	3	4
4	385	4	9
5	548	5	15
6	179	3	12
7	433	4	1
8	432	4	6
9	406	4	8
OUT	3,285	35	
10	304	4	11
11	428	4	3
12	374	4	7
13	165	3	16
14	453	4	5
15	385	4	10
16	437	4	2
17	151	3	18
18	525	5	13
IN	3,226	35	
TOTAL	6,511	70	

The clubhouse has a full bar and dining facilities; there is also a delightful historical display in the lounge (don't miss it). There are locker rooms and changing facilities; a separate pro shop (small but well stocked); and a putting green and driving range.

LEVEL OF MAINTENANCE: This is a very well maintained parkland course. The greens are robust, the bunkers unique and well cared for, the building facilities clean and functional. An excellent drainage system keeps this course remarkably dry throughout the year and therefore eminently playable in all seasons.

COURSE DESCRIPTION: Carlow is a parkland course with rolling, sometimes undulating, terrain; stands of mature trees define the fairways. The greens are in wonderful condition, generally following the natural contours of the ground with only a slight elevation. The trapping is always interesting, and often there are traps up to 30 yards in front of the holes to capture shots not reaching the green. Some water hazards and abundant gorse add additional challenge to this course. Views of the Blackstairs Mountains, complete with snow-capped peaks, are terrific. The course has an old, classic, intuitive layout and provides a wonderful Irish Experience. Carlow is a challenging test of golf and a lot of fun to play. Enjoy yourself.

UNIQUE FEATURE: The location of bunkering throughout the course is unique.

ACCOMMODATION INFORMATION

Standard hotel: Dolman Hotel (Carlow), 353 503 42002

Local hotel/guesthouse/B&B: Seven Oaks Hotel (Carlow), 353 503 31308

Restaurant/pub: Reddy's Pub and Restaurant, 353 503 42224 or Teach Dolman Pub, 353 503 30911

GREEN FEES:
Moderate

EQUIPMENT RENTAL
Buggies: yes
Trolleys: yes
Caddies: yes
Clubs: yes

DATE FOUNDED: 1899

ARCHITECTS: Thomas Barcroft (1922); 10 greens and most bunkers redesigned by Tom Simpson (1937)

TYPE: Parkland

FACILITIES
Clubhouse at turn: yes
Restrooms on course: no

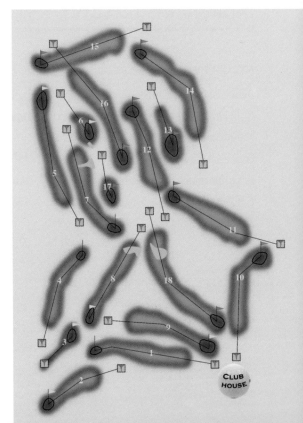

Mount Wolseley Golf Club

GREEN FEES:
Moderate

EQUIPMENT RENTAL
Buggies: yes
Trolleys: yes
Caddies: yes
Clubs: yes

DATE FOUNDED: 1996

ARCHITECT:
Christy O'Connor Jr.

TYPE: Parkland

FACILITIES
Clubhouse at turn: yes
Restrooms on course: no

*T*his is an estate course, with all the former estate buildings utilized in a beautiful fashion. The clubhouse is fully stocked, and changing facilities are top-notch. The on-site hotel and restaurant are quite lovely. The three practice holes are complete with manicured greens and fairways, just behind the clubhouse. The club also has a putting green and a driving range.

ADDRESS:
Tullow (Tullagh),
County Carlow,
Ireland

TELEPHONE:
353 503 51674

FAX:
353 503 52123

WEB PAGE:
www.golfclubireland.com/
mtwolseley/index.htm

E-MAIL: wolseley@iol.ie

LEVEL OF MAINTENANCE: This now-resort course is maintained accordingly. The clubhouse facilities and golf course are immaculate.

COURSE DESCRIPTION: This majestic parkland course is long and grueling and all Christy O'Connor Jr. Unless you are a scratch golfer, consider tees other than the back. The course is extremely well manicured and landscaped. There are excellent large tee boxes. The greens are devilishly difficult; most are tiered, and unless you are playing to the pin, you could have some unmerciful putts. The water hazards, typical O'Connor bunkers, and occasional mature stands of trees add to an exceptionally difficult course. This beautiful course should not be missed.

UNIQUE FEATURE: There are three practice holes. Everybody always wants to take either a mulligan or a mulligan hole. Well, here's your chance!

ACCOMMODATION INFORMATION
Standard hotel: Mount Wolseley Hotel (on site), 353 503 51674

Local hotel/guesthouse/B&B: Sherwood Park House (guesthouse) (Carlow), 353 503 59117

Restaurant/pub: Mount Wolseley Clubhouse, 353 503 51674

DIRECTIONS TO COURSE:
Just southeast of Tullow town on the Ardattin Road. Watch for excellent signage.

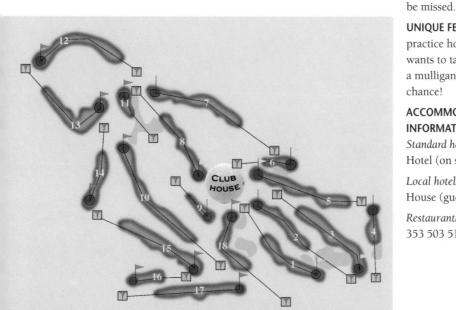

SCORECARD			
HOLE	YDG	PAR	INDEX
1	411	4	9
2	447	4	5
3	447	4	1
4	273	4	1
5	499	5	7
6	210	3	13
7	542	5	11
8	440	4	3
9	191	3	17
OUT	3,460	36	
10	592	5	6
11	207	3	10
12	519	5	18
13	427	4	14
14	339	4	12
15	449	4	2
16	226	3	16
17	457	4	4
18	413	4	8
IN	3,646	36	
TOTAL	7,106	72	

County Cavan Golf Club

ADDRESS:
Drumelis,
Cavan, County
Cavan, Ireland

TELEPHONE:
353 49 4331388

FAX:
353 49 4331541

WEB PAGE: www.cavangolf.ie

E-MAIL: info@cavangolf.ie

DIRECTIONS TO COURSE: Follow the Killshandra Road (R198) 1.5 miles west of the town of Cavan. Follow the course signage.

This is an estate course, and the clubhouse is the old manor house. It is all warm, neat, and tidy. The club has a separate, well-stocked pro shop, driving range, and putting green. There is a PGA professional on site, along with full restaurant and bar facilities and changing rooms.

LEVEL OF MAINTENANCE: This is a well-maintained course with good turf development and good greens. The bunkering is marginal but well kept.

COURSE DESCRIPTION: County Cavan Golf Club is generally on hilly terrain that has tree-lined fairways of various-aged trees. The greens range from flat to severely sloped and make it difficult to get a good read. The 9th green can be practically impossible, and there are a few crisscrossing holes to negotiate. The finishing holes can provide some real challenge, and when the new plantings mature, this course could become extremely difficult. Nice signage throughout the course guides you on your way.

UNIQUE FEATURE: Green types vary extremely, from flat to tiered to severely sloping.

ACCOMMODATION INFORMATION

Standard hotel: Hotel Kilmore (3 star) (Cavan), 353 49 4332288

Local hotel/guesthouse/B&B: Hilltop Farm Farmhouse (Belturbet), 353 49 9522114

Restaurant/pub: Clubhouse on site, 353 49 4331388

GREEN FEES:
Low

EQUIPMENT RENTAL
Buggies: yes
Trolleys: yes
Caddies: yes
Clubs: yes

DATE FOUNDED: 1894

ARCHITECT:
Redesigned to 18 holes by Eddie Hackett

TYPE: Parkland

FACILITIES
Clubhouse at turn: yes
Restrooms on course: no

SCORECARD

HOLE	YDG	PAR	INDEX
1	313	4	11
2	317	4	13
3	404	4	3
4	175	3	15
5	381	4	3
6	339	4	7
7	531	5	17
8	355	4	5
9	186	3	9
OUT	3,006	35	
10	205	3	6
11	330	4	12
12	371	4	14
13	144	3	16
14	415	4	8
15	410	4	2
16	389	4	4
17	487	5	18
18	378	4	10
IN	3,134	35	
TOTAL	6,140	70	

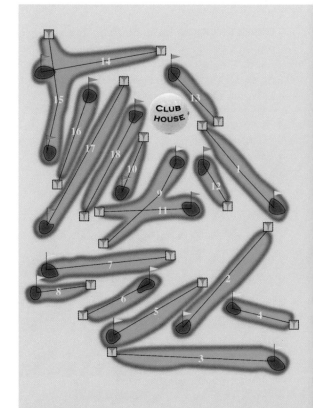

Slieve Russell Hotel, Golf and Country Club

GREEN FEES:
Moderate
EQUIPMENT RENTAL
Buggies: yes
Trolleys: yes
Caddies: yes
Clubs: yes

DATE FOUNDED: 1992
ARCHITECT:
Patrick Merrigan
TYPE: Parkland
FACILITIES
Clubhouse at turn: yes
Restrooms on course: no

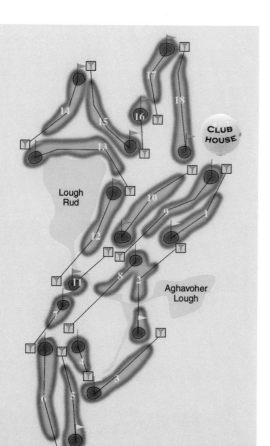

Lough
Rud

CLUB
HOUSE

Aghavoher
Lough

This is a 5-star golf resort and hotel, complete with all the amenities expected from such a complex. These include practice range, putting green, leisure center, club storage and cleaning, and so on. The hotel even has its own helicopter and pad. Suffice it to say there is opulence everywhere.

LEVEL OF MAINTENANCE: This resort was established in 1992. It is still growing and is taken care of with kid gloves.

COURSE DESCRIPTION: Slieve Russell is set on beautiful, rolling parkland terrain. The tee boxes are huge and diligently kept. The greens are undulating with superb turf; bunkering is spectacular; and water hazards are frequent. There are many mature tree plantings, as well as a plethora of new plantings. Views of the surrounding hills (all glacial in origin) are gorgeous, and landscaping on the course and the rest of the grounds is spectacular. It would be difficult to find a better parkland course to play.

UNIQUE FEATURE: The clock tower adds some unique charm to an already perfectly charming resort.

ACCOMMODATION INFORMATION

Standard hotel: Slieve Russell Hotel, Golf and Country Club (5 star) (on site), 353 49 26444

Local hotel/guesthouse/B&B: Angler's Rest (Ballyconnell), 353 49 26391

Restaurant/pub: Brackley Restaurant (Slieve Russell Hotel), 353 49 26444

ADDRESS:
Ballyconnell,
County Cavan,
Ireland
TELEPHONE:
353 49 26444
FAX:
353 49 26474
WEB PAGE: NA
E-MAIL: slieve-russell@sqgroup.com
DIRECTIONS TO COURSE: From Ballyconnell, follow the Belturbet Road (N87). The course is just outside (east) of Ballyconnell.

SCORECARD			
HOLE	YDG	PAR	INDEX
1	428	4	10
2	434	4	1
3	398	4	6
4	167	3	16
5	436	4	3
6	512	5	18
7	220	3	8
8	389	4	14
9	552	5	12
OUT	3,536	36	
10	411	4	2
11	193	3	11
12	442	4	4
13	529	5	9
14	374	4	17
15	453	4	5
16	176	3	7
17	399	4	15
18	540	5	13
IN	3,517	36	
TOTAL	7,053	72	

Dromoland Golf and Country Club

ADDRESS:
Newmarket-on-Fergus, County Clare, Ireland

TELEPHONE: 353 61 70368444

FAX: 353 61 70368498

WEB PAGE: NA

E-MAIL: Dromonan@dromoland.ie

DIRECTIONS TO COURSE: The course and castle are directly off the N18, between the towns of Shannon and Ennis.

Oromoland Golf Club (pronounced "Drum UH lund") offers splendid, top-notch facilities set amid the grounds of the Dromoland Castle Hotel. The entire complex is elegant and well appointed. The clubhouse is warm and rich, with dark wood paneling. The bar is very attractive. Locker rooms are spacious, clean, and have showers. A practice green is near the clubhouse.

LEVEL OF MAINTENANCE: Every aspect of this course, clubhouse, and hotel is top-notch and immaculate. The greens are excellent and the turf well established throughout the course. The fairways are quite good, and the secondary rough is expansive.

COURSE DESCRIPTION: Dromoland is set amid classic, hilly, forested terrain with a natural lake. Throughout the course are wonderful views of the restored castle (now the hotel) and vistas of the River Shannon and River Rine, the latter flowing through the estate. The castle in itself is remarkable to see, as are many old-growth trees. Note especially the double tree at the end of hole 2. The castle is beautifully restored, with manicured English-type gardens.

If this is your first day in Ireland, Dromoland provides a nice transition, allowing you to rest from jet lag but still get in some golf. This is not an especially challenging layout but is a stunning walking course. Unfortunately, some of it is located near a rather noisy highway.

UNIQUE FEATURE: Bird life is abundant on this course. Watch especially for pheasants, grouse, and all sorts of ducks—a real treat.

ACCOMMODATION INFORMATION

Standard hotel: Dromoland Castle Hotel (on site), 353 61 70368144

Local hotel/guesthouse/B&B: The Clare Inn Golf and Leisure Hotel (Dromoland), 353 61 7074503

Restaurant/pub: Durty Nellies in Bunratty Village (very popular; book well in advance), 353 61 7036481

GREEN FEES:
Moderate

EQUIPMENT RENTAL
Buggies: yes
Trolleys: yes
Caddies: yes
Clubs: yes

DATE FOUNDED: 1963

ARCHITECT:
Robert Trent Jones Sr.

TYPE: Parkland

FACILITIES
Clubhouse at turn: yes
Restrooms on course: no

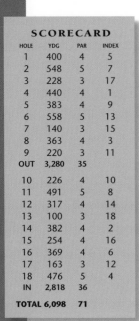

SCORECARD

HOLE	YDG	PAR	INDEX
1	400	4	5
2	548	5	7
3	228	3	17
4	440	4	1
5	383	4	9
6	558	5	13
7	140	3	15
8	363	4	3
9	220	3	11
OUT	3,280	35	
10	226	4	10
11	491	5	8
12	317	4	14
13	100	3	18
14	382	4	2
15	254	4	16
16	369	4	6
17	163	3	12
18	476	5	4
IN	2,818	36	
TOTAL	6,098	71	

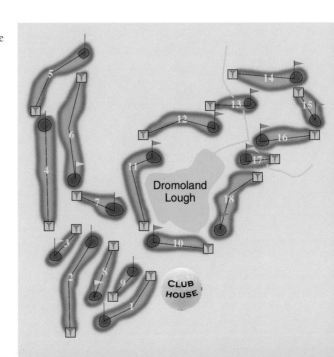

East Clare Golf Club

GREEN FEES:
Low

EQUIPMENT RENTAL
Buggies: yes
Trolleys: yes
Caddies: no
Clubs: yes

DATE FOUNDED: 1991

ARCHITECT: Back 9, opened in 1997, by Arthur Spring

TYPE: Parkland

FACILITIES
Clubhouse at turn: yes
Restrooms on course: no

East Clare offers a small but comfortable clubhouse. Its lunchroom offers drinks and sandwiches; there is no pro shop.

LEVEL OF MAINTENANCE: This course is adequately maintained, has good turf development and very good greens.

COURSE DESCRIPTION: East Clare is a parkland course with many newly planted trees, which, when mature, will add another level of difficulty to this open course. The wind can affect the degree of difficulty dramatically. The course sets up high, with stunning views of the surrounding countryside, including farmsteads and hills. In places, there are 360-degree views, along with several ponds with ducks and swans. Some informational signage is inconsistent, but the course offers a fairly intuitive layout. In the end, if you're looking for a quintessential Emerald Isle panorama, this is the course to visit and play.

UNIQUE FEATURE: Hole 9 offers high risks and rewards—a real thinking golfer's hole, requiring many decisions.

ACCOMMODATION INFORMATION
Standard hotel: Old Ground Hotel (Ennis), 353 65 28127

Local hotel/guesthouse/B&B: Magowna House Hotel (Ennis), 353 65 39009

Restaurant/pub: Cloister Restaurant (Ennis), 353 65 29521

ADDRESS:
Coolreigh, Bodyke
County Clare,
Ireland

TELEPHONE:
353 61 921322

FAX:
353 61 921717

WEB PAGE: NA

E-MAIL: pnesbitt@iol.ie

DIRECTIONS TO COURSE: The course is just east of Bodyke (east of Ennis) on the R352; it has easily identifiable signage. The road to the course is quite narrow and may seem more like a farmstead driveway than a public road.

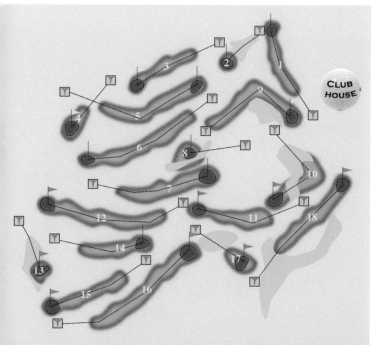

SCORECARD			
HOLE	YDG	PAR	INDEX
1	354	4	14
2	176	3	11
3	373	4	5
4	182	3	7
5	531	5	17
6	488	5	9
7	456	4	3
8	142	3	18
9	427	4	1
OUT	3,134	35	
10	354	4	10
11	380	4	4
12	511	5	15
13	225	3	2
14	360	4	12
15	409	4	8
16	467	5	16
17	193	3	13
18	416	4	6
IN	3,320	36	
TOTAL	6,454	71	

Kilkee Golf Club

ADDRESS: East End, Kilkee, County Clare, Ireland

TELEPHONE: 353 65 9056048

FAX: 353 65 9056977

WEB PAGE: NA

E-MAIL: NA

DIRECTIONS TO COURSE: In the town of Kilkee, watch club directional signage. The road to the course goes along the seashore and is visible from the town.

Kilkee offers a clubhouse best described as lovely and old, comfy and friendly. Full facilities include a cozy bar and restaurant serving dinners and sometimes offering dancing and entertainment. Changing rooms have showers. The staff is extremely helpful, and there is a small pro shop.

LEVEL OF MAINTENANCE: This course is well maintained, with good greens. Signage is adequate, and distance markers and turf development are good.

GREEN FEES: Low

EQUIPMENT RENTAL
Buggies: yes
Trolleys: yes
Caddies: yes
Clubs: yes

DATE FOUNDED: 1896

ARCHITECTS: 18 holes by Eddie Hackett and Arthur Spring (1995)

TYPE: Seaside

FACILITIES
Clubhouse at turn: no
Restrooms on course: no

COURSE DESCRIPTION: Kilkee is not a classic links course, nor is it particularly challenging for the low handicapper, but it has some of the more remarkable vistas of the rugged Atlantic coastline that you will see anywhere in Ireland. Of particular note are holes 3 and 4, which follow the very edge of the sea cliff. One distinguishing feature of this course is that each hole stays in visual contact with massive cliffs and deep azure blue Atlantic water, which alone is well worth the trip. One distracting element, often characteristic of Eddie Hackett–designed courses, is the artificially placed and appearing mounds on otherwise flat fairways.

UNIQUE FEATURE: Get ready for the 4th hole, with its massive drive over a precipitous cliff, sure to test the concentration of any golfer. For the first-time visitor, the drive really doesn't matter, because this is one of the great views in Ireland.

ACCOMMODATION INFORMATION
Standard hotel: Strand Guesthouse (4 star) (Kilkee), 353 65 9056177

Local hotel/guesthouse/B&B: Stella Maris Hotel (Kilkee), 353 65 9056455

Restaurant/pub: Manuel's Seafood Restaurant (Kilkee), 353 65 9056211

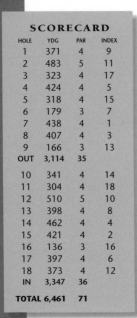

SCORECARD

HOLE	YDG	PAR	INDEX
1	371	4	9
2	483	5	11
3	323	4	17
4	424	4	5
5	318	4	15
6	179	3	7
7	438	4	1
8	407	4	3
9	166	3	13
OUT	3,114	35	
10	341	4	14
11	304	4	18
12	510	5	10
13	398	4	8
14	462	4	4
15	421	4	2
16	136	3	16
17	397	4	6
18	373	4	12
IN	3,347	36	
TOTAL	6,461	71	

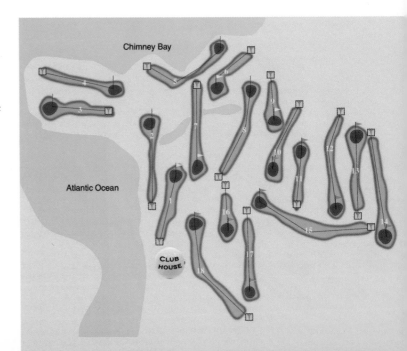

Chimney Bay

Atlantic Ocean

CLUB HOUSE

Lahinch Golf Club (Castle Course)

GREEN FEES:
Moderate

EQUIPMENT RENTAL
Buggies: yes
Trolleys: yes
Caddies: yes
Clubs: yes

DATE FOUNDED: 1975

ARCHITECT: NA

TYPE: Links

FACILITIES
Clubhouse at turn: no
Restrooms on course: no

The Castle Course has its own small "clubhouse," which includes restrooms and a starter's office. Full bar and restaurant facilities are across the street in the clubhouse of the Old Course (see page 90). A drinking fountain is near the 8th tee.

LEVEL OF MAINTENANCE: The Castle Course is very well maintained by the same excellent greenkeeper crews who take care of Lahinch's Old Course. The small clubhouse is clean and well presented.

COURSE DESCRIPTION: The Castle Course was originally designed to accommodate players unable to get onto the Old Course. Many players, however, report that they enjoy playing the Castle Course after being brutalized by the Old Course and its grueling links. We recommend playing Castle Course to soothe a battered ego after undergoing what is often a rigorous match across the street. The course itself is flat and does not have the towering dunes of the Old Course, but it does have clusters of low moguls. The picturesque ruins of O'Brien Castle, built in 1452, are found at the 8th tee.

UNIQUE FEATURE: It's a thrill to get so close to the ruins of O'Brien's Castle and to think that when its lords and ladies were living within its walls, North America had just been "discovered" by European explorers.

ACCOMMODATION INFORMATION
Standard hotel: Aberdeen Arms Hotel (3 star) (Lahinch), 353 65 7081100

Local hotel/guesthouse/B&B: Sancta Maria (Lahinch), 353 65 7081529

Restaurant/pub: Atlantic Hotel Restaurant (Lahinch), 353 65 7081049

ADDRESS:
Lahinch, County Clare, Ireland

TELEPHONE:
353 65 7081003

FAX:
353 65 7081592

WEB PAGE: NA

E-MAIL: NA

DIRECTIONS TO COURSE: Lahinch Golf Club is immediately north of the town of Lahinch on the Atlantic Coast. Take road R478 north, and watch for the Old Course on the ocean side. You will need to go to the green fees office of the Old Course in order to get a tee time for the smaller Castle Course, which is across from the Old Course.

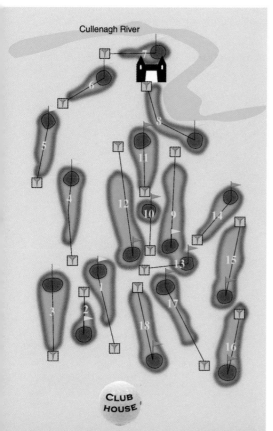

Cullenagh River

CLUB HOUSE

SCORECARD			
HOLE	YDG	PAR	INDEX
1	358	4	2
2	193	3	8
3	262	4	14
4	446	5	10
5	248	4	18
6	214	3	4
7	114	3	16
8	267	4	12
9	493	5	6
OUT	2,600	35	
10	163	3	15
11	362	4	5
12	438	4	1
13	148	3	17
14	275	4	13
15	511	5	11
16	334	4	7
17	388	4	3
18	350	4	9
IN	2,974	35	
TOTAL	**5,574**	**70**	

Lahinch Golf Club (Old Course)

ADDRESS:
Lahinch,
County Clare,
Ireland

TELEPHONE:
353 65 7081003

FAX:
353 65 7081592

WEB PAGE: NA

E-MAIL: NA

DIRECTIONS TO COURSE: The course is immediately north of the town of Lahinch, on the Atlantic Coast. Take road R478 north, and watch for the course on the ocean side of the road.

SCORECARD

HOLE	YDG	PAR	INDEX
1	385	4	4
2	512	5	14
3	151	3	16
4	428	4	2
5	482	5	12
6	155	3	18
7	399	4	6
8	350	4	10
9	384	4	8
OUT	3,246	36	
10	451	4	1
11	138	3	17
12	475	4	7
13	373	4	11
14	488	5	13
15	462	4	3
16	195	3	15
17	437	4	5
18	533	5	9
IN	3,452	36	
TOTAL	**6,698**	**72**	

The Lahinch Old Course is a top-notch facility. Although the clubhouse lends itself to the terrain and is generally adequate, plans are to replace it in the near future. In addition to views of several of the holes and the Atlantic Ocean, you'll find full bar and restaurant facilities and spacious locker rooms with showers. Adjacent to the 1st hole are the well-stocked pro shop and starter's office. There is also a practice green.

LEVEL OF MAINTENANCE: Even during the off-season, this course is excellently maintained, with healthy greens, neatly mowed fairways, and well-cared-for bunkers. The undisturbed rough (dunegrass) adds to great golf. The building facilities are well presented, and the entire greenkeeping staff is exceptionally friendly.

COURSE DESCRIPTION: Lahinch is a must-play course. It is one of the best classic links courses in Ireland, with a great architectural pedigree, spectacular tall dunes, and wonderful bunkering. Many of its holes overlook the Atlantic Ocean and Liscannor Bay. Secure a caddy for your first round, or play with someone familiar with the course, as there are some tricky holes with blind shots. Holes 5 (Klondyke) and 6 (the Dell), from the original course as laid out by Old Tom Morris, are historical gems.

UNIQUE FEATURE: A black billy goat, his buff-colored mate, and any one of their offspring are resident goats.

ACCOMMODATION INFORMATION

Standard hotel: Atlantic Hotel (3 star) (Lahinch), 353 65 7081049

Local hotel/guesthouse/B&B: Liscannor Bay Hotel (Liscannor Bay), 353 65 7081186

Restaurant/pub: O'Looneys Pub (a local must-do) (Lahinch), 353 65 7081414, or Black Oak Restaurant (gourmet cuisine), 353 65 7084403

GREEN FEES:
Moderate

EQUIPMENT RENTAL
Buggies: yes
Trolleys: yes
Caddies: yes
Clubs: yes

DATE FOUNDED: 1892

ARCHITECTS: Old Tom Morris (1892); Alister MacKenzie (1927)

TYPE: Links

FACILITIES
Clubhouse at turn: no
Restrooms on course: yes (10th hole)

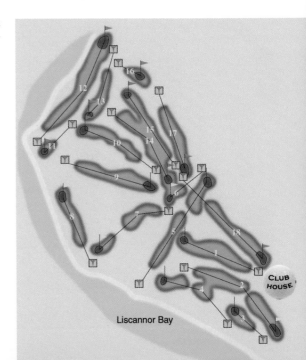

Liscannor Bay

Shannon Golf Club

GREEN FEES:
Moderate

EQUIPMENT RENTAL
Buggies: yes
Trolleys: yes
Caddies: yes
Clubs: yes

DATE FOUNDED: 1966

ARCHITECT: John D. Harris

TYPE: Parkland

FACILITIES
Clubhouse at turn: no
Restrooms on course: no

The Shannon Club has a fully equipped club-house with a restaurant and bar. The well-stocked pro shop is complete with club repair. On site, you will also find a putting green, practice area, and attractive landscaping and gardens.

LEVEL OF MAINTENANCE: This is a well-maintained course with beautifully manicured grounds. The fairways and bunkers are all well tended, as are the greens. The building facilities are neat and clean.

ADDRESS:
Shannon, County
Clare, Ireland

TELEPHONE:
353 61 471849

FAX:
353 61 471507

WEB PAGE: NA

E-MAIL: NA

DIRECTIONS TO COURSE: The Shannon Club is about 1 mile beyond the Shannon Airport terminal building; follow the signs.

COURSE DESCRIPTION: The Shannon course is a lovely, mature parkland tract with tree-lined fairways and many bunkers—all providing an excellent test on this championship course. It is a long course with many water hazards and frequent mounding. There are lovely views of the River Shannon estuary, and water is definitely a feature on a number of the holes. In fact, its signature hole is the 17th, a 224-yard par-3 hole with a carry over the Shannon estuary. Be sure to check out the photographs in the clubhouse halls of the early days of Ballesteros, Faldo, Langer, Lyle, Norman, and Christy O'Connor Jr.

UNIQUE FEATURE: This may be one of the few times that you'll play an excellent championship course laid between a major river and a country's major airport.

ACCOMMODATION INFORMATION
Standard hotel: Shannon Great Southern Hotel (3 star) (Shannon Airport), 353 61 471122

Local hotel/guesthouse/B&B: Carrygerry Country House (3 star) (Newmarket-on-Fergus, 10 minutes from the airport), 353 61 363739

Restaurant/pub: The Carvery at the Shannon Great Southern Hotel (see above), 353 61 471122

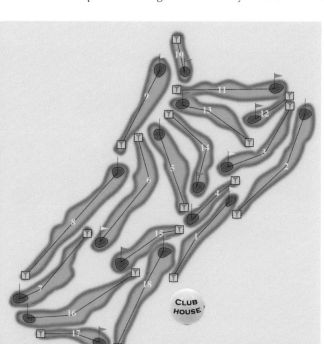

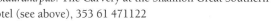

CLUB HOUSE

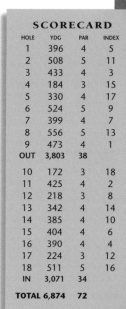

SCORECARD			
HOLE	YDG	PAR	INDEX
1	396	4	5
2	508	5	11
3	433	4	3
4	184	3	15
5	330	4	17
6	524	5	9
7	399	4	7
8	556	5	13
9	473	4	1
OUT	3,803	38	
10	172	3	18
11	425	4	2
12	218	3	8
13	342	4	14
14	385	4	10
15	404	4	6
16	390	4	4
17	224	3	12
18	511	5	16
IN	3,071	34	
TOTAL	6,874	72	

Spanish Point Golf and Sports Club

ADDRESS:
Miltown
Malbay, County
Clare, Ireland

TELEPHONE:
353 65 7084198

FAX:
353 65 7084219

WEB PAGE: NA

E-MAIL: dkfitzgerald@tinet.ie

DIRECTIONS TO COURSE: The course is 2 miles southwest of the town of Miltown Malbay (on Mal Bay), off the N67 (Quilty Road). Follow signs.

This very small 9-hole course is reminiscent of days gone by. The clubhouse includes a cozy bar with bar food, along with changing rooms. There is no pro shop.

LEVEL OF MAINTENANCE: All aspects of this course are adequately maintained.

COURSE DESCRIPTION: Spanish Point, just down the road from the grueling Lahinch Club, is a welcome addition to your itinerary if you're in the area. Don't be surprised if you pay green fees through an "honest box." In the summer, however, the clubhouse is open until 11:00 p.m., serving snacks in a quaint and friendly manner. This is a 9-hole classic links course with a fascinating combination of six par 3s and three par 4s, located on sometimes elevated and sometimes low-lying greens. When the winds blow, as they always do, this can be as challenging a course as you would want to play. There are gorgeous views of Mal Bay and the Atlantic Ocean, along with classic sand dunes through which the course is played.

UNIQUE FEATURE: You can easily fantasize that this is the 1890s and you're playing Irish golf on a classic links—good, clean fun!

GREEN FEES:
Low; if no one is in the clubhouse, look for envelopes inside an "honest box."

EQUIPMENT RENTAL
Buggies: yes
Trolleys: yes

Caddies: yes
Clubs: yes

DATE FOUNDED: 1896

ARCHITECT: NA

TYPE: Links

FACILITIES
Clubhouse at turn: yes
Restrooms on course: no

ACCOMMODATION INFORMATION

Standard hotel: Armada Hotel (3 star) (Miltown Malbay), 353 65 7084110

Local hotel/guesthouse/B&B: Bellbridge House Hotel (3 star) (Miltown Malbay), 353 65 7084038

Restaurant/pub: Cape Restaurant in the Armada Hotel (see above), 353 65 7084110

SCORECARD

HOLE	YDG	PAR	INDEX
1	334	4	13
2	196	3	9
3	404	4	7
4	223	3	5
5	421	4	1
6	369	4	3
7	312	4	11
8	109	3	15
9	148	3	17
OUT	2,520	32	
10	334	4	14
11	196	3	10
12	404	4	8
13	223	3	6
14	421	4	2
15	369	4	4
16	312	4	12
17	109	3	16
18	148	3	18
IN	2,520	32	
TOTAL	5,040	64	

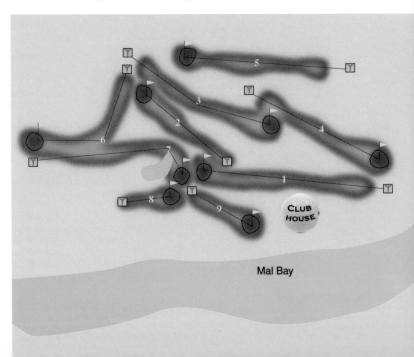

Mal Bay

Woodstock House Golf and Country Club

GREEN FEES:
Moderate

EQUIPMENT RENTAL
Buggies: yes
Trolleys: yes
Caddies: yes
Clubs: yes

DATE FOUNDED: 1993

ARCHITECT: Arthur Spring

TYPE: Parkland

FACILITIES
Clubhouse at turn: yes
Restrooms on course: no

Woodstock provides an attractive, Georgian-style clubhouse. The upstairs bar and restaurant offer an excellent balcony view of the course and adjoining countryside. The club has a moderately stocked pro shop and changing rooms. If no one is in the pro shop, head for the bar/restaurant; the pro may be serving as barkeeper (off-season).

LEVEL OF MAINTENANCE: While the clubhouse and adjoining changing room facilities are attractively styled, they woefully lack in upkeep and maintenance. Signage is inconsistent, and there are no fairway markers on the back 9 holes. The course itself is adequately maintained with regard to turf, greens, and bunkering.

COURSE DESCRIPTION: Woodstock is a typical parkland course with many new plantings that will require maturing before this course truly comes into its own. It is situated on 150 acres of well-drained soil, making it playable virtually all year long. A series of four to five holes leads to lakes with swans and gorgeous views. A couple of the greens are undulating. Don't be surprised if townsfolk, dogs, and hikers use the course. There is a nice opening hole, and the course's difficulty is moderate until you reach the 7th hole, a world-class par 4 at 425 yards.

UNIQUE FEATURE: The 7th hole at Woodstock is a real gem. A longish par 4, it wraps around a small lake, complete with swans, to an interesting green.

ACCOMMODATION INFORMATION

Standard hotel: Old Ground Hotel (3 star) (Ennis), 353 65 6828127

Local hotel/guesthouse/B&B: Cill Eoin House (3-star guesthouse) (Ennis), 353 65 6841668

Restaurant/pub: Ruby Tuesday's (Ennis), 353 65 6840474

ADDRESS:
Shanaway Road,
Ennis, County
Clare, Ireland

TELEPHONE:
353 65 7029463

FAX:
353 65 7020304

WEB PAGE: NA

E-MAIL: NA

DIRECTIONS TO COURSE: This club is 2 miles west of downtown Ennis, just off the N85 (Ennistymon and Lahinch Road). Watch for the club's sign on the N85 indicating a left-hand turn (coming from Ennis), with the club about ¾ mile on the left.

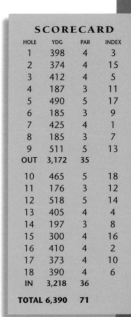

SCORECARD			
HOLE	YDG	PAR	INDEX
1	398	4	3
2	374	4	15
3	412	4	5
4	187	3	11
5	490	5	17
6	185	3	9
7	425	4	1
8	185	3	7
9	511	5	13
OUT	3,172	35	
10	465	5	18
11	176	3	12
12	518	5	14
13	405	4	4
14	197	3	8
15	300	4	16
16	410	4	2
17	373	4	10
18	390	4	6
IN	3,218	36	
TOTAL	**6,390**	**71**	

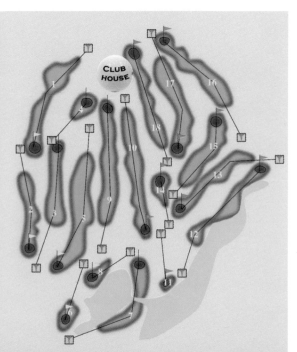

CLUB HOUSE

Bantry Bay Golf Club

ADDRESS:
Bantry Bay, West Cork, County Cork, Ireland

TELEPHONE:
353 27 50579

FAX:
353 27 50579

WEB PAGE: NA

E-MAIL:
greenfee@bantrygolfclub.iol.ie

DIRECTIONS TO COURSE: The course is 2 miles west of Bantry on the Glengariff Road (N71).

Bantry Bay has a modern and modest clubhouse, complete with changing rooms, bar, and grill. There is also a putting green.

LEVEL OF MAINTENANCE: This is basically a municipal course, maintained at the level you would expect at such courses. The turf, including the greens, is adequate, and the traps, when present, are low and flat.

COURSE DESCRIPTION: This course has many elevation changes, large greens, and few traps. Mature tree stands and many new plantings define the holes. On many of the holes, there are panoramic views of Bantry Bay and, in the distance, the Bearna Mountains. These views, along with a few water hazards, add interest. This course presents a fair challenge to all levels of player and, coupled with the fine views, would be an enjoyable round for anyone.

UNIQUE FEATURE: The course enjoys a close proximity to Bantry Bay.

ACCOMMODATION INFORMATION

Standard hotel: West Lodge Hotel (Bantry), 353 27 50360

Local hotel/guesthouse/B&B: Atlanta House Hotel (Bantry), 353 27 50237

Restaurant/pub: J. J. Crowley's (Bantry), 353 27 50029

GREEN FEES:
Low

EQUIPMENT RENTAL
Buggies: yes
Trolleys: yes
Caddies: yes
Clubs: yes

DATE FOUNDED: 1975

ARCHITECTS: Eddie Hackett and Christy O'Connor Jr.

TYPE: Parkland

FACILITIES
Clubhouse at turn: no
Restrooms on course: no

SCORECARD

HOLE	YDG	PAR	INDEX
1	162	3	12
2	490	5	16
3	359	4	8
4	401	4	6
5	320	4	14
6	413	4	2
7	303	4	10
8	413	4	4
9	137	3	18
OUT	3,002	35	
10	405	4	7
11	530	5	13
12	444	4	1
13	153	3	15
14	402	4	5
15	373	4	9
16	457	4	3
17	204	3	11
18	465	5	17
IN	3,438	36	
TOTAL	6,440	71	

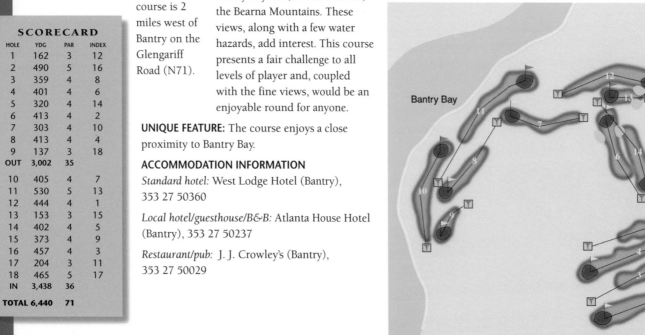

Bantry Bay

Cork Golf Club

GREEN FEES:
Moderate

EQUIPMENT RENTAL
Buggies: no
Trolleys: yes
Caddies: yes
Clubs: yes

DATE FOUNDED: 1888

ARCHITECTS: Alister MacKenzie (1927); new 5th hole by Dave Thomas (1985)

TYPE: Parkland

FACILITIES
Clubhouse at turn: no
Restrooms on course: no

Cork has a lovely clubhouse with a full bar and restaurant, locker rooms with showers, and a separate well-stocked pro shop. It also has a practice ground and putting green. A special feature is the cupola clock on the pro shop that faces the course.

LEVEL OF MAINTENANCE: This is an extremely well maintained course; the greens, traps, and fairways are all pristine. The venerable clubhouse is warm, friendly, and clean.

COURSE DESCRIPTION: This is a mature parkland course that has many stands of old-growth trees and numerous patches of gorse. The course itself is a rolling to slightly hilly tract that works its way to and from the River Lee. In between, you will run into the famous Cork limestone quarry. Several holes are affected by this geographical feature, including the 7th, a par 3, which is actually on the floor of the quarry. This Alister MacKenzie course possesses some of his signature characteristics with respect to bunkers and greens—that is, undulating and rolling greens and always intelligently placed bunkers. Another characteristic of MacKenzie's European courses is the crisscrossing fairways, of which there are more than seems necessary at this course.

UNIQUE FEATURE: Local lore purports that many New York and Boston buildings obtained their limestone from the Cork Golf Club quarry in the middle of the course.

ACCOMMODATION INFORMATION
Standard hotel: Jury's Hotel (4 star) (Cork), 353 21 276622

Local hotel/guesthouse/B&B: Doughcloyne Hotel (3 star) (Cork), 353 21 312535

Restaurant/pub: Jacques Restaurant (gourmet restaurant) (Cork), 353 21 277387

ADDRESS:
Little Island,
County Cork,
Ireland

TELEPHONE:
353 21 353451

FAX:
353 21 353410

WEB PAGE: NA

E-MAIL: NA

DIRECTIONS TO COURSE: Take the N25 east of the town of Cork; watch for signs to Little Island. There, follow the Cork Golf Club sign to the course.

SCORECARD

HOLE	YDG	PAR	INDEX
1	367	4	7
2	504	5	15
3	264	4	17
4	446	4	1
5	575	5	3
6	329	4	13
7	184	3	9
8	417	4	5
9	196	3	11
OUT	3,286	36	
10	407	4	2
11	491	5	18
12	327	4	12
13	171	3	16
14	427	4	10
15	410	4	6
16	343	4	14
17	385	4	8
18	418	4	4
IN	3,383	36	
TOTAL	6,669	72	

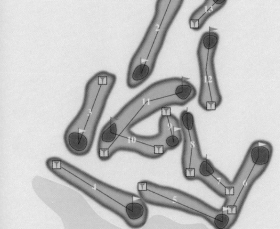

CLUB HOUSE

Lee River

Foza Island Golf Club

ADDRESS:
Carrigtwohill,
County Cork,
Ireland

TELEPHONE:
353 21 883700

FAX:
353 21 883710

WEB PAGE: NA

E-MAIL: fotagolf@iol.ie

DIRECTIONS TO COURSE: Take the N25 east of Cork city. Watch very closely for road signs to Fota Island, and follow the signage directly to the course.

In 1999, Fota Island did an extensive renovation, which precluded a review of this course. It is an important course, however, and has received a great deal of positive acclaim. We are therefore including it with the best information available at the time of publication.

LEVEL OF MAINTENANCE: Before the renovation, Fota Island was renowned for the exquisite care that the course and the facilities received. These same high standards of maintenance are likely to continue.

COURSE DESCRIPTION: This was a championship-quality course prior to renovations in 1999, with the Irish Amateur Open and the Irish PGA Championship being held here. The course is undergoing extensive renovations to both the shape and location of the holes. All 18 greens will be rebuilt to PGA specifications, as will the tees, with a minimum of 4 for each hole. Water will play a significant role in the new course layout. Everything indicates that this will be an outstanding course.

UNIQUE FEATURE: This club is located on a 780-acre estate cited in the "Inventory of Outstanding Landscapes of Ireland."

ACCOMMODATION INFORMATION

Standard hotel: Bayview Hotel (4 star) (Ballycotton), 353 21 646746

Local hotel/guesthouse/B&B: Lotamore House (Cork), 353 21 822344

Restaurant/pub: Riverview Restaurant (in the Metropole Hotel, Cork), 353 21 508122

GREEN FEES:
Moderate

EQUIPMENT RENTAL
Buggies: yes
Trolleys: yes
Caddies: no
Clubs: yes

DATE FOUNDED: 1883

ARCHITECTS: Christy O'Connor Jr. and Peter McEvoy; Jeff Howes, formerly of Nicklaus Associates (1999)

TYPE: Parkland

FACILITIES
Clubhouse at turn: NA
Restrooms on course: NA

SCORECARD

HOLE	YDG	PAR	INDEX
1	428	4	2
2	435	4	6
3	182	3	14
4	501	5	18
5	577	5	8
6	375	4	12
7	170	3	10
8	484	5	16
9	425	4	4
OUT	3,577	37	
10	502	5	9
11	201	3	17
12	425	4	3
13	183	3	13
14	440	4	1
15	445	4	5
16	417	4	7
17	209	3	15
18	492	5	11
IN	3,314	35	
TOTAL	**6,891**	**72**	

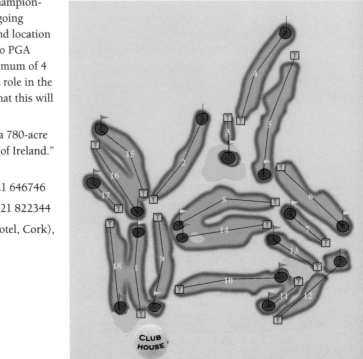

CLUB HOUSE

Kinsale Golf Club

GREEN FEES:
Moderate
EQUIPMENT RENTAL
Buggies: yes
Trolleys: yes
Caddies: yes
Clubs: yes

DATE FOUNDED: 1912
ARCHITECT: Jack Kenneally (1995)
TYPE: Parkland
FACILITIES
Clubhouse at turn: yes
Restrooms on course: no

Kinsale Golf Club has a modern, new, very functional clubhouse with restaurant and bar facilities. There are also showers and dressing rooms and a separate pro shop. A practice ground and putting green are available to the public.

LEVEL OF MAINTENANCE: This well-maintained course has very nice greens and good bunkering. The turf is still a little thin in places, as the course is fairly new. Generally, though, the course is in good condition year-round. Building facilities are clean, well presented, and welcoming to visitors.

COURSE DESCRIPTION: Kinsale (Farringalway Course) is a parkland course that has a number of water hazards to add a great deal of interest to what is otherwise a generally flat landscape. Many new plantings are liberally sprinkled throughout this course. The greens are generally large and gently rolling, with some very good and intelligently placed bunkering. Large, level tees, always a delight, are in abundance at Kinsale. The cupola clock tower adds a nice touch, and the scenic views make for an interesting visual experience. This course is relatively short and can yield some good scores for players in the groove. The old course, Ringenane, is a 9-hole parkland course just off the R600, about 2 miles north of Kinsale. Ringenane is much older (1912), with many pleasant views and mature trees. Many locals still prefer this course over the new one.

UNIQUE FEATURE: The 8th and 9th on the Farringalway Course are back-to-back par 5s, both in excess of 550 yards.

ACCOMMODATION INFORMATION
Standard hotel: Moorings (4 star) (Kinsale), 353 21 772376

Local hotel/guesthouse/B&B: Kilcaw House (3-star guesthouse) (Kinsale), 353 21 774155

Restaurant/pub: Blue Haven Restaurant (Kinsale), 353 21 772209

ADDRESS:
Belgooly, County Cork, Ireland
TELEPHONE:
353 21 772197
FAX:
353 21 773114
WEB PAGE: NA
E-MAIL: kinsaleg@indigo.ie
DIRECTIONS TO COURSE: Take the R600 3 miles north of Kinsale to Belgooly. Follow signs west to Kinsale Golf Club.

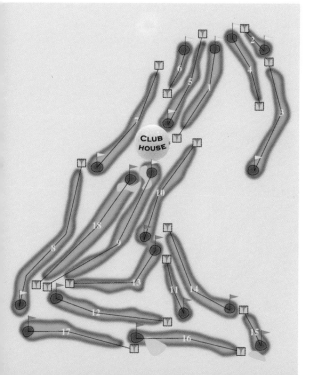

SCORECARD			
HOLE	YDG	PAR	INDEX
1	372	4	13
2	123	3	17
3	415	4	2
4	280	4	16
5	368	4	11
6	175	3	18
7	431	4	3
8	556	5	12
9	560	5	6
OUT	3,280	36	
10	405	4	8
11	216	3	7
12	438	4	5
13	395	4	4
14	421	4	14
15	183	3	9
16	368	4	10
17	411	4	1
18	492	5	15
IN	3,329	35	
TOTAL	**6,609**	**71**	

Lee Valley Golf and Country Club

ADDRESS:
Clashanure, Ovens, County Cork, Ireland

TELEPHONE:
353 21 331721

FAX:
353 21 331695

WEB PAGE: NA

E-MAIL: NA

DIRECTIONS TO COURSE: Lee Valley is located about 8 miles west of Cork on the N22 (Cork-Killarney Road). The course is about 1½ miles off the N22; watch for signage.

The Lee Valley Club offers a stunningly beautiful and opulent clubhouse, complete with a full-service restaurant and elegant bar. There are locker rooms and a well-stocked pro shop. Also on site are a sheltered fifteen-bay floodlit driving range and a large putting green.

LEVEL OF MAINTENANCE: This course is maintained with an eye toward detail. Greens and traps are excellent, and the building facilities are both high quality and exceptionally well kept.

COURSE DESCRIPTION: Lee Valley is another gem of Christy O'Connor Jr. He has designed a wonderful course with almost every imaginable kind of sand trap, water hazard, green, and intelligently placed bunker. Even a couple of ring forts add a sense of antiquity and charm to this wonderful course. It is definitely of championship quality and offers up a challenging game to any golfer. The course is nestled in the Lee Valley, surrounded by panoramic views of the nearby Kerry Mountains, a true Irish Experience. That great, unseen hazard, the wind, plays a big role on this delightful hilltop course.

UNIQUE FEATURE: Two ring forts, also known as "fairy forts," possibly date to 400 A.D. These historic structures were used as occupation sites and were often surrounded by ditches and banks for fortification.

ACCOMMODATION INFORMATION
Standard hotel: Arbutus Lodge (3 star) (Montenotte, Cork), 353 21 501237

Local hotel/guesthouse/B&B: Innishannon House Hotel (3 star) (Innishannon), 353 21 775121

Restaurant/pub: Tatler Jack Bar and Restaurant (near the course), 353 21 731659

GREEN FEES:
Moderate

EQUIPMENT RENTAL
Buggies: yes
Trolleys: yes
Caddies: yes
Clubs: yes

DATE FOUNDED: 1993

ARCHITECT:
Christy O'Connor Jr.

TYPE: Parkland

FACILITIES
Clubhouse at turn: no
Restrooms on course: no

SCORECARD

HOLE	YDG	PAR	INDEX
1	363	4	11
2	344	1	7
3	179	3	13
4	528	5	15
5	475	4	1
6	169	3	17
7	451	4	3
8	538	5	9
9	315	4	5
OUT	3,352	36	
10	347	4	18
11	549	5	6
12	178	3	16
13	379	4	10
14	407	4	12
15	536	5	4
16	171	3	14
17	407	4	2
18	399	4	8
IN	3,373	36	
TOTAL	**6,725**	**72**	

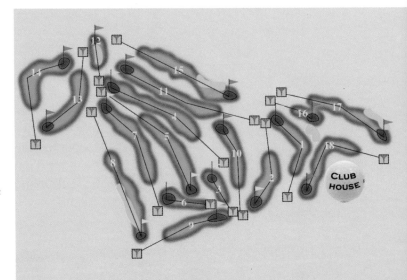

Macroom Golf Club

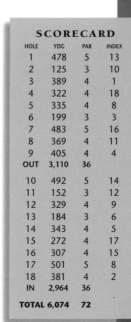

GREEN FEES:
Low

EQUIPMENT RENTAL
Buggies: no
Trolleys: yes
Caddies: yes
Clubs: yes

DATE FOUNDED: 1924

ARCHITECTS: Old 9 by Eddie Hackett (1976); extended to full 18 by Jack Kenneally (1992)

TYPE: Parkland

FACILITIES
Clubhouse at turn: yes
Restrooms on course: no

Macroom offers a lovely new clubhouse, complete with full bar and restaurant. Built in 1996, it also includes changing rooms. There is no pro shop, but there is a putting green.

LEVEL OF MAINTENANCE: This course is very well maintained, with excellent turf and greens. The clubhouse is well presented, friendly, and generally a nice facility.

COURSE DESCRIPTION: The Macroom Club has an entryway that alone is worth a visit to the course. Driving through the castle gates and along the winding road through the course and historic grounds proves to be a fascinating experience in itself. This is one of those Irish parkland courses set amid old estate grounds. Thus, the old-growth trees and lush natural landscaping are spectacular. The two halves of the course are as different as black and white. The first 9 are very hilly, sometimes rather severe, with few sand traps and plenty of mature trees. The back 9 are flatter but with many sand traps, and the River Sullane is always a threat. There are beautiful views of the Kerry Mountains, along with many historic features dotting this course.

UNIQUE FEATURE: Macroom has a most unique entrance through the old castle grounds; enter it and you will feel steeped in history.

ACCOMMODATION INFORMATION

Standard hotel: Castle Hotel and Leisure Centre (Macroom), 353 26 41074

Local hotel/guesthouse/B&B: Mills Inn (Ballyvourney, Macroom), 353 26 45237

Restaurant/pub: Castle Hotel Restaurant (see above), 353 26 41074

ADDRESS:
Lackaduve,
Macroom,
County Cork,
Ireland

TELEPHONE:
353 26 41072

FAX:
353 26 41391

WEB PAGE: NA

E-MAIL: mcroomgc@iol.ie

DIRECTIONS TO COURSE: This course is located on the castle demesne (or grounds), right in the center of Macroom. You will go through a stone archway and then follow a lovely single-lane historic road to the course.

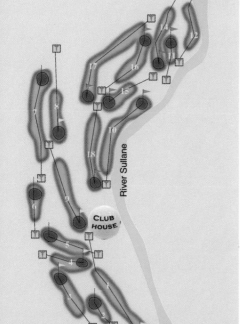

River Sullane

CLUB HOUSE

SCORECARD			
HOLE	YDG	PAR	INDEX
1	478	5	13
2	125	3	10
3	389	4	1
4	322	4	18
5	335	4	8
6	199	3	3
7	483	5	16
8	369	4	11
9	405	4	4
OUT	3,110	36	
10	492	5	14
11	152	3	12
12	329	4	9
13	184	3	6
14	343	4	5
15	272	4	17
16	307	4	15
17	501	5	8
18	381	4	2
IN	2,964	36	
TOTAL	6,074	72	

Mallow Golf Club

ADDRESS:
Ballyellis,
Mallow, County
Cork, Ireland

TELEPHONE:
353 22 21145

FAX:
353 22 42501

WEB PAGE: NA

E-MAIL: NA

DIRECTIONS TO COURSE: Mallow Golf Club is located on the Mallow-Killavullen Road, about 1 mile east of the town of Mallow.

The Mallow Club offers an older-style clubhouse with a separate small but fully equipped pro shop. It has a practice ground and putting green. The clubhouse includes a traditional full bar and restaurant, along with changing rooms, and a very friendly staff. As an added bonus, there are squash courts, sauna facilities, and floodlit tennis courts.

LEVEL OF MAINTENANCE: This club and its facilities are quite well maintained, with excellent turf and very good greens.

COURSE DESCRIPTION: Mallow Golf Club is a parkland course with great views of the Mushera and Galtee Mountains, along with the Blackwater Valley. These features combine to make Mallow a lovely visual experience. There are mature tree–lined fairways with rolling terrain; indeed, some strong slopes can produce real challenges. The course has five par 3s, some of which are very challenging.

UNIQUE FEATURE: This is a well-rounded recreational facility with golf, squash, tennis, and sauna.

ACCOMMODATION INFORMATION

Standard hotel: Longueville House and Presidents Restaurant (Mallow), 353 22 47156

Local hotel/guesthouse/B&B: Springfort Hall (Mallow), 353 22 21278

Restaurant/pub: Presidents Restaurant in Longueville House (see above), 353 22 47156

GREEN FEES:
Moderate

EQUIPMENT RENTAL
Buggies: yes
Trolleys: yes
Caddies: no
Clubs: yes

DATE FOUNDED: 1947

ARCHITECT:
Redesigned by John D. Harris (1996)

TYPE: Parkland

FACILITIES
Clubhouse at turn: no
Restrooms on course: no

SCORECARD

HOLE	YDG	PAR	INDEX
1	399	4	7
2	189	3	9
3	488	5	11
4	187	3	15
5	378	4	3
6	503	5	13
7	450	4	1
8	473	5	17
9	369	4	5
OUT	3,441	37	
10	428	4	6
11	168	3	12
12	540	5	8
13	412	4	2
14	312	4	16
15	382	4	4
16	126	3	18
17	485	5	14
18	196	3	10
IN	3,055	35	
TOTAL	6,496	72	

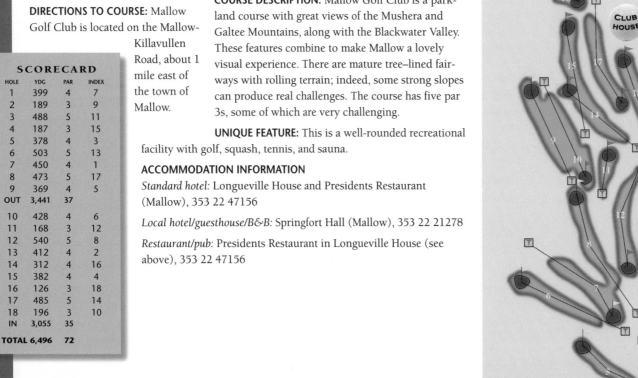

Old Head Golf Links

GREEN FEES:
High

EQUIPMENT RENTAL
Buggies: yes
Trolleys: yes
Caddies: yes
Clubs: no

DATE FOUNDED: 1997

ARCHITECTS: Ron Kirby, Joe Carr, Eddie Hackett, Patrick Merrigan, and Liam Higgins

TYPE: Seaside

FACILITIES
Clubhouse at turn: yes
Restrooms on course: yes

The clubhouse, designed by local architect Patrick Byrne, is reminiscent of Frank Lloyd Wright, blending perfectly with the landscape. The spacious restaurant offers stunning panoramic views, gourmet cuisine, and tables made of fossil ammonites. The elegant gift center offers basic golf needs, along with luxury items. Nearby, there are putting and chipping greens, and a driving range.

LEVEL OF MAINTENANCE: Despite this course's youth, the level of care in all areas demonstrates commitment to the highest of standards.

COURSE DESCRIPTION: Old Head is a seaside course with incomparable views. The course showcases its surroundings with understated but challenging bunkers and traps. Six sets of tees on each hole are changed every morning, depending on playing conditions. At 6,756 yards, the back tees set up a challenging course regardless of weather. Old Head is clearly a course that sets new standards for play and respect for the environment. The personnel are friendly and helpful. Be prepared to catch your breath as you approach this awesome course.

UNIQUE FEATURE: The Old Head protrudes into the ocean and offers refuge for hundreds of species of birds. This peninsula was important during Neolithic times, and the geological features give you glimpses of Earth's earliest stages.

ACCOMMODATION INFORMATION
Standard hotel: Old Bank House (4-star hotel) (Kinsale), 353 21 774075

Local hotel/guesthouse/B&B: Kilcaw House (3-star guesthouse) (Kinsale), 353 21 774155

Restaurant/pub: The Old Head Bar and Restaurant, 353 21 778444

ADDRESS:
Kinsale, County Cork, Ireland

TELEPHONE:
353 21 778444

FAX:
353 21 778022

WEB PAGE:
www.oldheadgolflinks.com

E-MAIL: info@oldheadgolf.ie

DIRECTIONS TO COURSE: Old Head is 7 miles south of Kinsale. Take the R600 through Kinsale and follow closely the road signs directing you to Old Head. Once you get to the course, a gatekeeper will meet you, because these grounds are protected.

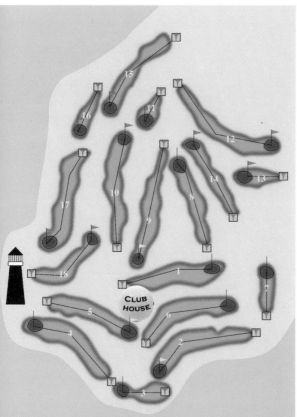

Celtic Sea

SCORECARD

HOLE	YDG	PAR	INDEX
1	420	4	7
2	387	4	5
3	153	3	15
4	407	4	3
5	405	4	9
6	488	5	13
7	164	3	11
8	496	5	17
9	449	4	1
OUT	3,369	36	
10	493	5	16
11	180	3	12
12	498	5	14
13	222	3	8
14	429	4	2
15	340	4	18
16	186	3	10
17	628	5	4
18	411	4	6
IN	3,387	36	
TOTAL	**6,756**	**72**	

Skibbereen and West Carbery Golf Club

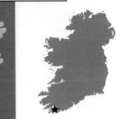

ADDRESS:
Licknavar,
Skibbereen,
County Cork,
Ireland

TELEPHONE:
353 28 21227

FAX:
353 28 22994

WEB PAGE: www.westcorkweb.ie
/skibbereen/skibgolf

E-MAIL: NA

DIRECTIONS TO COURSE:
This course is 1.1 miles southwest of Skibbereen, off the R595 to Baltimore. Follow signage to the course.

The Skibbereen and West Carbery Club offers a small clubhouse with changing rooms and a bar and grill with snack foods but no pro shop. It has a putting green and practice area.

LEVEL OF MAINTENANCE: This facility is adequately maintained, on the level of most municipal courses.

COURSE DESCRIPTION: The Skibbereen and West Carbery Club is one of those ubiquitous Irish municipal courses, making golf in Ireland accessible and convenient. While this course is a wide-open parkland tract that's great for the high handicapper and beginner, its rolling land with good greens provide interesting golf for the more accomplished golfer as well. There is one water hazard, and the bunkering is rather weak; but aside from that, you will find a generally interesting course. The surrounding countryside is typically Irish, including Lough Ine and the Mount Gabriel hills. This course has excellent drainage, making it playable year-round.

UNIQUE FEATURE: The course has four challenging par-3 holes.

ACCOMMODATION INFORMATION
Standard hotel: West Cork Hotel (3 star) (Skibbereen), 353 28 21277

Local hotel/guesthouse/B&B: Eldon Hotel (Skibbereen), 353 28 22000

Restaurant/pub: Clipper Restaurant (in the Baltimore Harbour Resort Hotel, Baltimore), 353 28 20361

GREEN FEES:
Low

EQUIPMENT RENTAL
Buggies: no
Trolleys: yes
Caddies: no
Clubs: no

DATE FOUNDED: 1905

ARCHITECT: NA

TYPE: Parkland

FACILITIES
Clubhouse at turn: no
Restrooms on course: yes
(8th and 16th holes)

SCORECARD			
HOLE	YDG	PAR	INDEX
1	418	4	1
2	159	3	15
3	424	4	5
4	276	4	17
5	494	5	10
6	358	4	9
7	319	4	11
8	200	4	7
9	384	3	3
OUT	3,032	35	
10	418	4	2
11	159	3	16
12	424	4	6
13	276	4	18
14	494	5	14
15	358	4	10
16	319	4	12
17	200	3	8
18	384	4	4
IN	3,032	35	
TOTAL	**6,064**	**70**	

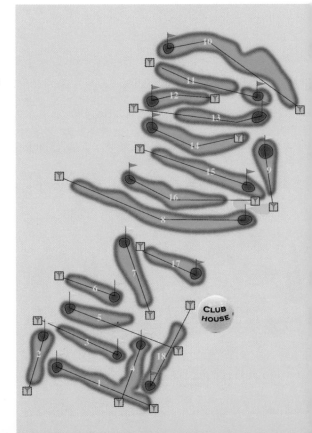

Youghal Golf Club

GREEN FEES:
Low

EQUIPMENT RENTAL
Buggies: no
Trolleys: yes
Caddies: yes
Clubs: yes

DATE FOUNDED: 1898

ARCHITECTS: John D. Harris; redesigned by Eddie Hackett

TYPE: Parkland

FACILITIES
Clubhouse at turn: no
Restrooms on course: no

This course's clubhouse has a bar and a very nice restaurant, locker rooms, and a modestly stocked pro shop. The club also has a practice range and putting green.

LEVEL OF MAINTENANCE: This municipal course is maintained accordingly. The building facilities are maintained quite well, however. The clubhouse is clean, warm, and inviting.

COURSE DESCRIPTION: The Youghal Club is a parkland course with some of the most dazzling panoramic views you will see anywhere in Ireland. The problem is with the course itself—the tract is pretty uninteresting and not particularly well maintained. Despite this, views of Youghal Bay and the mouth of the River Blackwater estuary may make it worth a trip. In any event, at least come up and have a Guinness and a toasty (see glossary) in the restaurant and appreciate the incredible views.

UNIQUE FEATURE: A wonderful stone sundial in front of the clubhouse was given to the Youghal Club on its 1998 centennial.

ACCOMMODATION INFORMATION

Standard hotel:
Aherne's Seafood Restaurant and Accommodation (4 star) (Youghal), 353 24 92424

Local hotel/guesthouse/B&B:
Barnabrow Country House (premier guesthouse) (Cloyne), 353 21 652534

Restaurant/pub:
Aherne's Seafood Restaurant and Accommodation (see above), 353 24 92424

ADDRESS:
Knockaverry,
Youghal, County
Cork, Ireland

TELEPHONE:
353 24 92787

FAX:
353 24 92641

WEB PAGE: NA

E-MAIL: NA

DIRECTIONS TO COURSE: There is no simple way to describe how to find this course. Off the N25, take the "business loop," and go to the Tides Restaurant. Keep heading the best you can to the top of the hill, where you will find the Youghal (pronounced "Yowl") Club.

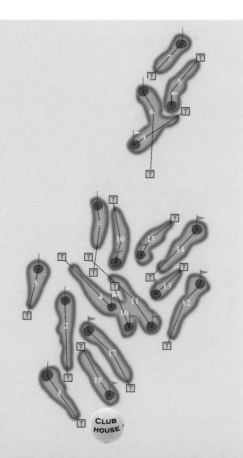

SCORECARD			
HOLE	YDG	PAR	INDEX
1	299	4	14
2	491	5	10
3	154	3	16
4	404	4	3
5	437	4	5
6	348	4	7
7	306	4	12
8	415	4	1
9	264	4	18
OUT	3,122	36	
10	403	4	4
11	358	4	13
12	329	4	17
13	164	3	15
14	415	4	2
15	365	4	11
16	199	3	9
17	380	4	8
18	415	4	6
IN	3,031	34	
TOTAL	6,153	70	

CLUB HOUSE

Ballyliffin Golf Club (Glashedy Links)

ADDRESS:
Ballyliffin,
Inishowen,
County
Donegal, Ireland

TELEPHONE:
353 77 76119

FAX:
353 77 76672

WEB PAGE: NA

E-MAIL: NA

DIRECTIONS TO COURSE: Out of Ballyliffin, take the R238 for 2 miles. The course will be on your left; follow the signage.

The present clubhouse is in the process of being replaced by a new one. The new complex will boast multiple restaurants and bars, locker rooms with shower facilities, and a pro shop. There are three practice holes, putting greens, and a practice range amicably shared with some sheep.

LEVEL OF MAINTENANCE: The Glashedy course is still evolving. This course appears to be better maintained than the Old Course. The prevailing philosophy at Ballyliffin is that of a natural links, which translates into "less is more." So, in the eyes of those who seek perfect fairways and greens, the Glashedy course may actually deteriorate. But for those who seek the purer experience of turn-of-the-century golf, this course will get better over time.

COURSE DESCRIPTION: Glashedy is a wonderful course played over some extraordinary linksland. The front 9 is truly splendid; the 7th hole offers spectacular views of Glashedy Rock in the nearby bay, the Atlantic Ocean, and the rugged mountains of the Inishowen Peninsula. At 7,135 yards, Glashedy is a long course; with the wind, it can become a monster. Many of the greens are large and gently rolling; others are two-tiered. All have subtle and difficult breaks. A number of revetted bunkers add to the beauty. These range from potlike to large gaping bunkers, some of which are difficult to see until you are on top of them. Anyone will be challenged by the long, relatively tight par 4s.

UNIQUE FEATURE: The panoramic views are just magnificent. This course is a visual pleasure and a wonderful test of golf.

ACCOMMODATION INFORMATION
Standard hotel: Ballyliffin Hotel (Ballyliffin), 353 77 76106

Local hotel/guesthouse/B&B: Strand Hotel (Ballyliffin), 353 77 76107

Restaurant/pub: Ubiquitous Chip Restaurant (Buncrana), 353 77 62530

GREEN FEES:
Moderate

EQUIPMENT RENTAL
Buggies: yes
Trolleys: yes
Caddies: yes
Clubs: yes

DATE FOUNDED: 1995

ARCHITECTS:
Pat Ruddy and Tom Craddock

TYPE: Links

FACILITIES
Clubhouse at turn: yes
Restrooms on course: no

SCORECARD

HOLE	YDG	PAR	INDEX
1	426	4	11
2	432	4	7
3	428	4	2
4	479	5	13
5	177	3	15
6	361	4	18
7	183	3	9
8	422	4	4
9	382	4	6
OUT	3,290	35	
10	397	4	8
11	419	4	14
12	448	4	3
13	572	5	10
14	183	3	17
15	440	4	1
16	426	4	5
17	549	5	12
18	411	4	16
IN	3,845	37	
TOTAL	7,135	72	

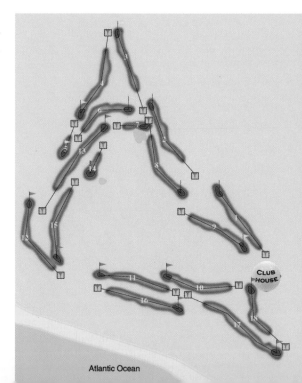

Atlantic Ocean

Ballyliffin Golf Club (Old Links)

GREEN FEES:
Low
EQUIPMENT RENTAL
Buggies: yes
Trolleys: yes
Caddies: yes
Clubs: yes

DATE FOUNDED: 1947
ARCHITECT: NA
TYPE: Links
FACILITIES
Clubhouse at turn: yes
Restrooms on course: no

The present clubhouse is in the process of being replaced by a new one. The new complex will boast multiple restaurants and bars, locker rooms with shower facilities, and a pro shop. There are three practice holes, putting greens, and a practice range amicably shared with some sheep.

LEVEL OF MAINTENANCE: Ballyliffin's Old Course prides itself on being a natural links. This means that the fairways are rugged, oftentimes bumpy, with many different grasses. The greens are less than perfect by today's standards, but are no doubt equal to the best of the courses of the 1920s. Likewise, the bunkers are somewhat old-fashioned.

COURSE DESCRIPTION: The Old Course lies in a low mogul-ridden basin within the extensive duneland that makes up the Ballyliffin complex. At 6,612 yards, the course is not particularly long, unless, of course, the wind blows—and the wind always blows. Let your imagination run and you can feel what it was like in the early days of the game. Here, there is literally no such thing as a level lie, with the exception of the sand bunkers and sometimes the greens. The moguls are strategically challenging. This course is quirky, unique and fun—so don't take yourself too seriously.

UNIQUE FEATURE: The Old Course is a throwback to golf of 100 years ago—catch the nostalgia.

ACCOMMODATION INFORMATION
Standard hotel: Ballyliffin Hotel (Ballyliffin), 353 77 76106

Local hotel/guesthouse/B&B: Strand Hotel (Ballyliffin), 353 77 76107

Restaurant/pub: Kealeys Seafood Restaurant (Buncrana), 353 77 81010

ADDRESS:
Ballyliffin, Inishowen.
County Donegal,
Ireland
TELEPHONE:
353 77 76119
FAX:
353 77 76672
WEB PAGE: NA
E-MAIL: NA
DIRECTIONS TO COURSE: Proceed north out of Ballyliffin on the R238. Continue for 2 miles, and you will see the course on the left-hand side.

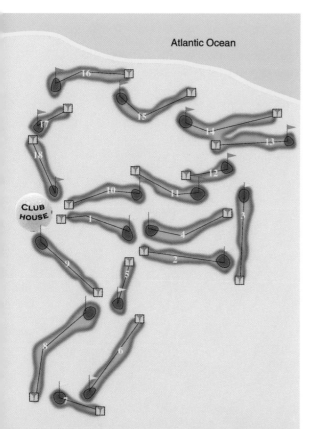

Atlantic Ocean

CLUB HOUSE

SCORECARD			
HOLE	YDG	PAR	INDEX
1	393	4	8
2	422	4	2
3	354	4	14
4	491	5	10
5	176	3	16
6	378	4	12
7	211	3	18
8	409	4	6
9	389	4	4
OUT	3,223	35	
10	334	4	15
11	395	4	5
12	206	3	13
13	426	4	3
14	535	5	9
15	435	4	1
16	344	4	11
17	160	3	17
18	554	5	7
IN	3,389	36	
TOTAL	6,612	71	

Bundoran Golf Club

ADDRESS:
Bundoran,
County
Donegal,
Ireland

TELEPHONE:
353 72 41302

FAX:
353 72 42014

WEB PAGE: NA

E-MAIL: NA

DIRECTIONS TO COURSE: Go to the north edge of Bundoran town, following the signs to the Great Northern Hotel. The club is right on the ocean adjacent to the hotel.

The clubhouse of this course has a bar with snacks only. The Great Northern Hotel overlooks the course and provides full restaurant facilities. There is a small but adequate pro shop in the clubhouse, along with modest changing rooms. There is also a putting green.

LEVEL OF MAINTENANCE: The course itself is well maintained, with very good greens. The clubhouse is a bit old and in spots tattered. The hotel is old and gracious, quite lovely.

COURSE DESCRIPTION: Bundoran is a very old, wide-open, resort-type course. Its holes run east-west over a large crest. There are some truly great views of the seashore to the west and of the Atlantic Ocean. The holes are basically featureless, but the test of the course comes from the wind. On a calm day, the course plays very easy, as it is short, but with wind, shot making is at a premium. This course has quite a bit of history attached to it. Harry Vardon designed it as one of his resort courses. Christy O'Connor Sr. was the course professional during the 1960s. Because it has changed little over the years, Bundoran, then, is a great location to see what early resort golf looked and played like.

UNIQUE FEATURE: This course has a nice history and surrounds the venerable and opulent Victorian-style Great Northern Hotel, a treat in itself.

ACCOMMODATION INFORMATION

Standard hotel: Great Northern Hotel (Bundoran), 353 72 41204

Local hotel/guesthouse/B&B: Holyrood Hotel (Bundoran), 353 72 41232

Restaurant/pub: Restaurants in the Great Northern Hotel (do check them out), 353 72 41204

GREEN FEES:
Low (but residents of Great Northern Hotel are not charged green fees)

EQUIPMENT RENTAL
Buggies: no
Trolleys: yes
Caddies: yes
Clubs: yes

DATE FOUNDED: 1894

ARCHITECT:
Harry Vardon

TYPE: Seaside

FACILITIES
Clubhouse at turn: yes
Restrooms on course: no

SCORECARD

HOLE	YDG	PAR	INDEX
1	356	4	8
2	500	5	15
3	127	3	18
4	360	4	6
5	214	3	9
6	196	3	14
7	354	4	7
8	387	4	4
9	387	4	13
OUT	2,886	34	
10	396	4	2
11	418	4	3
12	344	4	11
13	230	3	10
14	398	4	5
15	425	4	1
16	154	3	17
17	493	5	16
18	353	4	12
IN	3,216	35	
TOTAL	6,102	69	

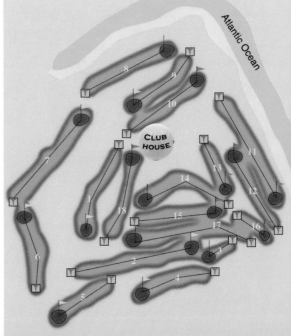

Donegal Golf Club

GREEN FEES:
Low
EQUIPMENT RENTAL
Buggies: yes
Trolleys: yes
Caddies: yes
Clubs: yes

DATE FOUNDED: 1960
ARCHITECT: Eddie Hackett
TYPE: Links
FACILITIES
Clubhouse at turn: yes
Restrooms on course:yes
(7th green)

The Donegal Club (sometimes referred to as "Murvagh") offers an elegant and well-designed clubhouse, complete with clean and spacious locker rooms and showers. It has a small but well-stocked pro shop, a practice range, and a great putting green.

LEVEL OF MAINTENANCE: This course enjoys a very high level of maintenance, including careful attention to the greens, making them quite spectacular. You will also find thick and lush turf. The clubhouse is immaculate, elegant, and inviting to visitors.

COURSE DESCRIPTION: As soon as you turn off the N15 and start traveling toward the course through a lovely tree-lined estate drive, you know you're in for a fine round of golf and a true Irish Experience. Once you arrive, you encounter a wide-open, expansive linksland of mostly low dunes with occasional views of the Atlantic Ocean. The course, on 180 acres at the end of a peninsula, provides good links golf set in scenic countryside unmarred by houses, trailer parks, holiday homes, or development. Some questionable bunkers bear Eddie Hackett's signature, as do some artificially placed fairway division moguls. The greens are first-rate, and the play of the links is hard and fast.

UNIQUE FEATURE: Watch for lazybeds (see glossary) that line the 1st hole fairway. Other special features are the superb quality of the greens and the five par 5s.

ACCOMMODATION INFORMATION
Standard hotel: St. Ernan's House Hotel (4 star; no children under 6) (Donegal town, but on its own private island), 353 73 21065

Local hotel/guesthouse/B&B: Hyland Central Hotel (3 star) (Donegal town), 353 73 21027

Restaurant/pub: Donegal Clubhouse, or restaurants at either of the hotels listed (see above)

ADDRESS:
Murvagh, Ballinta,
Donegal,
County Donegal,
Ireland

TELEPHONE:
353 73 34054
FAX:
353 73 34377
WEB PAGE: NA
E-MAIL: NA

DIRECTIONS TO COURSE: Take the N15 south out of Donegal town. The course is about halfway between Rossnowlagh and Donegal, with good signage.

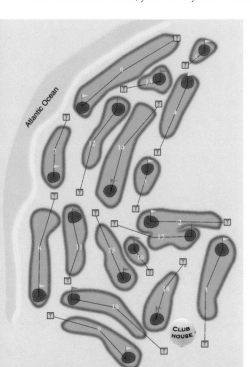

SCORECARD			
HOLE	YDG	PAR	INDEX
1	521	5	15
2	461	4	1
3	207	3	7
4	475	4	5
5	189	3	9
6	521	5	17
7	437	4	11
8	543	5	3
9	399	4	13
OUT	3,757	37	
10	348	4	12
11	397	4	4
12	596	5	14
13	158	3	18
14	546	5	10
15	403	4	6
16	227	3	2
17	358	4	16
18	397	4	8
IN	3,445	36	
TOTAL	**7,202**	**73**	

Narin and Portnoo Golf Club

ADDRESS:
Portnoo, Nerne, County Donegal, Ireland

TELEPHONE:
353 75 45107

FAX:
353 75 45185

WEB PAGE: NA

E-MAIL: NA

DIRECTIONS TO COURSE: This course is a challenge to find, but worth the effort! Take R261 out of Ardara, to Portnoo. Take the beach road; go through gates marked "private." Stay on the dirt road through the trailer ("caravan") park. You'll see the single-story clubhouse and the course itself.

SCORECARD

HOLE	YDG	PAR	INDEX
1	314	4	17
2	490	5	6
3	186	3	12
4	453	4	1
5	387	4	7
6	203	3	9
7	318	4	3
8	141	3	13
9	320	4	15
OUT	2,817	34	
10	387	4	2
11	196	3	5
12	330	4	11
13	185	3	16
14	518	5	10
15	490	5	8
16	119	3	18
17	404	4	4
18	349	4	14
IN	2,983	35	
TOTAL	**5,800**	**69**	

Narin and Portnoo Club provides a primitive but functional clubhouse and a putting green. The whole setup is best described as "spartan," with the absence of a pro shop and limited snack foods available.

LEVEL OF MAINTENANCE: The course itself is generally well maintained. Money is obviously put into maintaining the course and equipment rather than the building facilities. Be prepared for "barnyard matter" dotting the fairways and roughs.

COURSE DESCRIPTION: The Narin and Portnoo course, located on the outer reaches of County Donegal, presents one of the most unique golfing experiences you're likely to have in Ireland. You enter the course through a cattle gate. The putting green is surrounded by an electrified fence. You shortly discover that you're sharing the front and back ends of the course with a small herd of cattle and a few sheep! To its credit, this club protects its greens; they are well kept and run true. On the 3rd hole, you go through a second cattle gate and begin the ascent to the dunes and to some spectacular golf. The 10th hole, with its breathtaking view of Gweebarra Bay, unfortunately dips back away from the ocean too quickly. The course is relatively short but challenging, with consistent signage. It is a don't-miss, Irish Experience.

UNIQUE FEATURE: Be sure to bring your camera for pictures of the cattle and the dramatic coastline.

ACCOMMODATION INFORMATION
Standard hotel: Woodhill House (3-star country house hotel) (Ardara), 353 75 41112

Local hotel/guesthouse/B&B: The Highlands Hotel (Glenties), 353 75 51111

Restaurant/pub: Woodhill House Restaurant (see above), 353 75 41112

GREEN FEES:
Low

EQUIPMENT RENTAL
Buggies: no
Trolleys: no
Caddies: no
Clubs: no

DATE FOUNDED: 1930

ARCHITECT:
Phillip Carr

TYPE: Links

FACILITIES
Clubhouse at turn: no
Restrooms on course: yes (5th green)

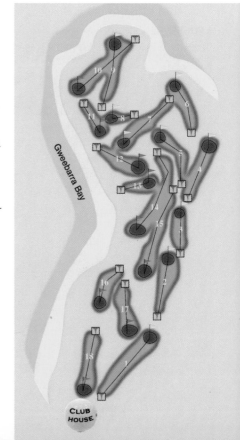

Portsalon Golf Club

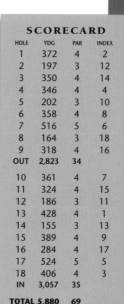

GREEN FEES:
Low

EQUIPMENT RENTAL
Buggies: no
Trolleys: yes
Caddies: no
Clubs: no

DATE FOUNDED: 1891

ARCHITECT: Thompson

TYPE: Links

FACILITIES
Clubhouse at turn: no
Restrooms on course: no

Portsalon offers a new and welcoming clubhouse, complete with bar, restaurant, and changing rooms with lockers. There is no pro shop, and green fees are paid in the office. The clubhouse overlooks the Ballymastocker Bay, with a backdrop of the Knockalla Mountains. Check out the historic photographs on the stairwell walls going up to the bar.

LEVEL OF MAINTENANCE: This is a well-maintained links course with good greens, sand bunkers, and fairway turf. The clubhouse facilities are maintained with pride and consequently are clean and very presentable.

COURSE DESCRIPTION: To play Portsalon links, you will need to use every club in your bag. It's a short, quirky little course that will test your golfing and orienting skills. Its members and staff are extraordinarily friendly. There are a number of blind shots, crisscrossing fairways, and a few trees, but also some great golf and beautiful views of Ballymastocker Bay, the Fanad Peninsula, and the Knockalla Mountains. The 3rd hole is unchanged from 1891, and the rest of the course makes its way through the sand dunes. The course has recently purchased an additional 37 acres, leading to local disagreement about whether to straighten out some of the quirks.

UNIQUE FEATURE: This quintessential Irish Experience offers a bell on the 15th tee to alert players on the 4th that you are about to hit your ball.

ACCOMMODATION INFORMATION

Standard hotel: Rosapenna Golf Hotel (4 star) (Rosapenna), 353 74 55301

Local hotel/guesthouse/B&B: Fort Royal Hotel (3 star) (Rathmullen), 353 74 58100

Restaurant/pub: Restaurants in either of the two hotels listed (see above)

ADDRESS:
Portsalon, Fanad,
County Donegal,
Ireland

TELEPHONE:
353 74 59459

FAX:
353 74 59459

WEB PAGE: NA

E-MAIL: NA

DIRECTIONS TO COURSE: Head for the town of Portsalon, on the R246. The course is on your right, just before you reach the town. Watch closely for the course; there is no signage for the access road.

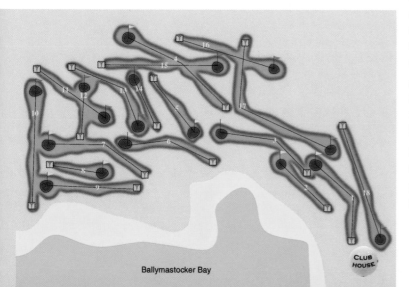

Ballymastocker Bay

CLUB HOUSE

SCORECARD			
HOLE	YDG	PAR	INDEX
1	372	4	2
2	197	3	12
3	350	4	14
4	346	4	4
5	202	3	10
6	358	4	8
7	516	5	6
8	164	3	18
9	318	4	16
OUT	2,823	34	
10	361	4	7
11	324	4	15
12	186	3	11
13	428	4	1
14	155	3	13
15	389	4	9
16	284	4	17
17	524	5	5
18	406	4	3
IN	3,057	35	
TOTAL	5,880	69	

Rosapenna Golf Club

ADDRESS:
Downings,
County
Donegal, Ireland

TELEPHONE:
353 74 55301

FAX:
353 74 55128

WEB PAGE: NA

E-MAIL: rosapenna@tinet.ie

DIRECTIONS TO COURSE: On R425, the Rosapenna Hotel and Golf Links is 2 miles northwest of Carrigart. Follow signage to the hotel and course.

The clubhouse is the beautiful Rosapenna Hotel, built after the original hotel was destroyed by fire in 1962. The pro shop is just inside the lobby. From the moment you meet its owners/managers, Frank and Hilary Casey, you'll notice the exceedingly friendly atmosphere. The hotel includes a spacious dining room, with exceptional food and service. Don't miss the golfing memorabilia in the bar. Also on site are a covered-bay practice range, putting green, and changing facilities for nonresidents.

LEVEL OF MAINTENANCE: Rosapenna provides very well maintained fairways and bunkers. The greens are unusually smooth for a links course, and the tees of highest quality. The building facilities are tended with an eye to detail.

COURSE DESCRIPTION: The links part of the course is set amid a valley between high dunelands and Sheephaven Bay. The fairways are wide and the gently rolling greens are spacious with subtle breaks. Bunkering is intelligently placed. Some of the tees are carved out of sand dunes and offer great views of the linksland. The last 8 holes leave the valley and head up and around a hill to Mulroy Bay. On the 18th hole, you'll pass by Villa Lough to complete a day of lovely resort golf. Rosapenna offers golf clinics March through August; check the hotel for package details.

UNIQUE FEATURE: In 1891, Lord Leitrim invited Scotland's Old Tom Morris to look at another piece of ground for a course. During the train trip, Morris spotted the present site and convinced Leitrim to build the course there. As you play Rosapenna, immerse yourself in this connection with Old Tom.

ACCOMMODATION INFORMATION

Standard hotel: Rosapenna Hotel and Golf Links (4 star) (on site), 353 74 55301

Local hotel/guesthouse/B&B: Hotel Carrigart (Carrigart), 353 74 55114

Restaurant/pub: The bar and restaurant in Rosapenna Hotel (unsurpassed), 353 74 55301

GREEN FEES:
Moderate

EQUIPMENT RENTAL
Buggies: yes
Trolleys: yes
Caddies: yes
Clubs: yes

DATE FOUNDED: 1893

ARCHITECTS: Old Tom Morris (1891); later modifications and extensions to 18 holes by James Braid and Harry Vardon

TYPE: Links/Parkland

FACILITIES
Clubhouse at turn: no
Restrooms on course: no

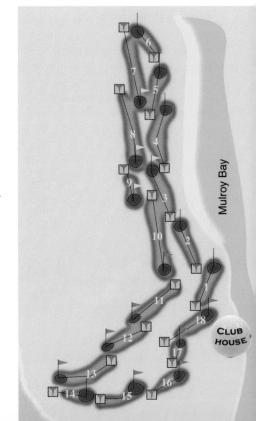

SCORECARD

HOLE	YDG	PAR	INDEX
1	298	4	11
2	428	4	5
3	446	4	1
4	386	4	9
5	255	4	15
6	167	3	17
7	367	4	3
8	485	5	7
9	185	3	13
OUT	3,017	35	
10	543	5	10
11	427	4	2
12	342	4	14
13	455	4	6
14	128	3	18
15	418	4	4
16	216	3	16
17	358	4	12
18	367	4	8
IN	3,254	35	
TOTAL	6,271	70	

City West Hotel, Conference Centre and Golf Resort

GREEN FEES:
Moderate

EQUIPMENT RENTAL
Buggies: yes
Trolleys: yes
Caddies: yes
Clubs: yes

DATE FOUNDED: 1994

ARCHITECT: Christy O'Connor Jr.

TYPE: Parkland

FACILITIES
Clubhouse at turn: yes
Restrooms on course: yes (10th tee)

City West is a lovely resort facility whose hotel and pro shop are joined. Adjacent to the pro shop are the shower and changing rooms; restaurant and bar facilities are in the hotel. City West has a wonderful covered driving range, also the home of the McGregor Golf Academy. The putting green is excellent, and the landscaping around the hotel and course is wonderful. Overall, this facility is quite appealing and very functional.

LEVEL OF MAINTENANCE: City West is a resort course that is maintained accordingly. The building facilities are well cared for and clean. Indeed, all aspects of the course are first-rate.

COURSE DESCRIPTION: This classic parklands course is delightful to look at and play. The holes are pure Christy O'Connor, interestingly shaped with great bunkers and expansive greens. All greens are excellent surfaces to putt on and roll true. A few water hazards and a multitude of new plantings will have a dramatic effect on the course in the future. Directly in front of the 18th hole is a lovely lake that creates the kind of drama O'Connor likes in his courses. A new 18 holes, scheduled to be built at this site, also by Christy O'Connor, should open for play in 2001.

UNIQUE FEATURE: The practice facility and McGregor Golf Academy are wonderful assets to this fine course.

ACCOMMODATION INFORMATION

Standard hotel: The City West Hotel (on site), 353 1 458 8566

Local hotel/guesthouse/B&B: Shelbourne (Dublin City), 353 1 661 6006

Restaurant/pub: Facilities on site (see above)

ADDRESS:
Saggart, County Dublin, Ireland

TELEPHONE:
353 1 458 8566

FAX:
353 1 458 8565

WEB PAGE: NA

E-MAIL: info@citywest-hotel.iol.ie

DIRECTIONS TO COURSE: The resort is near the city center of Saggart (just outside Dublin), a very small community, and there is good signage to follow.

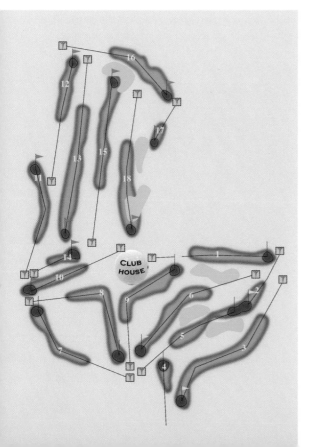

SCORECARD			
HOLE	YDG	PAR	INDEX
1	386	4	9
2	197	3	13
3	541	5	7
4	220	3	11
5	398	4	15
6	454	4	1
7	380	4	17
8	457	4	3
9	430	4	5
OUT	3,463	35	
10	200	3	10
11	369	4	12
12	400	4	4
13	555	5	8
14	178	3	18
15	536	5	14
16	397	4	6
17	158	3	16
18	435	4	2
IN	3,228	35	
TOTAL	6,691	70	

Corballis Public Golf Course

ADDRESS:
Donabate,
County Dublin,
Ireland

TELEPHONE:
353 1 843 6583

FAX: NA

WEB PAGE: NA

E-MAIL: NA

DIRECTIONS TO COURSE: North of Dublin, take the N1 toward Belfast. Follow good signage toward Donabate (don't actually go through Donabate); additional good signage directs you to the course.

Corballis's clubhouse is currently a marginal facility and provides basics (e.g., snacks). There is a putting green. Above and beyond that, one must realize that this is a municipal course run by a municipality (Fingal County Council).

LEVEL OF MAINTENANCE: The greens are weak; sand traps are nicely placed but unkempt; and the cleanliness of the clubhouse is marginal.

COURSE DESCRIPTION: Two prominently placed signs on the gravel road leading toward the course, reading "Danger, Golf In Progress," provide an apt warning of things to come. At first glance, one sees the classic links terrain with rolling sand dunes and green fairways, all of which can be exciting to the eye. But as one plays past the 1st hole, the layout quickly speaks to what could be a very dangerous golfing experience: blind shots, a tight and constricted layout, crossing greens, and numerous golfers with apparently high handicaps. This course was probably a wonderful 9-hole links course that got stretched to the breaking point when it was converted to 18 holes. Thus, the first 9 holes, although tight, fit comfortably in linksland. The second 9 holes take a perilous course. They snake behind housing developments, around small lakes and public roads, and offer eminent danger to the occasional cottage screened in with netting. Play this course very much mindful of your own risk.

UNIQUE FEATURE: The first 9 holes are quirky, delightful, bending, turning, undulating linksland that would be a treat for any seasoned golfer. Beware, however; this is an exceedingly dangerous course.

ACCOMMODATION INFORMATION

Standard hotel: Deer Park Hotel (Howth), 353 1 832 2624

Local hotel/guesthouse/B&B: The Dunes (across from the course), 353 1 843 6153

Restaurant/pub: Pub at the Dunes Hotel (see above), 353 1 843 6153

GREEN FEES:
Low

EQUIPMENT RENTAL
Buggies: no
Trolleys: yes
Caddies: no
Clubs: no

DATE FOUNDED: 1973

ARCHITECT:
Dublin County Council

TYPE: Links

FACILITIES
Clubhouse at turn: yes
Restrooms on course: no

SCORECARD

HOLE	YDG	PAR	INDEX
1	155	3	12
2	251	4	18
3	465	4	2
4	155	3	16
5	389	4	4
6	183	3	6
7	188	3	8
8	264	4	14
9	494	5	10
OUT	2,544	33	
10	132	3	15
11	374	4	9
12	405	4	3
13	264	4	17
14	191	3	11
15	196	3	5
16	392	4	1
17	140	3	7
18	333	4	13
IN	2,427	32	
TOTAL	**4,971**	**65**	

Irish Sea

CLUB HOUSE

Deer Park Hotel and Golf Courses

GREEN FEES:
Low

EQUIPMENT RENTAL
Buggies: yes
Trolleys: yes
Caddies: yes
Clubs: yes

DATE FOUNDED: 1973

ARCHITECT: Frederick W. Hawtree

TYPE: Parkland

FACILITIES
Clubhouse at turn: no
Restrooms on course: no

Deer Park's clubhouse is actually part of the larger hotel complex. Although somewhat dated, the bar and restaurant facilities of the adjoining hotel are more than adequate. A separate pro shop is modestly stocked. The hotel offers such amenities as a large and attractive swimming pool, complete with relaxing sauna and steam room, and conference and function rooms.

ADDRESS:
Howth, County Dublin, Ireland

TELEPHONE:
353 1 832 2624

FAX:
353 1 839 2405

WEB PAGE:
www.deerpark-hotel.ie

E-MAIL: sales@deerpark.iol.ie, or jjdoran@indigo.ie

DIRECTIONS TO COURSE: Take the N32 toward Malahide; go through Baldoyle. At the T junction, turn left. After about 1½ miles, the sign for the hotel is on the right.

LEVEL OF MAINTENANCE: This course is very well maintained, with the exception of some of the fringe areas, such as a few of the sand traps. Although wonderfully placed and designed, the borders of some of the traps are uneven and broken down. The turf and greens are well kept.

COURSE DESCRIPTION: Deer Park is a parkland course with spectacular views of Howth (pronounced "Hooth") Castle and the Howth peninsula. This is Ireland's largest golf complex, with a number of parkland courses from which to choose. These include a pitch and putt, two 18-hole courses, and a short 12-hole course. The main course, called Deer Park Course, is well bunkered, with open fairways lined by mature and stately trees. The greens are flat and occasionally tiered. The course also presents an intuitive layout with good signage. This is a pleasant venue for any handicap. The hotel complex is a good "base camp" to use when playing the many courses in this area of County Dublin.

UNIQUE FEATURE: The 18th hole is a blockbuster of a finishing hole, as it is 550 yards, par 5. This hole requires three good shots to get you in position for par.

ACCOMMODATION INFORMATION
Standard hotel: Deer Park Hotel (on site), 353 1 832 2624

Local hotel/guesthouse/B&B: Howth Lodge Hotel (Howth), 353 1 832 1010

Restaurant/pub: Howth Lodge Hotel restaurant, 353 1 832 1010

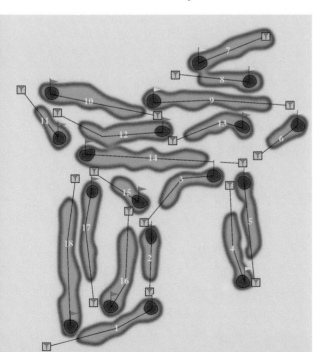

SCORECARD			
HOLE	YDG	PAR	INDEX
1	416	4	9
2	221	3	5
3	350	4	11
4	365	4	13
5	405	4	3
6	207	3	7
7	509	5	15
8	430	4	1
9	519	5	17
OUT	3,426	36	
10	434	4	2
11	193	3	12
12	392	4	14
13	318	4	16
14	555	5	4
15	166	3	18
16	339	4	10
17	428	4	8
18	550	5	6
IN	3,381	36	
TOTAL	6,807	72	

Forrest Little Golf Club

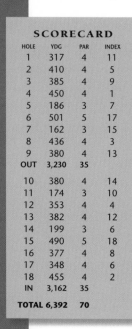

ADDRESS:
Cloghran,
County Dublin,
Ireland

TELEPHONE:
353 1 840 1763

FAX:
353 1 840 1000

WEB PAGE: NA

E-MAIL: NA

DIRECTIONS TO COURSE: Take the N1 to St. Margaret's roundabout exit; the course is directly across from the Dublin Airport, with good signage to follow.

Forrest Little provides excellent facilities, including a well-stocked pro shop complete with a full club-making shop. The clubhouse offers bar and dining facilities, with a lovely dining room overlooking the golf course. Locker rooms are available, along with an excellent practice facility, including putting and chipping greens and a driving range.

LEVEL OF MAINTENANCE: This course is very well maintained, and all aspects of the clubhouse are inviting, clean, and immaculate.

COURSE DESCRIPTION: Forrest Little is a mature parkland course with quaint bridges, streams, and beautiful landscaping throughout the grounds. In all aspects, it is a visual treat. There are many areas of mature trees, unique for most parkland settings. The bunkering is intelligently placed and a real challenge. The course offers a good, intuitive layout, along with excellent hole signage. Forrest Little is one of the prequalifying courses for the Irish Open. One unfortunate feature results from the course being directly across from the Dublin Airport; some typical airport-related noise is a true test for your concentration. Otherwise, this is a great course on which to test your golf when you first land on Irish soil.

UNIQUE FEATURE: A stream running through the course comes into play on a number of holes and adds dramatic beauty to this lovely course.

ACCOMMODATION INFORMATION

Standard hotel: Forte Posthouse (4 star) (near the Dublin Airport), 353 1 808 0500

Local hotel/guesthouse/B&B: Great Southern Hotel (at the Dublin Airport), 353 1 844 6000

Restaurant/pub: Restaurants in either of the two hotels listed (see above)

GREEN FEES:
Moderate

EQUIPMENT RENTAL
Buggies: yes
Trolleys: yes
Caddies: no
Clubs: yes

DATE FOUNDED: 1940

ARCHITECT:
Frederick G. Hawtree

TYPE: Parkland

FACILITIES
Clubhouse at turn: yes
Restrooms on course: no

SCORECARD

HOLE	YDG	PAR	INDEX
1	317	4	11
2	410	4	5
3	385	4	9
4	450	4	1
5	186	3	7
6	501	5	17
7	162	3	15
8	436	4	3
9	380	4	13
OUT	3,230	35	
10	380	4	14
11	174	3	10
12	353	4	4
13	382	4	12
14	199	3	6
15	490	5	18
16	377	4	8
17	348	4	6
18	455	4	2
IN	3,162	35	
TOTAL	**6,392**	**70**	

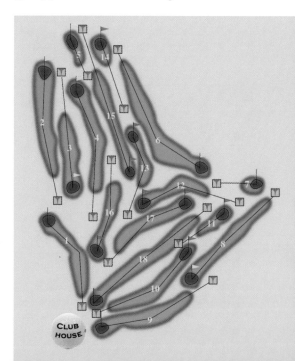

Howth Golf Club

GREEN FEES:
Low

EQUIPMENT RENTAL
Buggies: no
Trolleys: yes
Caddies: yes
Clubs: yes

DATE FOUNDED: 1911
ARCHITECT: James Braid
TYPE: Parkland
FACILITIES
Clubhouse at turn: no
Restrooms on course: no

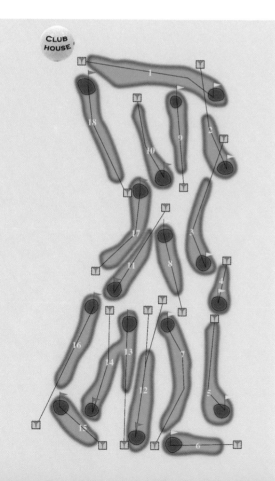

owth (pronounced "Hooth") offers a modern clubhouse with bar and snack-food facilities, along with a moderately well stocked pro shop and changing rooms. The site also includes a nice practice area.

LEVEL OF MAINTENANCE: This is a well-kept course with community course standards. The greens and traps are neat and interesting.

COURSE DESCRIPTION: Howth has some wonderful views of Dublin Bay because of its high elevation. Many interesting elevation changes make it a difficult course to traverse. Several of the fairways have low middle areas that may affect the course's playability in rainy periods. Howth also presents itself well, with a very friendly and helpful staff.

UNIQUE FEATURE: Howth's spectacular views include vistas of Dublin Bay; watch especially for the large island called Eye of Ireland.

ACCOMMODATION INFORMATION
Standard hotel: Deer Park Hotel (3 star) (Howth), 353 1 832 2624

Local hotel/guesthouse/B&B: Howth Lodge Hotel (3 star) (Howth), 353 1 832 1010

Restaurant/pub: The Bloody Stream (Howth), 353 1 839 5076

ADDRESS:
Carrickbrack Road.
Sutton, Dublin 13,
County Dublin,
Ireland

TELEPHONE:
353 1 832 3055

FAX:
353 1 832 1793

WEB PAGE: NA

E-MAIL: NA

DIRECTIONS TO COURSE: This club is 9 miles northeast of Howth city center and 2 miles from Sutton Cross. Watch closely for the sparse signage.

SCORECARD

HOLE	YDG	PAR	INDEX
1	341	4	10
2	341	4	4
3	450	5	14
4	163	3	8
5	446	4	2
6	306	4	12
7	525	5	6
8	155	3	16
9	275	4	18
OUT	3,006	36	
10	335	4	7
11	342	4	3
12	495	5	15
13	430	4	1
14	355	4	11
15	149	3	17
16	325	4	9
17	392	4	5
18	348	4	13
IN	3,176	36	
TOTAL	6,182	72	

The Island Golf Club

ADDRESS:
Corballis,
Donabate,
County Dublin,
Ireland

TELEPHONE:
353 1 843 6104

FAX:
353 1 843 6860

WEB PAGE: NA

E-MAIL: NA

DIRECTIONS TO COURSE: This course is on the N1, about 7 miles north of Dublin Airport on the Corballis Peninsula. Turn right on Donabate Road, and follow the signage.

The Island provides a beautiful, modern clubhouse with full amenities, including a bar and restaurant and fully appointed locker rooms. There is a large practice area with putting green.

LEVEL OF MAINTENANCE: This top-notch operation provides excellent management of its superb links course. The greens, fairways, and bunkers are exceptional, the signage is consistent and helpful, and the whole course is a pleasure to play. The building facilities are inviting and very well maintained.

COURSE DESCRIPTION: The Island is classic linksland with no two holes alike. Each is a special treat to play, with challenges and great visual appeal. The course is surrounded on three sides by the Atlantic Ocean. The challenges on this course range from the diabolic length of the 18th hole to the needle-and-thread accuracy needed for the 14th, which has one of the narrowest fairways you will ever play. The Island, almost completely situated in the dunes, is one of the best golfing treats in Ireland.

UNIQUE FEATURE: The Island provides 18 entirely different holes to test your game and ability to concentrate.

ACCOMMODATION INFORMATION
Standard hotel: The Grand Hotel (4 star) (Malahide), 353 1 845 0000

Local hotel/guesthouse/B&B: Belcamp Hutchinson (high-standard guesthouse) (Malahide), 353 1 846 0843

Restaurant/pub: The Island Clubhouse, or restaurants at either of the two hotels listed (see above)

GREEN FEES:
Moderate

EQUIPMENT RENTAL
Buggies: yes
Trolleys: yes
Caddies: yes
Clubs: yes

DATE FOUNDED: 1890

ARCHITECTS: Redesigned by Frederick W. Hawtree and Eddie Hackett (1990)

TYPE: Links

FACILITIES
Clubhouse at turn: yes
Restrooms on course: no

SCORECARD

HOLE	YDG	PAR	INDEX
1	431	4	5
2	395	4	7
3	441	4	1
4	348	4	11
5	366	4	9
6	327	4	13
7	439	4	3
8	307	4	15
9	173	3	17
OUT	3,230	35	
10	545	5	14
11	309	4	18
12	412	4	4
13	208	3	8
14	343	4	16
15	552	5	12
16	152	3	10
17	422	4	6
18	446	4	2
IN	3,394	36	
TOTAL	6,224	71	

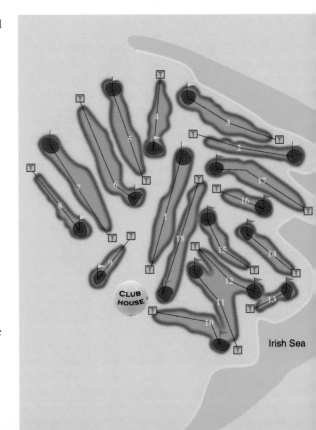

Irish Sea

Luttrellstown Castle Golf and Country Club

GREEN FEES:
Moderate

EQUIPMENT RENTAL
Buggies: yes
Trolleys: yes
Caddies: yes
Clubs: yes

DATE FOUNDED: 1993

ARCHITECTS: Nicholas Bielenberg and Eddie Connaughton

TYPE: Parkland

FACILITIES
Clubhouse at turn: no
Restrooms on course: no

This club offers a unique split-log, multigabled clubhouse, complete with elegant dining room, excellent cuisine, full bar, conference rooms, and snooker room. The well-stocked pro shop has a very friendly staff. On site are a practice gound, putting green, and archery and clay pigeon ranges. The club organizes corporate programs with lodging and catering. The nearby Luttrellstown Castle is an internationally renowned facility for corporate rental.

ADDRESS:
Castleknock,
Dublin 15,
County Dublin,
Ireland

TELEPHONE:
353 1 808 9988

FAX:
353 1 808 9989

WEB PAGE: www.luttrellstown.ie

E-MAIL: golf@luttrellstown.ie

LEVEL OF MAINTENANCE: This is an exquisite facility, highly maintained in all aspects. Nothing is left to chance, making it a real treat to play.

COURSE DESCRIPTION: This course comprises rolling parkland situated on 560 acres, laid out with minimal disturbance of the topography. The greens are sand based and playable even during the wetter winter months. As an old estate, the course features many mature trees, along with a multitude of new plantings. At present the course is fairly wide open, with many bunkers and interesting water hazards, including a river with swans and geese. Water comes into play on 6 holes, demanding accurate tee shots.

DIRECTIONS TO COURSE: From Dublin, take the N4 west toward Lucan. At the M50 and N4 junction, turn right onto M50, cross the River Liffey, and go to Castleknock village. At the first traffic light, turn right, and watch for the club on your left.

UNIQUE FEATURE: The impressive ivy-clad castle comes into view at the 12th hole. Of unknown age, it passed out of the Luttrell family in 1811.

ACCOMMODATION INFORMATION
Standard hotel: Glenroyal Hotel, Leisure Club and Conference Center (3 star) (Maynooth), 353 1 629 0909

Local hotel/guesthouse/B&B: Finnstown Country House Hotel (3 star) (Lucan), 353 1 628 0644

Restaurant/pub: Luttrellstown Clubhouse (a must-do for ambience and great food), 353 1 808 9988

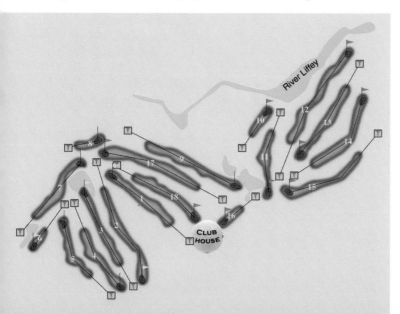

SCORECARD			
HOLE	YDG	PAR	INDEX
1	419	4	10
2	517	5	14
3	423	4	4
4	388	4	8
5	396	4	6
6	224	3	12
7	393	4	2
8	138	3	18
9	556	5	16
OUT	3,454	36	
10	187	3	17
11	347	4	11
12	579	5	7
13	440	4	5
14	436	4	1
15	462	4	3
16	171	3	15
17	533	5	13
18	412	4	9
IN	3,567	36	
TOTAL	7,021	72	

Portmarnock Golf Club

ADDRESS:
Portmarnock,
County
Dublin, Ireland

TELEPHONE:
353 1 846 2968

FAX:
353 1 846 2601

WEB PAGE: NA

E-MAIL: secretary@
portmarnockgolfclub.ie

DIRECTIONS TO COURSE: The
course lies about 10 miles north of Dublin and just south of Malahide. Watch for signs in the village of Portmarnock on the R106. (Don't confuse this club with its younger neighbor Portmarnock Hotel and Golf Links.)

Beyond a doubt, this is one of Ireland's classic clubs. Its tradition-steeped clubhouse exudes history and grandeur. It offers an elegant bar, full restaurant, locker rooms with showers, a separate pro shop, fine putting green, and adequate practice area.

LEVEL OF MAINTENANCE: This world-class venue provides superb maintenance, though, when we visited, a couple of the sod-lined sand bunkers had gone to seed. Nonetheless, expect this course to meet your every linksland dream.

COURSE DESCRIPTION: Portmarnock is a classic links course with its turn at the 9. At 27 holes, there is room for even more. This links lacks the dramatic views and elevation changes found in the west (e.g., at Lahinch and Ballybunion), but it does offer classic blind drives and difficult approach shots. Some of the greens are quirky, others elevated, and all undulate. The numerous classic bunkers offer a tremendous test, as can the wind which is always a factor. The club hosted the first Irish Open Amateur Championship in 1896 and the Walker Cup in 1991. Ireland's own Joe B. Carr and Christy O' Connor Sr. have been tested by these amazing links.

UNIQUE FEATURE: Get ready for links golf at its best on this spectacular promontory.

ACCOMMODATION INFORMATION
Standard hotel: Sutton Castle Hotel (3 star) (Sutton), 353 1 832 2688

Local hotel/guesthouse/B&B: Marine Hotel (4 star) (Sutton Cross), 353 1 839 0000

Restaurant/pub: Golfer's Link (Portmarnock), 353 1 846 0129

GREEN FEES: High (open only to members on Wednesdays)

EQUIPMENT RENTAL
Buggies: yes
Trolleys: yes
Caddies: yes
Clubs: yes

DATE FOUNDED: 1894

ARCHITECT: W. C. Pickeman

TYPE: Links

FACILITIES
Clubhouse at turn: yes
Restrooms on course: no

SCORECARD

HOLE	YDG	PAR	INDEX
1	392	4	13
2	409	4	15
3	396	4	11
4	471	4	1
5	395	4	5
6	600	5	9
7	182	3	17
8	399	4	7
9	436	4	3
OUT	3,686	36	
10	368	4	8
11	425	4	2
12	154	3	18
13	563	5	14
14	409	4	6
15	189	3	12
16	575	5	16
17	470	4	4
18	409	4	10
IN	3,568	36	
TOTAL	**7,254**	**72**	

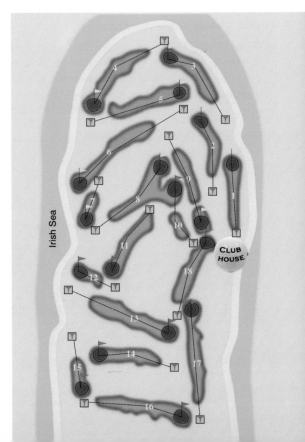

Irish Sea

CLUB HOUSE

Portmarnock Hotel and Golf Links

GREEN FEES:
Moderate

EQUIPMENT RENTAL
Buggies: no
Trolleys: yes
Caddies: yes
Clubs: yes

DATE FOUNDED: 1993

ARCHITECTS: Bernard Langer and Stan Eby

TYPE: Links

FACILITIES
Clubhouse at turn: no
Restrooms on course: no

Portmarnock Links offers facilities that are superb in every sense. Be sure to have a Cream Tea in the elegant dining area by the fireplace. The clubhouse is incorporated into the hotel, an opulent building that was once the family home of John Jameson, the Irish whiskey magnate. The club offers a well-stocked pro shop, beautiful putting green and practice area, and first-rate landscaping.

LEVEL OF MAINTENANCE: This venue is exceedingly well maintained. The only exception is that some of the greens are a little spotty with multiple grasses, but the greenkeeping staff is working toward a solution.

COURSE DESCRIPTION: This is a fine course to play, although the first 7 holes can be subject to flooding, as they were built on agricultural land in 1993. Holes 8 through 14 are entirely in the gorgeous dunes. You'll be challenged by 90 intelligently placed bunkers, many of which are in the classic Scottish revetted style. There is a good, intuitive layout. While the course is not always in visual contact with the ocean, there are wooden steps up to vantage points, which you should not miss.

UNIQUE FEATURE: Aside from the opulence of the hotel and beauty of the links, this club boasts of being the only PGA European Tour course in Ireland.

ACCOMMODATION INFORMATION
Standard hotel: Portmarnock Hotel and Golf Links (on site), 353 1 846 0611

Local hotel/guesthouse/B&B: St. Lawrence Hotel (Harbour Road in Howth),
353 1 832 2643

Restaurant/pub: The hotel on site (elegant fare), 353 1 846 0611, or the Golf Links Bar and Restaurant (near the course),
353 1 846 0129

ADDRESS: Portmarnock, County Dublin, Ireland

TELEPHONE:
353 1 846 1800

FAX:
353 1 846 1077

WEB PAGE: NA

E-MAIL: NA

DIRECTIONS TO COURSE: Portmarnock Links (not to be confused with its venerable neighbor, Portmarnock Golf Club) is located near the town of Portmarnock on the R106 north of Dublin. Head for Howth on the R105, then take a left onto R106 to Portmarnock. Watch for the hotel and links just off the road.

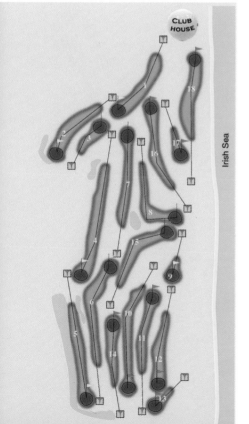

SCORECARD			
HOLE	YDG	PAR	INDEX
1	385	4	14
2	392	4	10
3	193	3	12
4	574	5	6
5	469	4	2
6	529	5	18
7	449	4	4
8	372	4	8
9	169	3	16
OUT	3,538	36	
10	527	5	15
11	456	4	1
12	358	4	5
13	149	3	17
14	345	4	13
15	396	4	7
16	404	4	11
17	201	3	9
18	444	4	3
IN	3,285	35	
TOTAL	6,823	71	

The Royal Dublin Golf Club

ADDRESS:
North Bull Island, Dollymount, Dublin 3, County Dublin, Ireland

TELEPHONE: 353 1 833 6346

FAX: 353 1 833 6504

WEB PAGE: NA

E-MAIL: royaldublin@ clubi.ie

DIRECTIONS TO COURSE: 3 miles northeast of Dublin city, head for North Bull Island via the Coast Road to Clontarf. Signage is excellent.

The Royal Dublin provides an opulent clubhouse with an elegant dining room, a members-only bar and another bar open to visitors. The locker rooms offer every amenity, including a male attendant in the men's area (there are no women members). A separate pro shop is very well stocked. A practice area and putting green are also provided.

LEVEL OF MAINTENANCE: The course and building facilities are maintained to the standards of a first-class operation.

COURSE DESCRIPTION: The Royal Dublin is a classic links course with a linear layout very similar to that at St. Andrews in Scotland: 9 out and 9 in. The course has some of St. Andrews's subtleties, such as exceptional bunkering, rolling greens, and sometimes-vicious winds. In terms of course management, the distances are on the sprinkler heads, unusual for an Irish course. This classic Harry S. Colt design is a strikingly beautiful linksland course. For history buffs, Bull Island was built by William Bligh, before he sailed on the Bounty, as a sea wall to protect Dublin.

UNIQUE FEATURE: The back 9 is adjacent to some untrammeled ground that offers a glimpse of pre-development linksland.

ACCOMMODATION INFORMATION

Standard hotel: Howth Lodge Hotel (Howth, pronounced "Hooth"), 353 1 832 1010

Local hotel/guesthouse/B&B: Deer Park Hotel and Golf Courses (Howth), 353 1 832 2624

Restaurant/pub: The Grill Room in the Clubhouse (on site), 353 1 833 6346

GREEN FEES: Moderate

EQUIPMENT RENTAL
Buggies: yes
Trolleys: yes
Caddies: yes
Clubs: yes

DATE FOUNDED: 1885

ARCHITECT: Harry S. Colt (1893)

TYPE: Links

FACILITIES
Clubhouse at turn: no
Restrooms on course: no

SCORECARD			
HOLE	YDG	PAR	INDEX
1	393	4	8
2	484	5	17
3	395	4	5
4	177	3	13
5	460	4	3
6	196	3	14
7	368	4	10
8	506	5	11
9	178	3	15
OUT	3,163	35	
10	465	4	1
11	537	5	7
12	204	3	12
13	462	4	2
14	495	5	16
15	432	4	6
16	267	4	18
17	376	4	9
18	493	4	4
IN	3,736	37	
TOTAL	6,899	72	

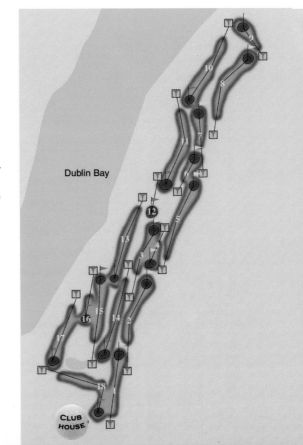

Dublin Bay

CLUB HOUSE

Rush Golf Club

GREEN FEES:
Low
EQUIPMENT RENTAL
Buggies: no
Trolleys: no
Caddies: no
Clubs: yes

DATE FOUNDED: 1943

ARCHITECT: NA

TYPE: Links

FACILITIES
Clubhouse at turn: yes
Restrooms on course: no

The Rush Club includes an old, warm, and quaint clubhouse with a small bar and snacks. There are modest changing rooms, but no pro shop.

LEVEL OF MAINTENANCE: This well-cared-for course is primarily used by locals. Consequently, it is not tourist oriented but is worth the time and effort to find it.

COURSE DESCRIPTION: Rush is actually a 9-hole course with two sets of tees (except at the two par 3s) to complete the 18-hole layout. This is a lovely links with a few great ocean views. The fairways are well moguled, with natural dunes and grasses. The greens are slightly undulating, protected by pot bunkers, and fun to play. Bunkering can be tricky—watch out! As a links course, it is playable year-round. This is an out-of-the-way course primarily meant for links aficionados. Be the only one on your block to have played it!

UNIQUE FEATURE: Rush qualifies as one of Ireland's quaint-and-quirky courses unlike what you will find back home, or anywhere else for that matter.

ACCOMMODATION INFORMATION
Standard hotel: Grand Hotel (4 star) (Malahide), 353 1 845 0000

Local hotel/guesthouse/B&B: Island View Hotel (Malahide), 353 1 845 0099

Restaurant/pub: Coachman's Bar and Lounge (Rush), 353 1 840 1227

ADDRESS:
Corr's Lane, Rush,
County Dublin,
Ireland

TELEPHONE:
353 1 843 8177

FAX:
353 1 8438177

WEB PAGE: NA

E-MAIL: NA

DIRECTIONS TO COURSE: In the village of Rush, find Sand Road; then drive north to just past the Rush Credit Union, and turn left at Corr's Lane. This may look like a driveway, but fear not; keep traveling to the end. You will probably get lost hunting for this course. Don't be afraid to stop someone and ask directions.

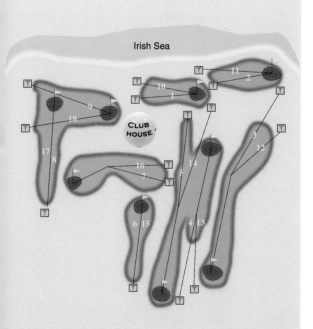

Irish Sea

CLUB HOUSE

SCORECARD			
HOLE	YDG	PAR	INDEX
1	321	4	13
2	367	4	3
3	571	5	9
4	383	4	7
5	359	4	11
6	209	3	5
7	403	4	1
8	148	3	17
9	252	4	15
OUT	3,017	35	
10	308	4	14
11	392	4	2
12	568	5	10
13	378	4	12
14	390	4	8
15	209	3	6
16	395	4	4
17	148	3	18
18	291	4	16
IN	3,084	35	
TOTAL	6,101	70	

St. Anne's Golf Club

ADDRESS:
North Bull Island, Dollymount, Dublin 5, County Dublin, Ireland

TELEPHONE:
353 1 833 6471

FAX: 353 1 833 4618

WEB PAGE: NA

E-MAIL: NA

DIRECTIONS TO COURSE:
St. Anne's Club is located 4 miles northeast from Dublin city center along the coast road to Bull Island. Watch for excellent signage.

St. Anne's Club includes a pleasant clubhouse with full facilities. It has a bar and restaurant, changing rooms, and a putting green, but no pro shop.

LEVEL OF MAINTENANCE: This facility is very well maintained. The very attractive landscaping includes an absolutely beautiful drive and entry into the course. Watch out for golfers as you enter the clubhouse parking lot.

COURSE DESCRIPTION: St. Anne's is a lovely links course with intelligent bunkering, good signage, and well-kept greens. Although very close to Dublin, it is far enough out on North Bull Island that you feel you're out of the hustle and bustle of the city. The course is located in a wonderful bird sanctuary with abundant avian life (and "birders"). There are a couple of testing holes with difficult greens—notably, holes 10 and 18. As always on a links course, wind can be a definite factor.

UNIQUE FEATURE: You may want to read up on the history of North Bull Island—fascinating because Captain William Bligh built the pier that resulted in the formation of the island, well before he sailed on the Bounty.

ACCOMMODATION INFORMATION
Standard hotel: Clontarf Castle Hotel (recently refurbished) (Clontarf), 353 1 832 2321

Local hotel/guesthouse/B&B: Sutton Castle Hotel (3 star) (Sutton), 353 1 832 2688

Restaurant/pub: Templars Bistro in the Clontarf Castle Hotel (see above), 353 1 832 2321

GREEN FEES:
Moderate

EQUIPMENT RENTAL
Buggies: no
Trolleys: yes
Caddies: yes
Clubs: yes

DATE FOUNDED: 1921

ARCHITECT: Redesigned to 18 holes by Eddie Hackett (1980s)

TYPE: Links

FACILITIES
Clubhouse at turn: no
Restrooms on course: no

SCORECARD

HOLE	YDG	PAR	INDEX
1	504	5	15
2	385	4	9
3	163	3	13
4	396	4	3
5	373	4	11
6	156	3	17
7	468	4	1
8	405	4	7
9	392	4	5
OUT	3,248	35	
10	161	3	16
11	551	5	10
12	372	4	6
13	479	5	8
14	232	3	12
15	410	4	2
16	309	4	18
17	192	3	14
18	411	4	4
IN	3,123	35	
TOTAL	**6,371**	**70**	

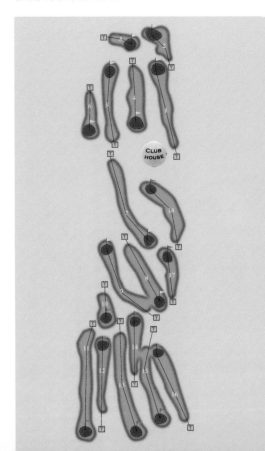

St. Margaret's Golf and Country Club

GREEN FEES:
Moderate

EQUIPMENT RENTAL
Buggies: yes
Trolleys: yes
Caddies: yes
Clubs: yes

DATE FOUNDED: 1992

ARCHITECTS: Pat Ruddy and Tom Craddock

TYPE: Parkland

FACILITIES
Clubhouse at turn: yes
Restrooms on course: no

St. Margaret's Club provides an elegant, modern, tastefully designed and built clubhouse that includes a spacious restaurant, bar, and conference center. The whole facility is rich, warm, and inviting. It has a well-stocked pro shop, practice green, and driving range.

LEVEL OF MAINTENANCE: As might be expected with such a first-rate venue, all aspects of the building facilities and grounds are extremely well maintained. This includes excellent turf development and beautifully manicured greens and plantings.

COURSE DESCRIPTION: St. Margaret's is a beautiful new course that utilizes sculptured mounding and is a delight to play. The fairways are wide, with many young trees planted throughout. When mature, they will prove to be even more of a test. A number of the par 4s are grueling tests of strength and distance. There are several water hazards: the 12th hole crosses a stream, the 8th crosses part of a lake, and the 18th green has a sizable lake nearby. This is a very good test of golf in a beautiful setting.

UNIQUE FEATURE: Clearly, the use of water hazards sets this course apart, making it a challenge and a delight to play.

ACCOMMODATION INFORMATION

Standard hotel: Forte Posthouse (near Dublin airport), 353 1 808 0500

Local hotel/guesthouse/B&B: Ashling Hotel (Dublin 8), 353 1 677 2324

Restaurant/pub: Clubhouse on site, 353 1 864 0400

ADDRESS:
St. Margaret's,
County
Dublin, Ireland

TELEPHONE:
353 1 864 0400

FAX:
353 1 864 0289

WEB PAGE:
www.fusio.ie/web/stmargarets

E-MAIL: stmarggc@indigo.ie

DIRECTIONS TO COURSE: From Dublin, take the N1 northeast toward the airport. Go past the airport, and follow the clear signage to the course.

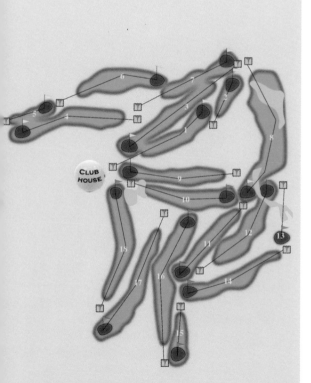

SCORECARD			
HOLE	YDG	PAR	INDEX
1	358	4	13
2	149	3	17
3	509	5	15
4	456	4	1
5	174	3	11
6	458	4	3
7	374	4	5
8	525	5	9
9	398	4	7
OUT	3,401	36	
10	395	4	10
11	366	4	8
12	474	5	18
13	194	3	14
14	402	4	6
15	180	3	16
16	423	4	2
17	512	5	12
18	458	4	4
IN	3,404	36	
TOTAL 6,805		72	

Athenry Golf Club

ADDRESS:
Palmerstown, Oranmore, County Galway, Ireland

TELEPHONE:
353 91 841922

FAX:
353 91 841671

WEB PAGE: NA

E-MAIL: NA

DIRECTIONS TO COURSE: The course is located between Athenry and Galway towns, 8 miles west of Galway and 6 miles from Athenry, on the N6. Follow signage to the course.

SCORECARD

HOLE	YDG	PAR	INDEX
1	377	4	3
2	350	4	13
3	173	3	5
4	283	4	17
5	362	4	7
6	154	3	15
7	441	4	1
8	511	5	11
9	380	4	9
OUT	3,035	35	
10	482	5	18
11	373	4	16
12	190	3	10
13	401	4	2
14	372	4	12
15	381	4	4
16	399	4	6
17	155	3	14
18	360	4	8
IN	3,119	35	
TOTAL	6,154	70	

Athenry has a nice clubhouse with excellent facilities that are clean and attractive. A well-stocked pro shop, a full bar, and dining facilities are all presented in a warm and inviting way.

LEVEL OF MAINTENANCE: This course is well cared for, with good signage. All aspects of Athenry club show attention and care.

COURSE DESCRIPTION: This parkland course is well established, with excellent, very attractive landscaping and new tree plantings. Trees and bunkers are all well positioned, and the greens are fairly large and undulating. Although the two 9s are distinct and clearly built in different eras, the difference does not detract from the enjoyment of playing this tract. All in all, Athenry presents a good challenge without being unfair. This is a solid parkland venue.

UNIQUE FEATURE: This enjoyable parkland course has very interesting greens and bunkering.

ACCOMMODATION INFORMATION

Standard hotel: Hotel Sacre-Coeur (Galway), 353 91 523355

Local hotel/guesthouse/B&B: New Park Hotel Cross, 353 91 844035

Restaurant/pub: Ann Barrett Pub, 353 91 844120

GREEN FEES:
Low

EQUIPMENT RENTAL
Buggies: no
Trolleys: yes
Caddies: yes
Clubs: no

DATE FOUNDED: 1902
(first 9 holes)

ARCHITECT: Second 9 holes by Eddie Hackett

TYPE: Parkland

FACILITIES
Clubhouse at turn: no
Restrooms on course: no

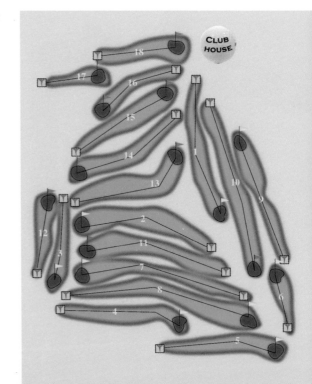

Ballinasloe Golf Club

GREEN FEES:
Low
EQUIPMENT RENTAL
Buggies: no
Trolleys: yes
Caddies: no
Clubs: no

DATE FOUNDED: 1894
ARCHITECT: Eddie Connaughton
TYPE: Parkland
FACILITIES
Clubhouse at turn: no
Restrooms on course: no

Ballinasloe has a newly remodeled clubhouse with full bar and restaurant. The whole facility is clean and pleasant, including the locker rooms and showers. The pro shop is modestly stocked.

LEVEL OF MAINTENANCE: Ballinasloe is a well-maintained community course. The greens are in good shape, and signage on the course is consistent and helpful.

COURSE DESCRIPTION: This course is a nifty little community golf course with many mature plantings and some new growth. It is well drained, making it playable year-round. This is somewhat unusual for an inland parkland course. Ballinasloe's members and staff are friendly and pleasant. If you're in the area, this is a nice course to play.

UNIQUE FEATURE: Six of the 9 holes built in 1984 are on a bog that has been reclaimed. The process has involved extensive planning and work, and the members are deservedly proud of the effort.

ACCOMMODATION INFORMATION
Standard hotel: Castledaly Manor (Athlone), 353 902 81211

Local hotel/guesthouse/B&B: Hayden's Hotel (Ballinasloe), 353 905 42347

Restaurant/pub: Garbally Restaurant in Hayden's Hotel (see above), 353 905 42347

ADDRESS:
Rossgrove,
Ballinasloe,
County Galway,
Ireland

TELEPHONE:
353 905 42126

FAX:
353 905 42538

WEB PAGE: NA

E-MAIL: NA

DIRECTIONS TO COURSE: Take the Ballinasloe-Portumna Road. The course is about 2 miles south of Ballinasloe; watch for signage.

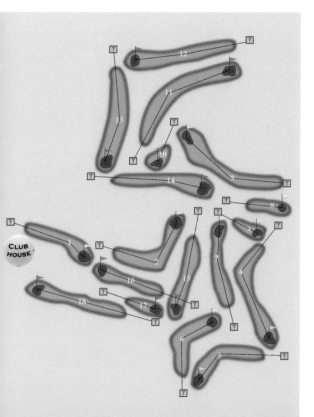

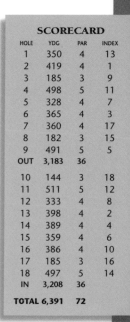

SCORECARD			
HOLE	YDG	PAR	INDEX
1	350	4	13
2	419	4	1
3	185	3	9
4	498	5	11
5	328	4	7
6	365	4	3
7	360	4	17
8	182	3	15
9	491	5	5
OUT	3,183	36	
10	144	3	18
11	511	5	12
12	333	4	8
13	398	4	2
14	389	4	4
15	359	4	6
16	386	4	10
17	185	3	16
18	497	5	14
IN	3,208	36	
TOTAL	6,391	72	

Bearna Golf Club

ADDRESS:
Corboley,
Bearna (some
maps say
Barna), County
Galway, Ireland

TELEPHONE:
353 91 592677

FAX: NA

WEB PAGE: NA

E-MAIL: NA

DIRECTIONS TO COURSE: This course is 2 miles west of Bearna (or Barna), on R336. Watch for signage to the course.

Bearna has an imposing, modern-style clubhouse overlooking the course. This lovely building has full facilities, including a large restaurant and bar with a varied and interesting menu, locker rooms with showers, and a well-stocked pro shop. All are tasteful and well appointed. There is also a putting green.

LEVEL OF MAINTENANCE: This course is new, and as with all new courses, many more things need to be completed. Drainage and parking remain issues, with construction and improvements still being done. The greens and turf are beginning to come in quite nicely.

COURSE DESCRIPTION: First and foremost, this is purely an Irish Golf Experience. You will not encounter a course like this anywhere else in the world. For that reason, it should not be missed. The Connemara region—with its beautiful outcroppings of stone (resembling a lunar surface), numerous water hazards, and abundant heather and gorse—makes this a classic moorland course and a fascinating challenge. There are also great views of Galway Bay, the Burren, and the Aran Islands. Bearna, however, is immature and, strictly from a golfing perspective, needs a few more years to reach its full potential. The sand traps appear as afterthoughts and will need attention. But do include this course on your itinerary if you are in the area.

UNIQUE FEATURE: The landscape of the Connemara region seems to be one that would make laying out a golf course impossible, making Bearna an unlikely but lovely experience.

ACCOMMODATION INFORMATION

Standard hotel: Twelve Pins Hotel and Restaurant (Bearna),
353 91 592368

Local hotel/guesthouse/B&B: Spinnaker House Hotel (Bearna),
353 91 525425

Restaurant/pub: Twelve Pins Restaurant (see above), 353 91 592368

GREEN FEES:
Low

EQUIPMENT RENTAL
Buggies: no
Trolleys: yes
Caddies: no
Clubs: yes

DATE FOUNDED: 1996

ARCHITECT:
Robert Browne

TYPE: Moorland

FACILITIES
Clubhouse at turn: no
Restrooms on course: no

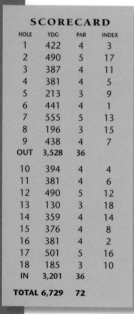

SCORECARD			
HOLE	YDG	PAR	INDEX
1	422	4	3
2	490	5	17
3	387	4	11
4	381	4	5
5	213	3	9
6	441	4	1
7	555	5	13
8	196	3	15
9	438	4	7
OUT	3,528	36	
10	394	4	4
11	381	4	6
12	490	5	12
13	130	3	18
14	359	4	14
15	376	4	8
16	381	4	2
17	501	5	16
18	185	3	10
IN	3,201	36	
TOTAL	6,729	72	

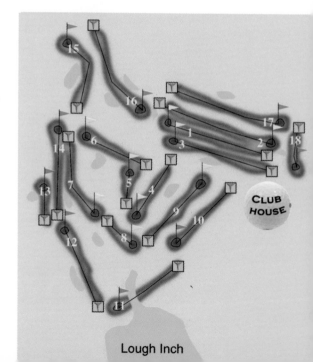

CLUB HOUSE

Lough Inch

Connemara Golf Club

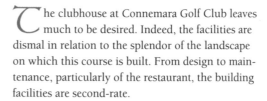

GREEN FEES:
Moderate

EQUIPMENT RENTAL
Buggies: yes
Trolleys: yes
Caddies: yes
Clubs: yes

DATE FOUNDED: 1973

ARCHITECTS: Eddie Hackett and Tom Craddock

TYPE: Links

FACILITIES
Clubhouse at turn: yes
Restrooms on course: yes
(13th tee)

The clubhouse at Connemara Golf Club leaves much to be desired. Indeed, the facilities are dismal in relation to the splendor of the landscape on which this course is built. From design to maintenance, particularly of the restaurant, the building facilities are second-rate.

LEVEL OF MAINTENANCE: The course is generally well maintained despite inconsistent signage. The greens and bunkers are cared for, and the fairways are classic tight links, cropped close; the tees are reasonably good.

COURSE DESCRIPTION: Connemara Golf Club offers a classic links course with flat, windswept terrain and a challenging length. Bring your chipping and putting game. The course is wide open, with a rough that does not penalize you. The lack of consistent signage leading to the next tees creates minor inconveniences, although the course has a good layout. There is no map of the course, either on the scorecard or otherwise, so consult the map outside the pro shop or the layout in this guide. Holes 13, 14, and 15 offer spectacular views, with the tee at 14 an outstanding visual experience. Pot bunkers, deep and menacing, are frequent throughout the course.

UNIQUE FEATURE: Keep an eye out for the very large hares and their huge holes in the hillside as you walk down the 14th fairway.

ACCOMMODATION INFORMATION
Standard hotel: Ardagh Hotel and Restaurant (Clifden), 353 95 21384

Local hotel/guesthouse/B&B: The Station House Hotel and Restaurant (Clifden), 353 95 21699

Restaurant/pub: The King's Bar and Restaurant (Clifden), 353 95 21085

ADDRESS:
Ballyconneely,
Clifden,
County Galway,
Ireland

TELEPHONE:
353 95 23505

FAX:
353 95 23662

WEB PAGE: NA

E-MAIL: links@iol.ie

DIRECTIONS TO COURSE: The course is 9 miles south of Clifden (there are no signs for it in Clifden). Watch for a course sign in Ballyconneely.

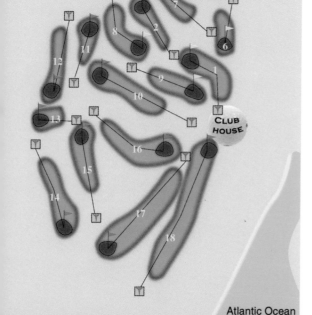

Atlantic Ocean

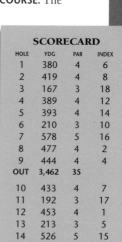

SCORECARD			
HOLE	YDG	PAR	INDEX
1	380	4	6
2	419	4	8
3	167	3	18
4	389	4	12
5	393	4	14
6	210	3	10
7	578	5	16
8	477	4	2
9	444	4	4
OUT	3,462	35	
10	433	4	7
11	192	3	17
12	453	4	1
13	213	3	5
14	526	5	15
15	399	4	9
16	454	4	3
17	534	5	11
18	540	5	13
IN	3,744	37	
TOTAL	7,206	72	

Connemara Isles Golf Club

ADDRESS:
Eanach Mheain, Annaghvane Isles, Leitir Moir (English: Lettermore), County Galway, Ireland

TELEPHONE:
353 91 572498

FAX: 353 91 572214

WEB PAGE: NA

E-MAIL: NA

DIRECTIONS TO COURSE:
Out of Maam, take the R336 south through Maam Cross to Costelloe. There, take the R343 to the island of Lettermore (Leitir Moir). Look for a large sign directing you to the course, down a dirt road.

SCORECARD

HOLE	YDG	PAR	INDEX
1	314	4	12
2	340	4	5
3	170	3	9
4	280	4	18
5	380	5	6
6	165	3	16
7	282	4	10
8	425	5	13
9	165	3	3
OUT	2,521	35	
10	324	4	11
11	315	4	7
12	158	3	14
13	330	4	8
14	440	5	2
15	155	3	17
16	270	4	15
17	470	5	4
18	185	3	1
IN	2,647	35	
TOTAL	**5,168**	**70**	

Connemara Isles offers Ireland's only thatch-roofed clubhouse, complete with peat-burning fireplace and all signage in Gaelic ("Irish"). This clubhouse is the original farmhouse of the farm on which the course was built; it is a quaint, old family dwelling. Changing rooms are small, but clean and adequate. There is no pro shop.

LEVEL OF MAINTENANCE: This course offers rather poorly maintained fairways, and the greens are a little rough. But the reason to play this course is for its beauty, not for the perfection of its golf facilities.

COURSE DESCRIPTION: Connemara Isles Golf Club offers one of the more unusual and spectacular Irish Experiences in golf and is beyond categorization. Strictly from a golfing perspective, the course is interesting but of marginal design. Several of the greens are simply laid on top of the ground, are too small, and undulate too severely. From an aesthetic point of view, however, this course is the essence of your reason for crossing the Atlantic. It is rugged and stunningly beautiful, with barren rock and an estuary. This is absolutely an incredible piece of land on which to play golf. The course is relatively difficult to find, but if you want to play a course that you will not encounter anyplace else, it is well worth the effort.

UNIQUE FEATURE: Enjoy Ireland's only thatch-roofed clubhouse and the breathtaking landscape.

ACCOMMODATION INFORMATION
Standard hotel: Park Lodge Hotel (Carraroe), 353 91 553159

Local hotel/guesthouse/B&B: Hotel Carraroe (Carraroe), 353 91 595116

Restaurant/pub: Trigger Martyns Bar (Carraroe), 353 91 561294

GREEN FEES:
Low

EQUIPMENT RENTAL
Buggies: no
Trolleys: yes
Caddies: no
Clubs: yes

DATE FOUNDED: 1995

ARCHITECTS: Tom Craddock and Pat Ruddy

TYPE: Links

FACILITIES
Clubhouse at turn: yes
Restrooms on course: no

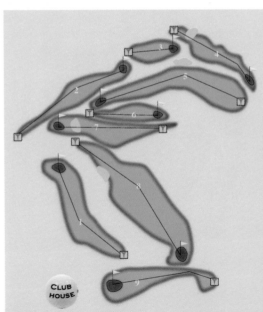

Galway Bay Golf and Country Club

GREEN FEES:
Moderate
EQUIPMENT RENTAL
Buggies: yes
Trolleys: yes
Caddies: yes
Clubs: no

DATE FOUNDED: 1993

ARCHITECT:
Christy O'Connor Jr.

TYPE: Parkland
FACILITIES
Clubhouse at turn: yes
Restrooms on course: no

Galway Bay provides a first-rate clubhouse and course. The elegant clubhouse has the best of amenities, including a well-designed and inviting restaurant, bar, and an exceptionally well stocked pro shop. Very charming round stone huts, complete with traditional thatched roofs, provide shelter. These are a great Irish touch.

LEVEL OF MAINTENANCE: All aspects of Galway Bay Golf and Country Club are immaculate.

COURSE DESCRIPTION: Galway Bay is a visually spectacular course; mounding, bunkers, and greens are set picturesquely on Galway Bay, with the Atlantic Ocean on three sides. Human-made ponds bring additional beauty and difficulty to many of the holes. At first sight, this parkland course appears to be wide open, with forgiving rough. But the wind and the length of this course challenge players of any level. The course is well marked and enjoyable to play. Our lone criticism is that it is very American in feel, from its decidedly unlinkslike terrain and layout to its precision-manicured greens and fairways.

UNIQUE FEATURE: Watch for historic stone huts behind the 16th tee, an ancient ring fort between the 2nd and 10th greens, and a copper mine of the 1500s at the 13th hole.

ACCOMMODATION INFORMATION
Standard hotel: Galway Bay Golf and Country Club Hotel (on site), 353 91 790500

Local hotel/guesthouse/B&B: Galway Great Southern Hotel (4 star) (Galway town), 353 91 564041

Restaurant/pub: Paddy Burke's The Oyster Inn (just outside Galway), 353 91 796226

ADDRESS:
Renville, Roanmore.
County Galway,
Ireland

TELEPHONE:
353 91 790500

FAX:
353 91 790510

WEB PAGE: NA

E-MAIL: Gbaygolf@iol.ie

DIRECTIONS TO COURSE: Galway Bay Golf and Country Club (not to be confused with Galway Golf Club) is located 6 miles from Galway city. Take the N18 (Limerick-Galway Road) to Oranmore. Follow signage (about 2 miles from Oranmore) to the course.

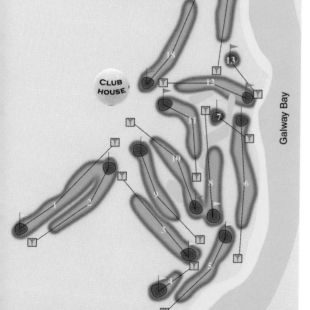

SCORECARD			
HOLE	YDG	PAR	INDEX
1	551	5	14
2	445	4	2
3	421	4	10
4	168	3	16
5	366	4	8
6	524	5	12
7	150	3	18
8	455	4	6
9	436	4	4
OUT	3,520	36	
10	447	4	5
11	410	4	7
12	436	4	1
13	172	3	15
14	546	5	13
15	187	3	17
16	540	5	11
17	380	4	9
18	478	4	3
IN	3,600	36	
TOTAL	7,120	72	

Galway Golf Club

ADDRESS:
Blackrock,
Salthill, County
Galway, Ireland

TELEPHONE:
353 91 522033

FAX:
353 91 529783

WEB PAGE: NA

E-MAIL: NA

DIRECTIONS TO COURSE: Galway
Golf Club (not to be confused with
Galway Bay
Golf and
Country
Club) is
located 3
miles west of
Galway city
on the R339.
It is situated
just outside
the small vil-
lage of
Salthill, in
which you
will find good
signage to the
course.

SCORECARD

HOLE	YDG	PAR	INDEX
1	312	4	13
2	149	3	11
3	405	4	5
4	385	4	7
5	437	4	1
6	427	4	3
7	504	5	17
8	352	4	15
9	201	3	9
OUT	3,176	35	
10	441	4	2
11	185	3	10
12	496	5	14
13	129	3	18
14	396	4	6
15	388	4	8
16	417	4	4
17	342	4	16
18	381	4	12
IN	3,180	35	
TOTAL	**6,356**	**70**	

Galway Golf Club provides an older, well-estab-lished clubhouse with a nice sense of tradition and quiet elegance. Full facilities include a bar and a large dining room. The pro shop is very well stocked, and there is a putting green.

LEVEL OF MAINTENANCE: This course is old, steeped with tradition, and very well kept. The greens, bunkers, and fairways are all in excellent condition, and the turf is thick and healthy. The clubhouse and its facilities are inviting and immaculate.

COURSE DESCRIPTION: Galway Golf Club is a well-established course with an excellent pedigree. It is, after all, an Alister MacKenzie design. The trees are mature and grand, and the traps are well placed. Since bunkers were one of the great MacKenzie's spe-cialties, it's not surprising that they are carefully tended. There are some great views of the Aran Islands, Galway Bay, and the Burren. A good iron game is well rewarded; some of the greens are tiered, and all are difficult but fair. A variety of mounds and water hazards lends a great deal of interest to this wonderful course. Come prepared for some chal-lenge and some fun.

UNIQUE FEATURE: One of many nice features throughout this course is the close visual proximity to Galway Bay.

ACCOMMODATION INFORMATION
Standard hotel: Ardilaun House Hotel (4 star hotel) (Salthill), 353 91 521433

Local hotel/guesthouse/B&B: Gentien Hill House (Salthill), 353 91 521427

Restaurant/pub: Tigh Neachtain Bar and Seafood Bistro (Galway), 353 91 568820

GREEN FEES:
Moderate

EQUIPMENT RENTAL
Buggies: no
Trolleys: yes
Caddies: yes
Clubs: yes

DATE FOUNDED: 1895

ARCHITECT:
Alister MacKenzie (1926)

TYPE: Parkland

FACILITIES
Clubhouse at turn: yes
Restrooms on course: no

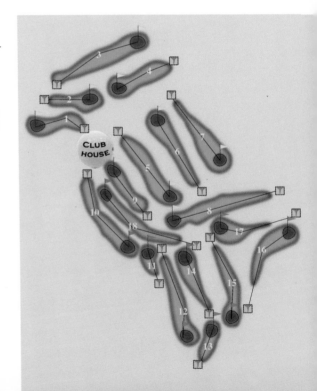

GORT GOLF CLUB

GREEN FEES:
Low

EQUIPMENT RENTAL
Buggies: no
Trolleys: yes
Caddies: yes
Clubs: yes

DATE FOUNDED: 1924

ARCHITECT: Redesigned by Christy O'Connor Jr. (1996)

TYPE: Parkland

FACILITIES
Clubhouse at turn: yes
Restrooms on course: no

Gort offers a spacious clubhouse with very nice locker room facilities, including oak-paneled lockers. The bar and restaurant overlook the course and provide both snacks and a full menu. The club has a well-stocked pro shop and a putting green.

LEVEL OF MAINTENANCE: This course shows attention to detail, with all aspects of the course and building facilities maintained to high standards.

COURSE DESCRIPTION: Gort Golf Club is definitely not your typical parkland course. It is set on the outskirts of the world-famous Burren, with its moonscape appearance, and just a short distance from the Kilmachduagh abbey ruins. Views of the Clare hills are spectacular, and the course's terrain is replete with old stone walls, ancient outbuildings used for sheds, and lakes. The sense is truly of being amid a sylvan setting. Numerous gentle slopes result in interesting undulations and transitions from tee to green. Indeed, each hole stands out with its own particular character. There are many well-established mature groves of holly and apple orchards, along with numerous new plantings. Except for the thinness of the turf, it would be difficult to spot this as a relatively new course. The layout is fairly intuitive, and signage is good. Warm up well for the 1st hole, a test even to the experienced golfer. It is a dogleg left with a very elevated green and takes two strong shots to reach.

UNIQUE FEATURE: The course offers exceptionally beautiful parkland terrain with panoramic views.

ACCOMMODATION INFORMATION
Standard hotel: O'Deas Hotel (3 star) (Loughrea), 353 91 841611

Local hotel/guesthouse/B&B: Glynn's Country Inn Hotel (Gort), 353 91 631047

Restaurant/pub: O'Donell's Traditional Pub (Gort), 353 91 631923

ADDRESS:
Castlequarter, Gort,
County Galway,
Ireland

TELEPHONE:
353 91 632244

FAX: NA

WEB PAGE: NA

E-MAIL: NA

DIRECTIONS TO COURSE: This course is located 2 miles north of Gort town on the Kilmachduagh Road. On the N18 slightly north of Gort, take the R460, and watch for the Kilmachduagh Road sign, which also has a Gort Golf Course sign on it. Follow the abundant signage to the course.

SCORECARD			
HOLE	YDG	PAR	INDEX
1	377	4	9
2	455	4	5
3	411	4	3
4	362	4	7
5	168	3	15
6	318	4	17
7	454	4	1
8	175	3	13
9	562	5	11
OUT	3,287	35	
10	346	4	6
11	413	4	2
12	330	4	8
13	182	3	14
14	539	5	16
15	341	4	10
16	169	3	18
17	514	5	12
18	389	4	4
IN	3,229	36	
TOTAL	**6,516**	**71**	

Loughrea Golf Club

ADDRESS:
Craigu,
Loughrea,
County Galway,
Ireland

TELEPHONE:
353 91 841049

FAX: NA

WEB PAGE: NA

E-MAIL: NA

DIRECTIONS TO COURSE: The Loughrea course is located about 1 mile southeast of the town of Loughrea on the Mountbellew Road (R350). Watch closely for signage.

This traditional golf club provides an elegant, old-style clubhouse with full bar and restaurant facilities. The locker rooms are very clean. On site also are a putting green and driving range. There is no pro shop.

LEVEL OF MAINTENANCE: This very tidy community club obviously takes pride in its course and building facilities.

COURSE DESCRIPTION: Loughrea Club is a mature parkland course with plenty of full-grown trees, very good turf, well-kept greens, and clear signage. The rough is challenging and deep, putting a premium on accurate shot making. Elevation changes throughout the course make it an interesting test of golf. Loughrea is another of Ireland's good community courses.

UNIQUE FEATURE: Five par 3s of varying length make Loughrea a real test of your iron shots.

ACCOMMODATION INFORMATION
Standard hotel: O'Deas Hotel (3 star) (Loughrea), 353 91 841611

Local hotel/guesthouse/B&B: Flannery's Hotel (Loughrea), 353 91 755111

Restaurant/pub: The Dugout Bar (Loughrea), 353 91 841948

GREEN FEES:
Low

EQUIPMENT RENTAL
Buggies: no
Trolleys: yes
Caddies: no
Clubs: no

DATE FOUNDED: 1924

ARCHITECT: Redesigned to 18 holes by Eddie Hackett (1992)

TYPE: Parkland

FACILITIES
Clubhouse at turn: no
Restrooms on course: no

SCORECARD

HOLE	YDG	PAR	INDEX
1	366	4	11
2	408	4	7
3	427	4	3
4	203	3	9
5	422	4	1
6	385	4	5
7	283	4	17
8	130	3	13
9	281	4	15
OUT	2,911	34	
10	401	4	2
11	159	3	14
12	484	5	10
13	334	4	4
14	146	3	18
15	290	4	6
16	458	5	16
17	174	3	12
18	372	4	8
IN	2,823	35	
TOTAL	5,734	69	

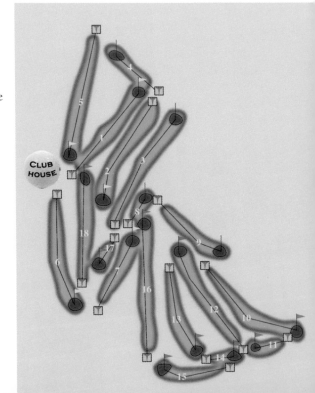

Oughterard Golf Club

GREEN FEES:
Low
EQUIPMENT RENTAL
Buggies: yes
Trolleys: yes
Caddies: yes
Clubs: no
DATE FOUNDED: 1974

ARCHITECTS: John Harris and Eddie Hackett; greens and tees upgraded by Patrick Merrigan (1999)

TYPE: Parkland
FACILITIES
Clubhouse at turn: no
Restrooms on course: no

Oughterard (pronounced "Ookh-tah-rhad") offers a brand new clubhouse which incorporates the former stone farmhouse with its cobblestone courtyard. It includes spacious, top-notch locker rooms with showers, an elegant bar, and full restaurant. The large pro shop is well stocked. Facilities also include a putting green and excellent practice area, with practice greens and bunkers.

LEVEL OF MAINTENANCE: At the time of our visit in 1999, Oughterard was being extensively renovated. With its history and reputation of being a very well maintained course, one can expect the same at its re-opening. The greens, fairways, and bunkers are in wonderful condition, as are the large tees. The building facilities are extremely clean and beautifully presented.

COURSE DESCRIPTION: This parkland course has mature trees throughout, and new USGA specification greens. The greens are large and undulating, providing an excellent roll and difficult read. The fairways, although not wide, are forgiving and in splendid condition. Intelligently placed hazards demand good course management. The trees lining many of the fairways make for a demanding drive but set up beautifully for your second shot. Oughterard is near Lough Corrib, making for some lovely scenery.

UNIQUE FEATURE: Recent high-standard renovation of the greens.

ACCOMMODATION INFORMATION
Standard hotel: Connemara Gateway Hotel (3 star) (Oughterard), 353 91 552328

Local hotel/guesthouse/B&B: Currarevagh House (4-star guesthouse) (Oughterard), 353 91 552312

Restaurant/pub: Drimcong Restaurant (Oughterard), 353 91 555115

ADDRESS:
Gortreevagh,
Oughterard,
County
Galway, Ireland
TELEPHONE:
353 91 552131
FAX:
353 91 552733
WEB PAGE: NA
E-MAIL: NA
DIRECTIONS TO COURSE: Take the N59 15 miles north from Galway city. The course is located just south of Oughterard town; watch for excellent signage.

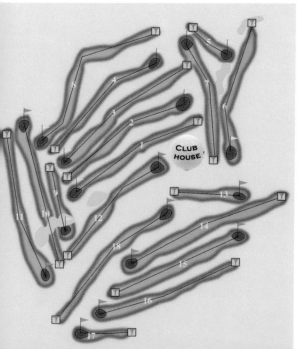

SCORECARD			
HOLE	YDG	PAR	INDEX
1	345	4	3
2	408	4	15
3	436	4	1
4	397	4	7
5	136	3	17
6	354	4	11
7	327	4	13
8	482	5	9
9	167	3	5
OUT	3,121	35	
10	389	4	10
11	392	4	6
12	405	4	12
13	98	3	14
14	484	5	16
15	419	4	8
16	429	4	2
17	278	4	18
18	427	4	4
IN	3,326	36	
TOTAL	6,447	71	

Portumna Golf Club

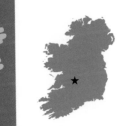

ADDRESS:
Woodford Road,
Portumna,
County Galway,
Ireland

TELEPHONE:
353 509 41059

FAX: NA

WEB PAGE: NA

E-MAIL: NA

DIRECTIONS TO COURSE: The course is 2 miles west of the town of Portumna on the R353; watch for road signs. It is adjacent to Portumna Forest Park.

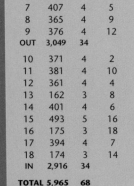

SCORECARD

HOLE	YDG	PAR	INDEX
1	442	4	3
2	180	4	13
3	441	4	1
4	327	4	15
5	152	3	17
6	356	4	11
7	407	4	5
8	365	4	9
9	376	4	12
OUT	3,049	34	
10	371	4	2
11	381	4	10
12	361	4	4
13	162	3	8
14	401	4	6
15	493	5	16
16	175	3	18
17	394	4	7
18	174	3	14
IN	2,916	34	
TOTAL	**5,965**	**68**	

Portumna Club has a new, modern clubhouse with complete facilities, including a wonderfully traditional bar and full restaurant amenities.

LEVEL OF MAINTENANCE: This is a lovely, well-maintained golf course. It offers very nice greens with some elevated tees.

COURSE DESCRIPTION: The Portumna Club is an old, established parklands course with some stately old-growth trees. It has the feel of an old estate grounds. There are a few elevated greens and limited bunkers. One can often see wild red deer on the course, which is adjacent to Portumna Forest Park. This is a short course defined by the mature trees and a pleasant tract to play.

UNIQUE FEATURE: The finishing hole is a par 3 to an elevated green, a challenge for any golfer.

ACCOMMODATION INFORMATION
Standard hotel: Shannon Oaks Hotel and Country Club (Portumna), 353 509 41777

Local hotel/guesthouse/B&B: Country Arms Hotel (Birr, County Offaly), 353 509 20791

Restaurant/pub: Idle Hour Bar and Restaurant in Shannon Oaks Hotel (see above), 353 509 41777

GREEN FEES:
Low

EQUIPMENT RENTAL
Buggies: yes
Trolleys: yes
Caddies: yes
Clubs: yes

DATE FOUNDED: 1913

ARCHITECT: NA

TYPE: Parkland

FACILITIES
Clubhouse at turn: no
Restrooms on course: no

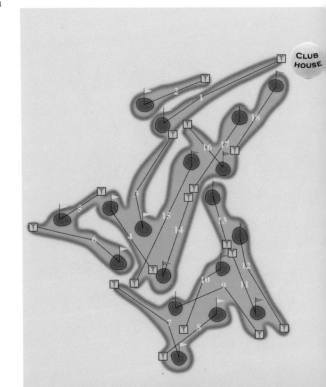

CLUB HOUSE

Tuam Golf Club

GREEN FEES: Low; members only on weekends (closed to visitors)
EQUIPMENT RENTAL
Buggies: 2
Trolleys: yes
Caddies: call ahead
Clubs: yes

DATE FOUNDED: 1907
ARCHITECT: 18 holes by Eddie Hackett (1974)
TYPE: Parkland
FACILITIES
Clubhouse at turn: no
Restrooms on course: no

This is a very nice clubhouse with friendly members and staff: modest but with full facilities, including changing rooms, a pro shop, a bar, and a restaurant. A wonderful practice range is complete with practice green, sand trap, and putting green.

LEVEL OF MAINTENANCE: The membership obviously keeps the course the best it can. Greens and bunkers are well maintained, and the clubhouse is clean and inviting.

COURSE DESCRIPTION: This is an oddly laid out parkland course; there are some old stands of pines and many new plantings. It is on gently rolling terrain, as are the greens. Some good, well-positioned traps challenge the golfer and test his or her shot-making skill. This course is purportedly laid out on naturally occurring gravel, resulting in a tract that can be played all year long. Tuam is a fun community course made inviting by the warmth of its patrons.

UNIQUE FEATURE: This is one of designer Eddie Hackett's many good community courses.

ACCOMMODATION INFORMATION
Standard hotel: Imperial Hotel (Tuam), 353 93 24188

Local hotel/guesthouse/B&B: Kilmore House (Tuam), 353 93 28118

Restaurant/pub: Cre na Cille (Tuam), 353 93 28232

ADDRESS:
Barnacurragh, Tuam.
County Galway,
Ireland
TELEPHONE:
353 93 28993
FAX:
353 93 24126
WEB PAGE: NA
E-MAIL: NA
DIRECTIONS TO COURSE: Take the N17, 2 miles south of Tuam (pronounced "Toom"); follow the brown signs.

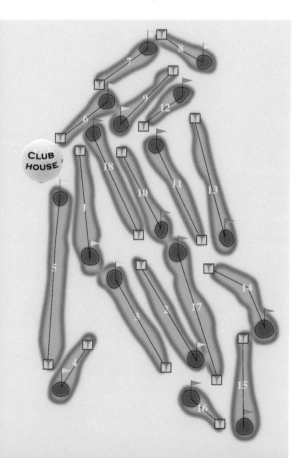

SCORECARD			
HOLE	YDG	PAR	INDEX
1	401	4	5
2	511	5	15
3	418	4	3
4	339	4	9
5	527	5	13
6	187	3	11
7	415	4	1
8	144	3	17
9	380	4	7
OUT	3,326	36	
10	360	4	18
11	371	4	16
12	199	3	6
13	521	5	12
14	336	4	8
15	377	4	4
16	165	3	14
17	529	5	10
18	401	4	2
IN	3,262	36	
TOTAL	**6,588**	**72**	

Ballybunion Golf Club (Cashen Course)

ADDRESS:
Sandhill Road,
Ballybunion,
County Kerry,
Ireland

TELEPHONE:
353 68 27146

FAX:
353 68 27387

WEB PAGE: NA

E-MAIL: BBGOLF@IOL.IE

DIRECTIONS TO COURSE: The Cashen Course is adjacent to Ballybunion's Old Course. Both are south from Ballybunion town center; there is ample signage.

The Cashen Course shares the same venue as the Old Course at Ballybunion. The first-rate clubhouse has an opulent bar and two restaurants. Locker rooms are impressively appointed, and the pro shop is well stocked. The clubhouse has an imperious appearance, but the staff is friendly.

LEVEL OF MAINTENANCE: The course and its facilities conform to the highest levels of maintenance. The greens are in excellent condition, and the bunkers are well maintained. The tee boxes are in good condition and also delightfully level.

COURSE DESCRIPTION: The Cashen Course was born of controversy. Although Robert Trent Jones Sr. declared it the best work of his life, the members were so unhappy with the length of the layout and the difficulty of the walk that they changed some of the holes. Cashen is a long, difficult, spectacular links course. Apparently the main bone of contention is how the greens receive the approach shots. Europeans like to bump and run, whereas Americans like to fly it in the air. Cashen requires you to fly it in to the many elevated greens. Thus, most of the locals prefer the Old Course, but many Americans seem to prefer the Cashen. Nonetheless, both the Old and Cashen Courses are extraordinary, and both should be played if at all possible. The mammoth dunes that make up Cashen are worth the price of admission in themselves.

UNIQUE FEATURE: Robert Trent Jones Sr. has framed many of the greens among the dunes. At times, you feel you're part of an epic poem. Play heroically.

ACCOMMODATION INFORMATION

Standard hotel: The Golf Hotel (Ballybunion), 353 68 27111

Local hotel/guesthouse/B&B: The Cliff House (Ballybunion), 353 68 27777

Restaurant/pub: Roof Top Restaurant in the Golf Hotel (see above), 353 68 27111

GREEN FEES:
Moderate

EQUIPMENT RENTAL
Buggies: yes
Trolleys: yes
Caddies: yes
Clubs: yes

DATE FOUNDED: 1993

ARCHITECT: Robert Trent Jones Sr.

TYPE: Links

FACILITIES
Clubhouse at turn: yes
Restrooms on course: no

SCORECARD

HOLE	YDG	PAR	INDEX
1	450	5	10
2	377	4	4
3	154	3	18
4	350	4	8
5	314	4	16
6	155	3	12
7	378	4	6
8	605	5	2
9	478	5	14
OUT	3,243	37	
10	324	4	11
11	146	3	17
12	210	3	13
13	395	4	1
14	400	4	7
15	487	5	3
16	164	3	15
17	479	5	9
18	368	4	5
IN	2,973	35	
TOTAL	**6,216**	**72**	

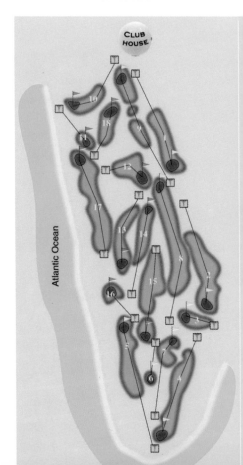

Ballybunion Golf Club (Old Course)

GREEN FEES:
Moderate

EQUIPMENT RENTAL
Buggies: yes
Trolleys: yes
Caddies: yes
Clubs: yes

DATE FOUNDED: 1893

ARCHITECTS: Original course laid out by members; minor modifications by Tom Simpson (1937) and Tom Watson (1995)

TYPE: Links

FACILITIES
Clubhouse at turn: no
Restrooms on course: yes

This course is unusual for Irish golf in that there are restrooms and a snack shop between the 6th and 9th holes. The elegant clubhouse has a bar and two restaurants. There are spacious locker rooms and a very well stocked pro shop.

LEVEL OF MAINTENANCE: This is one of Ireland's jewels, and the whole of it—building facilities, course, bunkers, greens, fairways, and signage—are all maintained to the highest of standards.

COURSE DESCRIPTION: Much has been written and said about this course. Tom Watson's love of it has made Ballybunion world renowned. It is a lovely piece of linksland and an extremely challenging course, with spectacular views of the Atlantic Ocean and constant sounds of the surf. As with any links course, wind is a factor. Be prepared to deal with gusty or sustained winds. Astonishingly, two large and unsightly trailer parks ("holiday homes") are encroaching upon this gem. One would like to dismiss them, but they overwhelm the eye and detract from the glorious setting. Nonetheless, this is a can't-miss national treasure. Call early for booking. If you can't get on the Old Course, do not turn down an opportunity to play the newer Cashen Course.

UNIQUE FEATURE: The entire course is set within the dunes.

ACCOMMODATION INFORMATION
Standard hotel: The Golf Hotel (Ballybunion), 353 68 27111

Local hotel/guesthouse/B&B: The Cliff House (Ballybunion), 353 68 27777

Restaurant/pub: Roof Top Restaurant in the Golf Hotel (see above), 353 68 27111

ADDRESS:
Sandhill Road,
Ballybunion,
County
Kerry, Ireland

TELEPHONE:
353 68 27146

FAX:
353 68 27387

WEB PAGE: NA

E-MAIL: BBGOLFC@IOL.IE

DIRECTIONS TO COURSE: Go to the town of Ballybunion. There is plenty of signage to the course, which is south of town on Sandhill Road, adjacent to the Atlantic Ocean.

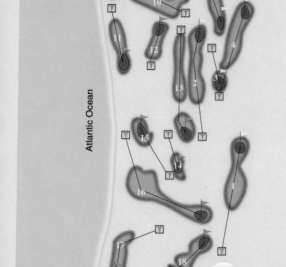

SCORECARD			
HOLE	YDG	PAR	INDEX
1	392	4	11
2	445	4	1
3	220	3	9
4	520	5	17
5	524	5	15
6	364	4	7
7	432	4	5
8	153	3	13
9	454	4	3
OUT	3,495	36	
10	359	4	10
11	453	4	2
12	192	3	8
13	484	5	16
14	131	3	18
15	216	3	4
16	499	5	14
17	385	4	6
18	379	4	12
IN	3,098	35	
TOTAL	6,593	71	

Cheann Sibeal Golf Club

ADDRESS: Baile an Fheirtearaigh (English: Bally-ferriter), County Kerry, Ireland

TELEPHONE: 353 66 56255

FAX: 353 66 56409

WEB PAGE: NA

E-MAIL: NA

DIRECTIONS TO COURSE: From the town of Dingle, take Baile an Fheirtearaigh Road for about 9 miles. Watch for signs to the course, and take in the gorgeous fuchsia and blackberry bramble–lined roadway designated by the signage.

Cheann Sibeal (Dingle) offers a very clean club-house, including a restaurant with a good menu and great views of the course. There is a pro shop within the clubhouse, along with locker rooms. This is in the heart of one of the Gaelic-speaking areas of Ireland, so all road signs and this course's scorecard are in Gaelic ("Irish").

LEVEL OF MAINTENANCE: This course is generally well maintained. The fairways and first cut of rough are well tended. The greens are somewhat below average, with multiple grasses resulting in some bumpiness.

COURSE DESCRIPTION: Cheann Sibeal is a links course in a spectacular setting of steep cliffs jutting out into the ocean and gently rolling dune terrain. Sheep from adjacent farmsteads are on the course in places. Cheann Sibeal is surrounded by some of Ireland's tallest mountains, including Mount Brandon, with views of Smerwick Harbour and the Atlantic Ocean. This is a relatively wide-open course whose greatest difficulties are the wind, dunegrasses, and a river that runs through the course. The par 3s are torturously long, and there are a couple of strong par 4s. One other hazard—don't be distracted by the beauty! This is a fun course to play.

UNIQUE FEATURE: This is the most westerly course in Ireland. The 14th hole offers a spectacular view of the whole of Dingle.

ACCOMMODATION INFORMATION

Standard hotel: Milltown Guesthouse (a must-do guesthouse if you're in the area!) (Dingle), 353 66 51372

Local hotel/guesthouse/B&B: Benner's Hotel (Dingle), 353 66 51638

Restaurant/pub: Danno's Restaurant (Dingle), 353 66 51855

GREEN FEES: Low

EQUIPMENT RENTAL
Buggies: no
Trolleys: yes
Caddies: yes
Clubs: yes

DATE FOUNDED: 1924

ARCHITECTS: Eddie Hackett and Christy O'Connor Jr.

TYPE: Links

FACILITIES
Clubhouse at turn: yes
Restrooms on course: no

SCORECARD

HOLE	YDG	PAR	INDEX
1	395	4	3
2	201	3	9
3	376	4	7
4	378	4	15
5	202	3	11
6	565	5	13
7	425	4	5
8	370	4	17
9	427	4	1
OUT	3,340	35	
10	197	3	8
11	523	5	14
12	156	3	16
13	479	5	12
14	342	4	18
15	405	4	2
16	373	4	4
17	371	4	6
18	504	5	10
IN	3,350	37	
TOTAL	6,690	72	

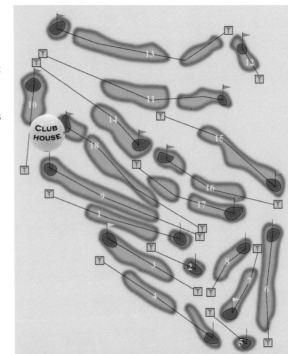

Dooks Golf Club

GREEN FEES:
Low
EQUIPMENT RENTAL
Buggies: no
Trolleys: yes
Caddies: yes
Clubs: yes

DATE FOUNDED: 1895

ARCHITECTS: Redesigned by Donald Steel and club members

TYPE: Links

FACILITIES
Clubhouse at turn: no
Restrooms on course: no

Dooks boasts a lovely clubhouse, complete with full bar, restaurant, and a very friendly staff. Locker rooms have showers. An excellent putting green and small practice area are available to the public.

LEVEL OF MAINTENANCE: The course and building facilities are all very well maintained. There are excellent greens, well-kept bunkers, and consistent yardage markers throughout the course.

COURSE DESCRIPTION: Dooks is a lovely links course set along Dingle Bay, with mountains on three sides. The holes lay out well, although not in a particularly dramatic fashion. Interesting combinations of features include high, elevated greens on some holes and flat, expansive greens on others. There are also trees, blind shots, and some flat and clearly visible holes. This is quite a combination, sure to test your creativity and shot-making skills. All goes well until the 18th hole, which appears contrived as the green slopes severely away from your incoming shot. But keep your sense of humor, and remember that the club's members created this.

UNIQUE FEATURE: This course underwent expansion in the 1980s, with each of a committee of nine club members designing one of the new back 9 holes. This course is also the breeding ground of the endangered Natterjack toad, which is the club's logo.

ACCOMMODATION INFORMATION

Standard hotel: Glenbeigh Hotel (Glenbeigh), 353 66 68333

Local hotel/guesthouse/B&B: The Caragh Lodge (4-star guesthouse) (Caragh Lake), 353 66 9769115

Restaurant/pub: Restaurant in the Glenbeigh Hotel (see above), 353 66 68333

ADDRESS:
Glenbeigh (on the Ring of Kerry), County Kerry, Ireland

TELEPHONE:
353 66 68205

FAX:
353 66 68476

WEB PAGE: NA

E-MAIL: NA

DIRECTIONS TO COURSE: The course is on the N70, just north of Glenbeigh town; follow signage to the course.

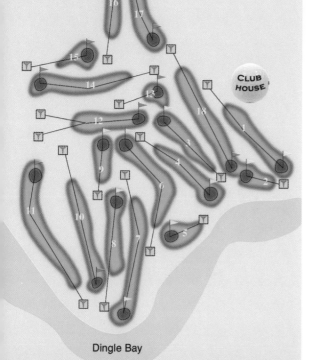

Dingle Bay

SCORECARD			
HOLE	YDG	PAR	INDEX
1	419	4	2
2	131	3	18
3	300	4	16
4	344	4	6
5	194	3	10
6	394	4	4
7	477	5	14
8	368	4	8
9	183	3	12
OUT	2,810	34	
10	406	4	1
11	531	5	7
12	370	4	3
13	150	3	15
14	375	4	11
15	213	3	5
16	348	4	13
17	313	4	17
18	494	5	9
IN	3,200	36	
TOTAL	6,010	70	

Kenmare Golf Club

ADDRESS:
Kenmare,
County Kerry,
Ireland

TELEPHONE:
353 64 41291

FAX:
353 64 42061

WEB PAGE: NA

E-MAIL: NA

DIRECTIONS TO COURSE: This course is just east of the town of Kenmare on the R569 (road to Kilgarvan). Watch for good signage.

Kenmare Golf Club (pronounced "Kenmarry") offers a modest clubhouse with simple, casual fare, including snacks and drinks. There are also changing rooms.

LEVEL OF MAINTENANCE: Kenmare course maintenance is moderate to good, even in the off-season.

COURSE DESCRIPTION: This club offers many beautiful vistas of the mountains (Roughty Valley) and Kenmare Bay. There are idyllic views of church spires and an ancient abbey, lovely views of the town of Kenmare, along with views of the verdant fields of adjacent farmlands, complete with sheep and mountain meadows. Numerous old-growth trees also help make this a stunning course visually. There is an unusual split in that the more recently added second 9 holes require you to cross a road and proceed through a housing addition. The several strenuous, high-incline hills are not for the faint of heart.

UNIQUE FEATURE: The clubhouse was originally a hunting lodge.

ACCOMMODATION INFORMATION
Standard hotel: Sheen Falls Lodge (5 star) (Kenmare), 353 64 41600 or Park Hotel Kenmare (5 star) (Kenmare), 353 64 41200

Local hotel/guesthouse/B&B: Foleys Shamrock Guesthouse (3 star) (Kenmare), 353 64 42162

Restaurant/pub: Cafe Indigo (Kenmare), 353 64 42357

GREEN FEES:
Low

EQUIPMENT RENTAL
Buggies: no
Trolleys: yes
Caddies: yes
Clubs: yes

DATE FOUNDED: 1903

ARCHITECT:
Eddie Hackett (1993)

TYPE: Parkland

FACILITIES
Clubhouse at turn: no
Restrooms on course: yes (7th hole)

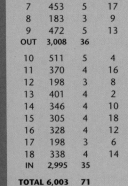

SCORECARD

HOLE	YDG	PAR	INDEX
1	341	4	11
2	172	3	7
3	406	4	1
4	308	4	15
5	348	4	3
6	325	4	5
7	453	5	17
8	183	3	9
9	472	5	13
OUT	3,008	36	
10	511	5	4
11	370	4	16
12	198	3	8
13	401	4	2
14	346	4	10
15	305	4	18
16	328	4	12
17	198	3	6
18	338	4	14
IN	2,995	35	
TOTAL	6,003	71	

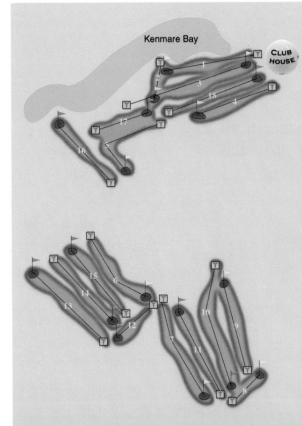

Killarney Golf and Fishing Club (Killeen Course)

GREEN FEES:
Moderate

EQUIPMENT RENTAL
Buggies: yes
Trolleys: yes
Caddies: yes
Clubs: yes

DATE FOUNDED: 1893

ARCHITECTS: Sir Guy Campbell; Earl of Kenmare; Frederick G. Hawtree; revised by Eddie Hackett and William O'Sullivan (1980s)

TYPE: Parkland

FACILITIES
Clubhouse at turn: no
Restrooms on course: yes
(14th hole)

The Killeen Course is adjacent to the other course (Mahony's Point) of the Killarney Golf and Fishing Club. The clubhouse for both courses is rich and warm, with excellent bar and restaurant facilities and a well-stocked pro shop. A practice range and putting green are available. Fishing lakes and equipment rental make for an enjoyable venue.

LEVEL OF MAINTENANCE: All aspects of this first-class site are superbly maintained. Thus, the greens and fairways are healthy, with good turf development. Excellent signage includes consistent distance markers on the sprinkler heads.

COURSE DESCRIPTION: Killarney Golf Club offers two parkland courses set amid the former 1,250-acre estate of the Earl of Kenmare. These courses, configured using portions of the original course, were opened for play in 1972. The longer and more difficult Killeen Course offers a very challenging tract with intelligent use of bunkers, stands of old-growth trees, and many water hazards. Most of the greens are large and gently undulating. Many holes follow the shores of Lough Leane, with the majestic mountains of Kerry rising in the distance. Abundant wildlife includes swans and deer. Many important competitions are played here most years.

UNIQUE FEATURE: The flora and fauna are spectacular; watch for several huge birch trees and prolific rhododendrons.

ACCOMMODATION INFORMATION
Standard hotel: The Lake Hotel (3 star, but feels more like 5 star) (Killarney), 353 64 31035

Local hotel/guesthouse/B&B: Killarney Royal Hotel (3 star) (Killarney), 353 64 31853

Restaurant/pub: Robertino's Italian Restaurant (Killarney), 353 64 34966

ADDRESS:
Mahony's Point,
Killarney, County
Kerry, Ireland

TELEPHONE:
353 64 31034

FAX:
353 64 33065

WEB PAGE: NA

E-MAIL: kgc@iol.ie

DIRECTIONS TO COURSE: This course is 2 miles west of the town of Killarney, on the N72 (Killorglin Road).

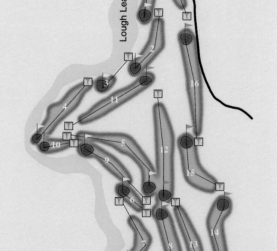

SCORECARD			
HOLE	YDG	PAR	INDEX
1	378	4	15
2	378	4	11
3	195	3	9
4	411	4	5
5	468	4	1
6	200	3	7
7	485	5	17
8	411	4	3
9	380	4	13
OUT	3,311	35	
10	168	3	16
11	506	5	14
12	472	4	6
13	440	4	2
14	384	4	12
15	419	4	10
16	517	5	18
17	385	4	8
18	447	4	4
IN	3,745	37	
TOTAL	7,056	72	

Killarney Golf and Fishing Club (Mahony's Point Course)

ADDRESS:
Mahony's Point,
Killarney,
County Kerry,
Ireland

TELEPHONE:
353 64 31034

FAX:
353 64 33065

WEB PAGE: NA

E-MAIL: kgc@iol.ie

DIRECTIONS TO COURSE: This course is on the N72 just to the north of Killarney. There are no signs in Killarney, but there is one on the N72 just out of Killarney town.

SCORECARD

HOLE	YDG	PAR	INDEX
1	371	4	12
2	440	4	2
3	469	4	4
4	153	3	14
5	488	5	16
6	392	4	6
7	184	3	8
8	579	5	10
9	322	4	18
OUT	3,402	36	
10	374	4	7
11	463	4	1
12	234	3	13
13	473	5	11
14	374	4	3
15	291	4	17
16	498	5	15
17	406	4	5
18	195	3	9
IN	3,315	36	
TOTAL	**6,717**	**72**	

Mahony's Point, along with the Killeen Course, is part of the Killarney Golf and Fishing Club. This top-notch facility includes a venerable clubhouse with an elegant bar and restaurant, a well-stocked pro shop, a driving range, and putting green. A snack shop is shared with the Killeen Course. You may also want to take advantage of the great fishing and boating opportunities.

LEVEL OF MAINTENANCE: The Killarney Club's building facilities, courses, and gardens are maintained to the highest of standards. Distance markers are consistent, and the greens are especially well maintained.

COURSE DESCRIPTION: Mahony's Point is the shorter of the two courses by some 300 yards. Both have some of the old holes from the original single course laid out in the 1930s. Most of this course plays through stands of old-growth forest, thereby challenging golfers to keep in the fairway. The greens offer significant undulation and can be particularly stern when they are cut short.

UNIQUE FEATURE: Romantic and picturesque lakes, along with old estate charm, make for a stunningly beautiful Irish Experience.

ACCOMMODATION INFORMATION
Standard hotel: Aghadoe Heights Hotel (5 star) (Killarney), 353 64 31766

Local hotel/guesthouse/B&B: Killarney Great Southern Hotel (4 star) (Killarney), 353 64 31262

Restaurant/pub: Malton Room in Killarney Great Southern Hotel (see above), 353 64 31262

GREEN FEES:
Moderate

EQUIPMENT RENTAL
Buggies: yes
Trolleys: yes
Caddies: yes
Clubs: yes

DATE FOUNDED: 1891

ARCHITECT: Redesigned by Sir Guy Campbell (1971)

TYPE: Parkland

FACILITIES
Clubhouse at turn: no
Restrooms on course: yes

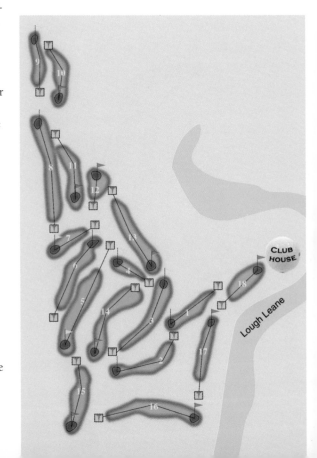

Ring of Kerry Golf and Country Club

GREEN FEES:
Moderate

EQUIPMENT RENTAL
Buggies: no
Trolleys: yes
Caddies: yes
Clubs: yes

DATE FOUNDED: 1993

ARCHITECTS: Designed by Eddie Hackett (1993); completed by Roger Jones and Associates (July 1998)

TYPE: Links

FACILITIES
Clubhouse at turn: yes
Restrooms on course: no

The Ring of Kerry course is one of Ireland's new, scenic golf venues. The clubhouse is a sleek-styled building that offers an upscale dining room and bar, locker rooms, and an adequately stocked pro shop. At the time of our visit, the course was still undergoing some construction with regard to signage and distance markers.

LEVEL OF MAINTENANCE: This was difficult to assess, given the construction. When this course gets into its full regime, its maintenance is likely to reflect the good care given to its design and quality of construction.

COURSE DESCRIPTION: The Ring of Kerry course is an example of the lengths to which golf architects will go in attempting to build a "links-like" course. Here, literally thousands of tons of sand were distributed over the entire course, not just its greens. Much of the soil was stripped away, so that the imported sand rests on sub-strata, to create a course playable year-round. There are some elements of parkland golf, such as streams and groves of ivy-covered trees. This is a gorgeous course, especially when the Irish mist creeps in. It is also an endurance test for the walking golfer.

UNIQUE FEATURE: The 18th green has a spectacular natural amphitheater, with your shot over a pond and sand bunker.

ACCOMMODATION INFORMATION
Standard hotel: Park Hotel Kenmare (Kenmare), 353 64 41200

Local hotel/guesthouse/B&B: Riversdale House Hotel (Kenmare), 353 64 41299

Restaurant/pub: Foley's Shamrock Pub and Bistro (Kenmare), 353 64 42162

ADDRESS:
Ring of Kerry,
Templenoe,
Kenmare,
County Kerry,
Ireland

TELEPHONE:
353 64 42000

FAX:
353 64 42533

WEB PAGE: NA

E-MAIL: NA

DIRECTIONS TO COURSE:
This course is 3½ miles north of the town of Kenmare, on the N70. Watch for signage.

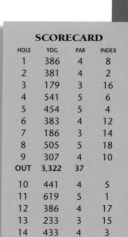

SCORECARD			
HOLE	YDG	PAR	INDEX
1	386	4	8
2	381	4	2
3	179	3	16
4	541	5	6
5	454	5	4
6	383	4	12
7	186	3	14
8	505	5	18
9	307	4	10
OUT	3,322	37	
10	441	4	5
11	619	5	1
12	386	4	17
13	233	3	15
14	433	4	3
15	425	4	7
16	430	4	9
17	435	4	13
18	199	3	11
IN	3,601	35	
TOTAL	6,923	72	

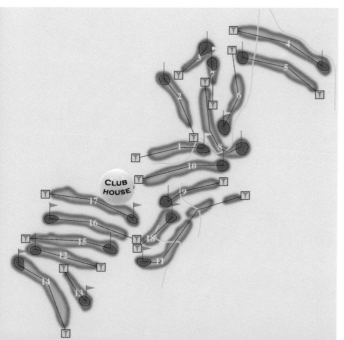

Tralee Golf Club at Barrow

ADDRESS: West Barrow, Ardfert, County Kerry, Ireland

TELEPHONE: 353 66 36379

FAX: 353 66 36008

WEB PAGE: NA

E-MAIL: NA

DIRECTIONS TO COURSE: Signage to this course is rather confusing, so allow ample time to find it. Go to the town of Ardfert and head southwest on the Fenit Road. Alternatively, you can head west out of Tralee on the R558 for about 8 miles. In either case, watch for blue-and-white Tralee Golf Club signs.

Tralee offers a splendid, warm clubhouse with a full bar and restaurant and a very helpful staff. The pro shop, remodeled in 1998, is well stocked. There is a good practice range, along with putting and chipping greens.

LEVEL OF MAINTENANCE: All aspects of this course are maintained to high standards, including great greens and well-managed fairways.

COURSE DESCRIPTION: Tralee is an extraordinary links course, both for the majestic setting as well as for the course itself. There are spectacular views of the Atlantic Ocean, Barrow Harbour, Dingle Peninsula, and Mount Brandon. Twelve holes track through the seaside sand dunes, each with a unique view. The back side has 5 holes along the ocean that are just breathtaking. This is a testing course, which deserves special credit for its use of the natural terrain without manipulating the land. Bring your A-game, since wind can be an ever-present factor. Holes 15, 16, and 17 are right on the cliffs, so wayward shots can end up in the cold, wet drink of the Atlantic Ocean.

UNIQUE FEATURE: The 12th hole has a menacing crater, from which a nearly vertical shot is needed to hit the green.

ACCOMMODATION INFORMATION

Standard hotel: Grand Hotel (3 star) (Tralee), 353 66 7121499

Local hotel/guesthouse/B&B: Brook Manor Lodge (4-star guesthouse) (Fenit Road, Tralee), 353 66 7120406

Restaurant/pub: The Tankard (Tralee), 353 66 36164

GREEN FEES: Moderate

EQUIPMENT RENTAL
Buggies: yes
Trolleys: yes
Caddies: yes
Clubs: yes

DATE FOUNDED: 1896

ARCHITECTS: 18-hole course designed by Arnold Palmer and Ed Seay (1984)

TYPE: Links

FACILITIES
Clubhouse at turn: yes
Restrooms on course: no

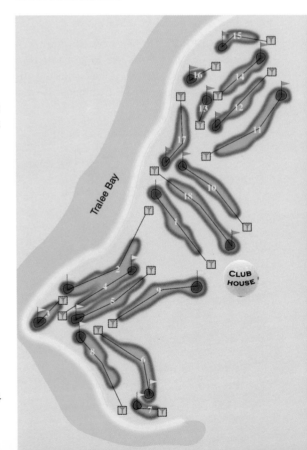

SCORECARD

HOLE	YDG	PAR	INDEX
1	401	4	12
2	589	5	2
3	133	3	14
4	422	4	8
5	425	4	4
6	423	4	10
7	155	3	18
8	385	4	6
9	491	5	16
OUT	3,432	36	
10	419	4	9
11	577	5	13
12	454	4	1
13	158	3	15
14	399	4	5
15	297	4	17
16	197	3	11
17	352	4	7
18	459	4	3
IN	3,316	35	
TOTAL	6,748	71	

Waterville Golf Links

GREEN FEES:
Moderate

EQUIPMENT RENTAL
Buggies: yes
Trolleys: yes
Caddies: yes
Clubs: yes

DATE FOUNDED: 1889

ARCHITECTS: Redesigned by Eddie Hackett and John Mulcahy (1973)

TYPE: Links

FACILITIES
Clubhouse at turn: yes
Restrooms on course: yes (13th hole)

Waterville is the site of a well-designed, attractive clubhouse, complete with friendly and helpful staff. Inside is an extremely well stocked pro shop, along with a full bar, a restaurant, and locker rooms with showers. There are also a driving range and chipping and putting greens. Watch for the statue of John Mulcahy (designer) just outside the clubhouse.

LEVEL OF MAINTENANCE: This course is maintained to excellent standards. The greens and fairways are in wonderful shape.

COURSE DESCRIPTION: The Waterville Club course is fairly wide open but is nonetheless challenging due to its length and intelligent bunkering. A number of artificial mounds dot the course, detracting from the beautiful natural terrain. Scenic views include cottages dotting adjacent hills, Ballinskelligs Bay and the Atlantic Ocean, gorse, earthy bogland, and natural duneland. The greens are mildly undulating and spacious. Despite its length, this course is not overly taxing to walk and is more than worth the effort. You will need to buy a strokesaver.

UNIQUE FEATURE: Read the facinating story on the sign at the 12th hole, called Mass Hole.

ACCOMMODATION INFORMATION
Standard hotel: Waterville House (4 star) (on site), 353 66 74102

Local hotel/guesthouse/B&B: Smuggler's Inn (3 star; excellent restaurant) (Waterville), 353 66 74330

Restaurant/pub: Sheilin Seafood Restaurant (Waterville), 353 66 74231

ADDRESS:
Waterville, Ring of Kerry, County Kerry, Ireland

TELEPHONE:
353 66 74102

FAX:
353 66 74482

WEB PAGE: NA

E-MAIL: wvgolf@iol.ie

DIRECTIONS TO COURSE: The Waterville course is located almost at the halfway mark on the Ring of Kerry, a scenic drive that loops between Killorglin and Kenmare (N70). Watch for course signs in the town of Waterville. The course is at the end of a side road and is fairly well marked.

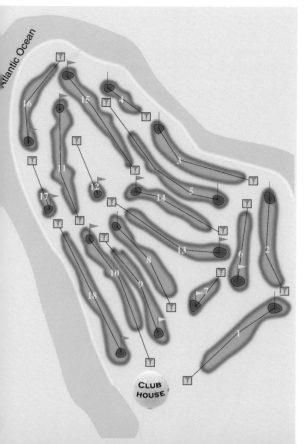

SCORECARD			
HOLE	YDG	PAR	INDEX
1	430	4	11
2	469	4	1
3	417	4	3
4	179	3	15
5	595	5	9
6	371	4	13
7	178	3	17
8	435	4	5
9	445	4	7
OUT	3,519	35	
10	475	4	2
11	496	5	10
12	200	3	18
13	518	5	14
14	456	4	4
15	392	4	6
16	350	4	12
17	196	3	16
18	582	5	8
IN	3,665	37	
TOTAL	7,184	72	

The Curragh Golf Club

ADDRESS:
Curragh Camp,
County Kildare,
Ireland

TELEPHONE:
353 45 441714

FAX: NA

WEB PAGE: NA

E-MAIL: NA

DIRECTIONS TO COURSE: Take the N7 east of Kildare (town). Follow excellent signage from the highway and through Curragh Camp to the clubhouse.

The Curragh has a venerable clubhouse, complete with gable clock on the front, a full bar and restaurant, locker rooms, and a well-stocked pro shop. It has a practice green, a practice hitting area, and very friendly staff.

LEVEL OF MAINTENANCE: This well-maintained parkland course is home to as many sheep as golfers. All fifteen bunkers are well tended. According to local lore, the scarcity of bunkers is due to the fact that sheep have trouble getting out of them. The Curragh land formation is naturally draining, making this course playable during wet months.

COURSE DESCRIPTION: The Curragh is a rolling, sometimes hilly course with good-size greens. The course is blessed with many mature trees and gorse that add to its difficulty and enjoyment. Roads crisscross a number of holes, which are laid out in intuitive fashion, so be careful. This course is the oldest golf course in Ireland, where purportedly golf was first played in 1852 by the Scottish army regiment stationed there. Do not be alarmed by the vast numbers of sheep on the course. They munch contentedly on the grassy rough and fairways, adding much to this bucolic setting. Another interesting feature is a series of trenches and foxholes left from turn-of-the-century army training days.

UNIQUE FEATURE: The Curragh is the oldest documented golf course in Ireland.

ACCOMMODATION INFORMATION

Standard hotel: The Standhouse House Hotel Leisure and Conference Centre (Curragh), 353 45 436177

Local hotel/guesthouse/B&B: Curragh Lodge Hotel (Kildare town), 353 45 522144

Restaurant/pub: The Silken Thomas Bar and Restaurant (Kildare town), 353 45 521695

GREEN FEES:
Low

EQUIPMENT RENTAL
Buggies: yes
Trolleys: yes
Caddies: yes
Clubs: yes

DATE FOUNDED: 1883

ARCHITECT: Redesigned by Gerry Burke

TYPE: Parkland

FACILITIES
Clubhouse at turn: no
Restrooms on course: no

SCORECARD

HOLE	YDG	PAR	INDEX
1	519	5	11
2	365	4	3
3	296	4	17
4	203	3	5
5	350	4	15
6	371	4	7
7	526	5	13
8	180	3	9
9	443	4	1
OUT	2,496	36	
10	185	3	10
11	436	4	4
12	425	4	8
13	310	4	12
14	501	5	16
15	500	5	14
16	135	3	18
17	449	4	2
18	374	4	6
IN	3,319	36	
TOTAL	**5,815**	**72**	

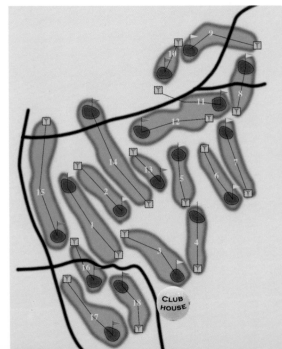

The K Club (Kildare Hotel and Country Club)

GREEN FEES:
High

EQUIPMENT RENTAL
Buggies: yes
Trolleys: yes
Caddies: yes
Clubs: yes

DATE FOUNDED: 1991

ARCHITECT:
Arnold Palmer

TYPE: Parkland

FACILITIES
Clubhouse at turn: yes
Restrooms on course: no

The Kildare Club, better known as the K Club, is a world-class facility. The clubhouse, which is separate from the 5-star hotel, has a bar and restaurant upstairs and a bar and grill just off the well-stocked pro shop. Its full amenities include a washroom attendant and staff to let you know personally when your tee time has arrived. The club has a practice area, driving range, putting and chipping areas. The hotel has a host of other facilities, such as five stocked fishing lakes.

LEVEL OF MAINTENANCE: The maintenance of this facility is as good as money can buy. It would be difficult to find a grass blade out of place on this course. If you enjoy posh, the K Club will meet your every expectation.

COURSE DESCRIPTION: The K Club will be the site for the 2005 Ryder Cup. Some controversy surrounds this, because many people would have expected a more Irish pedigree for Ireland's first Ryder Cup venue. As it is, the K club is an Arnold Palmer–designed American beauty. The River Liffey and some of the old-growth trees nicely counterpoint the human-made lakes and 40-foot transplanted trees. The bunkers are intelligently placed; the turf and greens are as good as you can find anywhere. Indeed, this entire facility is delightful—it's just not very Irish.

UNIQUE FEATURE: The hotel is Ireland's only 5-star hotel, and the course is probably the only course in Ireland where design changes today can be implemented to perfection tomorrow.

ACCOMMODATION INFORMATION
Standard hotel: Kildare Hotel and Country Club (5 star) (on site), 353 1 6017200

Local hotel/guesthouse/B&B: Finnstown Country House Hotel and Golf Course (3 star) (County Dublin), 353 1 6280644

Restaurant/pub: Kildare Hotel Restaurant (see above), 353 1 6017200

ADDRESS: Straffan, County Kildare, Ireland

TELEPHONE:
353 1 6273111

FAX:
353 1 6273990

WEB PAGE:
www.kclub.ie

E-MAIL: golf@kclub.ie or hotel@kclub.ie

DIRECTIONS TO COURSE: Head to the town of Straffan. The Club is just south of Straffan off the R406; watch for clear signage.

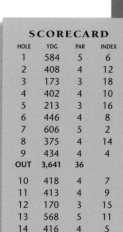

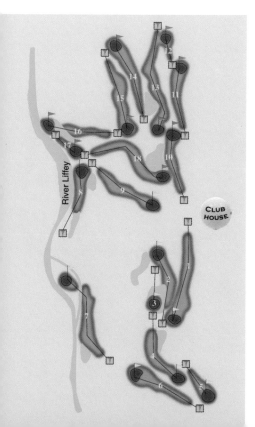

SCORECARD			
HOLE	YDG	PAR	INDEX
1	584	5	6
2	408	4	12
3	173	3	18
4	402	4	10
5	213	3	16
6	446	4	8
7	606	5	2
8	375	4	14
9	434	4	4
OUT	3,641	36	
10	418	4	7
11	413	4	9
12	170	3	15
13	568	5	11
14	416	4	5
15	447	4	3
16	395	4	1
17	173	3	17
18	537	5	13
IN	3,537	36	
TOTAL	7,178	72	

Kilkea Castle Hotel and Golf Club

ADDRESS:
Castledermot,
County Kildare,
Ireland

TELEPHONE:
353 503 45555

FAX:
353 503 45505

WEB PAGE:
www.kilkeacastlehotelgolf.com

E-MAIL: kilkeagolfclub@tinet.ie

DIRECTIONS TO COURSE: Take the N9 north from Castledermot about 2 miles; watch for signs.

Kilkea Castle, on site, is an extraordinary example of a hotel developed from an ancient castle. The facilities are first-rate and extensive. The clubhouse is separate, modern, and also beautifully presented. The club has a well-stocked pro shop, locker rooms, an elegant bar and restaurant, and a practice range and putting green. The staff is particularly eager to help.

LEVEL OF MAINTENANCE: This resort facility leaves nothing undone. It is top-notch in every respect.

COURSE DESCRIPTION: This is a relatively flat and open 18 holes of golf. Because the venue is a former estate, there are stands of old trees and many new plantings. When these numerous plantings mature, Kilkea Castle will be a completely different course. The greens are large, well shaped, and vary from rolling to double tiered. Very attractive mounding around some of the greens adds both interest and challenge. The River Griese runs throughout the course and affects 10 holes—beware, and place your shots with care. The bunkers are large and intelligently placed and present a real challenge.

UNIQUE FEATURE: This course is purported to surround the oldest inhabited castle in Ireland.

ACCOMMODATION INFORMATION

Standard hotel: Kilkea Castle Hotel (on site), 353 503 45156

Local hotel/guesthouse/B&B: Seven Oaks Hotel (Carlow), 353 503 31308

Restaurant/pub: Kilkea Castle Golf Club Clubhouse, 353 503 45555

GREEN FEES:
Moderate

EQUIPMENT RENTAL
Buggies: yes
Trolleys: yes
Caddies: yes
Clubs: yes

DATE FOUNDED: 1995

ARCHITECTS: Jack McDaid and Jim Cassidy

TYPE: Parkland

FACILITIES
Clubhouse at turn: yes
Restrooms on course: no

SCORECARD

HOLE	YDG	PAR	INDEX
1	402	4	16
2	543	5	4
3	369	4	13
4	180	3	10
5	543	5	15
6	161	3	18
7	425	4	6
8	452	4	2
9	396	4	7
OUT	3,476	36	
10	150	3	14
11	419	4	9
12	532	5	17
13	451	4	11
14	182	3	12
15	450	4	5
16	188	3	3
17	374	4	1
18	418	4	8
IN	3,169	34	
TOTAL	**6,645**	**70**	

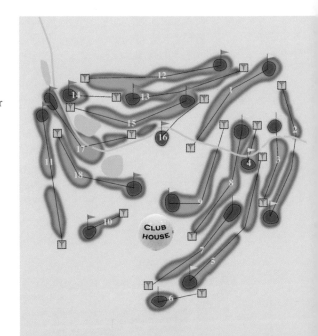

Kilkenny Golf Club

GREEN FEES:
Low
EQUIPMENT RENTAL
Buggies: no
Trolleys: yes
Caddies: yes
Clubs: yes

DATE FOUNDED: 1896
ARCHITECT: NA
TYPE: Parkland
FACILITIES
Clubhouse at turn: no
Restrooms on course: no

Kilkenny has a nice clubhouse with bar and restaurant facilities, as well as comfortable changing rooms with showers. It has a practice area and putting green, and a driving range a few hundred yards down the road.

LEVEL OF MAINTENANCE: This is a well-tended course. The greens and bunkers are well kept and the turf good. The building facilities are clean and attractive.

COURSE DESCRIPTION: Kilkenny is a mature parkland course with slightly rolling terrain. The interesting, intuitive layout has the feel of an older, well-established course. The course is fairly open, although some mature trees do provide difficulty and pleasant viewing. The three par 3s on the backside are treacherously long and require all you've got.

UNIQUE FEATURE: Thousands of trees were planted in the 1960s and 1970s, resulting in the well-established trees found throughout this course.

ACCOMMODATION INFORMATION
Standard hotel: Newpark Hotel (3 star) (Kilkenny), 353 56 22122

Local hotel/guesthouse/B&B: Butler House (3-star guesthouse), 353 56 65707

Restaurant/pub: Brannigans Glendine House (inn and restaurant), 353 56 21069

ADDRESS:
Glendine,
Kilkenny,
County Kilkenny,
Ireland

TELEPHONE:
353 56 65400

FAX:
353 56 65400

WEB PAGE: NA

E-MAIL: NA

DIRECTIONS TO COURSE: The course is 1 mile north of Kilkenny town, off the N77 or Castlecomer Road; watch for signage.

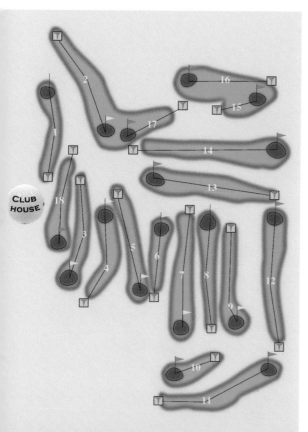

CLUB HOUSE

SCORECARD			
HOLE	YDG	PAR	INDEX
1	394	4	8
2	331	4	10
3	413	4	2
4	356	4	12
5	296	4	18
6	149	3	16
7	396	4	6
8	399	4	4
9	482	5	14
OUT	3,222	36	
10	209	3	3
11	434	4	1
12	485	5	17
13	422	4	3
14	498	5	13
15	197	3	11
16	385	4	5
17	176	3	15
18	352	4	9
IN	3,162	35	
TOTAL	6,384	71	

Mount Juliet Golf Club

ADDRESS:
Thomastown, County Kilkenny, Ireland

TELEPHONE:
353 56 24725

FAX:
353 56 24828

WEB PAGE: NA

E-MAIL: NA

DIRECTIONS TO COURSE: Take the N9 out of Thomastown toward Dublin for about 3 miles. Watch for possibly the best signage to a course you'll see in Ireland.

This is an estate resort with all the expected amenities, including elegant showers and changing rooms in the spacious and opulent clubhouse. A bar and grill are in the clubhouse area, and restaurants are in the hotel. The club has a well-appointed pro shop near the caddymaster, a covered driving range, and a large putting green. No expenses have been spared in converting this one-time country estate into elegant facilities. It also has an equestrian center, clay target shooting, fishing, archery, tennis, and croquet, along with a pool, spa, and gym.

GREEN FEES:
High

EQUIPMENT RENTAL
Buggies: no
Trolleys: yes
Caddies: yes
Clubs: yes

DATE FOUNDED: 1991

ARCHITECT:
Jack Nicklaus

TYPE: Parkland

FACILITIES
Clubhouse at turn: yes
Restrooms on course: yes (10th tee)

LEVEL OF MAINTENANCE: This facility is maintained to some of the highest standards you will find in Ireland.

COURSE DESCRIPTION: Mount Juliet is a beautiful rolling parkland course. The stately trees, liberally sprinkled throughout the course, create some difficulty. The real challenge, however, is the exceptional bunkering that is the genius of most Nicklaus courses. They range from small pot to gargantuan bunkers that surround half the green. Water is also a hazard, from meandering streams to large, graceful ponds (replete with numerous types of waterfowl). The turf on this course is superb and the greens of equal quality, although the latter are relatively flat and not particularly big. The final weapon in Mount Juliet's arsenal is its length. The 18th hole, for example, is a 474-yard demon par 4, with a lake and a huge sand trap to the left of the green.

UNIQUE FEATURE: This is the only Jack Nicklaus course in Ireland.

ACCOMMODATION INFORMATION
Standard hotel: Mount Juliet Estate (4 star) (on site), 353 56 73000

Local hotel/guesthouse/B&B: Butler House (3 star) (Kilkenny), 353 56 65707

Restaurant/pub: Broom's Bistro, in the Hotel Kilkenny (Kilkenny), 353 56 62000

SCORECARD

HOLE	YDG	PAR	INDEX
1	364	4	16
2	419	4	4
3	182	3	14
4	404	4	2
5	540	5	18
6	229	3	6
7	419	4	12
8	575	5	10
9	426	4	8
OUT	3,558	36	
10	553	5	7
11	169	3	17
12	411	4	9
13	433	4	1
14	195	3	11
15	370	4	15
16	433	4	5
17	516	5	13
18	474	4	3
IN	3,554	36	
TOTAL	**7,112**	**72**	

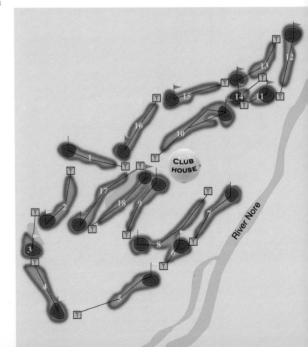

Waterford Golf Club

GREEN FEES: Moderate

EQUIPMENT RENTAL

Buggies: yes
Trolleys: yes
Caddies: no
Clubs: yes

DATE FOUNDED: 1912

ARCHITECTS: Willie Park Jr. (1913); James Braid (1934)

TYPE: Parkland

FACILITIES

Clubhouse at turn: no
Restrooms on course: no

Waterford has the usual clubhouse, with a nice bar and restaurant as well as a modestly stocked pro shop. The practice area and putting green are also very nice.

LEVEL OF MAINTENANCE: Waterford is a very well maintained course. Practice areas are well tended. The turf is excellent throughout the course, and the building facilities are clean and very functional.

ADDRESS:
Waterford, County Kilkenny (club members refer to themselves as in Waterford County), Ireland

TELEPHONE:
353 51 876748

FAX:
353 51 853405

WEB PAGE: NA

E-MAIL: NA

DIRECTIONS TO COURSE:
Off the N25, take the Newrath Road at the roundabout. The club is just north of the town of Waterford. The signage is spotty—you may need to ask directions.

COURSE DESCRIPTION: Waterford Club is a parkland course designed by the famous James Braid and Willie Park Jr. One of the common features of a Braid course is that the back collars of the greens cup up at the far end of the hole, thus keeping the ball near the green. This course is no exception. There is rolling to hilly terrain throughout the course, and traditional small bunkers are intelligently placed. Putting surfaces are first-rate and a lot of fun. There are also a number of blind shots throughout the course, typical of golf course design during Braid's time. Another feature is the many stands of old trees and thickets of gorse sprinkled across the landscape. The 18th hole is 400+ yards; it is downhill and lined on both sides by gorse. Stray on this hole and you will pay the penalties. This is a fun course, and if you bring your A-game, you can score well and have an enjoyable day.

UNIQUE FEATURE: The 18th tee offers a 360-degree view of five adjacent counties.

ACCOMMODATION INFORMATION

Standard hotel: Granville Hotel (3 star) (Meagher Quay, Waterford), 353 51 305555

Local hotel/guesthouse/B&B: Diamond Hill Country House (3-star guesthouse) (Slieveue, Waterford), 353 51 873531

Restaurant/pub: McCluskey's Bistro (Waterford), 353 51 857766

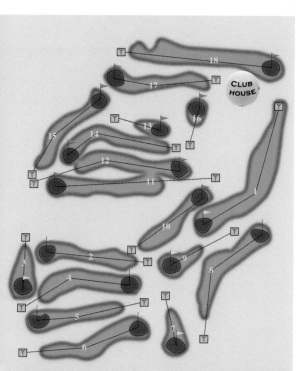

SCORECARD			
HOLE	YDG	PAR	INDEX
1	418	4	5
2	363	4	11
3	129	3	17
4	413	4	1
5	403	4	7
6	393	4	3
7	178	3	15
8	538	5	9
9	185	3	13
OUT	3,025	34	
10	293	4	14
11	492	5	10
12	482	5	6
13	193	3	12
14	433	4	2
15	478	5	8
16	139	3	18
17	293	4	16
18	401	4	4
IN	3,211	37	
TOTAL	**6,236**	**71**	

Heath Golf Club

ADDRESS: The Heath, Portlaoise, County Laois, Ireland

TELEPHONE: 353 502 46533

FAX: NA

WEB PAGE: NA

E-MAIL: NA

DIRECTIONS TO COURSE: The Heath course is 3 miles northeast of Portlaoise off N7. Follow excellent signage.

This course has a modest but adequate clubhouse with changing rooms, a small pro shop, a bar, and a full restaurant. It has a fully illuminated driving range and putting green.

LEVEL OF MAINTENANCE: This course is well maintained—especially the greens and bunkering. The clubhouse, however, is marginal in places (in particular, the men's bathrooms).

COURSE DESCRIPTION: Heath (pronounced "Heat"), a parkland course, has good bunkering, water hazards, and mature stands of trees. Some long holes make this a challenging and difficult test of golf. You'll need your A-game to score well here. The course does drain extremely well and can get a little hard and "bouncy" when dry. The heather and gorse are ever-present and will cause you the worst kind of headache if you don't respect them. There are some spectacular views of the County Laois (pronounced "Leesh") hills surrounding this course.

UNIQUE FEATURE: This club is purported to be the seventh-oldest golf course in Ireland.

ACCOMMODATION INFORMATION

Standard hotel: Killeshin Hotel (3 star) (Portlaoise), 353 502 21663

Local hotel/guesthouse/B&B: O'Loughlin's Hotel (Portlaoise), 353 502 21305

Restaurant/pub: Treacy's Pub and Restaurant (said to be Ireland's oldest pub using the original family name), 353 502 46781

GREEN FEES: Low

EQUIPMENT RENTAL
Buggies: no
Trolleys: yes
Caddies: no
Clubs: yes

DATE FOUNDED: 1890

ARCHITECT: NA

TYPE: Parkland

FACILITIES
Clubhouse at turn: yes
Restrooms on course: no

SCORECARD			
HOLE	YDG	PAR	INDEX
1	513	5	10
2	182	3	12
3	397	4	4
4	504	5	16
5	331	4	14
6	409	4	6
7	409	4	8
8	417	4	2
9	187	3	18
OUT	3,355	36	
10	380	4	11
11	178	3	17
12	393	4	13
13	434	4	1
14	392	4	9
15	412	4	3
16	540	5	15
17	195	3	7
18	386	4	5
IN	3,315	35	
TOTAL	**6,670**	**71**	

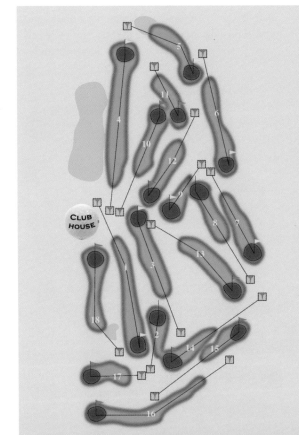

Adare Manor Golf Club

GREEN FEES:
Low
EQUIPMENT RENTAL
Buggies: no
Trolleys: yes
Caddies: yes
Clubs: yes

DATE FOUNDED: 1900

ARCHITECTS: Ben Sayers and Eddie Hackett (1992)

TYPE: Parkland
FACILITIES
Clubhouse at turn: yes
Restrooms on course: no

This is a small but complete facility, including bar and restaurant. This course does not have a practice range, but there is a putting green.

LEVEL OF MAINTENANCE: Building facilities are very well maintained. Likewise, the course is well kept, with excellent landscaping, tremendous turf, and excellent greens.

COURSE DESCRIPTION: This parkland course is set in historic surroundings, including a complete abbey built in 1464 and an ivy-clad tower, the ruins of Desmond Castle (ca. 1200 A.D.). Adare Manor is a modest course but is quite lovely, often joining up with the River Maigue to provide some beautiful scenery. There are six par 3s of varying length and difficulty. The old-growth trees contribute to the classic beauty of this course. It's great fun to play.

UNIQUE FEATURE: The historic buildings and cemetery on the site may make concentrating on your game difficult. They definitely make for an Irish Experience.

ACCOMMODATION INFORMATION
Standard hotel: Dunraven Arms Hotel (Adare), 353 61 396633

Local hotel/guesthouse/B&B: Fitzgerald's Woodlands House Hotel (Adare), 353 61 396118

Restaurant/pub: The Inn Between, 353 61 396633

ADDRESS:
Adare, County Limerick, Ireland

TELEPHONE:
353 61 396204

FAX:
353 61 396800

WEB PAGE: NA

E-MAIL: NA

DIRECTIONS TO COURSE: The course is on the N20, northeast of the town of Adare; watch for a sudden turnoff (dangerous intersection).

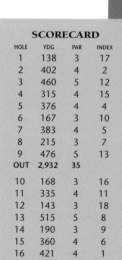

SCORECARD			
HOLE	YDG	PAR	INDEX
1	138	3	17
2	402	4	2
3	460	5	12
4	315	4	15
5	376	4	4
6	167	3	10
7	383	4	5
8	215	3	7
9	476	5	13
OUT	2,932	35	
10	168	3	16
11	335	4	11
12	143	3	18
13	515	5	8
14	190	3	9
15	360	4	6
16	421	4	1
17	272	4	14
18	370	4	3
IN	2,774	34	
TOTAL	5,706	69	

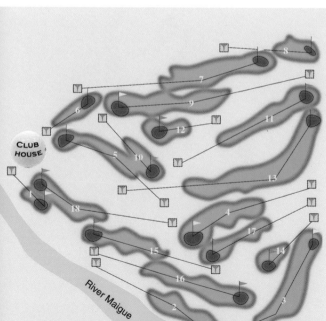

Adare Manor Hotel and Golf Club

ADDRESS:
Adare, County Limerick, Ireland

TELEPHONE:
353 61 395044

FAX:
353 61 396987

WEB PAGE: www.adaremanor.ie

E-MAIL: NA

DIRECTIONS TO COURSE: In Adare town, head for the city center and watch for good signage to the course.

This gorgeous estate is currently being remodeled. The hotel portion is the Adare Manor, built in 1832. There is a world-class practice area, along with full facilities and the hotel's complete amenities of sauna bath, clay pigeon shooting, heated pool, horseback riding, fishing, and much more.

LEVEL OF MAINTENANCE: Adare Manor Hotel is a top-notch facility with a wonderful eye to, and sense of, detail. This location is quite a treat and worth the effort, even if all you do is enjoy some tea or a beer in the hotel lounge.

COURSE DESCRIPTION: Adare Manor Hotel and Golf Club is a parkland course with gorgeous lakes and the Maigue River running throughout the course. A heavy sprinkling of old-growth trees makes it an absolutely beautiful and idyllic setting. The course has the typical Robert Trent Jones Sr. bunkering (i.e., numerous and in unusual shapes) and undulating greens. The course is also typically long and challenging from tee to green. Four sets of tees allow all levels of players to enjoy this course. Adare Manor Hotel is simply a lovely facility that should definitely be on your parkland courses must-play list.

UNIQUE FEATURE: Four sets of tees on each hole and all of Robert Trent Jones's wizardry make this lovely course a treat for all skill levels.

ACCOMMODATION INFORMATION
Standard hotel: Adare Manor Hotel (5 star), 353 61 396566
FAX: 353 61 396124

Local hotel/guesthouse/B&B: Dunraven Arms Hotel (Adare), 353 61 396633

Restaurant/pub: The Wild Geese, 353 61 396451

GREEN FEES:
Moderate

EQUIPMENT RENTAL
Buggies: yes
Trolleys: yes
Caddies: yes
Clubs: yes

DATE FOUNDED: 1995

ARCHITECT:
Robert Trent Jones Sr.

TYPE: Parkland

FACILITIES
Clubhouse at turn: yes
Restrooms on course: no

SCORECARD

HOLE	YDG	PAR	INDEX
1	433	4	5
2	413	4	9
3	403	4	13
4	180	3	17
5	419	4	1
6	205	3	15
7	537	5	7
8	427	4	3
9	577	5	11
OUT	3,594	36	
10	441	4	10
11	187	3	14
12	550	5	8
13	442	4	6
14	425	4	4
15	370	4	16
16	170	3	12
17	415	4	18
18	544	5	2
IN	3,544	36	
TOTAL	**7,138**	**72**	

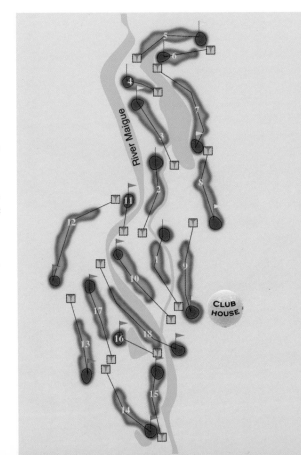

Limerick County Golf and Country Club

GREEN FEES:
Moderate

EQUIPMENT RENTAL
Buggies: no
Trolleys: yes
Caddies: yes
Clubs: yes

DATE FOUNDED: 1993

ARCHITECT: Des Smyth

TYPE: Parkland

FACILITIES
Clubhouse at turn: yes
Restrooms on course: no

Limerick County Golf and Country Club provides a large, modern, circular clubhouse with full-scale bar and restaurant facilities. There are some great views of the course from this elegant clubhouse, along with locker rooms and a well-stocked pro shop. On site, you will also find a driving range, a 3-hole short game practice area, and a large putting green. Several 4-star holiday cottages are on the course (phone 353 61 351881).

LEVEL OF MAINTENANCE: This is a very well maintained course, new and modern. The greens and fairways are in great shape and the bunkers well tended. In sum, nothing about this course is shabby.

COURSE DESCRIPTION: Limerick County offers a long course that is fairly wide open with many newly planted trees. The stands of trees will definitely make this course a greater test when they have matured. Bunkers are well placed and artfully designed. The greens are large and undulating, and a number are tiered. The greens are sand based, blessing this course with excellent drainage, always a factor for parkland courses during the rainy months. The water hazards make this an interesting inland course and a good, stiff challenge to play.

UNIQUE FEATURE: This course is laid out upon sandy terrain, giving it good drainage year-round.

ACCOMMODATION INFORMATION
Standard hotel: Dunraven Arms Hotel (4 star) (Adare), 353 61 396633

Local hotel/guesthouse/B&B: Alexandra Guest House (3 star) (Limerick town), 353 61 318472

Restaurant/pub: Clubhouse on site (excellent cuisine), 353 61 351881

ADDRESS:
Ballyneety, County Limerick, Ireland

TELEPHONE:
353 61 351881

FAX:
353 61 351384

WEB PAGE: NA

E-MAIL: lcgolf@iol.ie

DIRECTIONS TO COURSE: The course is 5 miles south of Limerick town on the R512; watch closely for signage.

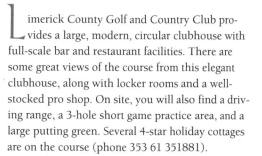

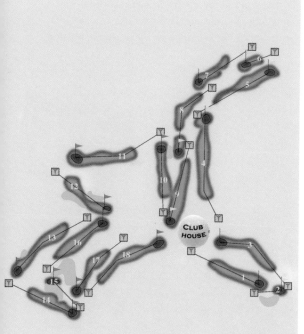

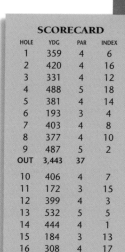

SCORECARD			
HOLE	YDG	PAR	INDEX
1	359	4	6
2	420	4	16
3	331	4	12
4	488	5	18
5	381	4	14
6	193	3	4
7	403	4	8
8	377	4	10
9	487	5	2
OUT	3,443	37	
10	406	4	7
11	172	3	15
12	399	4	3
13	532	5	5
14	444	4	1
15	184	3	13
16	308	4	17
17	420	4	9
18	412	4	11
IN	3,283	35	
TOTAL	6,726	72	

155

Newcastle West Golf Club

ADDRESS:
Newcastle West, Ardagh, County Limerick, Ireland

TELEPHONE:
353 69 76500

FAX:
353 69 76511

WEB PAGE: NA

E-MAIL: NA

DIRECTIONS TO COURSE: From the town of Newcastle West, take the R521 north toward Ardagh. Follow the brown signs to the golf club and Ardagh Heritage Centre. This course is a bit difficult to find, but is another one of those Irish Experiences.

The Newcastle West Golf Club near Ardagh was at one time a beautiful estate. The club puts to good use the old buildings throughout the grounds. The clubhouse offers a full bar and restaurant facilities, along with locker rooms and a small pro shop. The buildings are unique, given their former uses. A great driving range and putting green are near the clubhouse.

LEVEL OF MAINTENANCE: This course provides generally well maintained greens, but overall maintenance of the course and grounds is otherwise a bit spotty.

COURSE DESCRIPTION: The 150-acre Newcastle West Golf Club was laid out upon a former estate that was, for the most part, cleared for farming. There are gently rolling hills, and the underlying soil is predominantly sandy, making this parkland course playable most of the year. The course is fairly wide open, with many new plantings and some stands of older trees. The greens are large and interesting, the bunkers well placed. The streams and lakes add challenge and interest to this tract. This course is a bit out of the way, which may hamper its convenience to the tourist golfer.

UNIQUE FEATURE: This course is worth the trip just to see the wonderful old outbuildings. You can imagine this as a former grand estate with its spacious grounds.

ACCOMMODATION INFORMATION
Standard hotel: Courtenay Lodge Hotel (3 star) (Newcastle West), 353 69 62244

Local hotel/guesthouse/B&B: Devon Inn Hotel (3 star) (Newcastle West), 353 69 84122

Restaurant/pub: Courtenay Lodge Hotel Restaurant (see above), 353 69 62244

GREEN FEES:
Low

EQUIPMENT RENTAL
Buggies: no
Trolleys: yes
Caddies: no
Clubs: yes

DATE FOUNDED: 1938

ARCHITECT:
Arthur Spring

TYPE: Parkland

FACILITIES
Clubhouse at turn: yes
Restrooms on course: no

SCORECARD

HOLE	YDG	PAR	INDEX
1	465	5	17
2	356	4	12
3	191	3	10
4	330	4	13
5	412	4	2
6	187	3	4
7	381	4	8
8	506	5	15
9	370	4	6
OUT	3,198	36	
10	185	3	14
11	399	4	3
12	358	4	7
13	310	4	16
14	507	5	11
15	335	4	18
16	407	4	1
17	183	3	9
18	435	4	5
IN	3,119	35	
TOTAL	6,317	71	

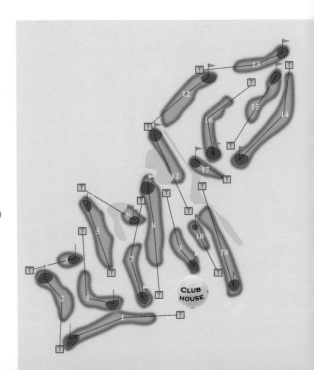

County Longford Golf Club

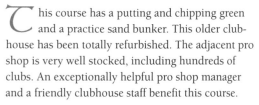

GREEN FEES:
Low
EQUIPMENT RENTAL
Buggies: yes
Trolleys: yes
Caddies: yes
Clubs: yes
DATE FOUNDED: 1900

ARCHITECTS: Eddie Hackett; 18 brand-new greens and tees by Declan Branigan (1999)

TYPE: Parkland
FACILITIES
Clubhouse at turn: no
Restrooms on course: no

This course has a putting and chipping green and a practice sand bunker. This older clubhouse has been totally refurbished. The adjacent pro shop is very well stocked, including hundreds of clubs. An exceptionally helpful pro shop manager and a friendly clubhouse staff benefit this course.

LEVEL OF MAINTENANCE: The course will have 18 new greens and tees in the very near future. You may want to call ahead to check on the status of the course relative to its reconstruction.

COURSE DESCRIPTION: This is a well-tended course as is and should be a real treat when renovation is complete. The terrain is slightly hilly, with some mature tree stands and many new plantings that define the fairways. Pleasant views overlook Longford city. A number of water hazards add interest to the course, and a pleasant creek meanders through it. For now, we'll look forward to the renovations. A nice driving range facility is just beyond the course, on the R393.

UNIQUE FEATURE: Drainage is good for an inland course.

ACCOMMODATION INFORMATION
Standard hotel: Longford Arms Hotel (3 star) (Longford), 353 43 46296

Local hotel/guesthouse/B&B: Richmond Court Guesthouse (Longford), 353 43 46957

Restaurant/pub: Clubhouse on site, 353 43 46310

ADDRESS:
Longford, County Longford, Ireland
TELEPHONE:
353 43 46310
FAX:
353 43 47082
WEB PAGE: NA
E-MAIL: NA

DIRECTIONS TO COURSE: The club is on the R393 just out of the town of Longford. Follow the signs to the course.

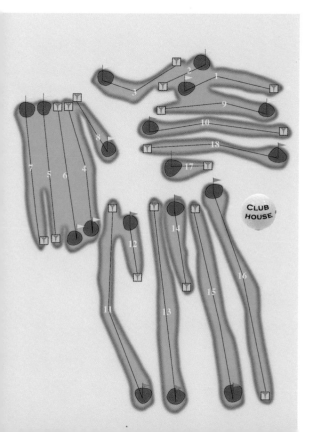

CLUB HOUSE

SCORECARD			
HOLE	YDG	PAR	INDEX
1	329	4	9
2	132	3	18
3	412	4	2
4	270	4	14
5	348	4	6
6	337	4	15
7	360	4	4
8	160	3	17
9	356	4	12
OUT	2,810	34	
10	433	4	1
11	376	4	11
12	191	3	7
13	403	4	3
14	304	4	8
15	493	5	13
16	476	5	10
17	126	3	16
18	408	4	5
IN	3,214	36	
TOTAL	6,024	70	

Ardee Golf Club

ADDRESS:
Townparks,
Ardee, County
Louth, Ireland

TELEPHONE:
353 41 6853227

FAX:
353 41 6856137

WEB PAGE: NA

E-MAIL: NA

DIRECTIONS TO COURSE: The course is just north of the town of Ardee, on the Woodville Road; watch for signs.

Ardee Golf Club has a modest clubhouse and no pro shop. There are adequate changing rooms and a bar serving snacks. A practice range and putting green are also available to the public.

LEVEL OF MAINTENANCE: Clubhouse facilities are marginally maintained. The buildings and grounds have the look and feel of a modest municipal course. The greens and turf are well developed, however, and the bunkers well maintained.

COURSE DESCRIPTION: Ardee is a parkland course set on a lovely rolling landscape, with stands of old trees. A stream runnng through the course adds interest and beauty. The greens putt well but are small and basically flat. Some good bunkers are scattered throughout, making this a reasonable, but not consistently interesting, test of golf.

UNIQUE FEATURE: The 13th hole is a 200-yard par 3 with much of it over a small lake—a good hole.

ACCOMMODATION INFORMATION

Standard hotel: Conyngham Arms Hotel (in Slane), 353 41 9884444

Local hotel/guesthouse/B&B: McQuaid's Guesthouse, 353 41 56905

Restaurant/pub: Auberge, McKeever's Bar and Restaurant, 353 41 53354

GREEN FEES:
Moderate

EQUIPMENT RENTAL
Buggies: yes
Trolleys: yes
Caddies: yes
Clubs: no

DATE FOUNDED: 1911

ARCHITECT: Eddie Hackett (redesigned)

TYPE: Parkland

FACILITIES
Clubhouse at turn: no
Restrooms on course: no

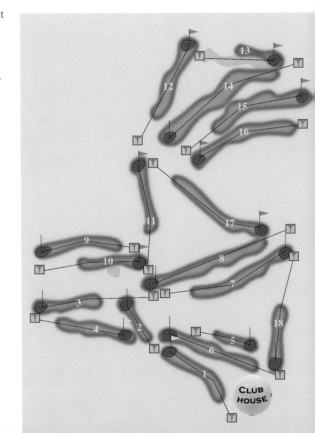

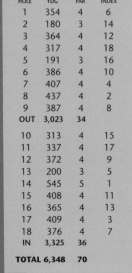

SCORECARD

HOLE	YDG	PAR	INDEX
1	354	4	6
2	180	3	14
3	364	4	12
4	317	4	18
5	191	3	16
6	386	4	10
7	407	4	4
8	437	4	2
9	387	4	8
OUT	3,023	34	
10	313	4	15
11	337	4	17
12	372	4	9
13	200	3	5
14	545	5	1
15	408	4	11
16	365	4	13
17	409	4	3
18	376	4	7
IN	3,325	36	
TOTAL	6,348	70	

County Louth Golf Club

GREEN FEES:
Moderate

EQUIPMENT RENTAL
Buggies: yes
Trolleys: yes
Caddies: yes
Clubs: yes

DATE FOUNDED: 1892

ARCHITECT: Tom Simpson

TYPE: Links

FACILITIES
Clubhouse at turn: yes
Restrooms on course: no

County Louth offers an old, classic clubhouse complete with a members-only bar as well as a full-service bar and restaurant for members and visitors alike. It serves excellent food (continental cuisine) and has an exceptional and elegant atmosphere. The well-stocked pro shop has a helpful and very courteous staff. The excellent practice facilities include chipping and putting greens and a driving range.

LEVEL OF MAINTENANCE: As would be expected from such a venerable club, all aspects of this course and its building facilities are maintained according to the highest standards.

COURSE DESCRIPTION: County Louth, a classic links course, does not have the west coast beauty of Lahinch but is a solid and challenging golfing venue. The fairways, bunkers, and greens are all excellently maintained, with the greens being some of the best you are likely to see in Ireland. Signage is good and consistent. There is also a natural placement of bunkers that will catch you if you're wayward, along with a good, intuitive layout. This is a course that requires the ability to think yourself through it as well as the ability to play around it—a great challenge and a perfect joy to play.

UNIQUE FEATURE: This is one of the few courses laid out by the famous architect Tom Simpson. Also, the intelligence required to play this course explains why it is respected and renowned.

ACCOMMODATION INFORMATION

Standard hotel: Westcourt Hotel (Drogheda), 353 41 9830965

Local hotel/guesthouse/B&B: Highfield House (a super guesthouse) (Baltray), 353 41 22172

Restaurant/pub: County Louth Clubhouse (excellent food), 353 41 22329

ADDRESS:
Baltray, Drogheda,
County Louth,
Ireland

TELEPHONE:
353 41 22329

FAX:
353 41 22969

WEB PAGE: NA

E-MAIL: baltray@indigo.ie

DIRECTIONS TO COURSE: The club is 5 miles northeast of Drogheda. Take the Baltray Road (R167), and watch for the course signage.

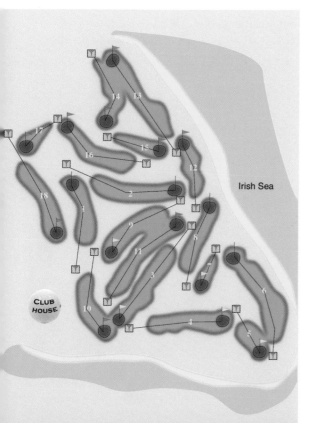

Irish Sea

CLUB HOUSE

SCORECARD			
HOLE	YDG	PAR	INDEX
1	433	4	3
2	482	5	17
3	544	5	9
4	344	4	15
5	158	3	13
6	531	5	7
7	163	3	5
8	407	4	11
9	419	4	1
OUT	3,481	37	
10	398	4	4
11	481	5	16
12	410	4	2
13	421	4	6
14	332	4	12
15	152	3	185
16	388	4	8
17	179	3	14
18	541	5	10
IN	3,302	36	
TOTAL 6,783		73	

Dundalk Golf Club

ADDRESS:
Blackrock,
Dundalk,
County Louth,
Ireland

TELEPHONE:
353 42 21731

FAX:
353 42 22022

WEB PAGE: NA

E-MAIL: NA

DIRECTIONS TO COURSE: Take the R172 to Blackrock village. There will be signs to follow; watch for them very closely.

This is an older, established club and clubhouse. The clubhouse facilities consist of a well-appointed bar, a restaurant, and locker rooms. In a separate building is a pro shop with very friendly staff. A good practice area and putting green are also available.

LEVEL OF MAINTENANCE: This club is very well maintained and lives up to its venerable reputation.

COURSE DESCRIPTION: Dundalk is a traditional Irish parkland course. It is particularly nice to play a mature course, with well-established trees and hazards. Many of the newer courses only have recently planted trees, which, while impressive, will take some years to grow and mature. The course terrain at Dundalk is rolling to hilly; the greens are gently rolling and putt true. The tee boxes are wonderful, and the panoramic views of Dundalk Bay and the Mourne Mountains in the near distance, spectacular. The layout of this course is very natural and has a good flow. Bring your A-game; some of the par 5s are very long and challenging. A couple of water hazards add to the enjoyment of the course. The bunkering will leave you scratching your head. All in all, this is a stern test and a great deal of fun.

UNIQUE FEATURE: Dundalk has a strong design pedigree and a great history of competitive events.

ACCOMMODATION INFORMATION

Standard hotel: Ballymascanlon House (3 star) (Dundalk), 353 42 9371124

Local hotel/guesthouse/B&B: Bellingham Castle Hotel (Dundalk), 353 42 9372176

Restaurant/pub: Beagans Bar and Restaurant, 353 42 37354

GREEN FEES:
Low

EQUIPMENT RENTAL
Buggies: yes
Trolleys: yes
Caddies: yes
Clubs: yes

DATE FOUNDED: 1904

ARCHITECTS: James Braid (1933); Peter Alliss and Dave Thomas of Golf Construction (1978)

TYPE: Parkland

FACILITIES
Clubhouse at turn: yes
Restrooms on course: no

SCORECARD

HOLE	YDG	PAR	INDEX
1	386	4	7
2	388	4	9
3	399	4	3
4	440	4	1
5	169	3	11
6	492	5	17
7	528	5	5
8	331	4	15
9	172	3	13
OUT	3,311	36	
10	492	5	16
11	423	4	2
12	503	5	8
13	174	3	12
14	317	4	18
15	388	4	6
16	424	4	4
17	187	3	14
18	345	4	10
IN	3,259	36	
TOTAL	6,570	72	

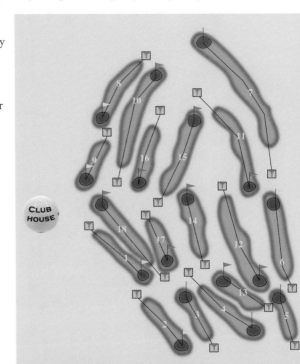

CLUB HOUSE

Greenore Golf Club

GREEN FEES:

Low

EQUIPMENT RENTAL

Buggies: no
Trolleys: yes
Caddies: yes
Clubs: yes

DATE FOUNDED: 1896

ARCHITECT: Redesigned by Eddie Hackett

TYPE: Links/Parkland

FACILITIES

Clubhouse at turn: no
Restrooms on course: no

Greenore boasts a beautiful, even opulent, clubhouse with full facilities and excellent amenities. The club includes a bar, a restaurant, and very well appointed locker rooms, but no pro shop.

LEVEL OF MAINTENANCE: This course is very well maintained, and the clubhouse is inviting and immaculate.

COURSE DESCRIPTION: Greenore is situated on the shores of Carlingford Lough, with scenic views of the Mourne Mountains. It is a links-like course that also has some parkland features, such as a stand of tall and stately pines that comes into play on seven of the holes. The famous 14th hole, Pig's Back (par 3), is a real test with its elevated tee. This course is low in places and therefore subject to drainage problems during wet periods; be sure to ask about conditions when you call to book a tee time.

UNIQUE FEATURE: This is one of Ireland's old, traditional courses at which you can relax in the clubhouse after your round and take in the spectacular views.

ACCOMMODATION INFORMATION

Standard hotel: Ballymascanlon House Hotel (Dundalk), 353 42 9371124

Local hotel/guesthouse/B&B: Derryhale Hotel (Dundalk), 353 42 9335471

Restaurant/pub: Beagans Bar and Restaurant (Dundalk), 353 42 37354

ADDRESS:

Greenore, County
Louth, Ireland

TELEPHONE:
353 42 73212

FAX:
353 42 73678

WEB PAGE: NA

E-MAIL: NA

DIRECTIONS TO COURSE: On the N1, go north through Drogheda toward Dundalk. Take the R173, or follow signs for Greenore. Watch for the course on your left, because there isn't any course signage. Once you see the course, take the first left-hand turn. Go to the dead end, where you'll find the club drive.

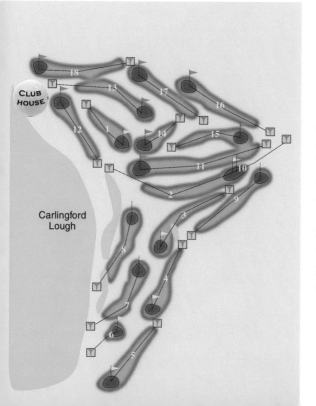

CLUB HOUSE

Carlingford Lough

SCORECARD

HOLE	YDG	PAR	INDEX
1	218	3	11
2	522	5	15
3	392	4	5
4	399	4	7
5	423	4	3
6	130	3	13
7	410	4	1
8	415	4	9
9	325	4	17
OUT	3,234	35	
10	157	3	14
11	527	5	18
12	372	4	6
13	436	4	4
14	139	3	12
15	357	4	8
16	435	4	2
17	487	5	16
18	370	4	10
IN	3,280	36	
TOTAL	6,514	71	

Seapoint Golf Club

ADDRESS:
Termonfeckin, County Louth, Ireland

TELEPHONE:
353 41 22333

FAX:
353 41 22331

WEB PAGE: NA

E-MAIL: golflinks@seapoint.ie

DIRECTIONS TO COURSE: Head for the village of Termonfeckin (just a little north of Drogheda, on the east coast); follow signs to the course.

Seapoint offers a very nice, modern, new clubhouse with a full bar and restaurant, as well as locker rooms. It has a well-stocked pro shop and a practice range and putting green.

LEVEL OF MAINTENANCE: Seapoint is maintained with care and high standards. The greens and turf are good and healthy and the sand traps well tended. The building facilities are very clean and presentable.

COURSE DESCRIPTION: The Seapoint Club is a course with many faces. The first four holes, complete with a housing development, have a parklike feel, with trees, ponds, and wide-open fairways. The rough, however, is punishing for a truly wayward shot. The middle ten holes are fairly wide open, straightforward, and rather nondescript. The last four holes are in lovely sand dunes, with a number of great views of the ocean and its wide, sandy beaches. In general, the whole course has a good, intuitive layout, along with good signage. The bunkers are well designed and placed, and clumps of rhododendrons make summers on this course gorgeous. One possible drawback is that evidence points to further housing development on the interior of the course, diminishing the aesthetics of Seapoint.

UNIQUE FEATURE: This course is a unique blend of parkland and links, with sand dunes, lakes, trees, and ocean views.

ACCOMMODATION INFORMATION
Standard hotel: Boyne Valley Hotel and Country Club (3 star) (Drogheda), 353 41 9837737

Local hotel/guesthouse/B&B: Highfield House (guesthouse) (Termonfeckin), 353 41 22172

Restaurant/pub: Seapoint Clubhouse, 353 41 22333

GREEN FEES:
Moderate

EQUIPMENT RENTAL
Buggies: yes
Trolleys: yes
Caddies: yes
Clubs: yes

DATE FOUNDED: 1993

ARCHITECT: Des Smyth

TYPE: Links/Parkland

FACILITIES
Clubhouse at turn: yes
Restrooms on course: yes (3rd hole)

SCORECARD

HOLE	YDG	PAR	INDEX
1	387	4	7
2	369	4	15
3	441	4	3
4	420	4	1
5	198	3	11
6	366	4	17
7	441	4	5
8	507	5	13
9	201	3	9
OUT	3,335	35	
10	523	5	16
11	374	4	10
12	443	4	4
13	449	4	2
14	418	4	6
15	159	3	14
16	363	4	8
17	178	3	18
18	493	5	12
IN	3,405	36	
TOTAL	**6,740**	**71**	

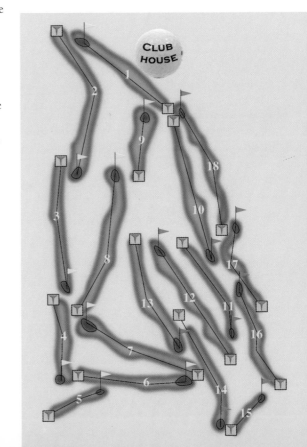

CLUB HOUSE

Ballinrobe Golf Club

GREEN FEES:
Low

EQUIPMENT RENTAL
Buggies: no
Trolleys: yes
Caddies: on request
Clubs: yes

DATE FOUNDED: 1895

ARCHITECT: New course by Eddie Hackett (1995)

TYPE: Parkland

FACILITIES
Clubhouse at turn: yes
Restrooms on course: no

This 250-year-old estate was a functioning farm and has many old outbuildings and courtyards. The buildings could potentially give this course a very unique flavor. They have not been developed to date, but intentions are to do so in the future. A very nice practice facility has a chipping green and practice sand trap, and there is a putting green. The clubhouse occupies what was the main home on this lovely estate, and the grounds are quite interesting, with the remains of cattle barns and paddocks. A bar, full restaurant, and changing rooms are in the clubhouse.

ADDRESS:
Cloonacastle,
County
Mayo, Ireland

TELEPHONE:
353 92 41118

FAX:
353 92 41889

WEB PAGE: NA

E-MAIL: NA

DIRECTIONS TO COURSE: Take Claremorris Road 3 miles west of Ballinrobe. Watch closely for the signage.

LEVEL OF MAINTENANCE: This parkland course seems to do all that it can. The greens and turf are good, and the traps are well maintained. The clubhouse and changing rooms are clean, and the restaurant is quaint and warm.

COURSE DESCRIPTION: Ballinrobe is a parkland course developed from an estate, which almost always means a few good stands of old trees and a lot of new plantings. This course is no exception. It has some very good bunkering and a few good long holes that are often doglegged and/or over water. The course has nine water hazards. The River Robe imparts much beauty to Ballinrobe and adds to the classic parkland nature of the course layout.

UNIQUE FEATURE: Cloonacastle Tower is on the course proper. The five stone sculptures at the driveway entrance are representative of 5,000 years of County Mayo. They are worth a look on your way into the course.

ACCOMMODATION INFORMATION
Standard hotel: Jennings Hotel (Castlebar), 353 94 23111

Local hotel/guesthouse/B&B: Daly's Hotel (Castlebar), 353 94 21961

Restaurant/pub: Flannery's Bar and Restaurant, 353 92 417244

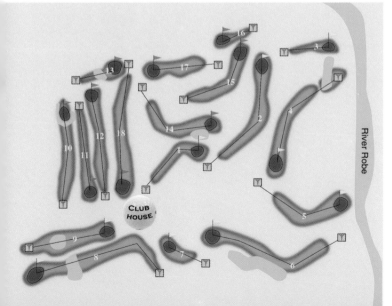

SCORECARD			
HOLE	YDG	PAR	INDEX
1	366	4	15
2	446	4	1
3	190	3	9
4	521	5	11
5	385	4	7
6	527	5	5
7	172	3	13
8	534	5	3
9	329	4	17
OUT	3,473	37	
10	397	4	2
11	396	4	8
12	379	4	10
13	169	3	12
14	534	5	16
15	379	4	6
16	169	3	14
17	409	4	4
18	482	5	18
IN	3,321	36	
TOTAL	**6,795**	**73**	

Ballyhaunis Golf Club

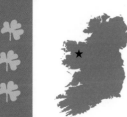

ADDRESS:
Ballyhaunis,
Coolnaha,
County Mayo,
Ireland

TELEPHONE:
353 92 41118

FAX: NA

WEB PAGE: NA

E-MAIL: NA

DIRECTIONS TO COURSE: Take the N83 north of Ballyhaunis for 2 miles. Directly off the highway, watch for a gate and a sign that appears rather suddenly.

Ballyhaunis offers a very small, modest clubhouse with a bar and grill. There is no pro shop, but there are changing rooms and a putting green.

LEVEL OF MAINTENANCE: This is a beautifully maintained course, with many bunkers, great greens, and good fairways. The clubhouse is clean and neat.

COURSE DESCRIPTION: This is a lovely 9-hole course with two sets of tees. The terrain is undulating around hills and drumlins (glacial features). The greens are elevated, with a number of bunkers. The course is a challenge to walk but worth every step. This is a great test of golf and a whole lot of fun, a 9-holer that should not be missed if at all possible.

UNIQUE FEATURE: Playing in and around the drumlins makes this course a hidden gem.

ACCOMMODATION INFORMATION
Standard hotel: The Cill Aodain Hotel (Kiltimagh), 353 94 81761

Local hotel/guesthouse/B&B: Knock International Hotel (Knock), 353 94 88466

Restaurant/pub: An Bialann (Knock), 353 94 88122

GREEN FEES:
Low

EQUIPMENT RENTAL
Buggies: no
Trolleys: yes
Caddies: no
Clubs: no

DATE FOUNDED: 1928

ARCHITECT: NA

TYPE: Parkland

FACILITIES
Clubhouse at turn: yes
Restrooms on course: no

SCORECARD

HOLE	YDG	PAR	INDEX
1	390	4	3
2	336	4	9
3	487	5	11
4	392	4	1
5	307	4	15
6	166	3	13
7	350	4	7
8	137	3	17
9	390	4	5
OUT	2,961	35	
10	405	4	4
11	367	4	6
12	449	5	14
13	385	4	2
14	297	4	16
15	162	3	18
16	328	4	10
17	161	3	12
18	381	4	8
IN	2,938	35	
TOTAL	5,899	70	

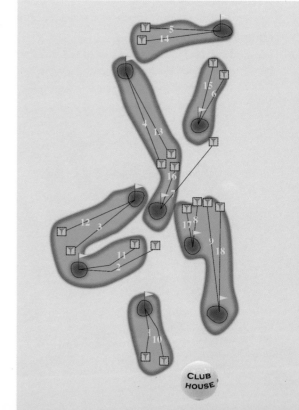

Carne (Belmullet) Golf Links

GREEN FEES: Moderate; (fairly complicated fee structure, depending on season, day of week, and number in party)

EQUIPMENT RENTAL
Buggies: yes
Trolleys: yes
Caddies: yes

Clubs: yes

DATE FOUNDED: 1925

ARCHITECT: Redesigned by Eddie Hackett

TYPE: Links

FACILITIES
Clubhouse at turn: yes
Restrooms on course: no

Carne has a large and well-appointed clubhouse, complete with bar and full-facility restaurant. There is no pro shop, but the club does have a good driving range and putting green.

LEVEL OF MAINTENANCE: This course is generally well maintained; however, there have been some difficulties with the greens in the recent past. Given the presentation of the rest of the course and the building facilities, we trust the greens issue will be resolved.

COURSE DESCRIPTION: This is a stunningly beautiful natural links course, a gorgeous tract, and a wonderful walk through some of the most beautiful dunelands you will see in Ireland. It is also out in the middle of nowhere (so be sure to make hotel reservations beforehand; you'll find few options in Belmullet). The course is clearly some of Eddie Hackett's best work, requiring little disturbance of the natural terrain. The greens were laid out and designed well but have had some problems recently. One has a great sense of being in the linksland while walking through the high dunes. This course would be an absolute don't-miss except for its remote location. If you are anywhere within striking distance, however, you won't be disappointed with whatever effort it takes to get to Carne.

UNIQUE FEATURE: The 9th hole is distracting in its beauty and a great way to end the outward half.

ACCOMMODATION INFORMATION
Standard hotel: Western Strand Hotel (Belmullet), 353 97 810964
Local hotel/guesthouse/B&B: Teach Iorrais (Geesala), 353 97 86888
Restaurant/pub: Clubhouse on site, 353 97 82292

ADDRESS:
Belmullet, County Mayo, Ireland

TELEPHONE:
353 97 82292

FAX:
353 97 81477

WEB PAGE: NA

E-MAIL: carngolf@iol.ie

DIRECTIONS TO COURSE: This course is 1.7 miles west of Belmullet on the Mullet Peninsula; watch for directional signs in the town of Belmullet.

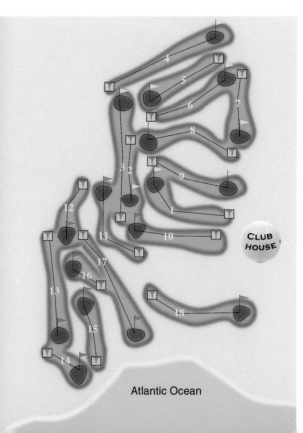

CLUB HOUSE

Atlantic Ocean

SCORECARD			
HOLE	YDG	PAR	INDEX
1	398	4	6
2	199	3	16
3	409	4	12
4	515	5	18
5	411	4	14
6	395	4	2
7	176	3	8
8	397	4	4
9	356	4	10
OUT	3,262	35	
10	506	5	15
11	361	4	5
12	327	4	13
13	525	5	9
14	144	3	11
15	398	4	3
16	167	3	17
17	434	4	1
18	539	5	7
IN	3,407	37	
TOTAL 6,669		72	

Castlebar Golf Club

ADDRESS:
Rocklands,
Castlebar,
County Mayo,
Ireland

TELEPHONE:
353 94 21649

FAX:
353 94 26088

WEB PAGE: NA

E-MAIL: NA

DIRECTIONS TO COURSE: Take the N84 south of Castlebar and then watch for brown information signs for the golf course.

A modest but adequate clubhouse has a bar and snack foods. There is no pro shop, but there are changing rooms. Facilities include a putting green and a small area for short-iron work.

LEVEL OF MAINTENANCE: The greens and turf are very weak at this course. The bunkering is decent, however. Clubhouse facilities are adequately maintained.

COURSE DESCRIPTION: This is a parkland course on gently rolling terrain. It has many old stands of trees, some new plantings, and some good bunkering. The greens also are gently rolling, and some are tiered.

UNIQUE FEATURE: Your introduction to this course, the opening hole, is 413 yards long and lined by sloping fairways.

ACCOMMODATION INFORMATION

Standard hotel: Breaffy House Hotel (3 star) (Castlebar), 353 94 22033

Local hotel/guesthouse/B&B: Daly's Hotel (Castlebar), 353 94 21961

Restaurant/pub: Mulberry Bar and Garden Restaurant, Breaffy House Hotel (see above), 353 94 22033

GREEN FEES:
Low

EQUIPMENT RENTAL
Buggies: yes
Trolleys: yes
Caddies: no
Clubs: no

DATE FOUNDED: 1910

ARCHITECT: NA

TYPE: Parkland

FACILITIES
Clubhouse at turn: yes
Restrooms on course: no

SCORECARD

HOLE	YDG	PAR	INDEX
1	413	4	9
2	386	4	5
3	319	4	17
4	333	4	15
5	168	3	11
6	394	4	1
7	503	5	3
8	159	3	13
9	343	4	7
OUT	3,023	35	
10	172	3	12
11	504	5	14
12	167	3	10
13	392	4	4
14	419	4	6
15	395	4	2
16	304	4	18
17	353	4	8
18	477	5	16
IN	3,187	36	
TOTAL	6,210	71	

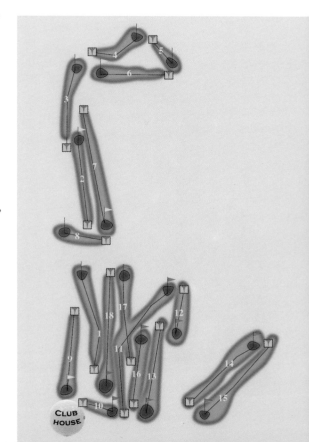

Mulranny Golf Club

GREEN FEES:
Low

EQUIPMENT RENTAL
Buggies: no
Trolleys: yes
Caddies: no
Clubs: yes

DATE FOUNDED: 1896

ARCHITECT: NA

TYPE: Links

FACILITIES
Clubhouse at turn: yes
Restrooms on course: no

The course at Mulranny is located on commonage, and as such, no permanent buildings can be placed. Consequently, in a very clever manner, a couple of mobile units have been brought on and made into a very nice, if modest, clubhouse. Inside you will find a green fees desk, a couple of very small changing rooms, a bathroom, and a quaint little area serving drinks and snacks. There is a putting green.

ADDRESS:
Mulranny, Newport.
County Mayo,
Ireland

TELEPHONE:
353 98 36262

FAX: NA

WEB PAGE: NA

E-MAIL: NA

LEVEL OF MAINTENANCE: Two men and a dog (Bart, a big yellow Labrador) take care of this place, and they do a great job. Seriously, this fun and fine links is clean and very well presented.

COURSE DESCRIPTION: Mulranny is actually a 9-hole links course with two sets of men's tees to make for 18 holes; the women play from one set of tees twice. The linksland here is subdued, gently rolling, and not particularly dramatic. The views of Clew Bay and the surrounding landscape are perfectly delightful, however. Some of the greens are huge and undulating, while others are raised and treacherous—barbed wired encompasses all to keep out the commonage sheep and cattle. Some testing par 4s and a par 3 or two will require all that you can muster. This is a delightful course to visit and a fun course to play.

DIRECTIONS TO COURSE: Take the N59 just south of Mulranny village, which is north of Westport town. Follow signage to the course.

UNIQUE FEATURE: This course started out as a 9 hole in 1896. Around 1970, it was increased to 18, but it was reduced back to 9 when a lease with area farmers ran out.

ACCOMMODATION INFORMATION
Standard hotel: Knockranny House Hotel (4 star) (Westport), 353 98 28600

Local hotel/guesthouse/B&B: Augusta Lodge (3 star) (Westport), 353 98 28900

Restaurant/pub: Welsh's Bridge Inn (Newport), 353 98 41524

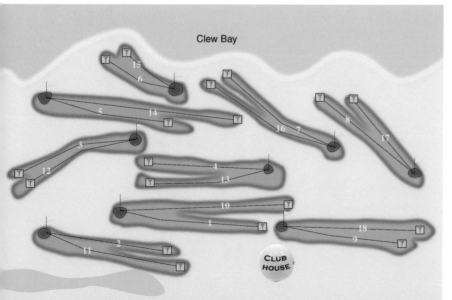

SCORECARD			
HOLE	YDG	PAR	INDEX
1	468	5	18
2	391	4	4
3	342	4	13
4	437	4	1
5	413	4	6
6	200	3	8
7	372	4	5
8	160	3	10
9	301	4	17
OUT	3,084	35	
10	498	5	16
11	375	4	9
12	336	4	12
13	420	4	2
14	481	5	15
15	165	3	14
16	405	4	3
17	150	3	11
18	341	4	7
IN	3,171	36	
TOTAL	6,255	71	

Westport Golf Club

ADDRESS:
Carrowholly,
Westport,
County Mayo,
Ireland

TELEPHONE:
353 98 28262

FAX:
353 98 27070

WEB PAGE: NA

E-MAIL: wpgolf@iol.ie

DIRECTIONS TO COURSE: Westport Club is located 2½ miles north of the town of Westport, off the N59. Watch for signs.

The Westport Club includes an excellent, clean, upscale clubhouse with a great bar and restaurant. The views of the surrounding countryside and ocean are breathtaking. The club has a well-stocked pro shop, locker rooms, a putting green, and a practice range.

LEVEL OF MAINTENANCE: All aspects of this club are maintained to the highest standards, including well-tended greens and bunkers.

COURSE DESCRIPTION: Westport is located in an exceptionally gorgeous part of Ireland overlooking Westport Bay, at the base of the holy mountain Croagh Patrick. The course encompasses 260 acres of the former Lord Sligo of Westport House estate. Westport has already made a name for itself by hosting many Irish cup championships. This is a good intuitive layout, and the first five holes provide a tranquil preamble to some of the toughness ahead. The course plays long but fair with five par 5s. One of these, the 580-yard 15th, has a demanding 160-yard carry over an inlet of Westport Bay. The 14th hole will offer a true test of your concentration as you gaze up at the impressive slopes of Croagh Patrick. When the wind blows, as it often does given the course's proximity to the ocean, even the longest hitters will find this course a challenge.

UNIQUE FEATURE: Croagh Patrick is reputedly the mountain site from which St. Patrick banished all reptiles from Ireland (an apocryphal tale, but intriguing nonetheless).

ACCOMMODATION INFORMATION

Standard hotel: Knockranny House Hotel (4 star) (Westport), 353 98 28600

Local hotel/guesthouse/B&B: Augusta Lodge (3-star guesthouse) (Westport), 353 98 28900

Restaurant/pub: The Towers Bar and Seafood Restaurant (Westport), 353 98 26534

GREEN FEES:
Moderate

EQUIPMENT RENTAL
Buggies: yes
Trolleys: yes
Caddies: yes
Clubs: yes

DATE FOUNDED: 1908

ARCHITECT: Frederick W. Hawtree (1973)

TYPE: Parkland

FACILITIES
Clubhouse at turn: yes
Restrooms on course: no

SCORECARD

HOLE	YDG	PAR	INDEX
1	344	4	14
2	345	4	8
3	168	3	16
4	502	5	18
5	360	4	10
6	463	4	4
7	529	5	12
8	472	4	2
9	208	3	6
OUT	3,391	36	
10	537	5	11
11	437	4	3
12	220	3	5
13	455	4	1
14	191	3	7
15	580	5	9
16	363	4	15
17	378	4	13
18	520	5	17
IN	3,695	37	
TOTAL	**7,086**	**73**	

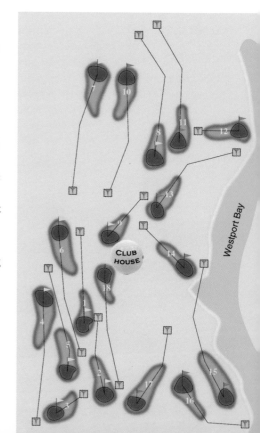

Black Bush Golf Club

GREEN FEES:
Low
EQUIPMENT RENTAL
Buggies: yes
Trolleys: yes
Caddies: yes
Clubs: yes

DATE FOUNDED: 1987
ARCHITECT:
Robert Browne
TYPE: Parkland
FACILITIES
Clubhouse at turn: yes
Restrooms on course: no

This is a truly elegant facility; remodeling of the clubhouse was completed as of spring 1999. Black Bush's clubhouse offers a top-notch restaurant, a bar, meeting rooms, snooker rooms, and locker rooms for visitors and members. The club also has a separate, well-stocked pro shop, an excellent teaching and practice facility, a covered driving range, and a practice and putting green.

LEVEL OF MAINTENANCE: Black Bush is a very industrious member-owned club which did a number of renovation activities in 1998–1999. The facilities and course are very well maintained, with good turf, great greens, and well-tended traps. All of the building facilities are first-rate.

COURSE DESCRIPTION: This course is located on gently rolling terrain with some mature trees and many new plantings. There are a couple of water hazards and some very nice bunkering. In addition, the length of the course makes this a challenging venue for all golfers. The greens are an excellent test of putting, with several of them undulating fairly significantly. The site presents 27 holes for your golfing pleasure.

UNIQUE FEATURE: The narrow drive on the 1st tee, over a lake, is one intimidating start!

ACCOMMODATION INFORMATION
Standard hotel: Wellington Court Hotel (Trim), 353 46 31516

Local hotel/guesthouse/B&B: Station House Hotel and Restaurant (Kilmessan), 353 46 25239

Restaurant/pub: Station House Hotel and Restaurant (Kilmessan), 353 46 25239

ADDRESS:
Thomastown,
Dunshaughlin,
County Meath,
Ireland
TELEPHONE:
353 825 0021
FAX:
353 825 0400
WEB PAGE: NA
E-MAIL: golf@blackbush.iol.ie
DIRECTIONS TO COURSE: In
Dunshaughlin town, take the R125 (Rotath Road) for about 1 mile, and watch for signage to the course.

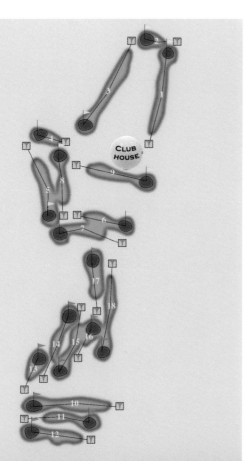

SCORECARD

HOLE	YDG	PAR	INDEX
COURSE A			
1	539	5	6
2	156	3	8
3	536	5	3
4	192	3	5
5	379	4	1
6	367	4	4
7	419	4	2
8	322	4	7
9	462	5	9
TOTAL 3,372		**37**	
COURSE B			
1	481	5	6
2	370	4	7
3	386	4	2
4	153	3	9
5	410	4	1
6	385	4	4
7	167	3	3
8	370	4	8
9	559	5	5
TOTAL 3,281		**36**	

HOLE	YDG	PAR	INDEX
COURSE C			
1	322	4	6
2	175	3	4
3	507	5	3
4	361	4	1
5	425	4	7
6	339	4	8
7	138	3	9
8	385	4	2
9	376	4	5
TOTAL 3,028		**35**	

County Meath Golf Club

ADDRESS:
Newtown-
moynagh, Trim,
County Meath,
Ireland

TELEPHONE:
353 46 31463

FAX:
353 46 37554

WEB PAGE: NA

E-MAIL: NA

DIRECTIONS TO COURSE: The
course is 3
miles south of
Trim town
center, on the
Longwood
Road. Follow
the excellent
signage to the
course.

County Meath (pronounced "Meat") has an elegant new clubhouse surrounded by extensive and attractive landscaping. The club has a large, well-appointed bar and full restaurant, very nice locker rooms with showers, a well-stocked pro shop, a putting green, and an excellent 7-acre practice facility.

LEVEL OF MAINTENANCE: This course and its building facilities are all very well maintained. The greens are excellent, as are the bunkers and turf. The clubhouse is extremely clean and inviting.

COURSE DESCRIPTION: County Meath is a parkland course that has a multitude of hazards—grass bunkers, sand bunkers, water hazards, and trees. The greens are rolling and particularly well tended, making them a joy to play. The whole course is set on picturesque, rolling landscape and is, given the multitude and variety of hazards, a very stern test of golf. Either bring your A-game or just relax and enjoy the experience.

UNIQUE FEATURE: A great variety of hazards are liberally sprinkled throughout this course.

ACCOMMODATION INFORMATION

Standard hotel: Highfield House Bed-and-Breakfast (Trim), 353 46 36386

Local hotel/guesthouse/B&B: Wellington Court Hotel (2 star, with a very accommodating and helpful staff)(Trim), 353 46 31516

Restaurant/pub: Abbey Lodge Restaurant (Trim), 353 46 31285

GREEN FEES:
Low

EQUIPMENT RENTAL
Buggies: yes
Trolleys: yes
Caddies: no
Clubs: yes

DATE FOUNDED: 1898

ARCHITECTS: Redesigned and converted to 18 holes by Eddie Hackett and Tom Craddock (1990)

TYPE: Parkland

FACILITIES
Clubhouse at turn: yes
Restrooms on course: no

SCORECARD

HOLE	YDG	PAR	INDEX
1	190	3	8
2	532	5	6
3	482	5	15
4	339	4	17
5	415	4	2
6	382	4	4
7	160	3	12
8	366	4	10
9	490	5	14
OUT	3,361	37	
10	287	4	18
11	357	4	9
12	196	3	7
13	370	4	5
14	343	4	11
15	347	4	16
16	424	4	3
17	462	4	1
18	534	5	13
IN	3,325	36	
TOTAL	6,686	73	

Headfort Golf Club

GREEN FEES:
Moderate

EQUIPMENT RENTAL
Buggies: yes
Trolleys: yes
Caddies: yes
Clubs: yes

DATE FOUNDED: 1928

ARCHITECT: Extended to 18 holes by Christy O'Connor Jr. (1994)

TYPE: Parkland

FACILITIES
Clubhouse at turn: yes
Restrooms on course: no

headfort has a stunningly beautiful clubhouse, built in 1994; its design is very unusual for Ireland. There are full bar and restaurant facilities, along with a member's bar and snooker rooms. Locker rooms, on the main level, are spacious and inviting. A separate, very well stocked pro shop, along with both a practice and putting green, are also on site. This club has an extremely helpful and friendly staff.

ADDRESS:
Kells, County Meath, Ireland

TELEPHONE:
353 46 40146

FAX:
353 46 49282

WEB PAGE: NA

E-MAIL: NA

DIRECTIONS TO COURSE: The course is on the N3, just east of the town of Kells; watch for signage.

LEVEL OF MAINTENANCE: This course and its buildings are very well maintained; it is a top-notch facility in every respect. Attention to course maintenance is high quality, and the buildings are well organized and clean.

COURSE DESCRIPTION: Headfort is a lovely parkland course with mature trees and fine fairways that make it extremely enjoyable. This course is pure Christy O'Connor, with particularly wonderful greens owing to their great mounding and well-placed bunkering. The greens are a pleasure to putt on and offer a great challenge for the best of putters. The trees help define the holes but are not so dense as to create too many lost-balls or impossible shot situations. You will not be disappointed in the playability of this course, regardless of your handicap. A second 18, currently being built, is also a Christy O'Connor Jr. design. From all appearances, this new course will also be wonderful.

UNIQUE FEATURE: Headfort presents an unusual, almost Oriental-style clubhouse surrounded by gorgeous flower beds that are well attended.

ACCOMMODATION INFORMATION
Standard hotel: Arboyne Hotel (Navan), 353 46 23119

Local hotel/guesthouse/B&B: Headfort Arms Hotel (Kells), 353 46 40063

Restaurant/pub: The Round Tower Restaurant (Kells), 353 46 40144

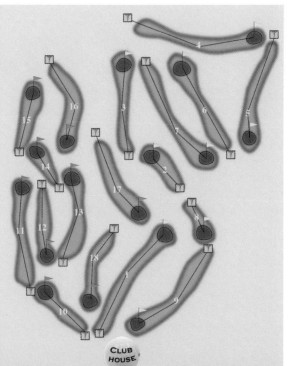

CLUB HOUSE

SCORECARD			
HOLE	YDG	PAR	INDEX
1	477	5	17
2	188	3	12
3	402	4	5
4	483	5	8
5	429	4	1
6	415	4	3
7	475	5	18
8	156	3	14
9	346	4	10
OUT	3,375	37	
10	186	3	16
11	534	5	13
12	387	4	4
13	382	4	6
14	186	3	11
15	328	4	15
16	405	4	2
17	355	4	7
18	367	4	9
IN	3,134	35	
TOTAL	6,509	72	

Laytown and Bettystown Golf Club

ADDRESS:

Bettystown,
County Meath,
Ireland

TELEPHONE:
353 41 27170

FAX:
353 41 28506

WEB PAGE: NA

E-MAIL: NA

DIRECTIONS TO COURSE: This
course is about 30 miles north of
Dublin and
about 4 miles
south of the
town of
Drogheda on
the R151. The
course is
right on the
road, impos-
sible to miss.

SCORECARD

HOLE	YDG	PAR	INDEX
1	320	4	13
2	338	4	10
3	405	4	3
4	481	5	14
5	360	4	8
6	162	3	15
7	401	4	6
8	401	3	11
9	178	4	2
OUT	3,050	35	
10	413	4	5
11	377	4	1
12	457	4	4
13	386	4	16
14	341	3	17
15	394	4	7
16	192	3	9
17	303	4	18
18	477	5	12
IN	3,345	35	
TOTAL	**6,395**	**70**	

Laytown and Bettystown offers a wonderfully clean clubhouse with a full bar and dining facilities, along with a well-stocked pro shop. Locker rooms require keyless locks (get the combination in the pro shop).

LEVEL OF MAINTENANCE: The building facilities are maintained to high standards, and the course is adequately maintained. The greens are in good shape and offer a good roll.

COURSE DESCRIPTION: The Laytown and Bettystown Club presents a course that can best be described as a very narrow links course with many appealing features. Unfortunately, the overall feeling is of a municipal course rather than a classic links course. Part of this is because the course sits right across the street from a heavily populated area with a busy thoroughfare, resulting in typical traffic noises. The wind will be to your back as you go out and then in your face as you head in. Greens are decent and the bunkering intelligently placed, with long stretches of sand dune moguls. The bunkers make this course an adequate challenge, and they can definitely penalize the wayward drive. The front 9 holes are situated in appealing dunes, but the back 9 are closer to the crowded road and its noise. This course does not require precision golf but is still a challenge.

UNIQUE FEATURE: This course offers stunning views of the Mourne Mountains and the Irish Sea.

ACCOMMODATION INFORMATION

Standard hotel: Boyne Valley Hotel and Country Club (3 star) (Drogheda), 353 41 37737

Local hotel/guesthouse/B&B: Waterunder Guest House (Drogheda), 353 41 38495

Restaurant/pub: Boyne Valley Hotel Restaurant (see above), 353 41 37737

GREEN FEES:

Moderate

EQUIPMENT RENTAL

Buggies: no
Trolleys: yes
Caddies: no
Clubs: yes

DATE FOUNDED: 1909

ARCHITECT: NA

TYPE: Links

FACILITIES

Clubhouse at turn: no
Restrooms on course: no

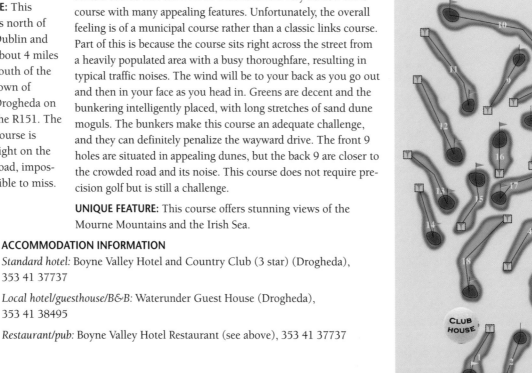

Royal Tara Golf Club

GREEN FEES:
Low

EQUIPMENT RENTAL
Buggies: yes
Trolleys: yes
Caddies: yes
Clubs: yes

DATE FOUNDED: 1923

ARCHITECTS: redesigned in 1960; 18 new holes added by Des Smyth and Associates (1994)

TYPE: Parkland

FACILITIES
Clubhouse at turn: yes
Restrooms on course: no

This member-owned club currently offers a modest clubhouse that is nonetheless fully appointed with a bar and restaurant, along with changing rooms and a well-stocked pro shop. Plans are to build a larger, more modern clubhouse. There are three 9-hole loops from which to choose: the Cluide Nine, the Tara Nine, and the Bellinter Nine.

LEVEL OF MAINTENANCE: This is a very well maintained course with excellent turf and good greens, along with well-cared-for bunkers. The building facilities are clean and presentable.

COURSE DESCRIPTION: Royal Tara is a parkland course with many mature tree stands. In 1994, the members planted an additional two thousand trees, resulting in well-defined fairways; accurate shot making is a must. The strategically bunkered, rolling greens require good work to score well. The River Skane skirts along four of the holes, adding interest and difficulty. Despite its name, there is no "royal" connection with the club aside from its geographical location near the Hill of Tara and its historical roots with Irish kings. The site presents 27 holes for your golfing pleasure.

UNIQUE FEATURE: This course is adjacent to the renowned Hill of Tara, ancient home of various early Irish kings. While in this general vicinity, you might want to check out the spectacular Newgrange Neolithic tomb off the N2. It is just south of Slane, northeast of Navan on the N51.

ACCOMMODATION INFORMATION
Standard hotel: Ardboyne Hotel (Navan), 353 46 23119

Local hotel/guesthouse/B&B: Mountainstown Guesthouse (restored 17th-century house) (Navan), 353 46 54154

Restaurant/pub: Hudson's Bistro (Navan), 353 46 29231

ADDRESS:
Bellinter, Navan,
County Meath,
Ireland

TELEPHONE:
353 46 25508

FAX:
353 46 25508

WEB PAGE: NA

E-MAIL: NA

DIRECTIONS TO COURSE: To find the Royal Tara Golf Club, head south from the town of Navan on the N3 and take the Hill of Tara exit. Go for about 3 miles, and watch for the club's signage.

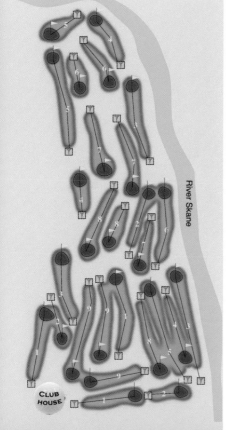

River Skane

CLUB HOUSE

SCORECARD

HOLE	YDG	PAR	INDEX
CLUIDE NINE			
1	473	5	6
2	411	4	2
3	484	5	3
4	296	4	8
5	139	3	9
6	333	4	7
7	437	4	1
8	181	3	5
9	500	5	4
TOTAL	**3,260**	**37**	
TARA NINE			
1	432	4	1
2	172	3	9
3	396	4	3
4	176	3	8
5	513	5	6
6	191	3	7
7	420	4	2
8	377	4	4
9	493	5	5
TOTAL	**3,175**	**35**	

HOLE	YDG	PAR	INDEX
BELLINTER NINE			
1	363	4	8
2	199	3	3
3	514	5	7
4	374	4	4
5	405	4	2
6	305	4	9
7	211	3	5
8	433	4	1
9	380	4	6
TOTAL	**3,189**	**35**	

Nuremore Hotel and Country Club

ADDRESS:
Carrickmacross,
County
Monaghan,
Ireland

TELEPHONE:
353 42 9661438

FAX:
353 42 9661853

WEB PAGE: www.nuremore-hotel.ie

E-MAIL: nuremore@tinet.ie

DIRECTIONS TO COURSE: The club is 1 mile southeast from Carrickmacross on the Dublin Road (N2); follow the signs.

Nuremore epitomizes "resort golf." The pro shop and clubhouse are separate from the hotel complex. All these facilities were built in 1991 or later, and all are in premium condition. The hotel is a full resort, with the usual amenities: masseuse, formal and informal restaurants, leisure complex, etc. The clubhouse offers a bar and grill, complete with beautiful changing rooms and shower facilities.

LEVEL OF MAINTENANCE: This is an extremely well maintained facility; the buildings are luxurious. The course is immaculate, with beautiful greens, well-kept fairways, and interesting traps.

COURSE DESCRIPTION: This parkland course has rolling to hilly terrain, with some great elevation changes. Bunkering is very good, and the greens range from slightly rolling to undulating. Landscaping is beautiful, and many water hazards add challenge to your game. There are some mature tree stands, along with a number of new plantings. Nuremore is laid out very intuitively and has excellent signage, including strokesaver-type information on each tee box.

UNIQUE FEATURE: Views of five counties, including Counties Meath, Cavan, Monaghan, Down, and Armagh.

ACCOMMODATION INFORMATION

Standard hotel: Nuremore Hotel and Country Club (on site), 353 42 9661438

Local hotel/guesthouse/B&B: Cabra Castle Hotel (Kingscourt, County Cavan), 353 42 67030

Restaurant/pub: Fiddler's Elbow (Carrickmacross), 353 43 9663863

GREEN FEES:
Moderate

EQUIPMENT RENTAL
Buggies: yes
Trolleys: yes
Caddies: yes
Clubs: yes

DATE FOUNDED: 1964

ARCHITECT: Eddie Hackett (1991); renovated 1992–1995

TYPE: Parkland

FACILITIES
Clubhouse at turn: yes
Restrooms on course: no

SCORECARD

HOLE	YDG	PAR	INDEX
1	407	4	7
2	482	5	17
3	403	4	1
4	164	3	15
5	402	4	3
6	184	3	9
7	359	4	5
8	357	4	11
9	363	4	13
OUT	3,126	35	
10	335	4	16
11	171	3	12
12	397	4	4
13	382	4	8
14	559	5	6
15	537	5	10
16	135	3	18
17	320	4	14
18	432	4	2
IN	3,272	36	
TOTAL	6,398	71	

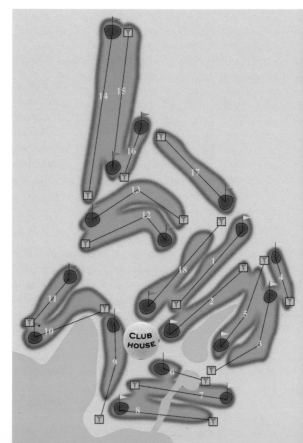

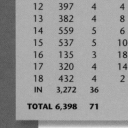

Rossmore Golf Club

GREEN FEES:

Low

EQUIPMENT RENTAL

Buggies: no

Trolleys: yes

Caddies: no

Clubs: no

DATE FOUNDED: 1916

ARCHITECT: Des Smyth (1993)

TYPE: Parkland

FACILITIES

Clubhouse at turn: no

Restrooms on course: no

This course has a very modest clubhouse with a small dining room and bar. There are changing rooms, but no pro shop.

LEVEL OF MAINTENANCE: The building facilities are very clean and well kept. The course reflects this kind of care as well. The bunkering is well tended as are the greens and fairways.

COURSE DESCRIPTION: This course was laid out upon undulating, hilly terrain, resulting in some interesting elevation changes throughout. The bunkering is challenging, and you play in and out of old-growth trees. A number of water hazards add interest, especially on the 11th hole. The course has nice views of the distant hills and is quiet—all lending to a relaxing and enjoyable day of golf. Down the road from this course, south on the R188, is a golf range.

UNIQUE FEATURE: This is a good example of a golf course featuring drumlins (see chapter 9, "Golf and Geology in Ireland").

ACCOMMODATION INFORMATION

Standard hotel: The Four Seasons Hotel (3 star) (Coolshannagh, Monaghan), 353 47 81888

Local hotel/guesthouse/B&B: Lisdaraagh House (next to the course), 353 47 81473

Restaurant/pub: Hillgrove Hotel Restaurant (Monaghan), 353 47 81288

ADDRESS:

Coothill Road,
Monaghan,
County
Monaghan,
Ireland

TELEPHONE:

353 47 81316

FAX: NA

WEB PAGE: NA

E-MAIL: NA

DIRECTIONS TO COURSE: Take the R188 1½ miles south of Monaghan and watch for the course signs.

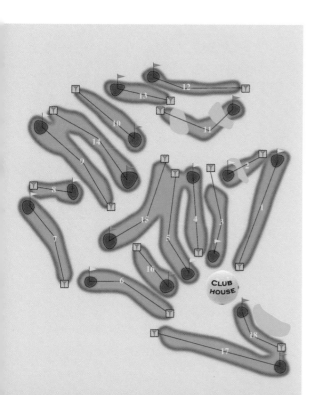

SCORECARD

HOLE	YDG	PAR	INDEX
1	512	5	12
2	171	3	10
3	428	4	5
4	292	4	16
5	421	4	1
6	366	4	8
7	379	4	3
8	122	3	15
9	479	5	18
OUT	3,174	36	
10	337	4	13
11	360	4	6
12	362	4	2
13	128	3	14
14	373	4	7
15	379	4	4
16	174	3	11
17	405	4	9
18	305	4	17
IN	2,828	34	
TOTAL	6,002	70	

Birr Golf Club

ADDRESS:
Glenns, Birr,
County Offaly,
Ireland

TELEPHONE:
353 509 26082

FAX:
353 509 22155

WEB PAGE: NA

E-MAIL: NA

DIRECTIONS TO COURSE: Take R439 west out of Birr for 2 miles. Watch for signs; go about ½ mile down a country lane that looks like a driveway. You will probably see sheep on both sides of the road.

This nice, modern clubhouse has full facilities, including locker rooms, a restaurant and bar, warm, dark wood accents, and a very friendly atmosphere. A well-stocked pro shop, separate driving range, and putting green create an enjoyable first impression.

LEVEL OF MAINTENANCE: Building facilities are clean and well kept. The Birr Club (sometimes referred to as the Glenns) is a first-rate community golf course. All aspects of the course are well maintained, adding to the enjoyment of the round.

COURSE DESCRIPTION: Birr is a relatively short course, with lots of elevation changes. The greens are generally small and gently rolling. While some are elevated, most are not. The course purportedly has sandy subsoil, which allows for good drainage and year-round play. The course has some stands of mature trees and numerous new plantings that will add a great deal of difficulty in years to come. Currently, the major challenges of the course are the elevation changes, some very difficult and long par 3s, and more than a few blind shots.

UNIQUE FEATURE: For a short course, this one has taken its par 3s seriously: one is 185 yards, another 188 yards, yet another 248!

ACCOMMODATION INFORMATION

Standard hotel: County Arms Hotel (Birr), 353 509 20791

Local hotel/guesthouse/B&B: Dooley's Hotel (Birr), 353 509 20032

Restaurant/pub: Riverbank Restaurant (absolutely excellent!) (Riverstown), 353 509 21528

GREEN FEES:
Low

EQUIPMENT RENTAL
Buggies: no
Trolleys: yes
Caddies: no
Clubs: yes

DATE FOUNDED: 1893

ARCHITECT: NA

TYPE: Parkland

FACILITIES
Clubhouse at turn: yes
Restrooms on course: no

SCORECARD

HOLE	YDG	PAR	INDEX
1	342	4	13
2	353	4	5
3	143	3	17
4	356	4	7
5	501	5	15
6	479	5	11
7	399	4	3
8	185	3	9
9	454	4	1
OUT	3,212	36	
10	337	4	14
11	429	4	2
12	391	4	12
13	400	4	4
14	188	3	10
15	248	3	6
16	342	4	16
17	334	4	18
18	436	4	8
IN	3,105	34	
TOTAL	6,317	70	

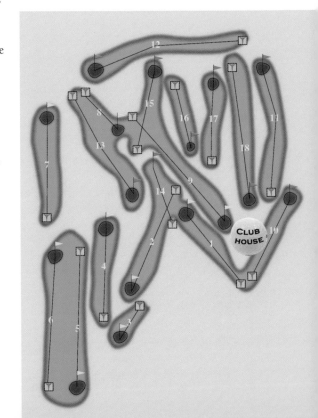

Edenderry Golf Club

GREEN FEES:
Low
EQUIPMENT RENTAL
Buggies: no
Trolleys: yes
Caddies: no
Clubs: yes

DATE FOUNDED: 1910
ARCHITECT: New 9 holes by Eddie Hackett
TYPE: Parkland
FACILITIES
Clubhouse at turn: yes
Restrooms on course: no

Edenderry has a very attractive, if modest, new brick clubhouse with bar and restaurant, along with changing facilities. It also has a putting green and practice ground. The grounds and course are all very well landscaped.

LEVEL OF MAINTENANCE: This municipal course is maintained to good standards.

COURSE DESCRIPTION: Edenderry is a fairly flat parkland course with some mature trees and numerous new plantings. There are well-placed bunkers and a river running along the far reaches of the course. Although it doesn't really come into play, the river does add some visual interest.

UNIQUE FEATURE: This course is purportedly built entirely on fen peat—a form of peat bog composed of grasses, unlike other types of peat bog, which are made of decomposed and compressed ancient trees.

ACCOMMODATION INFORMATION
Standard hotel: Bloomfield House Hotel (Mullingar), 353 44 40894

Local hotel/guesthouse/B&B: Rynella House Bed and Breakfast (Mullingar), 353 44 64137

Restaurant/pub: Galileo's Restaurant (Edenderry), 353 405 32965

ADDRESS:
Kishawanny,
Edenderry,
County Offaly,
Ireland
TELEPHONE:
353 405 31072
FAX: NA
WEB PAGE: NA
E-MAIL: NA
DIRECTIONS TO COURSE: The course is 1 mile north of Edenderry. Go to the town center, and watch for signage. You may need to ask directions, because the signs are difficult to locate.

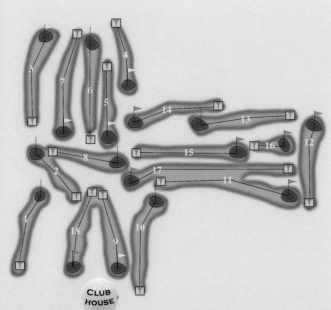

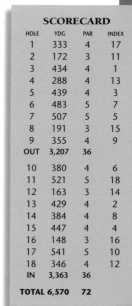

SCORECARD			
HOLE	YDG	PAR	INDEX
1	333	4	17
2	172	3	11
3	434	4	1
4	288	4	13
5	439	4	3
6	483	5	7
7	507	5	5
8	191	3	15
9	355	4	9
OUT	3,207	36	
10	380	4	6
11	521	5	18
12	163	3	14
13	429	4	2
14	384	4	8
15	447	4	4
16	148	3	16
17	541	5	10
18	346	4	12
IN	3,363	36	
TOTAL	6,570	72	

CLUB HOUSE

Esker Hills Golf and Country Club

ADDRESS:
Ballykilmurray,
Tullamore,
County Offaly,
Ireland

TELEPHONE:
353 506 55999

FAX:
353 506 55021

WEB PAGE: NA

E-MAIL: NA

DIRECTIONS TO COURSE: Esker Hills is just off the N80; watch for signs for Clara Road, 3 miles west of Tullamore. Follow the signage to the course.

Esker Hills, as of 1999, offers only temporary clubhouse facilities. Plans are to start building a permanent clubhouse in 2000. At the time of writing, there was a small coffee shop with limited snack food, along with restrooms. A practice area and putting green are also available.

LEVEL OF MAINTENANCE: This is a well-maintained course with good turf and generally well kept transition areas. It is a young course that seems to be developing quite well.

COURSE DESCRIPTION: Esker Hills is a Christy O'Connor Jr. course that displays his usual flair: undulating fairways with excellent bunker placement and always interesting greens. There are a number of challenging doglegs, some practically 90 degrees, and two huge holes (number 3, 490 yards, par 4; and number 17, 450 yards, par 4). Both are deep doglegs. As if that weren't enough, four lakes add to the interest and difficulty of this fine course. The course is generally open, although many trees have been planted that will eventually tighten it and add even more difficulty when they mature. The naturally well draining terrain makes this course playable year-round.

UNIQUE FEATURE: This course is built on top of drumlins and eskers, the humps and ridges of rocky tailings left behind after the glaciers melted some 13,000 years ago. Consequently, the course rests on natural sand and gravel. The high mounds and ridges often define a hole and cause interesting lies if shots aren't carefully played.

ACCOMMODATION INFORMATION

Standard hotel: Tullamore Court Hotel (Tullamore), 353 506 46666

Local hotel/guesthouse/B&B: Moorhill Country House Hotel (Tullamore), 353 506 21395

Restaurant/pub: Phoenix Arms Inn (Tullamore), 353 506 21066

GREEN FEES:
Low

EQUIPMENT RENTAL
Buggies: yes
Trolleys: yes
Caddies: no
Clubs: yes

DATE FOUNDED: 1996

ARCHITECT:
Christy O'Connor Jr.

TYPE: Parkland

FACILITIES
Clubhouse at turn: yes
Restrooms on course: no

SCORECARD

HOLE	YDG	PAR	INDEX
1	493	5	17
2	355	4	11
3	490	4	13
4	393	4	5
5	171	3	15
6	535	5	9
7	428	4	3
8	355	4	13
9	181	3	7
OUT	3,401	36	
10	307	4	18
11	390	4	4
12	396	4	6
13	201	3	16
14	360	4	10
15	191	3	8
16	580	5	14
17	450	4	2
18	393	4	12
IN	3,268	35	
TOTAL	**6,669**	**71**	

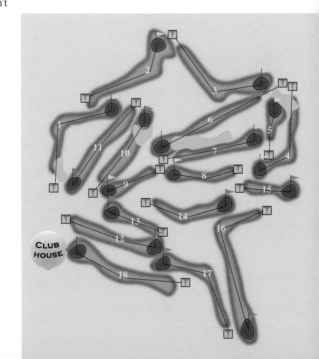

Tullamore Golf Club

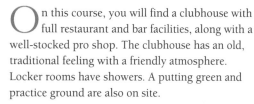

GREEN FEES:
Low

EQUIPMENT RENTAL
Buggies: no
Trolleys: yes
Caddies: yes
Clubs: yes

DATE FOUNDED: 1886

ARCHITECT: Full 18 holes opened in 1926; redesigned by James Braid (1938)

TYPE: Parkland

FACILITIES
Clubhouse at turn: no
Restrooms on course: no

On this course, you will find a clubhouse with full restaurant and bar facilities, along with a well-stocked pro shop. The clubhouse has an old, traditional feeling with a friendly atmosphere. Locker rooms have showers. A putting green and practice ground are also on site.

LEVEL OF MAINTENANCE: This is a very well-maintained course with excellent greens and well-kept bunkers. The building facilities are clean and presentable.

COURSE DESCRIPTION: Tullamore is a well-established parkland course with many stands of mature trees that frequently define the holes. It has a number of water hazards, including a stream that meanders throughout the course, adding both beauty and interest. There is nice bunkering, and while the greens are neatly kept, they are generally flat. In terms of local scenery, the Slieve Bloom Mountains in the background contribute to a lovely golfing experience.

UNIQUE FEATURE: If you're a golf history aficionado, you'll appreciate that the legendary James Braid redesigned this course in 1938.

ACCOMMODATION INFORMATION

Standard hotel: Tullamore Court Hotel (Tullamore), 353 506 46666

Local hotel/guesthouse/B&B: Sea Dew Guesthouse (3 star) (Tullamore), 353 506 52054

Restaurant/pub: Phoenix Arms Inn (Tullamore), 353 506 21066

ADDRESS:
Brookfield,
Tullamore,
County Offaly,
Ireland

TELEPHONE:
353 506 21439

FAX:
353 506 41806

WEB PAGE: NA

E-MAIL: NA

DIRECTIONS TO COURSE: The club is 3 miles south of the town of Tullamore on the N52 (Kinnitty Road). As you head south, the course will be on the right-hand side.

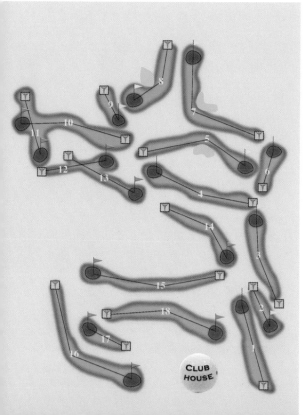

SCORECARD			
HOLE	YDG	PAR	INDEX
1	359	4	17
2	177	3	14
3	429	4	4
4	492	5	6
5	439	4	2
6	189	3	10
7	489	5	12
8	338	4	16
9	148	3	8
OUT	3,060	35	
10	382	4	9
11	325	4	17
12	197	3	11
13	387	4	13
14	474	4	1
15	548	5	7
16	419	4	3
17	184	3	15
18	452	4	5
IN	3,368	35	
TOTAL	6,428	70	

Athlone Golf Club

ADDRESS:
Hodson's Bay,
Athlone, County
Roscommon,
Ireland

TELEPHONE:
353 902 92073

FAX:
353 902 94080

WEB PAGE: NA

E-MAIL: NA

DIRECTIONS TO COURSE: The course is 1 mile outside of Athlone on the N61; watch for signage in Loughrea town.

Athlone has a beautiful clubhouse with rich, dark woods, giving it an opulent old-world feel, and a wonderful view of the course and Lough Ree. It has a bar, full restaurant, and a well stocked pro shop. The club also has a putting green and driving range.

LEVEL OF MAINTENANCE: All the facilities at Athlone are well maintained. The clubhouse locker rooms, for both members and visitors, are clean and spacious. The course also reflects excellent care and is thus a joy to play.

COURSE DESCRIPTION: Athlone is a mature parkland course with many old trees. A number of holes have an out-of-bounds hazard that requires accurately placed tee shots. Greens and turf are well developed, and the course displays intelligent bunkering. The greens are large, generally flat, but some are tiered. Elevation changes over this course provide for some fascinating and challenging shot making, which is no doubt why Athlone has hosted some prestigious tournaments. The three par 5s are short, providing some birdie possibilities. There are beautiful views of Lough Ree and the surrounding countryside.

UNIQUE FEATURE: Ten fairways have out-of-bounds to the right; coupled with the mature trees, they demand accurate shots.

ACCOMMODATION INFORMATION

Standard hotel: Hodson's Bay Hotel (very near the club), 353 902 92444

Local hotel/guesthouse/B&B: Villa St. John, 353 902 92490

Restaurant/pub: Athlone Clubhouse (beautiful!), 353 902 92073

GREEN FEES:
Low

EQUIPMENT RENTAL
Buggies: yes
Trolleys: yes
Caddies: yes
Clubs: yes

DATE FOUNDED: 1892

ARCHITECT: NA

TYPE: Parkland

FACILITIES
Clubhouse at turn: no
Restrooms on course: no

SCORECARD

HOLE	YDG	PAR	INDEX
1	377	4	11
2	165	3	7
3	288	4	15
4	424	4	4
5	548	5	9
6	462	5	17
7	424	4	5
8	436	4	2
9	187	3	13
OUT	3,316	36	
10	385	4	10
11	517	5	12
12	428	4	3
13	355	4	8
14	327	4	16
15	204	3	14
16	444	4	1
17	131	3	18
18	397	4	6
IN	3,193	35	
TOTAL	6,509	71	

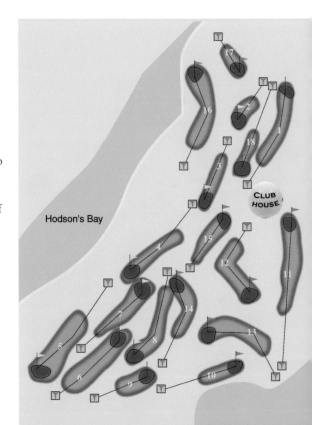

Hodson's Bay

CLUB HOUSE

Roscommon Golf Club

GREEN FEES:
Low

EQUIPMENT RENTAL
Buggies: yes
Trolleys: yes
Caddies: no
Clubs: no

DATE FOUNDED: 1904

ARCHITECT: Extended to 18 holes by Eddie Connaughton (1995)

TYPE: Parkland

FACILITIES
Clubhouse at turn: no
Restrooms on course: no

This is a beautiful clubhouse with lovely facilities, including a wonderful fireplace in the bar. It has a fine restaurant (completed in 1996) and locker rooms but no pro shop. You will also find a putting green and a venerable, huge clock on the course side of the clubhouse.

LEVEL OF MAINTENANCE: This is a very well maintained course; greens, traps, and turf are all in great condition. This course promises an enjoyable round of golf. The building facilities are well kept and beautifully appointed.

COURSE DESCRIPTION: Roscommon is an old 9-hole course that has recently been extended to 18. The two have been nicely integrated, with both 9s having some of the old mature trees and both having a number of new plantings, which will cause a good deal of trouble when they mature. Some well-positioned bunkers and a formidable lake on the 13th hole cause additional challenges. Roscommon is a good course that's fun to play. It has a very intuitive layout. The club intends to add another lake on the par-3 9th hole within a couple of years.

UNIQUE FEATURE: The lake on the 13th hole sits right in front of the green; it's a par-3, 149-yard hole—don't miss the green!

ADDRESS:
Mote Park,
Roscommon,
County
Roscommon,
Ireland

TELEPHONE:
353 903 26382

FAX: NA

WEB PAGE:
golfclubireland.com/Roscommon

E-MAIL: NA

DIRECTIONS TO COURSE:
The course is located on the south side of Roscommon, just outside of town. Watch for good signage. The course is directly off the road; you can't miss it.

ACCOMMODATION INFORMATION

Standard hotel: Abbey Hotel (Roscommon), 353 903 26240

Local hotel/guesthouse/B&B: Gleeson's Restaurant and Guesthouse (Roscommon), 353 903 26954

Restaurant/pub: Restaurant in Abbey Hotel (see above), 353 903 26240

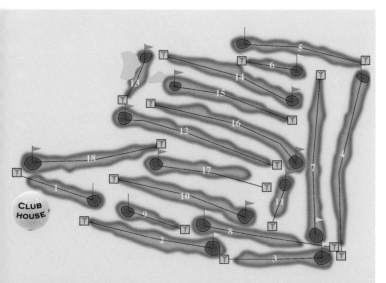

SCORECARD			
HOLE	YDG	PAR	INDEX
1	310	4	17
2	373	4	7
3	337	4	13
4	521	5	15
5	408	4	4
6	169	3	10
7	463	4	5
8	462	4	3
9	186	3	12
OUT	3,236	35	
10	440	4	1
11	135	3	18
12	507	5	16
13	149	3	11
14	437	4	6
15	401	4	8
16	519	5	9
17	358	4	14
18	418	4	2
IN	3,368	36	
TOTAL	**6,604**	**71**	

County Sligo Golf Club

ADDRESS:
Rosses Point, County Sligo, Ireland

TELEPHONE:
353 71 77186

FAX:
353 71 77460

WEB PAGE: NA

E-MAIL: cosligo@iol.ie

DIRECTIONS TO COURSE: The course is in Rosses Point, just west of the town of Sligo on the R291. Watch for good signage to the course.

The County Sligo clubhouse exudes history in a classic and venerable style. The club has a fully stocked pro shop, a full-service bar, and an elegant restaurant. There are locker rooms with showers and, throughout, a friendly and knowledgeable staff.

LEVEL OF MAINTENANCE: All aspects of this course are maintained to excellent standards. The bunkering is some of the best you will find in Ireland. Signage is consistent and good.

COURSE DESCRIPTION: County Sligo is a treat to play and a test for any golfer. The strategically placed bunkering on all holes, particularly the first three, is enough to make playing this course worthwhile. The quality and challenge continue throughout the entire course, though the extraordinary panoramic views peak at the start. The scenic vistas include the twelve "Bens" (mountains), Drumcliff Bay, and a majestic lighthouse. County Sligo is a classic links course in its length and layout (no facilities at the turn). Signage is very helpful on this already good, intuitive layout. As you might guess on a links course, some holes are strenuous and demanding. The play on this course is links all the way—hard, fast, and away you go!

UNIQUE FEATURE: This course has some of the most dramatic and panoramic views you will see in Ireland, especially on hole 2.

ACCOMMODATION INFORMATION

Standard hotel: Yeats Country Hotel Golf and Leisure Club (3 star) (right across from the golf course), 353 71 77211

Local hotel/guesthouse/B&B: Ballincar House Hotel and Restaurant (Rosses Point), 353 71 45361

Restaurant/pub: The Thatch Restaurant (Ballysodare), 353 71 67288

GREEN FEES:
Moderate

EQUIPMENT RENTAL
Buggies: yes
Trolleys: yes
Caddies: yes
Clubs: yes

DATE FOUNDED: 1894

ARCHITECT:
Harry S. Colt

TYPE: Links

FACILITIES
Clubhouse at turn: no
Restrooms on course: no

SCORECARD

HOLE	YDG	PAR	INDEX
1	378	4	8
2	308	4	11
3	497	5	15
4	163	3	12
5	477	5	17
6	412	4	6
7	428	4	1
8	407	4	5
9	166	3	13
OUT	3,236	36	
10	351	4	10
11	401	4	3
12	529	5	14
13	176	3	18
14	429	4	4
15	399	4	7
16	213	3	16
17	451	4	2
18	366	4	9
IN	3,350	35	
TOTAL	**6,586**	**71**	

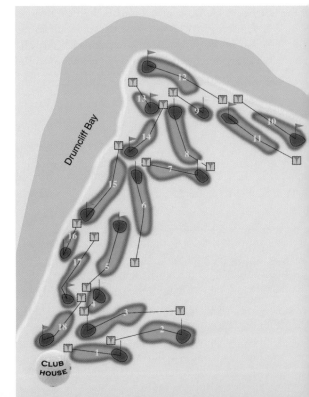

Enniscrone (Inniscrone) Golf Club

GREEN FEES:
Moderate

EQUIPMENT RENTAL
Buggies: yes
Trolleys: yes
Caddies: yes
Clubs: yes

DATE FOUNDED: 1918

ARCHITECT: Expanded to 18 holes by Eddie Hackett (1971); clubhouse built in 1989 and expanded in 1996

TYPE: Links

FACILITIES
Clubhouse at turn: no
Restrooms on course: no

Enniscrone offers a top-notch clubhouse with very friendly staff. It has a well-stocked pro shop, a practice area and putting green, a bar and full restaurant, and locker rooms.

LEVEL OF MAINTENANCE: This course is beautifully maintained, all the way from the fairways and greens to the immaculate and inviting clubhouse. Excellent maintenance and attention to detail are clearly emphasized.

COURSE DESCRIPTION: Enniscrone is a classic links course on natural dunes. It offers a full spectrum of links golf: thick rough, plenty of sand dunes, fast greens, and close proximity to the ocean. The first 7 holes fall along relatively flat landscape but have well-defined bunkers. By the 8th hole, you are well into the dunes, with backdrops of the Ox Mountains. Holes 17 and 18 overlook Killala Bay and the Atlantic. This course is a must-see/must-play venue; it's first-rate in all aspects. It offers challenging decisions for the good golfer but is fair for the average player as well. It offers an interesting layout, and the intelligent bunker placement requires careful planning by the golfer. A decision was made in 1998 to add 9 more holes in the duneland, with play estimated by 2003.

UNIQUE FEATURE: Hole 14 offers a spectacular panoramic view of the Atlantic Ocean and surrounding terrain.

ACCOMMODATION INFORMATION
Standard hotel: Castle Arms Hotel (Enniscrone), 353 96 36156

Local hotel/guesthouse/B&B: Ceol Na Mara Guesthouse (3 star) (Enniscrone), 353 96 36351

Restaurant/pub: Walsh's Restaurant and Pub (Enniscrone), 353 96 36110

ADDRESS:
Enniscrone,
County
Sligo, Ireland

TELEPHONE:
353 96 36297

FAX:
353 96 36657

WEB PAGE: NA

E-MAIL: enniscronegolf@kinet.ie

DIRECTIONS TO COURSE: The course is just off the R297, south of the town of Enniscrone (Inniscrone on some maps).

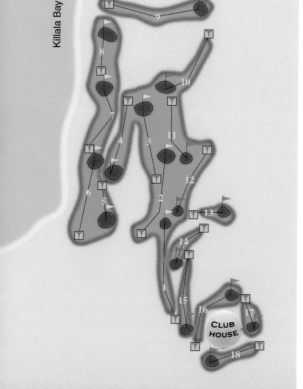

Killala Bay

SCORECARD			
HOLE	YDG	PAR	INDEX
1	551	5	9
2	535	5	11
3	395	4	2
4	534	5	13
5	170	3	17
6	395	4	5
7	374	4	7
8	170	3	15
9	345	4	4
OUT	3,469	37	
10	350	4	14
11	427	4	1
12	540	5	12
13	202	3	8
14	368	4	16
15	412	4	6
16	403	4	3
17	149	3	18
18	400	4	10
IN	3,251	35	
TOTAL 6,720		72	

Strandhill Golf Club

ADDRESS:
Strandhill,
County Sligo,
Ireland

TELEPHONE:
353 71 68188

FAX:
353 71 68811

WEB PAGE: NA

E-MAIL: NA

DIRECTIONS TO COURSE: This course is just outside the village of Strandhill on the R292, which is about 5 miles west of the town of Sligo.

The Strandhill Club offers a very attractive and clean clubhouse. It includes a modestly stocked pro shop, a bar and restaurant, and changing rooms for members and guests. Be aware that credit cards are not accepted for green fees, but they are accepted in the bar and restaurant.

LEVEL OF MAINTENANCE: The course itself is adequately maintained, but the signage is shabby despite being informative.

COURSE DESCRIPTION: Strandhill is one of the Irish courses redesigned to 18 holes by the prolific golf designer Eddie Hackett. The tract of land upon which it lays is truly beautiful duneland, ideal for a links course. Given these extraordinary surroundings, however, the course itself falls somewhat short of its promise. There are some outright dangerous holes, based on tee and green locations, so be warned. A shot from the 4th tee could hit someone on the 3rd green, for example. You get the impression that the course design is too large for this small amount of land. Some of the greens are severely undulating and in places a little rough. There are great views of the Knocknarea Mountains, the famous Benbulben, and the Atlantic Ocean. With more land and a modern design, Strandhill could be quite a venue.

UNIQUE FEATURE: Some of the greens are severely undulating, adding interest and challenge.

ACCOMMODATION INFORMATION

Standard hotel: Ocean View Hotel (3 star) (Strandhill), 353 71 68115

Local hotel/guesthouse/B&B: The Strand House Bar and Restaurant (Strandhill), 353 71 68140

Restaurant/pub: The Roof Top Restaurant (Strandhill), 353 71 44421

GREEN FEES:
Moderate

EQUIPMENT RENTAL
Buggies: no
Trolleys: yes
Caddies: yes
Clubs: yes

DATE FOUNDED: 1931

ARCHITECT: Redesigned to 18 holes by Eddie Hackett

TYPE: Links

FACILITIES
Clubhouse at turn: no
Restrooms on course: no

SCORECARD

HOLE	YDG	PAR	INDEX
1	421	5	13
2	142	3	17
3	337	4	11
4	310	4	9
5	460	5	1
6	338	4	5
7	370	4	3
8	306	4	7
9	180	3	15
OUT	2,871	36	
10	291	4	12
11	313	4	8
12	255	4	14
13	320	4	2
14	141	3	18
15	294	4	4
16	394	5	10
17	163	3	16
18	408	5	6
IN	2,586	36	
TOTAL	**5,457**	**72**	

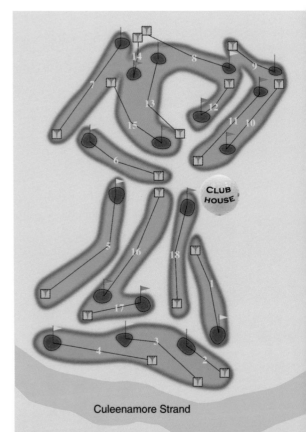

Culeenamore Strand

Ballykisteen Golf and Country Club

GREEN FEES:
Low
EQUIPMENT RENTAL
Buggies: no
Trolleys: yes
Caddies: yes
Clubs: no

DATE FOUNDED: 1995
ARCHITECT: Des Smyth
TYPE: Parkland
FACILITIES
Clubhouse at turn: yes
Restrooms on course: no

The Ballykisteen course is located on what used to be a horse stud farm. Along with the brand-new clubhouse (built in a mansion style), the stables give the facility a stately air. The clubhouse has a full complement of services, including full bar and restaurant, lockers with showers, and a small pro shop. Also on site are a well-constructed driving range and putting green.

LEVEL OF MAINTENANCE: The course and its facilities are extremely well maintained. The greens are excellent, and the bunkers well kept. The facilities are further enhanced by attractive flower beds and plantings, all well tended.

COURSE DESCRIPTION: Although this course is relatively new, the turf development and greens are wonderful. There are many stands of mature trees and even more new plantings. It is a somewhat long course, with several strong par 4s. A number of water hazards complete the challenge of this course. All in all, Ballykisteen is well designed and quite enjoyable. It is well worth the effort to search out, made all the more so by an extremely warm and friendly staff.

UNIQUE FEATURE: The stables and ambience of the old horse farm make this a true Irish Experience.

ACCOMMODATION INFORMATION
Standard hotel: The Royal Hotel (Tipperary), 353 62 33244
Local hotel/guesthouse/B&B: The Ballykisteen Lodge, 353 62 33403
Restaurant/pub: Derby Bar and Restaurant (on site), 353 62 33770

ADDRESS:
Monard, County
Tipperary, Ireland
TELEPHONE:
353 62 33333
FAX:
353 62 33668
WEB PAGE: NA
E-MAIL: NA
DIRECTIONS TO COURSE: The course is just off the N24, northwest of the city of Tipperary. Watch for the signage.

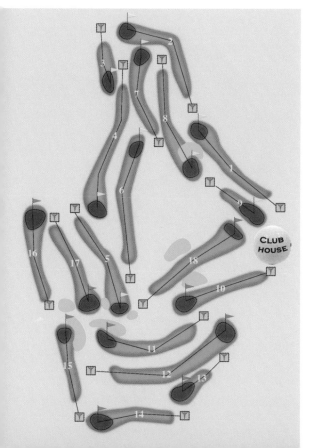

SCORECARD			
HOLE	YDG	PAR	INDEX
1	371	4	6
2	446	4	2
3	171	3	18
4	534	5	18
5	395	4	10
6	513	5	12
7	394	4	14
8	335	4	4
9	170	3	16
OUT	3,329	36	
10	415	4	1
11	417	4	3
12	509	5	15
13	169	3	13
14	394	4	11
15	226	3	7
16	389	4	17
17	371	4	5
18	546	5	9
IN	3,436	36	
TOTAL 6,765		72	

County Tipperary Golf Club

ADDRESS:
Dundrum,
Cashel, County
Tipperary,
Ireland

TELEPHONE:
353 62 71116

FAX:
353 62 71366

WEB PAGE: NA

E-MAIL: NA

DIRECTIONS TO COURSE: The course is just north of the town of Dundrum on the R661. Turn east at the Dundrum House Hotel, and watch for the course's large iron gates.

County Tipperary course, located on the estate grounds of an 18th-century manor house, has recently undergone extensive expansion. The club has a large putting green and driving range. The grounds are stately and expansive, with lovely flower gardens and plantings.

LEVEL OF MAINTENANCE: This course is very well maintained, including its fairways and greens; the bunkers are excellent, as is the turf.

COURSE DESCRIPTION: This is a fairly long parkland course. Two massive par 4s and one 562-yard par 5 present a real challenge for a long hitter. A number of water hazards add to the challenge, as does the River Multeen that snakes throughout this lovely sylvan course. County Tipperary boasts many stands of mature trees, along with a number of new plantings. In addition, there are some very interesting elevation changes—all in all, a good test for any golfer.

UNIQUE FEATURE: This is quite the Irish Experience course, with the grounds of an 18th-century manor and estate, and great golf.

ACCOMMODATION INFORMATION

Standard hotel: Dundrum House Hotel (3 star) (on site), 353 62 71116

Local hotel/guesthouse/B&B: The Rectory House Hotel (3 star) (Dundrum), 353 62 71266

Restaurant/pub: Dundrum House Hotel Restaurant (see above), 353 62 71116

GREEN FEES:
Moderate

EQUIPMENT RENTAL
Buggies: no
Trolleys: yes
Caddies: yes
Clubs: yes

DATE FOUNDED: 1993

ARCHITECT:
Philip Walton

TYPE: Parkland

FACILITIES
Clubhouse at turn: yes
Restrooms on course: no

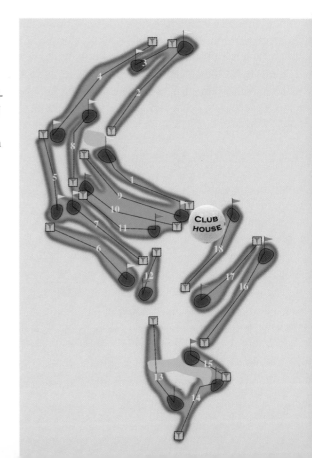

SCORECARD

HOLE	YDG	PAR	INDEX
1	432	4	3
2	510	5	7
3	168	3	17
4	562	5	5
5	342	4	15
6	366	4	11
7	357	4	13
8	378	4	9
9	470	4	1
OUT	3,607	37	
10	385	4	6
11	372	4	16
12	195	3	4
13	360	4	14
14	321	4	8
15	178	3	12
16	508	5	18
17	339	4	10
18	444	4	2
IN	3,102	35	
TOTAL	6,709	72	

Roscrea Golf Club

GREEN FEES:
Low

EQUIPMENT RENTAL
Buggies: no
Trolleys: yes
Caddies: no
Clubs: no

DATE FOUNDED: 1893

ARCHITECT: Arthur Spring

TYPE: Parkland

FACILITIES
Clubhouse at turn: no
Restrooms on course: no

The Roscrea Club is a mature parkland course with an older municipal-style clubhouse that includes a nice bar and restaurant. It does not have a pro shop or practice range, but there is a putting green.

LEVEL OF MAINTENANCE: While Roscrea offers rather old buildings, they are nonetheless well maintained. As for the course itself, it is, on the whole, adequately maintained; the greens are good, as are the few bunkers.

COURSE DESCRIPTION: Roscrea is an older parkland course with stands of mature trees and a sprinkling of new plantings. It is fairly wide open, with some rolling hills. The 5th hole, known locally as the Burma Road, is over 500 yards in length, with out-of-bounds down the left side. Beautiful old, huge trees line both sides of the fairway.

UNIQUE FEATURE: This club has an interesting variety of par-3 holes, especially the 4th, which, at 163 yards, is played over a lake.

ACCOMMODATION INFORMATION
Standard hotel: Racket Hall Country House Hotel (Roscrea), 353 505 21748

Local hotel/guesthouse/B&B: Tower Guesthouse (3 star) (Roscrea), 353 505 21774

Restaurant/pub: Riverbank Restaurant (excellent cuisine) (Riverstown), 353 509 21528

ADDRESS:
Derryvale,
Roscrea,
County
Tipperary,
Ireland

TELEPHONE:
353 505 21130

FAX:
353 505 23410

WEB PAGE: NA

E-MAIL: NA

DIRECTIONS TO COURSE:
The club is east of Roscrea town on the N7 (Dublin/Limerick Road). Watch for signs. The club is visible on the left side of the road.

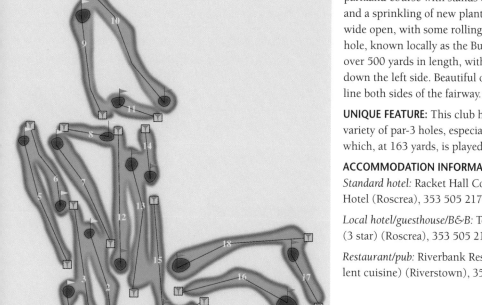

SCORECARD

HOLE	YDG	PAR	INDEX
1	296	4	18
2	496	5	14
3	403	4	6
4	163	3	10
5	513	5	8
6	339	4	12
7	404	4	4
8	148	3	16
9	421	4	2
OUT	3,188	36	
10	478	5	11
11	175	3	15
12	487	5	13
13	443	4	1
14	171	3	17
15	417	4	3
16	365	4	9
17	211	3	5
18	363	4	7
IN	3,114	35	
TOTAL	**6,302**	**71**	

Thurles Golf Club

ADDRESS:
Turtulla,
Thurles, County
Tipperary,
Ireland

TELEPHONE:
353 504 22466

FAX:
353 504 24647

WEB PAGE: NA

E-MAIL: NA

DIRECTIONS TO COURSE: Thurles Club is about 1 mile south of Thurles town on the R660 (Cork Road). Turn onto Horse and Jockey Road and watch for signage.

Thurles (pronounced "Turles") is an old club with a lovely, venerable clubhouse steeped in history. It has a full restaurant and bar, along with locker rooms and a well-stocked pro shop. The restaurant has a wonderful menu from which to select, with attentive and friendly service. The club also has a driving range and putting green. And, if you are so inclined, there are two championship squash courts.

LEVEL OF MAINTENANCE: All aspects of this course, from building facilities to the course itself, are top-notch and well maintained.

COURSE DESCRIPTION: Thurles is a mature parkland course set upon former estate grounds with generally flat but sometimes rolling terrain. The fairways are wide and lined with many mature trees and bushes, making for a punishing rough. There are several doglegs, four par 3s, and a very tight finishing hole. Thurles is a relatively long course at 6,465 yards. The first half is divided from the second by a road. Despite this, the whole tract has an old estate feel. The greens are very good, as is the turf throughout the course. Additionally, intelligent and well-placed bunkering make this course a joy to play and a challenge for any skill level.

UNIQUE FEATURE: This challenging and beautiful course starts out with two par 5s, 488 and 479 yards, respectively.

ACCOMMODATION INFORMATION

Standard hotel: Anner Hotel and Conference Centre (3 star) (Thurles), 353 504 21799

Local hotel/guesthouse/B&B: Inch House (historic guesthouse) (Thurles), 353 504 51348

Restaurant/pub: Thurles Clubhouse, 353 504 22466

GREEN FEES:
Low

EQUIPMENT RENTAL
Buggies: no
Trolleys: yes
Caddies: yes
Clubs: yes

DATE FOUNDED: 1909

ARCHITECT: Redesigned by Lionel Hewson (1944)

TYPE: Parkland

FACILITIES
Clubhouse at turn: yes
Restrooms on course: no

SCORECARD

HOLE	YDG	PAR	INDEX
1	488	5	6
2	479	5	16
3	338	4	10
4	396	4	4
5	115	3	18
6	414	4	2
7	305	4	14
8	194	3	12
9	389	4	8
OUT	3,118	36	
10	419	4	1
11	212	3	9
12	360	4	5
13	534	5	11
14	181	3	17
15	352	4	13
16	370	4	7
17	421	4	3
18	498	5	15
IN	3,347	36	
TOTAL	**6,465**	**72**	

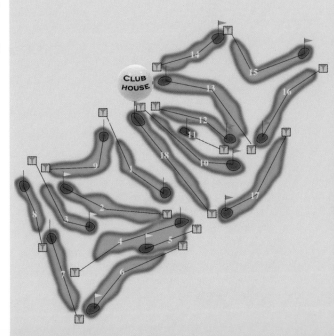

Dungarvan Golf Club

GREEN FEES:
Low
EQUIPMENT RENTAL
Buggies: yes
Trolleys: yes
Caddies: no
Clubs: yes

DATE FOUNDED: 1924
ARCHITECT: Maurice Fives (1993)
TYPE: Parkland
FACILITIES
Clubhouse at turn: yes
Restrooms on course: no

Oungarvan greets you with a very upscale, traditional, and friendly clubhouse. Inside you will find a gracious and elegant bar and a full restaurant, along with spacious locker rooms. A small but well-supplied pro shop has an adjacent practice range and putting green.

LEVEL OF MAINTENANCE: This club is extremely well maintained, from the immaculate clubhouse to the course itself. The fairways, greens, and traps are all in wonderful condition, attesting to a club that takes its maintenance seriously.

COURSE DESCRIPTION: Dungarvan is a beautiful rolling parkland course with a backdrop of the picturesque Comeragh Mountains and Dungarvan Bay. This is a truly championship course with nine water hazards, numerous well-designed traps, and grass mounds that are plentiful, well designed, and carefully built. The course is currently fairly open, but many new plantings, when mature, will make it very difficult. Tee boxes are wonderfully large, and all in all, the course is simply a treat to play. The views are lovely, and one gets a sense of being in a deeply rural setting. On a historical note, the original site for this club (founded in 1924) is the present location of the Gold Coast Golf Club's first 9 holes.

UNIQUE FEATURE: This course features numerous well-placed artificial hazards, sure to challenge the golfer at any level.

ACCOMMODATION INFORMATION
Standard hotel: Park Hotel (3 star) (Dungarvan), 353 58 42899

Local hotel/guesthouse/B&B: Lawlors Hotel (3 star) (Dungarvan), 353 58 41122

Restaurant/pub: Dungarvan Clubhouse, or restaurants at either of the hotels listed (see above)

ADDRESS:
Knocknagranagh,
Dungarvan,
County
Waterford,
Ireland

TELEPHONE:
353 58 43310

FAX:
353 58 44113

WEB PAGE: NA

E-MAIL:
dungarvangolf@cablesurf.com

DIRECTIONS TO COURSE:
Go 2 miles east of Dungarvan town, on the N25 to Waterford and Rosslare. Signage will direct you to the course.

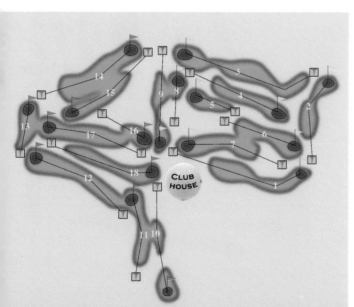

SCORECARD			
HOLE	YDG	PAR	INDEX
1	494	5	17
2	374	4	7
3	540	5	13
4	401	4	3
5	205	3	15
6	395	4	11
7	417	4	1
8	208	3	5
9	382	4	9
OUT	3,421	36	
10	393	4	8
11	383	4	4
12	507	5	10
13	139	3	18
14	462	4	2
15	361	4	16
16	173	3	12
17	416	4	6
18	501	5	14
IN	3,340	36	
TOTAL	6,761	72	

Dunmore East Golf Club

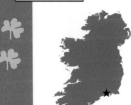

ADDRESS:
Dunmore East,
County
Waterford,
Ireland

TELEPHONE:
353 51 383151

FAX:
353 51 383151

WEB PAGE: NA

E-MAIL: NA

DIRECTIONS TO COURSE: Take the R684 from Waterford town to Dunmore East; follow the signs. The course overlooks the town and is approached by a rough, rocky road.

Dunmore East offers a very modest clubhouse without a pro shop. A small bar and grill serves snacks.

LEVEL OF MAINTENANCE: This municipal course is kept tidy.

COURSE DESCRIPTION: Dunmore East is a wide-open parkland course with few bunkers and great views of Tranmore Bay. Five of the holes skirt the water's edge, making for some lovely views. The 14th hole is a 196-yard par 3, with a dramatic drop from tee to green. Tranmore Bay is directly behind the green.

UNIQUE FEATURE: The 14th hole is visually spectacular.

ACCOMMODATION INFORMATION
Standard hotel: Haven Hotel (Dunmore East), 353 51 383150

Local hotel/guesthouse/B&B: Ocean Hotel (Dunmore East), 353 51 383136

Restaurant/pub: Jade Palace Restaurant (Dunmore East), 353 51 855611

GREEN FEES:
Low

EQUIPMENT RENTAL
Buggies: one
Trolleys: yes
Caddies: no
Clubs: no

DATE FOUNDED: 1993

ARCHITECT:
William Henry Jones

TYPE: Parkland

FACILITIES
Clubhouse at turn: no
Restrooms on course: no

SCORECARD

HOLE	YDG	PAR	INDEX
1	319	4	15
2	324	4	17
3	523	5	13
4	424	4	7
5	372	4	1
6	468	4	5
7	174	3	11
8	418	4	3
9	425	4	9
OUT	3,452	36	
10	480	5	10
11	392	4	4
12	503	5	16
13	577	5	6
14	196	3	8
15	431	4	2
16	99	3	18
17	329	4	14
18	141	3	12
IN	3,152	36	
TOTAL	6,604	72	

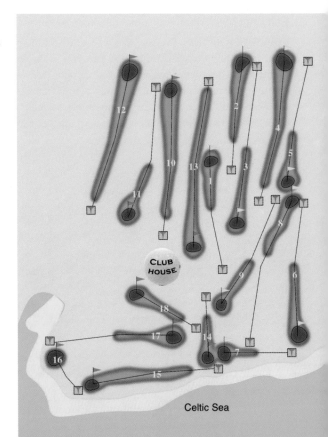

Celtic Sea

Faithlegg Golf Club

GREEN FEES:
Low
EQUIPMENT RENTAL
Buggies: yes
Trolleys: yes
Caddies: yes
Clubs: yes

DATE FOUNDED: 1993
ARCHITECT:
Patrick Merrigan
TYPE: Parkland
FACILITIES
Clubhouse at turn: no
Restrooms on course: no

Faithlegg Golf Club is located on an 18th-century estate. The mansion, which has been beautifully maintained and extensively restored, is a backdrop to the course. The club has a practice ground and putting green. The clubhouse is actually a remodeled coach house, with its own full bar and restaurant, locker rooms, and well-stocked pro shop. Faithlegg Hotel is a 4-star resort with a wide variety of amenities amid a restful, bucolic setting.

ADDRESS:
Faithlegg House,
Faithlegg, County
Waterford,
Ireland

TELEPHONE:
353 51 382241

FAX:
353 51 382664

WEB PAGE: NA

E-MAIL: NA

LEVEL OF MAINTENANCE: As one would expect with such a top-notch facility, the course and clubhouse are maintained to top standards.

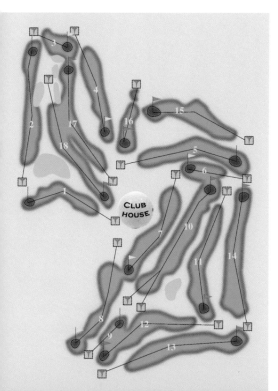

COURSE DESCRIPTION: This course is a championship-length course with many human-made and natural hazards. The course terrain is rolling; the greens are undulating and sometimes wicked. Water hazards and traps seem to come in bunches. There are many mature stands of trees and a number of new plantings. The 18th hole is a long par 4 that presents numerous problems along its dogleg. The challenges on the 18th don't end at the green. Once there, you still have to negotiate a vast two-tiered affair. Good fun! This excellent parkland facility is to be thoroughly enjoyed for its design, overall features, and attention to detail.

UNIQUE FEATURE: Faithlegg House dates to the year 1171, during the reign of King Henry II. This extraordinary piece of history surrounds you while you walk and play this lovely course.

ACCOMMODATION INFORMATION
Standard hotel: Faithlegg House Hotel (on site), 353 51 382241

Local hotel/guesthouse/B&B: Three Rivers Guesthouse (Cheekpoint), 353 51 382520

Restaurant/pub: Faithlegg House Hotel Restaurant (see above), 353 51 382241

DIRECTIONS TO COURSE: From Waterford town, take the Dunmore East Road to Cheekpoint village. The course is about 6 miles east of Waterford.

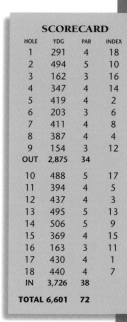

SCORECARD			
HOLE	YDG	PAR	INDEX
1	291	4	18
2	494	5	10
3	162	3	16
4	347	4	14
5	419	4	2
6	203	3	6
7	411	4	8
8	387	4	4
9	154	3	12
OUT	2,875	34	
10	488	5	17
11	394	4	5
12	437	4	3
13	495	5	13
14	506	5	9
15	369	4	15
16	163	3	11
17	430	4	1
18	440	4	7
IN	3,726	38	
TOTAL 6,601		72	

Gold Coast Golf Club

ADDRESS:
Ballinacourty,
Dungarvan,
County
Waterford,
Ireland

TELEPHONE:
353 58 44055

FAX: 353 58 42880

WEB PAGE:
www.amireland.com/clonea

E-MAIL:
clonea@
indigo.ie

**DIRECTIONS
TO COURSE:**
The club is
located 3
miles east of
the town of
Dungarvan
on the Coast
Road; watch
for good
signage.

SCORECARD

HOLE	YDG	PAR	INDEX
1	353	4	10
2	347	4	8
3	496	5	16
4	179	3	14
5	413	4	2
6	489	5	12
7	163	3	18
8	190	3	4
9	377	4	6
OUT	3,012	35	
10	436	4	3
11	367	4	17
12	384	4	11
13	369	4	15
14	214	3	9
15	393	4	5
16	523	5	13
17	468	4	1
18	555	5	7
IN	3,713	37	
TOTAL	**6,725**	**72**	

This course is associated with a large hotel complex. The hotel has the full complement of facilities, including a range of recreational and leisure options. These facilities are separate from the golf course. The course itself has its own pro shop, complete with changing rooms, and a practice range and putting green.

LEVEL OF MAINTENANCE: The Gold Coast Golf Club is a well-maintained course with good turf development and greens. It has quite a few well-placed and tended bunkers. All the club's building facilities are quite presentable, and the associated hotel's facilities are top-notch.

COURSE DESCRIPTION: The Gold Coast Golf Club was developed as two separate 9s. The older 9 holes (originally the Dungarvan Golf Course, founded in 1924) have a number of well-established stands of mature trees; the newer 9 are more open, with many new plantings. This course is bordered on three sides by Dungarvan Bay and the Celtic Sea. Consequently, in addition to the Comeragh Mountains in the background, there are some wonderful vistas. All these factors make this course interesting and fun to play.

UNIQUE FEATURE: The player is always in close proximity to views of water, either of Dungarvan Bay or the Celtic Sea. The course also has its own lighthouse just off the green of the 9th hole.

ACCOMMODATION INFORMATION

Standard hotel: Gold Coast Golf Hotel and Leisure Centre (3 star) (on site), 353 58 42249

Local hotel/guesthouse/B&B: Park Hotel (3 star) (Dungarvan), 353 58 42899

Restaurant/pub: Restaurants in either of the hotels listed (see above)

GREEN FEES:
Low

EQUIPMENT RENTAL
Buggies: yes
Trolleys: yes
Caddies: no
Clubs: yes

DATE FOUNDED: 1993

ARCHITECT: First 9 holes laid out in 1924; extended to 18 holes by Maurice Fives (1996)

TYPE: Parkland

FACILITIES
Clubhouse at turn: no
Restrooms on course: no

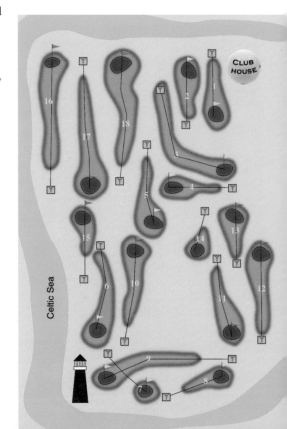

Tramore Golf Club

GREEN FEES:
Moderate

EQUIPMENT RENTAL
Buggies: no
Trolleys: yes
Caddies: yes
Clubs: yes

DATE FOUNDED: 1894

ARCHITECT: Redesigned and relocated by H. C. Tippett (1939)

TYPE: Parkland

FACILITIES
Clubhouse at turn: no
Restrooms on course: no

Tramore provides an older, traditional clubhouse, with a bar, restaurant facilities, and changing rooms. A separate pro shop is well stocked, and there are two practice areas, complete with a putting green.

LEVEL OF MAINTENANCE: This is a well-maintained course. The turf and greens are first-rate. The bunkering is well tended, but there is not much of it throughout the course. The building facilities are clean and pleasant.

COURSE DESCRIPTION: The Tramore Club is built on rolling terrain with many large, mature tree stands. The trees, however, do not define the course—indeed, it's generally an open course. The greens provide excellent putting surfaces, undulating only slightly. The tees are deep and therefore healthy. The course is noted for its 4th hole, a severe dogleg right, which calls for two long carries over gorse and very rough ground. This course is fun to play and one where you are likely to shoot your handicap. Take some time to savor the views of the Comeragh Mountains from the clubhouse.

UNIQUE FEATURE: The putting surfaces of this course are about as good as you'll find anywhere.

ACCOMMODATION INFORMATION

Standard hotel: Majestic Hotel (3 star) (Tramore), 353 51 381761

Local hotel/guesthouse/B&B: O'Shea's Hotel (3 star) (Tramore), 353 51 381246

Restaurant/pub: Seahorse Restaurant (Tramore), 353 51 386091

ADDRESS:
Newtown Hill,
Tramore, County
Waterford,
Ireland

TELEPHONE:
353 51 386170

FAX:
353 51 390961

WEB PAGE: NA

E-MAIL: tragolf@iol.ie

DIRECTIONS TO COURSE: The Tramore Golf Club is ½ mile west of Tramore town on the R675 (Dungarvan Coast Road). Watch for course signs on the right-hand side of the road.

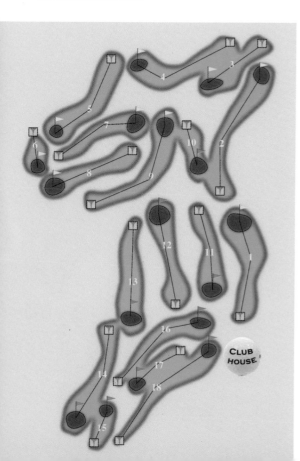

SCORECARD			
HOLE	YDG	PAR	INDEX
1	397	4	6
2	495	5	15
3	168	3	11
4	374	4	3
5	320	4	12
6	173	3	17
7	399	4	8
8	404	4	2
9	551	5	13
OUT	3,287	36	
10	189	3	16
11	398	4	4
12	343	4	10
13	398	4	7
14	442	4	1
15	127	3	18
16	545	5	9
17	377	4	5
18	489	5	14
IN	3,312	36	
TOTAL	6,599	72	

Waterford Castle Golf and Country Club

ADDRESS: The Island, Ballinakill, Waterford, County Waterford, Ireland

TELEPHONE: 353 51 871633

FAX: 353 51 871634

WEB PAGE: NA

E-MAIL: golf@waterfordcastle.com, or wcgolf@ici.ie

DIRECTIONS TO COURSE: This club is 2 miles east of Waterford city on the main road to Dunmore (R684). Go through the Regional Hospital roundabout, take the 4th turn to the left, and follow signs to the car ferry.

SCORECARD

HOLE	YDG	PAR	INDEX
1	419	4	7
2	191	3	17
3	405	4	3
4	387	4	5
5	518	5	15
6	367	4	11
7	210	3	9
8	492	5	13
9	415	4	1
OUT	3,409	36	
10	174	3	4
11	377	4	6
12	452	4	2
13	504	5	12
14	373	4	10
15	510	5	14
16	203	3	8
17	401	4	4
18	384	4	16
IN	3,382	36	
TOTAL	**6,791**	**72**	

The club has a modest clubhouse with a bar and limited snack foods. A heated swimming pool and tennis court are next to the clubhouse. You will find a full restaurant at Waterford Castle Tower Hotel, just down the road. On site are a putting green, driving range, and a small, modestly stocked pro shop.

LEVEL OF MAINTENANCE: This course is very well maintained and has a resort feel. Sand-based greens and tees make for year-round playability. The bunkering is superb and well tended.

COURSE DESCRIPTION: This parkland course has an utterly unique location: an island in an estuary of the River Suir, accessed by the course's own private ferry (free), with transport on demand during the summer. The 310 acres comprising this course were originally owned by the Fitzgerald family, ancestors of Strongbow. Since these were former estate grounds, there are stands of mature trees along with areas of more recent plantings. This championship-standard course is long and has many interesting and challenging hazards, including four artificial lakes. The layout is intuitive and promises a very enjoyable day of golf in a truly unusual setting.

UNIQUE FEATURE: This is Ireland's only golf course on an island accessible by private ferry.

ACCOMMODATION INFORMATION

Standard hotel: Waterford Castle Tower Hotel (5 star) (The Island), 353 51 878203

Local hotel/guesthouse/B&B: The Woodlands Hotel (Waterford), 353 51 304574

Restaurant/pub: The Old Strand Steak and Seafood Restaurant (Waterford), 353 51 879488

GREEN FEES: Moderate

EQUIPMENT RENTAL
Buggies: yes
Trolleys: yes
Caddies: yes
Clubs: yes

DATE FOUNDED: 1992

ARCHITECT: Des Smyth

TYPE: Parkland

FACILITIES
Clubhouse at turn: yes
Restrooms on course: no

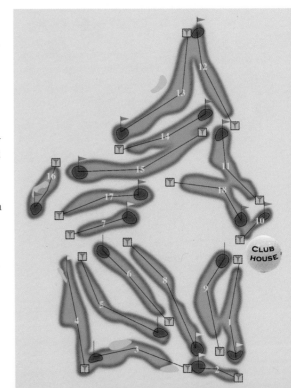

West Waterford Golf and Country Club

GREEN FEES:
Moderate
EQUIPMENT RENTAL
Buggies: yes
Trolleys: yes
Caddies: no
Clubs: yes

DATE FOUNDED: 1993
ARCHITECT: Eddie Hackett
TYPE: Parkland
FACILITIES
Clubhouse at turn: yes
Restrooms on course: no

West Waterford provides a lovely clubhouse, complete with full bar and restaurant, changing rooms, and a small but adequate pro shop. It has a putting green and practice range.

LEVEL OF MAINTENANCE: This facility is very well maintained, with excellent greens, good turf, and well-tended bunkers. The building is modern and very clean.

ADDRESS:
Coolcormack,
Dungarvan,
County
Waterford,
Ireland
TELEPHONE:
353 58 43216
FAX:
353 58 44343
WEB PAGE: NA
E-MAIL: NA
DIRECTIONS TO COURSE:
This club is located about 3 miles west of the town of Dungarvan on the N25. Turn onto Aglish Road, and the course is on the left-hand side.

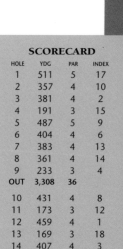

COURSE DESCRIPTION: This is an interesting parkland course with many new tree plantings that will provide quite a challenge when they mature. The 150 acres of former farmland upon which this course is built are rolling, with well-placed bunkering, making for interesting play. The holes around the Brickey River often have sightings of wildfowl, and the surrounding Comeragh Mountains and Knockmealdown Mountains offer gorgeous views. There are also many drumlins (see chapter 9, "Golf and Geology in Ireland"), making this course playable all year, with good natural drainage. Water hazards are a feature of this course, with the Brickey River coming into play on the 12th, 14th, 15th, and 16th holes.

UNIQUE FEATURE: This course is definitely an Irish Experience, with views of nearby patchwork fields, rolling farmlands, and mountains.

ACCOMMODATION INFORMATION
Standard hotel: Park Hotel (3 star) (Dungarvan), 353 58 42899

Local hotel/guesthouse/B&B: Failte House (guesthouse) (Dungarvan), 353 58 44170

Restaurant/pub: Mill Restaurant (Dungarvan), 353 58 45488

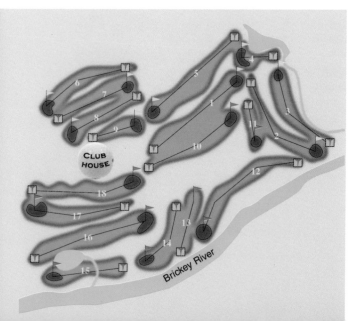

SCORECARD			
HOLE	YDG	PAR	INDEX
1	511	5	17
2	357	4	10
3	381	4	2
4	191	3	15
5	487	5	9
6	404	4	6
7	383	4	13
8	361	4	14
9	233	3	4
OUT	3,308	36	
10	431	4	8
11	173	3	12
12	459	4	1
13	169	3	18
14	407	4	3
15	333	4	11
16	523	5	16
17	424	4	5
18	575	5	7
IN	3,494	36	
TOTAL	6,802	72	

Glasson Golf and Country Club

ADDRESS:
Glasson,
Athlone, County
Westmeath,
Ireland

TELEPHONE:
353 902 85120

FAX:
353 902 85444

WEB PAGE: NA

E-MAIL: glasgolf@iol.ie

DIRECTIONS TO COURSE: Glasson is 6 miles north of the town of Athlone on the N55. Turn left at the Glasson Village Restaurant. The course is then about 1½ miles down a narrow road. Watch for good signage to the course.

Glasson boasts an exquisite clubhouse with a well-stocked pro shop and very friendly and helpful staff. The clubhouse includes a bar and spacious restaurant located within a notable 18th-century Georgian manor (Killinure House). All of this is part of a family estate.

LEVEL OF MAINTENANCE: The course and buildings are all very well maintained. The greens, traps, and fairways are of the highest standard, with excellent signage.

COURSE DESCRIPTION: This is an exceptionally well designed course situated on the Killinure Bay of Lough Ree, a large inland lake that connects to the River Shannon. Glasson has a lovely combination of mature trees and new plantings. A number of interesting elevation changes make the course a true challenge. Some creative green locations are near water's edge, some precariously placed on hillsides. The greens, generally undulating, are in excellent condition. The best is saved for last; the back tee on the 14th hole is placed on very high ground, offering splendid views of Killinure Bay. The course's length adds difficulty to an already challenging tract.

UNIQUE FEATURE: All 18 holes provide views of Lough Ree or Killinure Bay.

ACCOMMODATION INFORMATION
Standard hotel: Castledaly Manor Hotel (Castledaly), 353 902 81221

Local hotel/guesthouse/B&B: The Villa Bed and Breakfast (Glasson), 353 902 85277

Restaurant/pub: The Dog and Duck Bar (between Glasson and Athlone), 353 902 75797

GREEN FEES:
Moderate

EQUIPMENT RENTAL
Buggies: yes
Trolleys: yes
Caddies: yes
Clubs: yes

DATE FOUNDED: 1993

ARCHITECT:
Christy O'Connor Jr.

TYPE: Parkland

FACILITIES
Clubhouse at turn: no
Restrooms on course: no

SCORECARD

HOLE	YDG	PAR	INDEX
1	396	4	15
2	552	5	7
3	219	3	5
4	406	4	9
5	199	3	17
6	559	5	13
7	410	4	1
8	432	4	11
9	412	4	3
OUT	3,585	36	
10	513	5	18
11	183	3	14
12	406	4	16
13	397	4	6
14	566	5	12
15	185	3	8
16	452	4	4
17	450	4	2
18	383	4	10
IN	3,535	36	
TOTAL	7,120	72	

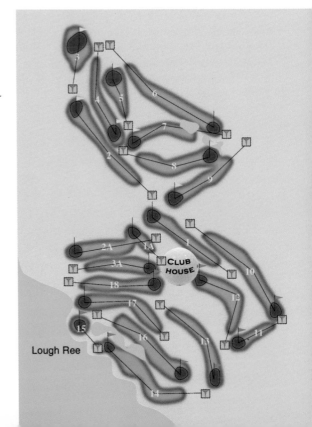

CLUB HOUSE

Lough Ree

Mount Temple Golf Club

GREEN FEES:
Low

EQUIPMENT RENTAL
Buggies: yes
Trolleys: yes
Caddies: no
Clubs: yes

DATE FOUNDED: 1991

ARCHITECT: Michael Dolan (owner and designer)

TYPE: Parkland

FACILITIES
Clubhouse at turn: yes
Restrooms on course: no

This is an estate course. The clubhouse is the former residence; the changing rooms are the former barn; and under the benches can be seen the old grain feed bins—all beautifully restored. This has clearly been the owner's labor of love. There is a practice range for short irons and wedges, complete with practice bunker and putting green. A modest but charming bar and dining facility offer several delightful seating areas.

LEVEL OF MAINTENANCE: Mount Temple is quaint, quaint, quaint, as well as clean and neat. The course is well maintained and a joy to play. Some really nice landscaping will add to your enjoyment.

COURSE DESCRIPTION: This course is located in a little farming village among eskers and generally rolling terrain. A pleasant little stream meanders through the course, and stands of mature trees intermingle with new plantings and some interesting bunkering. Some very challenging holes include the 16th—Heartbreak Hill, a 493-yard par 5, dogleg right, with a pond near the highly elevated green—a real monster. This course teems with history: old stone walls, ring forts, an old well, and a 14th-century abbey dripping with local lore. There are also remarkable views of up to 50 miles.

UNIQUE FEATURE: This course purportedly lies on unaltered terrain. The owners claim that they followed the "traditional" method of simply laying out the fairways and greens, then cutting them as they lay. The result, a natural-looking course with excellent drainage, is playable all year.

ACCOMMODATION INFORMATION
Standard hotel: Bloomfield House Hotel and Leisure Club (3 star) (Mullingar), 353 44 40894

Local hotel/guesthouse/B&B: Crookedwood House (4-star guesthouse) (Mullingar), 353 44 72165

Restaurant/pub: Egan's Pub (Mt. Temple), 353 902 281282

ADDRESS:
Mt. Temple Village, Moate, County Westmeath, Ireland

TELEPHONE:
353 902 81841

FAX:
353 902 81957

WEB PAGE: NA

E-MAIL: mttemple@iol.ie

DIRECTIONS TO COURSE:
The course is just north of Mt. Temple village; watch for signage. (The nearby town's name is pronounced "Mote.")

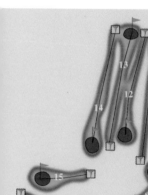

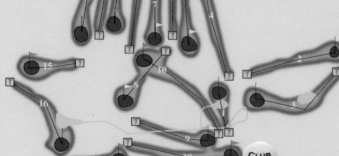

CLUB HOUSE

SCORECARD			
HOLE	YDG	PAR	INDEX
1	175	3	17
2	355	4	12
3	379	4	4
4	473	5	14
5	396	4	6
6	349	4	13
7	381	4	3
8	199	3	8
9	313	4	16
OUT	3,024	35	
10	432	4	1
11	498	5	15
12	405	4	5
13	433	4	2
14	395	4	7
15	128	3	18
16	493	5	9
17	155	3	11
18	490	5	10
IN	3,435	37	
TOTAL 6,459		72	

Mullingar Golf Club

ADDRESS:
Belvedere,
Mullingar,
County
Westmeath,
Ireland

TELEPHONE:
353 44 48366

FAX:
353 44 41499

WEB PAGE: NA

E-MAIL: NA

DIRECTIONS TO COURSE:
Mullingar Golf Club is located on the N52 South, about 3½ miles south of the town of Mullingar.

Mullingar offers a new and lovely clubhouse, with a separate, well-appointed pro shop, a practice green, and practice range. The clubhouse includes a full bar and restaurant facilities, along with changing rooms. The staff and members are very friendly and helpful.

LEVEL OF MAINTENANCE: This club clearly puts a premium on providing a very well maintained course, grounds, and building facilities. The greens are lovely, the traps carefully kept, and the fairways thick. The club has recently enlarged a number of the bunkers as well as the tees.

COURSE DESCRIPTION: Mullingar is a great parkland course with wonderful greens and well-positioned bunkers. One can immediately see why it is the site for some of Ireland's most noteworthy matches, including the 72-Hole Scratch Cups and the All Ireland Father and Son competitions. This course offers spectacular grounds and challenging golf. There are majestic stands of old-growth trees (beech and oak), flowering bushes (pink thorn and rhododendron), and a stream through the middle of the course—all contributing to a great golfing experience. As you look over your putt, beware the very subtle breaks; they can be score breakers.

UNIQUE FEATURE: Watch for the 2nd hole, a par 3 with 189 yards; it demands precision shooting off the tee onto an elevated green. If you are a golf history buff, note that this course was designed by the legendary James Braid.

ACCOMMODATION INFORMATION

Standard hotel: Bloomfield House Hotel and Leisure Club (3 star) (Mullingar), 353 44 40894

Local hotel/guesthouse/B&B: Crookedwood House (4-star guesthouse) (Mullingar), 353 44 72165

Restaurant/pub: Crookedwood House (see above), 353 44 72165

GREEN FEES:
Moderate

EQUIPMENT RENTAL
Buggies: yes
Trolleys: yes
Caddies: yes
Clubs: yes

DATE FOUNDED: 1894

ARCHITECT:
James Braid (1937)

TYPE: Parkland

FACILITIES
Clubhouse at turn: yes
Restrooms on course: no

SCORECARD

HOLE	YDG	PAR	INDEX
1	338	4	10
2	189	3	7
3	389	4	4
4	486	5	14
5	186	3	12
6	330	4	18
7	453	4	1
8	343	4	6
9	338	4	15
OUT	3,062	35	
10	433	4	2
11	388	4	9
12	152	3	16
13	370	4	5
14	480	5	17
15	162	3	13
16	493	5	8
17	417	4	3
18	511	5	11
IN	3,406	37	
TOTAL	**6,468**	**72**	

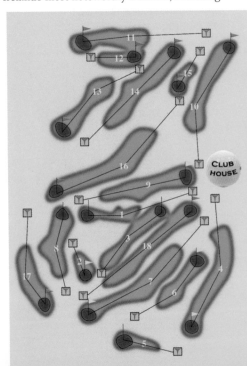

CLUB HOUSE

Enniscorthy Golf Club

GREEN FEES:
Low
EQUIPMENT RENTAL
Buggies: yes
Trolleys: yes
Caddies: no
Clubs: yes

DATE FOUNDED: 1908
ARCHITECT: Eddie Hackett
TYPE: Parkland
FACILITIES
Clubhouse at turn: no
Restrooms on course: no

*T*his club has the usual bar and grill/restaurant and a pro shop—all modest but adequate. It also has a putting green and practice area. Plans are to renovate the clubhouse and redesign some of the course. Check with the club regarding the status of the course for play.

LEVEL OF MAINTENANCE: Enniscorthy is a well-maintained municipal-type course. The greens are in good shape, and the bunkers well tended; building facilities are clean and fully functional.

COURSE DESCRIPTION: This parkland course has hilly terrain, gently rolling greens, and modest bunkering. Some great old stands of trees create difficulty and add beauty. This course lays out sometimes in an odd fashion—be careful, or follow someone who knows the course. The four par 3s are relatively long and testing.

UNIQUE FEATURE: The differential between the front and back 9s is odd in that the back is 400 yards longer.

ACCOMMODATION INFORMATION
Standard hotel: Riverside Park Hotel (3 star) (Enniscorthy), 353 54 37800

Local hotel/guesthouse/B&B: Murphy Flood's Hotel (Enniscorthy), 353 54 33413

Restaurant/pub: Millhouse Bar (part of Riverside Park Hotel), 353 54 378004

ADDRESS:
Knockmarshal,
Enniscorthy,
County
Wexford, Ireland
TELEPHONE:
353 54 33191
FAX:
353 54 37637
WEB PAGE: NA
E-MAIL: NA
DIRECTIONS TO COURSE: The course is 2 miles west of Enniscorthy town, on the N30 (the New Ross Road). Watch for signage to the course.

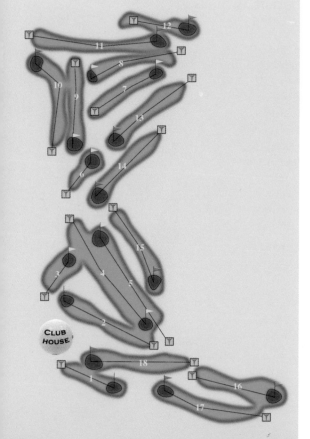

SCORECARD			
HOLE	YDG	PAR	INDEX
1	180	3	14
2	383	4	6
3	142	3	18
4	531	5	12
5	510	5	8
6	193	3	10
7	421	4	4
8	395	4	2
9	362	4	16
OUT	3,123	35	
10	527	5	9
11	551	5	17
12	179	3	15
13	373	4	7
14	381	4	5
15	438	4	1
16	342	4	13
17	399	4	3
18	346	4	11
IN	3,541	37	
TOTAL	6,664	72	

Rosslare Golf Club

ADDRESS:
Rosslare Strand,
Rosslare,
County
Wexford, Ireland

TELEPHONE:
353 53 32203

FAX:
353 53 32203

WEB PAGE: NA

E-MAIL: rgolfclb@iol.ie

DIRECTIONS TO COURSE: Off the N25, take the R740 to Rosslare and watch for signs.

SCORECARD

HOLE	YDG	PAR	INDEX
1	362	4	9
2	184	3	7
3	518	5	17
4	373	4	11
5	443	4	2
6	335	4	16
7	554	5	6
8	177	3	10
9	399	4	3
OUT	3,345	36	
10	167	3	13
11	469	4	1
12	472	5	15
13	282	4	8
14	160	3	14
15	403	4	12
16	377	4	4
17	420	4	5
18	482	5	18
IN	3,232	36	
TOTAL	**6,577**	**72**	

Rosslare Club, at the time of review, was under significant construction. It has a practice ground and putting green.

LEVEL OF MAINTENANCE: Because the clubhouse was under construction, the maintenance of the building facilities cannot be commented upon. The maintenance of the course, however, was woeful. Other than mowing, there seemed to be little attempt to do much of anything. The fairways were often indistinguishable from the rough; the divots were as plentiful as the wildflowers. The greens were not much better.

COURSE DESCRIPTION: Rosslare is a classic links with the "in-and-out" style. If you wanted to be generous, you could think of this course as the opportunity to play a bit of history, by virtue of its notable designers (Hawtree and Taylor), and by virtue of its approximation of original conditions (i.e., with very little maintenance). One could pretend that these are almost the exact conditions under which our forebears played: the putts were lined up with a daisy, you sometimes had to call up to get the greens mowed, and rabbit scrapes littered the fairways. Hawtree and Taylor did a nice job of laying out a maximum number of holes along the seaside. Thus, one can amble up and take a break from the devastation of the fairways to look over the seawalls and see the fine, clean, sandy beaches of the Irish Sea.

UNIQUE FEATURE: Despite the maintenance problems with this course, the sense of history is strong.

ACCOMMODATION INFORMATION

Standard hotel: Kelly's Resort Hotel (Rosslare), 353 53 32114

Local hotel/guesthouse/B&B: Churchtown House (4-star guesthouse; quite a treat) (in the village of Tagoat, just outside Rosslare), 353 53 32555

Restaurant/pub: La Marine Bistro in Kelly's Resort Hotel (see above), 353 53 32114

GREEN FEES:
Moderate

EQUIPMENT RENTAL
Buggies: no
Trolleys: yes
Caddies: yes
Clubs: yes

DATE FOUNDED: 1905

ARCHITECTS: First 18 holes by Frederick G. Hawtree and John Henry Taylor; 9 holes designed and added to the layout by Christy O' Connor Jr. (1992)

TYPE: Links

FACILITIES
Clubhouse at turn: no
Restrooms on course: no

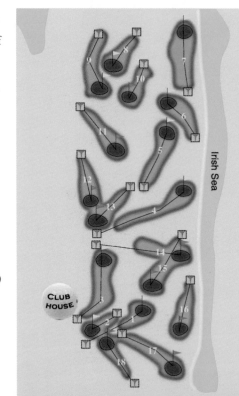

St. Helen's Bay Golf and Country Club

GREEN FEES:
Low

EQUIPMENT RENTAL
Buggies: yes
Trolleys: yes
Caddies: yes
Clubs: yes

DATE FOUNDED: 1993

ARCHITECT:
Philip Walton

TYPE: Links/Parkland

FACILITIES
Clubhouse at turn: yes
Restrooms on course: no

The clubhouse at St. Helen's underwent some renovation in 1999. It has a bar and full restaurant facilities, along with changing rooms and showers. The club also has a separate pro shop and a practice green. This operation has a number of self-catering cottages; call the course for details.

LEVEL OF MAINTENANCE: St. Helen's is a well-maintained course that has clean and inviting facilities. The greens, fairways, and bunkers are also kept in good condition.

COURSE DESCRIPTION: This is a mostly parkland course, but the final four holes are links holes. There are large tees, slightly rolling greens, and decent bunkering. Some of the traps, however, are nothing more than string bunkers. The course is wide open and not very interesting until it gets near the sea with the links holes—then, it changes dramatically. There are great views of the Irish Sea and other cliff-type vistas. The four par 3s on the course are all long and challenging. Indeed, the length of this course is its primary challenge.

UNIQUE FEATURE: Numerous palm trees are planted throughout this course. Ireland, amazingly, can grow palms, although they rarely get over 6 feet in height.

ACCOMMODATION INFORMATION

Standard hotel: Tuskar House Hotel (3 star) (Rosslare Harbour), 353 53 33363

Local hotel/guesthouse/B&B: Churchtown House (4-star guesthouse; a real treat) (Tagoat, just outside Rosslare Harbour), 353 53 32555

Restaurant/pub: Lobster Pot (Rosslare Harbour), 353 53 31110

ADDRESS:
Kilrane, Rosslare Harbour, County Wexford, Ireland

TELEPHONE:
353 53 33234

FAX:
353 53 33803

WEB PAGE: NA

E-MAIL: sthelens@iol.ie

DIRECTIONS TO COURSE: Start with the N25 to Rosslare Harbour and take the second turn right at the new school in Kilrane village; follow the St. Helen's Bay signs.

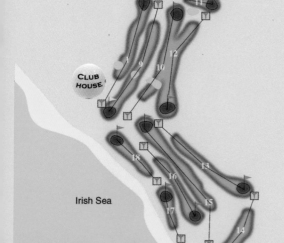

CLUB HOUSE

Irish Sea

SCORECARD			
HOLE	YDG	PAR	INDEX
1	446	5	17
2	412	4	6
3	209	3	10
4	313	4	18
5	332	4	8
6	335	4	16
7	179	3	13
8	449	4	2
9	521	5	7
OUT	3,201	36	
10	531	5	4
11	190	3	12
12	442	4	1
13	456	4	5
14	325	4	14
15	618	5	9
16	401	4	11
17	209	3	3
18	261	4	15
IN	3,437	36	
TOTAL 6,638		72	

Arklow Golf Club

ADDRESS:
Abbeylands,
Arklow, County
Wicklow,
Ireland

TELEPHONE:
353 402 32492

FAX: NA

WEB PAGE: NA

E-MAIL: NA

DIRECTIONS TO COURSE: Go to the town center of Arklow, and head just outside of town on the seacoast road. The course cannot be missed.

Arklow has recently renovated its clubhouse, bar, dining facilities, and changing rooms. A small putting green is just outside the clubhouse.

LEVEL OF MAINTENANCE: This is a well-maintained natural linksland course with a completely renovated clubhouse.

COURSE DESCRIPTION: This classic linksland course has all the "goodies": sand hills, marram grass, sand traps, gorse, and occasional crisscrossing holes. Arklow is a fairly short links course, so if you can guide your ball in the wind, you ought to score well here. If not, come to enjoy the linksland, the views, and the camaraderie.

UNIQUE FEATURE: A couple of streams meander through the course and eventually drain into Arklow Bay. They add even more interest to an already interesting layout.

ACCOMMODATION INFORMATION

Standard hotel: Arklow Bay Hotel (Arklow),
353 402 32309

Local hotel/guesthouse/B&B: Ostan Beag Hotel (Arklow),
353 402 33044

Restaurant/pub: Brook House Lounge (telephone number not available)

GREEN FEES:
Low

EQUIPMENT RENTAL
Buggies: yes
Trolleys: yes
Caddies: yes
Clubs: yes

DATE FOUNDED: 1927

ARCHITECTS: Frederick G. Hawtree and John Henry Taylor

TYPE: Links

FACILITIES
Clubhouse at turn: no
Restrooms on course: no

SCORECARD

HOLE	YDG	PAR	INDEX
1	403	4	7
2	376	4	6
3	163	3	15
4	328	4	11
5	429	4	2
6	412	4	3
7	138	3	18
8	298	4	13
9	184	3	9
OUT	2,734	33	
10	403	4	8
11	158	3	17
12	379	4	5
13	184	3	10
14	370	4	12
15	304	4	16
16	418	4	4
17	468	4	1
18	501	5	14
IN	3,188	35	
TOTAL	5,922	68	

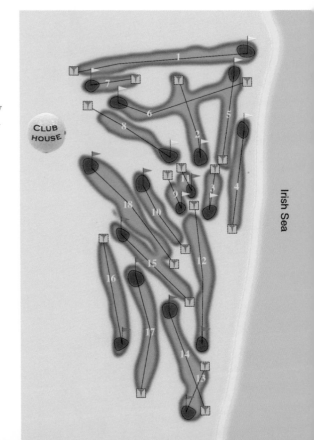

Blainroe Golf Club

GREEN FEES: Moderate (visitors can book primarily on Tuesdays and Thursdays)

EQUIPMENT RENTAL
Buggies: yes
Trolleys: yes
Caddies: yes
Clubs: yes

DATE FOUNDED: 1978

ARCHITECT: Charles Hawtree

TYPE: Seaside

FACILITIES
Clubhouse at turn: yes
Restrooms on course: no

This course has the standard clubhouse with full amenities, including bar and restaurant, locker rooms, and small, modestly stocked pro shop. There is a putting green.

LEVEL OF MAINTENANCE: This is a beautifully landscaped course from the moment you drive into it, carrying on throughout the course itself. It has extremely well maintained bunkers, and the greens are well tended. The facilities are clean and orderly.

COURSE DESCRIPTION: Blainroe is a gently rolling seaside parkland course with great sand bunkers, testing greens, and some good stands of mature trees and evergreens. The course has great signage, especially on the tees, and some of the views are breathtaking. The 14th hole is played from the cliff peninsula, for example. A small stream and lake add further elements of interest. Given its length, this can be a very challenging course. The management suggests that booking well ahead is necessary, as this is primarily a members' course with few visitors' times.

UNIQUE FEATURE: The course's seaside proximity and views of the Irish Sea make for a delightful visual experience.

ACCOMMODATION INFORMATION
Standard hotel: Blainroe Hotel (directly across the street), 353 404 67500

Local hotel/guesthouse/B&B: Old Rectory Country House and Restaurant (Wicklow town), 353 404 67048

Restaurant/pub: Blainroe Hotel restaurant facilities (see above), 353 404 67500

ADDRESS:
Blainroe, County Wicklow, Ireland

TELEPHONE:
353 404 68168

FAX:
353 404 69369

WEB PAGE: NA

E-MAIL: NA

DIRECTIONS TO COURSE: The course is 4 miles south of the town of Wicklow on the Dunbur Road.

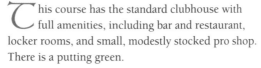

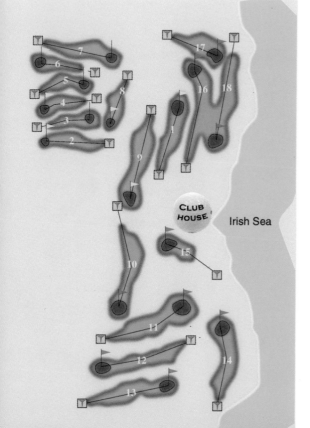

CLUB HOUSE

Irish Sea

SCORECARD

HOLE	YDG	PAR	INDEX
1	360	4	7
2	427	4	1
3	418	4	5
4	524	5	11
5	483	5	15
6	369	4	3
7	367	4	9
8	209	3	13
9	365	4	17
OUT	3,526	37	
10	378	4	6
11	382	4	12
12	427	4	4
13	394	4	10
14	330	4	14
15	227	3	8
16	455	4	2
17	120	3	18
18	487	5	16
IN	3,204	35	
TOTAL	**6,730**	**72**	

Druids Glen Golf Club

ADDRESS:
Newtown-mountkennedy, County Wicklow, Ireland

TELEPHONE:
353 1 287 3600

FAX:
353 1 287 3699

WEB PAGE: www.druidsglen.ie

E-MAIL: druids@indigo.ie

DIRECTIONS TO COURSE: Take the N11 to the Newtown-mount-kennedy exit; follow the ample and clearly marked signage to the course.

Druids Glen clubhouse (Woodstock House) and facilities could only be described as opulent, historic, and extremely posh. Everything you need is provided on site, even a practice area with three full-length holes.

LEVEL OF MAINTENANCE: Nothing is spared and nothing is left to your imagination. Suffice it to say, the Murphy's Irish Open was held here one year after the club's opening (1995) and has continued to be held here since.

COURSE DESCRIPTION: Druids Glen, a parkland course located on slightly hilly terrain, has an extensive new planting design complemented beautifully by the old existing trees. The liberally distributed water hazards and bunkers make this a challenging test of golf even before one factors in the prodigious length. The landscaping rivals Augusta's. Indeed, many of the holes hint of the best holes on other renowned courses, so do not be surprised by an occasional déjà vu. Druids Glen is more beautiful than it is Irish. This is an extremely busy course, so come prepared to play for a number of hours.

UNIQUE FEATURE: The stone bridges on this course are magnificent, as is the profuse and well-manicured landscaping.

ACCOMMODATION INFORMATION

Standard hotel: Ballyknocken House Farmhouse (Gleanealy, near Ashford, County Wicklow), 353 404 44627

Local hotel/guesthouse/B&B: The Chester Beatty Inn and Restaurant (Ashford), 353 404 40206

Restaurant/pub: The Sun Terrace, the Yellow Room, or the Spike Grill and Bar (clubhouse options), 353 1 287 3600

GREEN FEES: High (book well in advance)

EQUIPMENT RENTAL
Buggies: yes
Trolleys: yes (electric)
Caddies: yes
Clubs: yes

DATE FOUNDED: 1995

ARCHITECTS: Pat Ruddy and Tom Craddock

TYPE: Parkland

FACILITIES
Clubhouse at turn: yes
Restrooms on course: no

SCORECARD			
HOLE	YDG	PAR	INDEX
1	445	4	4
2	190	3	8
3	339	4	16
4	446	4	7
5	517	5	17
6	476	4	2
7	405	4	6
8	166	3	11
9	389	4	15
OUT	3,373	35	
10	440	4	10
11	522	5	13
12	174	3	12
13	471	4	1
14	399	4	14
15	456	4	9
16	538	5	18
17	203	3	5
18	450	4	3
IN	3,653	36	
TOTAL	**7,026**	**71**	

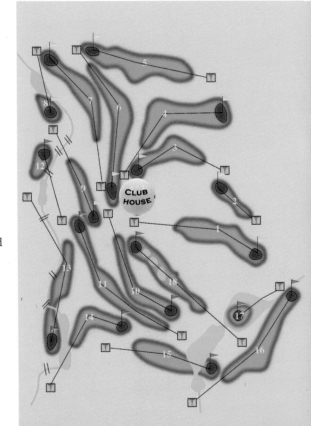

The European Club

GREEN FEES:
Moderate

EQUIPMENT RENTAL
Buggies: no
Trolleys: yes
Caddies: no
Clubs: no

DATE FOUNDED: 1987

ARCHITECT:
Pat Ruddy

TYPE: Links

FACILITIES
Clubhouse at turn: yes
Restrooms on course: no

This club has a modest clubhouse with a bar and dining room facilities, along with changing rooms. The owner/architect's philosophy is telling: "Our approach to golf is fundamentalist… you will not find fussy furniture on our links."

LEVEL OF MAINTENANCE: Consistent with this minimalist philosophy, this course is not fussed over or prissy, but it is well cared for and eminently playable. The greens and bunkers are in very good shape, and the building facilities are clean but not scrubbed. As Mr. Ruddy explains, "You might take it to be spartan, while we think it is akin to the way the game was in the beginning and as it should be now."

COURSE DESCRIPTION: The European Club is a beautiful linksland course. The rough is high, the gorse punishing, and the fairways wide. The greens are spacious, rolling, cropped short, and offer devilish breaks. The traps are intelligently placed and lined with railroad ties, except for the occasional pot bunker. Pat Ruddy claims that this style of bunkering is also a reminder of the early days. The holes near the ocean are so naturally laid out that you feel as though you are playing right on the beach. On this classic links course, you may be surprised to find water hazards on the 6th, 7th, 9th, and 18th holes. This course is evolving toward perfection.

UNIQUE FEATURE: Three holes are played along the beach, without impediments such as fences or walls.

ACCOMMODATION INFORMATION
Standard hotel: Tinakilly Country House and Restaurant (4 star) (Rathnew, near Wicklow), 353 404 69274

Local hotel/guesthouse/B&B: Gormanstown Manor Farm Guesthouse (near Brittas Bay; call for directions), 353 404 69432

Restaurant/pub: Jack White's Inn (Brittas Bay), 353 404 47106

ADDRESS: Brittas Bay, Wicklow, Ireland

TELEPHONE:
353 404 47415

FAX:
353 404 47449

WEB PAGE: NA

E-MAIL: NA

DIRECTIONS TO COURSE: Take Brittas Bay exit off the N11. Follow good signage for the course, and look carefully for the gates just off the road.

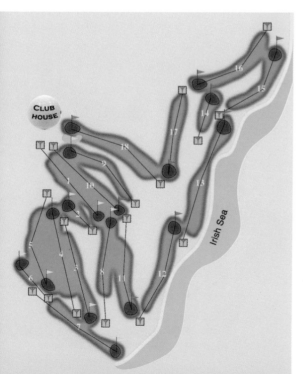

SCORECARD			
HOLE	YDG	PAR	INDEX
1	390	4	8
2	160	3	18
3	505	5	16
4	455	4	3
5	395	4	5
6	185	3	14
7	470	4	1
8	410	4	10
9	420	4	12
OUT	3,390	35	
10	415	4	2
11	385	4	9
12	420	4	6
13	540	5	15
14	165	3	17
15	380	4	13
16	415	4	11
17	390	4	4
18	445	4	7
IN	3,555	36	
TOTAL	6,945	71	

Old Conna Golf Club

ADDRESS:
Ferndale Road, Bray, County Wicklow, Ireland

TELEPHONE:
353 1 282 6055

FAX:
353 1 282 5611

WEB PAGE: NA

E-MAIL: NA

DIRECTIONS TO COURSE: The club is 2 miles northwest of Bray, on the Ferndale Road; watch for signage.

In 1999, a new clubhouse was erected. The facilities include a pro shop and a very nice bar and full-catering restaurant. There are also locker rooms and showers, a practice area, and a putting green.

LEVEL OF MAINTENANCE: Old Conna's building facilities are new, and the course is taken care of extremely well. The turf is good, as are the greens, and the signage throughout the course is excellent. The signage at the tee gives strokesaver-type information, particularly helpful if you have never played the course.

COURSE DESCRIPTION: Old Conna is a parkland course with hilly terrain and nice, mature wooded areas. The gently rolling greens are placed naturally throughout the course, which is to say they follow the terrain and are not built up. On a number of holes, streams coming into play add to the challenge, as do the well-positioned bunkers. The course layout is intuitive and the length moderate. If you are striking the ball well, you can score on this course. Old Conna can be fun, so enjoy your game and the spectacular views.

UNIQUE FEATURE: Striking hillside views of the Irish Sea and surrounding rugged Wicklow Mountains make Old Conna that special Irish Experience.

ACCOMMODATION INFORMATION

Standard hotel: Woodlands Court Hotel and Conference Centre (Bray), 353 1 276 0258

Local hotel/guesthouse/B&B: Royal Hotel and Leisure Centre (Bray), 353 1 286 2935

Restaurant/pub: Old Conna Clubhouse (unique Scandanavian design), 353 1 282 6055

GREEN FEES:
Low
EQUIPMENT RENTAL
Buggies: 1
Trolleys: yes
Caddies: no
Clubs: yes

DATE FOUNDED: 1987

ARCHITECT: Eddie Hackett

TYPE: Parkland
FACILITIES
Clubhouse at turn: yes
Restrooms on course: no

SCORECARD

HOLE	YDG	PAR	INDEX
1	384	4	10
2	240	3	4
3	326	4	12
4	550	5	14
5	585	5	2
6	385	4	8
7	376	4	6
8	116	3	18
9	350	4	16
OUT	3,312	36	
10	360	4	15
11	361	4	5
12	170	3	11
13	600	5	7
14	292	4	13
15	478	4	1
16	440	4	3
17	162	3	9
18	511	5	17
IN	3,374	36	
TOTAL	**6,686**	**72**	

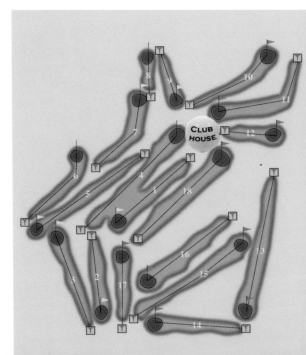

Powerscourt Golf Club

GREEN FEES:
Moderate

EQUIPMENT RENTAL
Buggies: yes
Trolleys: yes
Caddies: yes
Clubs: yes

DATE FOUNDED: 1996

ARCHITECT:
Peter McEvoy

TYPE: Parkland

FACILITIES
Clubhouse at turn: yes
Restrooms on course: no

*T*his graceful estate property offers a lovely bar and restaurant, locker rooms with showers, and full amenities. Powerscourt also has a modest pro shop, driving range, practice greens, and putting greens.

LEVEL OF MAINTENANCE: This is a superbly maintained resort complex. All aspects are flawless.

COURSE DESCRIPTION: Powerscourt is a beautiful parkland course that weaves in and out of stands of mammoth old trees. The rolling to hilly terrain offers some great challenges, not only from the trees but also from its prodigious length and incredible bunkering system. There are great views of the Irish Sea and Sugar Loaf Mountain in the distance. The course is fairly open but has a few water hazards. Given these and the other challenges, you had better play well, or your scores will balloon. This is truly a thinking golfer's course. Buy yourself a strokesaver and save a lot of headaches.

UNIQUE FEATURE: The tiered putting greens mandate shots close to the pin, or you may suffer through a number of three- and even four-putt greens.

ACCOMMODATION INFORMATION

Standard hotel: Glenview Hotel (Glen-o-the-Downs, Delgany), 353 1 287 3399

Local hotel/guesthouse/B&B: The Summerhill House Hotel, 353 1 286 7928

Restaurant/pub: Powerscourt Clubhouse Bar and Restaurant, 353 1 204 6033

ADDRESS: Powerscourt Estate, Enniskerry, County Wicklow, Ireland

TELEPHONE:
353 1 204 6033

FAX:
353 1 276 1303

WEB PAGE:
www.powerscourt.ie/golfclub

E-MAIL: golfclub@powerscourt.ie

DIRECTIONS TO COURSE: Off the N11, take the Enniskerry exit for 3 miles. Watch for excellent signage to the course.

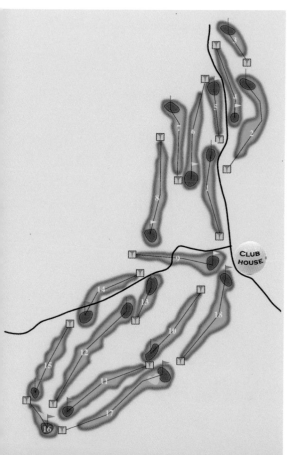

SCORECARD			
HOLE	YDG	PAR	INDEX
1	437	4	5
2	502	5	13
3	167	3	17
4	361	4	3
5	235	3	9
6	527	5	7
7	417	4	11
8	459	4	1
9	379	4	15
OUT	3,489	36	
10	421	4	6
11	416	4	8
12	542	5	12
13	181	3	16
14	381	4	14
15	388	4	4
16	158	3	18
17	592	5	2
18	424	4	10
IN	3,509	36	
TOTAL	6,998	72	

Rathsallagh Golf Club

ADDRESS:
Dunlavin,
County
Wicklow,
Ireland

TELEPHONE:
353 45 403316

FAX:
353 45 403295

WEB PAGE: NA

E-MAIL: info@rathsallagh.com

DIRECTIONS TO COURSE: From the N7, follow the Dunlavin signs. Near the town of Dunlavin, follow the Rathsallagh signage (good, but watch closely).

SCORECARD

HOLE	YDG	PAR	INDEX
1	571	5	10
2	454	4	2
3	400	4	18
4	173	3	12
5	396	4	16
6	502	5	8
7	176	3	14
8	382	4	6
9	447	4	4
OUT	3,501	36	
10	465	4	1
11	519	5	11
12	390	4	7
13	153	3	15
14	351	4	17
15	382	4	9
16	546	5	5
17	169	3	13
18	450	4	3
IN	3,415	36	
TOTAL	**6,916**	**72**	

This course includes the Rathsallagh House, a 4-star, Grade A country house surrounded by 530 acres. The separate clubhouse has a modest pro shop, a dining room and bar (complete with fireplace), and locker rooms. These facilities are elegant and well appointed, with an exceptionally helpful staff. The club has a practice range and putting green.

LEVEL OF MAINTENANCE: This is an extremely well maintained estate course with many bunkers that are given meticulous care. A creek meanders throughout the course, with well-clipped and neat turf-sodded banks. The clubhouse and facilities are lovely, well kept, and very clean.

COURSE DESCRIPTION: Rathsallagh is a long, challenging parkland course. The terrain is generally rolling, with a number of creeks and lakes adding both beauty and difficulty to this scenic treasure. The bunkering is some of the best in Ireland, both in terms of construction and intelligent placement. Unlike most estate courses, this one has an abundance of wonderfully mature trees throughout. Everything about this course requires thoughtful consideration and a fairly high level of execution. The combination of length, undulating terrain, variety of hazards, and interesting greens gives the golfer everything and sometimes more than he or she can handle. Bring your A-game and a sense of humor.

UNIQUE FEATURE: The number, position, and maturity of the trees on this course often define your approach to the holes.

ACCOMMODATION INFORMATION

Standard hotel: Rathsallagh House Hotel, 353 45 403112

Local hotel/guesthouse/B&B: Tynte House Farmhouse (Dunlavin), 353 45 401561

Restaurant/pub: Rathsallagh Golf Club Clubhouse, 353 45 403316

GREEN FEES:
Moderate

EQUIPMENT RENTAL
Buggies: yes
Trolleys: yes
Caddies: yes
Clubs: yes

DATE FOUNDED: 1993

ARCHITECTS: Christy O'Connor Jr. and Peter McEvoy

TYPE: Parkland

FACILITIES
Clubhouse at turn: yes
Restrooms on course: no

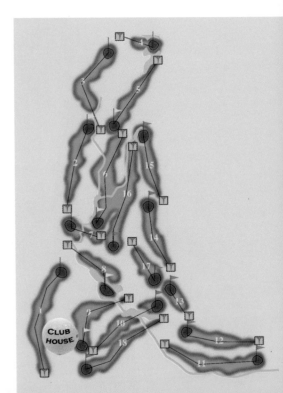

Wicklow Golf Club

GREEN FEES:
Low
EQUIPMENT RENTAL
Buggies: no
Trolleys: yes
Caddies: yes
Clubs: yes
DATE FOUNDED: 1904

ARCHITECTS: Redesigned and extended to 18 holes by Pat Ruddy and Tom Craddock (1994)
TYPE: Seaside
FACILITIES
Clubhouse at turn: yes
Restrooms on course: no

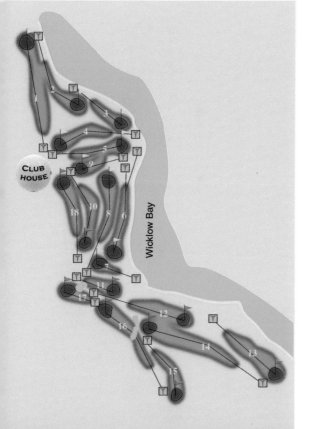

This course has a modest clubhouse, with a full bar and snack foods (order full meals before play). A separate, modestly stocked pro shop and a putting green are also available. There are changing rooms and shower facilities.

LEVEL OF MAINTENANCE: The club apparently puts its money into the course rather than the building facilities. The course is in good shape, including greens and traps.

COURSE DESCRIPTION: This seaside course is fairly open and has small, rolling greens. Some gorse and a few evergreens dot the course, but you will hardly spend much time looking at them, as the views of Wicklow Bay are gorgeous. This course, strung out along Wicklow Bay, is always in touch with the sea. The 6th hole (called Pebble Beach) gives you a carry over a small part of the bay. This is a relatively short course with few significant hazards. If you can keep your attention on your game rather than the beautiful surroundings, you should be able to score well. Have fun, and enjoy this seaside course.

UNIQUE FEATURE: The proximity to the seaside throughout the length of Wicklow Golf Club is a great visual pleasure.

ACCOMMODATION INFORMATION
Standard hotel: Old Rectory Country House and Restaurant (4 star) (Wicklow), 353 404 67048

Local hotel/guesthouse/B&B: Gormanstown Manor (farm guesthouse) (near Wicklow), 353 404 69432

Restaurant/pub: Restaurant and Grill Room in the Grand Hotel (Wicklow), 353 404 67337

ADDRESS:
Dunbur Road,
Wicklow, County
Wicklow, Ireland
353 404 66122
FAX: NA
WEB PAGE: NA
E-MAIL: NA

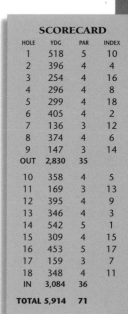

DIRECTIONS TO COURSE: Out of Wicklow town, take Dunbur Road south along the seacoast and watch for the signage.

SCORECARD			
HOLE	YDG	PAR	INDEX
1	518	5	10
2	396	4	4
3	254	4	16
4	296	4	8
5	299	4	18
6	405	4	2
7	136	3	12
8	374	4	6
9	147	3	14
OUT	2,830	35	
10	358	4	5
11	169	3	13
12	395	4	9
13	346	4	3
14	542	5	1
15	309	4	15
16	453	5	17
17	159	3	7
18	348	4	11
IN	3,084	36	
TOTAL	5,914	71	

Woodbrook Golf Club

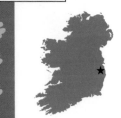

ADDRESS:
Dublin Road,
Bray, County
Wicklow,
Ireland

TELEPHONE:
353 1 282 4799

FAX:
353 1 282 1950

WEB PAGE: NA

E-MAIL: woodbrook@
internet-ireland.ie

DIRECTIONS TO COURSE:
Off the N11, take the Bray exit. Go to the first roundabout, and follow the signage; the course is just north of the roundabout on the east side.

This course has a lovely clubhouse, with all the usual amenities: full bar and restaurant facilities, ample locker rooms with showers, and well-stocked pro shop. There are two practice ranges, plus a large putting green and chipping green.

LEVEL OF MAINTENANCE: Woodbrook has recently been renovated to championship standards and is maintained accordingly. The turf and sand traps are in perfect condition, and the course is a joy to play.

COURSE DESCRIPTION: Woodbrook is a parkland course situated on gently rolling terrain. The greens are spacious, sometimes tiered, and always a challenge to your putting game. The bunkering on this course is extensive and creates a superb challenge for golfers of all levels. Stands of mature trees are sprinkled throughout the course. Given its length and conditions (i.e., challenging greens and bunkers), you had better bring your best game if you plan to score well. The golfer should also be prepared for the occasional train that barrels through the course, although the views of the Wicklow Mountains make up for any inconvenience.

UNIQUE FEATURE: The train was originally directed through the course because this used to be a cricket field. Until recently, members could pull a switch, and the next train would stop and pick them up if they needed transportation to Bray or Dublin. Unfortunately, this service is no longer available!

ACCOMMODATION INFORMATION
Standard hotel: The Royal Hotel and Leisure Centre (3 star) (Bray), 353 1 286 2935

Local hotel/guesthouse/B&B: The Esplanade Hotel (Bray), 353 1 286 2056

Restaurant/pub: The Tree of Idleness (Bray), 353 1 286 3498

GREEN FEES:
Moderate

EQUIPMENT RENTAL
Buggies: yes
Trolleys: yes
Caddies: yes
Clubs: yes

DATE FOUNDED: 1921

ARCHITECT: Redesigned by Peter McEvoy (1998)

TYPE: Seaside

FACILITIES
Clubhouse at turn: no
Restrooms on course: no

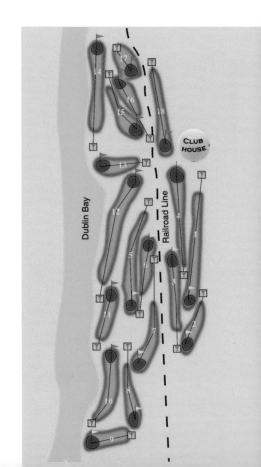

SCORECARD

HOLE	YDG	PAR	INDEX
1	506	5	17
2	194	3	9
3	383	4	11
4	449	4	3
5	576	5	7
6	401	4	13
7	482	4	1
8	385	4	5
9	157	3	15
OUT	3,533	36	
10	443	4	4
11	196	3	10
12	542	5	14
13	230	3	6
14	551	5	12
15	447	4	2
16	507	5	16
17	136	3	18
18	371	4	8
IN	3,423	36	
TOTAL	**6,956**	**72**	

Ballycastle Golf Club

GREEN FEES:
Moderate
EQUIPMENT RENTAL
Buggies: no
Trolleys: yes
Caddies: yes
Clubs: yes

DATE FOUNDED: 1891
ARCHITECT: NA
TYPE: Links/Parkland
FACILITIES
Clubhouse at turn: no
Restrooms on course: no

Ballycastle has a modest clubhouse composed of a bar and restaurant, locker rooms with showers, and a moderately stocked pro shop.

LEVEL OF MAINTENANCE: The course is adequately maintained. The turf, greens, and bunkers are all in good shape. The building facilities are clean and inviting.

ADDRESS:
Cushendall Road,
Ballycastle,
County Antrim,
Northern
Ireland BT54 6QP
TELEPHONE:
44 28 20762536
FAX:
44 28 20769909
WEB PAGE: NA
E-MAIL: NA
DIRECTIONS TO COURSE:

COURSE DESCRIPTION: Ballycastle is a quirky little course made up of links, parkland, seaside, and combinations thereof; the views are as good as anywhere in Ireland. This course is definitely an Irish Experience. Ballycastle has crisscrossing fairways, old ruins, and a meandering River Margy. The greens are good; the bunkers are deep, well cared for, and fun; some of the tees are highly elevated; and playing on some of the fairways is like hitting on top of an elephant's back. The cliffs are so steep that you'd better not look down, the holes are so close that you'd better be checking over your shoulder, and the history is so thick that you shouldn't mistake it for fog. The gorgeous views focus on Rathlin Island, where Robert of Bruce found sanctuary and coined the phrase "If at first you don't succeed, try and try again." The harbor below (sometimes 200 to 300 feet below) is where the Vikings first began plundering Ireland in the 790s, and the friary is a 16th-century ruin on the River Margy side of the road. In short, you won't find the best golf, but the visit is worth the effort and the views are quintessentially Irish.

UNIQUE FEATURE: The 17th tee is probably 150 feet above the 17th green, which seems to be directly below you even though it is a 180-yard hole.

ACCOMMODATION INFORMATION
Standard hotel: Bushmills Inn (3 star, a don't-miss hotel if you are in the area) (Bushmills), 44 28 20732339

Local hotel/guesthouse/B&B: Marine Hotel (3 star) (Ballycastle), 44 28 20762222

Restaurant/pub: Pub and restaurant in the Bushmills Inn (a unique and charming experience) (see above), 44 28 20732339

Take the A2 east out of Ballycastle town. Turn left onto the Cushendall Road, and then make an immediate left into the car park for the course.

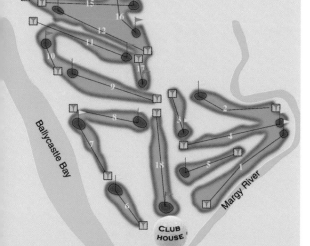

SCORECARD

HOLE	YDG	PAR	INDEX
1	492	5	9
2	349	4	7
3	166	3	13
4	403	4	5
5	262	4	17
6	267	4	15
7	401	4	3
8	329	4	11
9	353	4	1
OUT	3,022	36	
10	111	3	12
11	341	4	6
12	493	5	10
13	138	3	18
14	352	4	2
15	388	4	4
16	288	4	16
17	180	3	8
18	499	5	14
IN	2,790	35	
TOTAL	**5,812**	**71**	

Cairndhu Golf Club

ADDRESS: 192 Coast Road, Ballygally, Larne, County Antrim, Northern Ireland BT40 2QG

TELEPHONE: 44 28 28583324

FAX: 44 28 28583324

WEB PAGE: NA

E-MAIL: NA

DIRECTIONS TO COURSE: Go north on the A2 from Larne, approximately 1 mile before Ballygally, or 4 miles north of Larne. Watch for the course's sign on your left. The course is right next to the road, with a rather steep driveway.

Cairndhu's clubhouse has two dining rooms, a bar, a ballroom, shower and dressing room facilities, and a separate pro shop. The course also has a practice range and putting green and is affiliated with a private driving range down the road.

LEVEL OF MAINTENANCE: The folks at Cairndhu work hard to make the course presentable, and the buildings are clean and neat.

COURSE DESCRIPTION: Cairndhu is one of those special places you hope for but rarely find. Its members are exceptionally welcoming. The course itself is absolutely unique. It is extremely hilly, especially in the beginning, and should be approached only by those ready to tackle the challenge. The summit on hole 2 and the tee shot on number 3 are worth all your efforts to get there. As you gaze across the North Channel, Scotland's Mull of Kintyre looms in the hazy distance; the Maidens Hulin Rocks and lighthouse lie just out to sea. Below you is the beach of Ballygally, and inland, the gorgeous hills of Antrim. Past the summit, the golf gets wild and the bunkers menacing. Simply put, Cairndhu is a joy to play.

UNIQUE FEATURE: The 2nd hole, which is 159 yards, can be played either with a wedge or a driver, given the direction and velocity of the wind.

ACCOMMODATION INFORMATION

Standard hotel: Ballygally Castle Hotel (3 star) (Ballygally), 44 28 28583212

Local hotel/guesthouse/B&B: Manor Guest House (Larne), 44 28 28273305

Restaurant/pub: River Room Restaurant, Ballygally Castle Hotel (see above), 44 28 28583212

GREEN FEES: Moderate

EQUIPMENT RENTAL
Buggies: 1
Trolleys: yes
Caddies: yes
Clubs: yes

DATE FOUNDED: 1928

ARCHITECT: Moved to present site in 1958; course layout by John S. F. Morrison of Colt/Alison/Morrison Associates

TYPE: Seaside

FACILITIES
Clubhouse at turn: yes
Restrooms on course: no

SCORECARD

HOLE	YDG	PAR	INDEX
1	377	4	5
2	159	3	13
3	417	4	3
4	305	4	15
5	429	4	7
6	172	3	11
7	324	4	9
8	379	4	1
9	283	4	17
OUT	2,848	34	
10	408	4	4
11	214	3	8
12	445	4	2
13	154	3	14
14	494	5	12
15	419	4	6
16	299	4	16
17	536	5	10
18	292	4	18
IN	3,267	36	
TOTAL	**6,115**	**70**	

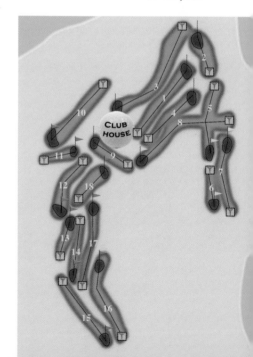

Galgorm Castle Golf and Country Club

Galgorm Castle

GREEN FEES:
Moderate

EQUIPMENT RENTAL
Buggies: yes
Trolleys: yes
Caddies: yes
Clubs: yes

DATE FOUNDED: 1997

ARCHITECT:
Simon Gidman

TYPE: Parkland

FACILITIES
Clubhouse at turn: yes
Restrooms on course: no

Galgorm's modern building contains two dining rooms (one of which is the Pavilion Restaurant), a well-stocked pro shop, changing rooms, and golf academy headquarters with three teaching pros. The course also offers a large, eighteen-bay, floodlit, landscaped driving range and putting green.

LEVEL OF MAINTENANCE: Galgorm is a well-maintained parkland course that is young and in a state of evolution. The greens are in very good condition, the turf is developing well, and the tees are wonderful. The bunkers are well kept, and attention to detail is obvious. Building facilities are well organized, clean, spacious, modern, and very inviting.

COURSE DESCRIPTION: This club is an estate course on 180 acres. Like so many other former estates on this island, it has many mature trees (some 200 to 300 years old) and also a vast number of new plantings. As indicated, this is a young course, but when it reaches maturity, it should be breathtaking. Two rivers (the Main and the Braid) come together to form two sides of the course. Artificial ponds add still more water hazards to the course. Each hole includes four sets of tees to challenge all levels of golfers. Thirty-nine sand bunkers complete the hazard arsenal of the Galgorm course. If you wish to score well, you must put forth your best game. The greens are generally rolling and full of subtle breaks. This is a fun course to play.

UNIQUE FEATURE: No expenses have been spared in constructing this course, including 40 miles of drains and a computerized irrigation system.

ACCOMMODATION INFORMATION
Standard hotel: Galgorm Manor (4 star) (on site), 44 28 25881001

Local hotel/guesthouse/B&B: Tullyglass House Hotel (3 star) (Ballymena), 44 28 25652639

Restaurant/pub: Pavilion Restaurant (on site), 44 28 25646161

ADDRESS:
Galgorm Castle,
Galgorm Road,
Ballymena,
County Antrim,
Northern Ireland
BT42 1HL

TELEPHONE:
44 28 25646161

FAX: 44 28 25661151

WEB PAGE: NA

E-MAIL: NA

DIRECTIONS TO COURSE:
From Ballymena town center, head west of town on the Galgorm Road. Go approximately 2 miles, and you will see the driving range to your left. Proceed to the roundabout. Follow signs to the course.

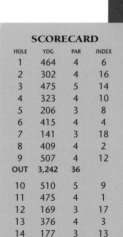

SCORECARD			
HOLE	YDG	PAR	INDEX
1	464	4	6
2	302	4	16
3	475	5	14
4	323	4	10
5	206	3	8
6	415	4	4
7	141	3	18
8	409	4	2
9	507	4	12
OUT	3,242	36	
10	510	5	9
11	475	4	1
12	169	3	17
13	376	4	3
14	177	3	13
15	382	4	11
16	409	4	7
17	446	4	5
18	550	5	15
IN	3,494	36	
TOTAL	6,736	72	

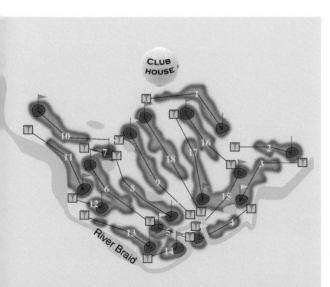

CLUB HOUSE

River Braid

Gracehill Golf Club

ADDRESS: 141 Ballinlea Road, Stranocum, Ballymoney, County Antrim, Northern Ireland BT53 8PX

TELEPHONE: 44 28 27651209

FAX: 44 28 27651074

WEB PAGE: NA

E-MAIL: NA

DIRECTIONS TO COURSE: On the A26 north from Ballymena, take the bypass around Ballymoney. Then take Ballintoy (or Kirk or B147) Road through Stranocum for about 3 miles; the course is on your left.

Gracehill offers a beautiful clubhouse that was part of an old family estate whose buildings date to the 1740s. The clubhouse includes a full bar and restaurant and locker rooms with showers. Also on site are a moderately stocked pro shop, a putting green, and practice range.

LEVEL OF MAINTENANCE: Although the transformation from estate to golf course is still incomplete, Gracehill looks to be a gem. The clubhouse facilities offer old-world charm in an updated, elegant style.

COURSE DESCRIPTION: Gracehill is a parkland course that has much promise of becoming a championship-quality site. The owners are doing exceptional work with water hazards and the placement of fairways and greens. The design calls for 8 of the holes to be played over water, and on a number of others, water is brought into play. On this estate course, ubiquitous new plantings accompany many mature stands of trees. The design calls for some very testing par 4s without a great deal of bunkering—but who needs bunkers when you've got such water and trees? The golfing world in Antrim looks forward to the completion of this course.

UNIQUE FEATURE: The artificial shaping of the water hazards throughout the course produces many interesting shots and tests for all levels of golfers.

ACCOMMODATION INFORMATION
Standard hotel: Bushmills Inn (3 star, a don't-miss experience) (Bushmills), 44 28 20732339

Local hotel/guesthouse/B&B: Cooleen Guesthouse (Ballymoney), 44 28 27663037

Restaurant/pub: Bell Tower Restaurant (on site), 44 28 27651074

GREEN FEES: Moderate

EQUIPMENT RENTAL
Buggies: no
Trolleys: yes
Caddies: no
Clubs: no

DATE FOUNDED: 1995

ARCHITECT: Frank Ainsworth

TYPE: Parkland

FACILITIES
Clubhouse at turn: no
Restrooms on course: no

SCORECARD

HOLE	YDG	PAR	INDEX
1	336	4	9
2	356	4	15
3	378	4	11
4	492	5	3
5	125	3	17
6	359	4	13
7	405	4	1
8	455	4	5
9	177	3	7
OUT	3,083	35	
10	467	5	12
11	410	4	2
12	235	3	4
13	155	3	18
14	365	4	10
15	182	3	8
16	386	4	6
17	486	5	14
18	161	3	16
IN	2,847	34	
TOTAL	5,930	69	

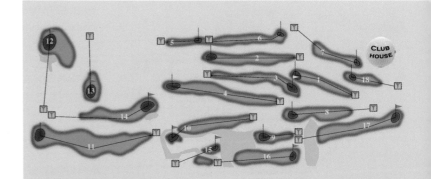

Royal Portrush Golf Club (Dunluce Course)

GREEN FEES:
High

EQUIPMENT RENTAL
Buggies: yes
Trolleys: yes
Caddies: yes
Clubs: yes

DATE FOUNDED: 1888

ARCHITECT: Harry S. Colt
(1929)

TYPE: Links

FACILITIES
Clubhouse at turn: no
Restrooms on course: yes
(10th hole)

The Dunluce Course sports a lovely modern clubhouse, with large bar and restaurant, and locker rooms with showers. It has a separate, well-stocked pro shop, a putting green, and a practice range. A snack bar and restroom are located at the 10th tee.

LEVEL OF MAINTENANCE: Royal Portrush figures to be one of the top courses in all of Ireland, with a high degree of maintenance. The turf practically sparkles. The traps, although not perfect, are lovely, and the greens well tended. The clubhouse is well presented, but the pro shop is a little disheveled.

COURSE DESCRIPTION: Some people wax eloquently about this course; we are not of that troop. Royal Portrush is a fine tract that offers a grinding test of golf for even the best player. But it doesn't maintain the level of interest and drama of other courses in Ireland. Many courses have better views, greens, sand traps, and length. Having said that, Royal Portrush is a fine links to play, presenting many faces: relatively short par 3s, long par 3s, monstrously long par 4s, undulating and tiered greens, and flat greens. The course has gorse, thick marram grass rough, buckthorn, some very good bunkering, and views of the Irish Sea and Scotland beyond.

UNIQUE FEATURE: This course, a Harry S. Colt design and original layout, has lots of history. It has seen the likes of Arnold Palmer and Gary Player and hosted the 1951 British Open, won by Max Faulkner.

ACCOMMODATION INFORMATION
Standard hotel: Royal Court Hotel (3 star) (Portrush), 44 28 70822236

Local hotel/guesthouse/B&B: Causeway Coast Hotel (3 star) (Portrush), 44 28 70822435

Restaurant/pub: Donovans Restaurant (Portrush), 44 28 70822063

ADDRESS:
Bushmills Road,
Portrush, County
Antrim, Northern
Ireland BT56 8JQ

TELEPHONE:
44 28 70822311

FAX:
44 28 70823139

WEB PAGE: NA

E-MAIL: NA

DIRECTIONS TO COURSE: On the A2 in Portrush, head east of the town center. Watch for the new large clubhouse looming on the sea side of the road.

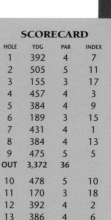

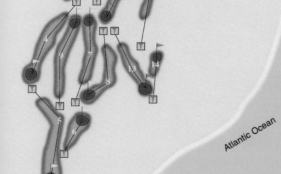

SCORECARD			
HOLE	YDG	PAR	INDEX
1	392	4	7
2	505	5	11
3	155	3	17
4	457	4	3
5	384	4	9
6	189	3	15
7	431	4	1
8	384	4	13
9	475	5	5
OUT	3,372	36	
10	478	5	10
11	170	3	18
12	392	4	2
13	386	4	6
14	210	3	16
15	365	4	12
16	428	4	4
17	548	5	14
18	469	4	8
IN	3,446	36	
TOTAL	**6,818**	**72**	

Royal Portrush Golf Club (Valley Links)

ADDRESS:
Bushmills Road, Portrush, County Antrim, Northern Ireland BT56 8JQ

TELEPHONE:
44 28 70822311

FAX: 44 28 70823139

WEB PAGE: NA

E-MAIL: NA

DIRECTIONS TO COURSE:
This course is on the A2 in Portrush. Watch for the separate, salmon pink clubhouse on the Portrush side of the larger main clubhouse.

The Valley Links offers a modest clubhouse with a small bar, grill, and changing rooms. A starter's shed is next to the putting green and practice area.

LEVEL OF MAINTENANCE: This is a very well maintained links course. The turf, greens, and few bunkers are well kept. As with Portrush's main course (Dunluce), the building facilities on the Valley Links are modern and inviting.

COURSE DESCRIPTION: The Valley Links course is located in some great duneland between the main Dunluce Course and the beach itself. The course is remarkably sheltered by these dunes, and often members of the Dunluce Course will come and play the Valley Links if the wind is really howling. There are only twenty bunkers on this 18-hole course, but it is nonetheless a challenge. The greens are rolling and the putts tricky, with subtle breaks. There's not much elevation change in the playing of the course, and the heather plays a role in the rough. Although this course is fun to play and visually stimulating, one suspects that the course's potential is greater than what the club presents.

UNIQUE FEATURE: Areas of this course are actually below sea level.

ACCOMMODATION INFORMATION
Standard hotel: Royal Court Hotel (3 star) (Portrush), 44 28 70822236

Local hotel/guesthouse/B&B: Causeway Coast Hotel (3 star) (Portrush), 44 28 70822435

Restaurant/pub: Donovans Restaurant (Portrush), 44 28 70822063

GREEN FEES:
Moderate

EQUIPMENT RENTAL
Buggies: yes
Trolleys: yes
Caddies: yes
Clubs: yes

DATE FOUNDED: 1888

ARCHITECT:
Harry S. Colt (1932)

TYPE: Links

FACILITIES
Clubhouse at turn: yes
Restrooms on course: no

SCORECARD

HOLE	YDG	PAR	INDEX
1	349	4	11
2	385	4	3
3	141	3	17
4	534	5	7
5	336	4	13
6	237	3	9
7	453	4	1
8	409	4	5
9	320	4	15
OUT	3,164	35	
10	496	5	2
11	140	3	18
12	465	4	4
13	486	5	8
14	421	4	12
15	165	3	14
16	360	4	10
17	384	4	6
18	192	3	16
IN	3,109	35	
TOTAL	6,273	70	

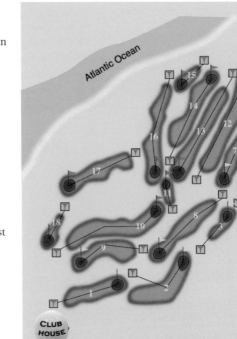

Atlantic Ocean

CLUB HOUSE

Craigavon Golf and Ski Centre (Silverwood Course)

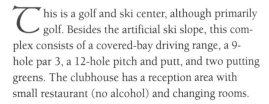

GREEN FEES:
Low

EQUIPMENT RENTAL
Buggies: no
Trolleys: yes
Caddies: no
Clubs: yes

DATE FOUNDED: 1974

ARCHITECT: NA

TYPE: Parkland

FACILITIES
Clubhouse at turn: no
Restrooms on course: no

This is a golf and ski center, although primarily golf. Besides the artificial ski slope, this complex consists of a covered-bay driving range, a 9-hole par 3, a 12-hole pitch and putt, and two putting greens. The clubhouse has a reception area with small restaurant (no alcohol) and changing rooms.

LEVEL OF MAINTENANCE: This municipal-owned complex is maintained to very acceptable standards. The facility receives a fair amount of traffic, especially from "societies" (see glossary), and a real effort is put forth to keep the complex properly maintained.

COURSE DESCRIPTION: This parkland course is purported to be on sand-based, well-drained terrain. It is a gently rolling affair that is basically open but has some mature tree stands and new plantings. A couple of streams and a pond add difficulty to this generally fair course for all handicaps.

UNIQUE FEATURE: Craigavon is primarily a multi-purpose golf and ski center. Expect a lot of youth and family activity at this site.

ACCOMMODATION INFORMATION
Standard hotel: Beechlawn House Hotel (Dunmurry, Belfast), 44 28 90612974

Local hotel/guesthouse/B&B: Balmoral Hotel (Dunmurry, Belfast), 44 28 90301234

Restaurant/pub: Cozy Corner (Craigavon), 44 28 38349678

ADDRESS:
Craigavon,
County Armagh,
Northern Ireland
BT66 6NG

TELEPHONE:
44 28 38326606

FAX: NA

WEB PAGE: NA

E-MAIL: NA

DIRECTIONS TO COURSE: Take the M1 southwest of Belfast; take the Lurgan exit; go south from the roundabout on Silverwood Road. You can see the course from the M1, so you will be turning immediately off Silverwood Road onto Tormoyra Lane; there is ample signage for this complex.

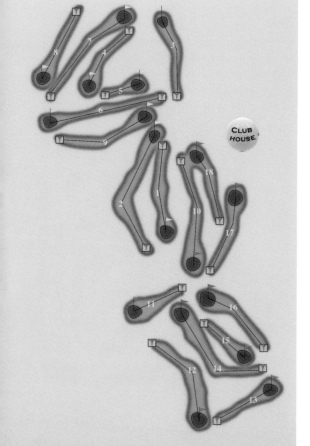

CLUB HOUSE

SCORECARD			
HOLE	YDG	PAR	INDEX
1	394	4	5
2	537	5	11
3	312	4	7
4	308	4	15
5	140	3	17
6	415	4	3
7	420	4	1
8	374	4	9
9	453	5	13
OUT	3,358	37	
10	484	5	10
11	156	3	14
12	333	4	6
13	301	4	18
14	428	4	2
15	202	3	4
16	301	4	8
17	309	4	16
18	287	4	12
IN	2,828	35	
TOTAL	6,186	72	

Belvoir Park Golf Club

ADDRESS:
Newtownbreda,
Belfast,
Northern
Ireland BT8
4AN

TELEPHONE:
44 28 90491693

FAX:
44 28 90646113

WEB PAGE: NA

E-MAIL: NA

DIRECTIONS TO COURSE:
On the A55 "outer ring" of eastern Belfast, take the Sainsbury Shopping Centre exit. Go past the shopping center, to a T junction. Turn left; go almost to the top of the hill; the club gate is to your right.

Belvoir (pronounced "Beaver") Park has a venerable old clubhouse with a clock on its front face. There are full restaurant and bar facilities, changing rooms with showers, a separate well-stocked pro shop, and a practice ground and putting green.

LEVEL OF MAINTENANCE: Belvoir Park is a course with a great deal of pride and is maintained accordingly. The building facilities are old but clean and well presented. The course itself just simply couldn't be better.

COURSE DESCRIPTION: Belvoir Park is a classic Harry Colt parkland course. Thankfully, the management over the years has had the wisdom not to change Colt's design. Great turf, super greens, and wonderful bunkering all make this course delightful. The trees, meandering streams, and difficult greens render the course extremely challenging. Belvoir Park is a great course, and you'd better have a great game if you intend to score well. There are some excellent views of the hills surrounding the course, and just the quality of the general landscape creates a visual pleasure wherever you are. This is a do-not-miss course. The friendly atmosphere put forth by the members and staff adds further enjoyment to this wonderful venue.

UNIQUE FEATURE: This is one of the few courses designed by an old master, Harry S. Colt, that has not been much tampered with in terms of its original layout. For that reason alone, it must be played and enjoyed.

ACCOMMODATION INFORMATION
Standard hotel: Stormont Hotel (4 star) (Belfast), 44 28 90658621

Local hotel/guesthouse/B&B: Beachlawn House Hotel (3 star) (Belfast), 44 28 90612974

Restaurant/pub: Either of the hotel restaurants (see above)

GREEN FEES:
Moderate

EQUIPMENT RENTAL
Buggies: no
Trolleys: yes
Caddies: yes
Clubs: yes

DATE FOUNDED: 1927

ARCHITECT:
Harry S. Colt

TYPE: Parkland

FACILITIES
Clubhouse at turn: yes
Restrooms on course: no

SCORECARD

HOLE	YDG	PAR	INDEX
1	278	4	18
2	406	4	6
3	435	4	2
4	192	3	8
5	509	5	14
6	390	4	10
7	439	4	3
8	137	3	16
9	488	5	12
OUT	3,274	36	
10	476	5	5
11	179	3	15
12	463	4	1
13	402	4	9
14	175	3	13
15	497	5	17
16	204	3	7
17	449	4	4
18	397	4	11
IN	3,242	35	
TOTAL	6,516	71	

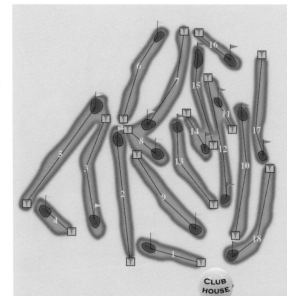

Malone Golf Club

GREEN FEES:
Moderate

EQUIPMENT RENTAL
Buggies: yes
Trolleys: yes
Caddies: yes
Clubs: yes

DATE FOUNDED: 1895

ARCHITECTS: Original course by C. Cotton; current site by Frederick W. and Martin Hawtree (1962)

TYPE: Parkland

FACILITIES
Clubhouse at turn: yes
Restrooms on course: no

Malone is a former estate. Its clubhouse, once the beautiful home of the landowner, is a Georgian building (ca. 1835). Inside, you'll find a formal restaurant, with strict jacket-and-tie requirements, and a casual restaurant and bar on the first floor. Changing rooms for visitors and an extremely well stocked pro shop are housed in the former outbuildings of the estate. In addition to a wonderful practice facility and two putting greens, the club offers its own bowling green with "secret garden," squash ground, fishing opportunities, and snooker room.

ADDRESS:
240 Upper
Malone Road,
Dunmurry,
Belfast, Northern
Ireland BT17 9LB

TELEPHONE:
44 28 90612758

FAX:
44 28 90431394

WEB PAGE: NA

E-MAIL: NA

DIRECTIONS TO COURSE:
This can be a difficult course to find. Take the A55 "outer ring" east and south of Belfast to the B103 (Finaghy/Dunmurray Road). Go past Sir Thomas and Lady Dixon Park, and follow club signs.

LEVEL OF MAINTENANCE: This is one of Belfast's premier courses, maintained to extremely high standards. The greens, tees, bunkers, and fairways are just perfect. The clubhouse and other buildings are immaculate and elegant, with beautiful landscaping.

COURSE DESCRIPTION: Malone is located in a "green belt area," free from further development. Consequently, this is a very pastoral setting. The terrain ranges from rolling to hilly, with great views of the surrounding area. This old estate has fabulous mature tree stands and a beautiful lake of roughly 25 acres. The River Lagan skirts the course but does not really come into play. The bunkering is intelligently placed, and the greens are large, interesting, and give the golfer an excellent roll.

UNIQUE FEATURE: Don't miss the "secret garden" just off the clubhouse.

ACCOMMODATION INFORMATION
Standard hotel: Clandeboye Lodge Hotel (3 star) (Bangor), 44 28 90852500

Local hotel/guesthouse/B&B: Strangford Arms Hotel (3 star) (Belfast), 44 28 90814141

Restaurant/pub: Restaurants at either of the hotels listed (see above)

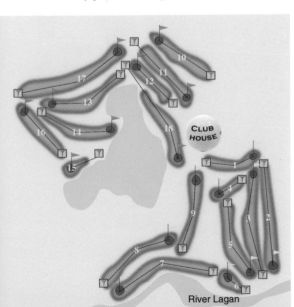
River Lagan

SCORECARD			
HOLE	YDG	PAR	INDEX
1	527	5	11
2	403	4	13
3	389	4	1
4	313	4	7
5	173	3	17
6	303	4	5
7	382	4	3
8	503	5	15
9	167	3	9
OUT	3,160	36	
10	527	5	12
11	403	4	14
12	389	4	2
13	313	4	8
14	173	3	18
15	303	4	6
16	382	4	4
17	503	5	16
18	167	3	10
IN	3,160	36	
TOTAL	6,320	72	

Ardglass Golf Club

ADDRESS: Castle Place, Ardglass, County Down, Northern Ireland BT30 7TP

TELEPHONE: 44 28 44841219

FAX: 44 28 44841841

WEB PAGE: NA

E-MAIL: NA

DIRECTIONS TO COURSE: On the A2, almost in the center of Ardglass town, along the beach, watch for signage and the ancient castle/fortification ruins.

SCORECARD

HOLE	YDG	PAR	INDEX
1	326	4	10
2	161	3	6
3	334	4	14
4	363	4	4
5	144	3	12
6	494	5	16
7	514	5	18
8	404	4	2
9	219	3	8
OUT	2,959	35	
10	439	4	1
11	181	3	5
12	397	4	7
13	382	4	11
14	490	5	13
15	392	4	3
16	361	4	9
17	119	3	17
18	345	4	15
IN	3,106	35	
TOTAL	**6,065**	**70**	

Part of the clubhouse at Ardglass comprises a 14th-century castle, and the rest has old-world charm. The building facilities include changing rooms with showers, a well-stocked pro shop, a bar, and a full restaurant. There is also a putting green.

LEVEL OF MAINTENANCE: Given the age of the castle and clubhouse, it is difficult to expect these facilities to conform to today's standards. They are perfectly quaint, however, and the four cannons out front make this a historic novelty not to be missed. The greens and bunkers are excellent, and the maintenance of the course is of high quality.

COURSE DESCRIPTION: Ardglass is a nearly classic "in-and-out" configuration over a rather hilly links tract. The course offers terrific views of both the Mourne Mountains and the Irish Sea; on a clear day, you can see the Isle of Man. Ardglass is blessed with a plethora of heather, gorse, dunes, humps, hollows, and deep frightening gorges; a wind that almost always blows; and all the other joys of links golf. Ardglass has many bunkers, some of which are very deep and swallow anything that gets near them. A stream meanders through the course, and elevation changes will maintain your attention. This course is relatively short, but given the links hazards, you'd better bring your A-game.

UNIQUE FEATURE: Your tee shot on the 161-yard hole 2 (par 3), Howd's Hole, is over a deep sea ravine; this shot is breathtaking.

ACCOMMODATION INFORMATION

Standard hotel: Abbey Lodge Hotel (Downpatrick), 44 28 44614511

Local hotel/guesthouse/B&B: The Cottage Bed and Breakfast (directly across from the course, in Ardglass), 44 28 44841080

Restaurant/pub: Aldo's Restaurant (opposite the course, in Ardglass), 44 28 44841315

GREEN FEES: Low

EQUIPMENT RENTAL
Buggies: yes
Trolleys: yes
Caddies: yes
Clubs: yes

DATE FOUNDED: 1896

ARCHITECT: NA

TYPE: Links

FACILITIES
Clubhouse at turn: no
Restrooms on course: no

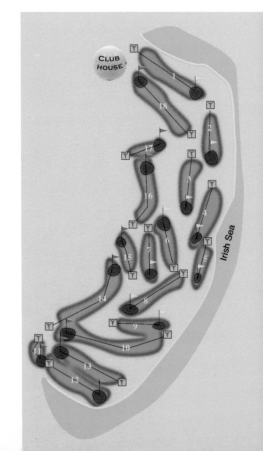

Blackwood Golf Centre (Hamilton Course)

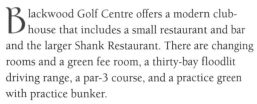

GREEN FEES:
Low
EQUIPMENT RENTAL
Buggies: yes
Trolleys: yes
Caddies: yes
Clubs: yes

DATE FOUNDED: 1994

ARCHITECT:
Simon Gidman

TYPE: Parkland

FACILITIES
Clubhouse at turn: yes
Restrooms on course: no

Blackwood Golf Centre offers a modern club-house that includes a small restaurant and bar and the larger Shank Restaurant. There are changing rooms and a green fee room, a thirty-bay floodlit driving range, a par-3 course, and a practice green with practice bunker.

LEVEL OF MAINTENANCE: This complex is main-tained to good municipal course standards. The club-house is modern and also well maintained, given the volume of adult and juvenile patrons.

COURSE DESCRIPTION: Blackwood is a training and learn-ing center as much as anything. The practice facilities are terrific; the par-3 course attracts novices of all ages and is an excellent opportunity for players of all levels to improve their game. This complex also appeals to those interested in family-type golf, where parents and children partake in a learning environment. The Hamilton Course is the standard course at this site and is on nice rolling to hilly terrain, with some mature trees, new plantings, and plenty of gorse. There are great views of the surrounding countryside. The greens are gently rolling with good turf and provide a good roll. Besides the mature trees, a num-ber of water hazards and a few well-placed bunkers create some interest on this course. It is relatively short and fairly open, so you can achieve a good score if your game is running well for you.

UNIQUE FEATURE: The effort to develop novice players is very nice, both in terms of coaching and facilities.

ACCOMMODATION INFORMATION
Standard hotel: Clandeboye Lodge Hotel (Bangor), 44 28 91852500
Local hotel/guesthouse/B&B: Royal Hotel (Bangor), 44 28 91271866
Restaurant/pub: Clandeboye Lodge Hotel restaurant, 44 28 91852500

ADDRESS:
Crawfordsburn
Road, Clandeboye
County Down,
Northern Ireland
BT19 1GB

TELEPHONE:
44 28 91853581

FAX:
44 28 91853785

WEB PAGE:
www.blackwoodgolf.co.uk

E-MAIL: NA

DIRECTIONS TO COURSE:
The course is 10 miles east of Belfast, just off the A2; follow the signs.

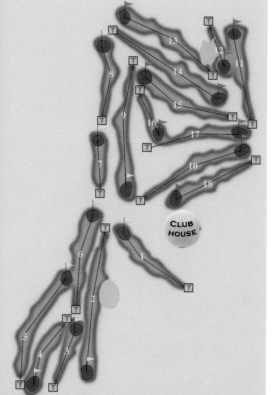

CLUB HOUSE

SCORECARD			
HOLE	YDG	PAR	INDEX
1	354	4	12
2	540	5	8
3	212	3	6
4	329	4	18
5	419	4	2
6	332	4	14
7	165	3	16
8	380	4	4
9	480	5	10
OUT	3,211	36	
10	436	4	3
11	354	4	15
12	166	3	9
13	436	4	1
14	491	5	17
15	404	4	5
16	180	3	7
17	365	4	11
18	349	4	13
IN	3,181	35	
TOTAL	**6,392**	**71**	

Clandeboye Golf Club (Dufferin Course)

ADDRESS:
Conlig,
Newtownards,
County Down,
Northern
Ireland BT23
4YH

TELEPHONE:
44 28 91271767

FAX: 44 28 91473711

WEB PAGE: NA

E-MAIL: NA

DIRECTIONS TO COURSE:
On the A21 south of Bangor, take the Conlig exit and go about 2 miles; turn at the Tower Road sign (also signed for golf club).

The beautiful clubhouse was renovated in 1999; the shower and changing room facilities are first-rate, the bar and restaurant excellent. The views from the clubhouse of the surrounding hills are breathtaking. There is a starter shed on the Dufferin Course. A good putting green and practice ground are close at hand.

LEVEL OF MAINTENANCE: The building facilities are immaculate, and the course, from the bunkers to the rough, is kept perfectly.

COURSE DESCRIPTION: The Dufferin Course is a parkland course. One is immediately struck by the rolling terrain, profuse gorse, precision lines on the bunkers, and the wonderful smoothness of the greens. The land once belonged to an estate, so the course has some wonderful old-growth trees. Many new plantings are strategically placed and will make this a tough tract soon. Although not dramatically long, the course does have some challenging par 4s. The tee boxes have good definition and are big enough to remain healthy. The signage throughout the course is excellent, with strokesaver-like qualities on each tee. Stunning views of the Irish Sea extend to the Scottish Coast. (A word on the shorter Ava Course: if you have time, it would not be misspent playing it.)

UNIQUE FEATURE: Watch for the specter of Scotland's Ailsa Craig (near the famous Turnberry Course).

ACCOMMODATION INFORMATION
Standard hotel: Clandeboye Lodge Hotel (Bangor), 44 28 91852500

Local hotel/guesthouse/B&B: Bangor Bay Inn (Bangor), 44 28 91270696

Restaurant/pub: Clubhouse on site (excellent continental cuisine), 44 28 91271767

GREEN FEES:
Moderate

EQUIPMENT RENTAL
Buggies: yes
Trolleys: yes
Caddies: yes
Clubs: yes

DATE FOUNDED: 1933

ARCHITECTS: W. R. Robinson. Redesigned by Baron Von Limburg, Peter Alliss, and Dave Thomas

TYPE: Parkland

FACILITIES
Clubhouse at turn: no
Restrooms on course: no

SCORECARD

HOLE	YDG	PAR	INDEX
1	388	4	7
2	172	3	5
3	417	4	9
4	389	4	1
5	183	3	13
6	521	5	17
7	360	4	15
8	452	4	3
9	397	4	11
OUT	3,279	35	
10	415	4	2
11	153	3	12
12	490	5	16
13	360	4	10
14	167	3	8
15	495	5	18
16	392	4	4
17	375	4	14
18	433	4	6
IN	3,280	36	
TOTAL	6,559	71	

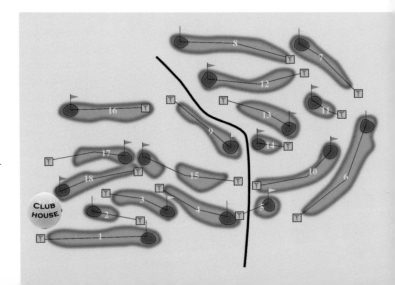

Downpatrick Golf Club

GREEN FEES:
Low
EQUIPMENT RENTAL
Buggies: yes
Trolleys: yes
Caddies: yes
Clubs: yes

DATE FOUNDED: 1930

ARCHITECT: Redesigned by Martin Hawtree (1975)

TYPE: Parkland
FACILITIES
Clubhouse at turn: no
Restrooms on course: no

Ownpatrick offers a modest but adequate clubhouse with a bar and grill, changing rooms, and a moderately stocked pro shop. The course has two putting greens, one for juveniles and another for adults, a large practice area, and a small chipping and wedge practice green, complete with sand trap.

LEVEL OF MAINTENANCE: The clubhouse is an older building with minimal maintenance. The course has excellent turf and very good greens. Traps are randomly placed and receive marginal care.

COURSE DESCRIPTION: Downpatrick is a mature parkland course with rolling to hilly terrain. There are many stands of mature trees, and most of the fairways are tree lined. The course is geometric, going north/south or east/west in straight lines. Although not particularly long, it has some massive par 4s, such as number 5 (Lough View), which is 457 yards. The par 3s are also a bit of a test in length. A small water hazard on this course adds some difficulty. Although the traps are fairly weak, the greens putt nicely. Given its rolling nature and subsoil, this course is playable all year.

UNIQUE FEATURE: On clear days, this course has views of the Isle of Man.

ACCOMMODATION INFORMATION
Standard hotel: Abbey Lodge Hotel (Downpatrick), 44 28 44614511

Local hotel/guesthouse/B&B: Swan Lodge Bed and Breakfast (Downpatrick), 44 28 44614452

Restaurant/pub: Abbey Lodge Hotel (see above), 44 28 44614511

ADDRESS:
43 Saul Road,
Downpatrick,
County Down,
Northern Ireland
BT30 6PA

TELEPHONE:
44 28 44615947

FAX: NA

WEB PAGE: NA

E-MAIL: NA

DIRECTIONS TO COURSE: Take the Saul Road northeast of Downpatrick town center. The course is about 1½ miles out of town. Watch for entry on your right; no signs direct you to the course from town.

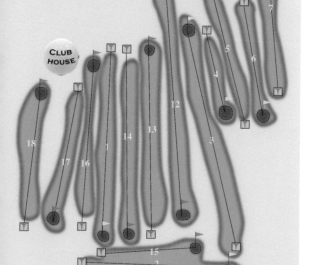

SCORECARD			
HOLE	YDG	PAR	INDEX
1	374	4	3
2	298	4	17
3	506	5	11
4	176	3	13
5	457	4	5
6	330	4	9
7	437	4	1
8	155	3	15
9	337	4	7
OUT	3,070	35	
10	362	4	10
11	181	3	12
12	544	5	4
13	390	4	6
14	424	4	2
15	171	3	16
16	364	4	14
17	278	4	18
18	336	4	8
IN	3,050	35	
TOTAL	**6,120**	**70**	

Kirkistown Castle Golf Club

ADDRESS: 142 Main Road, Cloughey, Kirkistown, County Down, Northern Ireland BT22 1JA

TELEPHONE: 44 28 42771233

FAX: 44 28 42771699

WEB PAGE: www.kcgc.org

E-MAIL: kirkistown@aol.com

DIRECTIONS TO COURSE: Take the A20 south from Newtownards. Go to Kirkcubbin and take the Kirkistown Road (east) all the way to a T junction. Turn right and go about ¾ mile; the course is on the right side of the road.

SCORECARD

HOLE	YDG	PAR	INDEX
1	512	5	10
2	403	4	4
3	300	4	18
4	148	3	14
5	389	4	2
6	423	4	8
7	318	4	16
8	147	3	12
9	381	4	6
OUT	3,025	35	
10	432	4	3
11	126	3	17
12	433	4	7
13	437	4	1
14	191	3	15
15	349	4	9
16	163	3	13
17	440	4	5
18	519	5	11
IN	3,095	34	
TOTAL	**6,120**	**69**	

Kirkistown's clubhouse offers the basic amenities, such as a bar and restaurant with full catering, changing rooms with showers, and a separate, well-stocked pro shop. The club has a putting green and a practice sand bunker with green.

LEVEL OF MAINTENANCE: Clubhouse facilities are extremely well maintained and clean. The Kirkistown Castle course is noted for the quality of its turf and greens. The bunkering is also well tended.

COURSE DESCRIPTION: Confusion reigns as to what exactly this course is: some call it links; others links-like; and still others a moorland course. Technicalities aside, this course plays like a links in that the fairways are hard and close cropped and there are dunelike hills and great views of the surrounding areas. The view of the Irish Sea is particularly interesting from a small hill next to the old Kirkistown Castle. The course has a fair amount of gorse, but generally it is very open and forgiving to play. Its status as a James Braid course gives it immediate credibility.

UNIQUE FEATURE: Course lore tells of the sale of gravel for construction of airfields during World War II, as a way to keep the course viable. Gravel was mined, and two "hollows" remain near the 1st tee and the 3rd green.

ACCOMMODATION INFORMATION

Standard hotel: Strangford Arms Hotel (3 star) (Newtownards), 44 28 42814141

Local hotel/guesthouse/B&B: Ganaway House B&B (Ballywalter), 44 28 42757096

Restaurant/pub: The Wildflower Inn (Gray Abbey), 44 28 42787307

GREEN FEES: Low (check with club about reductions based on the accommodation you use and the size of your group)

EQUIPMENT RENTAL
Buggies: no
Trolleys: yes

Caddies: yes
Clubs: yes

DATE FOUNDED: 1902

ARCHITECT: James Braid

TYPE: Links/Parkland

FACILITIES
Clubhouse at turn: yes
Restrooms on course: no

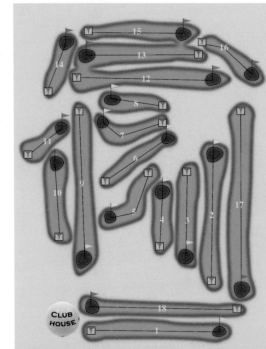

The Royal Belfast Golf Club

GREEN FEES:
Moderate

EQUIPMENT RENTAL
Buggies: no
Trolleys: yes
Caddies: no
Clubs: yes

DATE FOUNDED: 1881

ARCHITECT:
Harry S. Colt (1925)

TYPE: Parkland

FACILITIES
Clubhouse at turn: no
Restrooms on course: no

The Royal Belfast Golf Club is one of the oldest in Ireland. Its clubhouse is an elegant former manor house (ca. 1800). Heritage and tradition abound. Memorabilia are tucked here and there, including an Old Tom Morris driver and one of the original scarlet coats ("Hunting Pinks") worn by founding members. Facilities include a large restaurant and bar ("smart dress" required), pools and snooker rooms, tennis and squash courts, a separate well-stocked pro shop, putting green, and practice area.

LEVEL OF MAINTENANCE: All aspects of the course are excellently maintained, including closely cropped fairways, great putting surfaces, and well-tended bunkers.

COURSE DESCRIPTION: There's magic here—you can almost feel Harry Colt laying out a bunker or positioning a green. This rolling parkland course drifts down toward Belfast Lough, with great views of the blue hills of Antrim. Holes are carved out of the ancient woodlands; golf rarely gets better than this. Royal Belfast is a relatively short and open course, but the trees, sand, and elevation changes will challenge your game. This is a joy to play, and the staff are extraordinarily helpful and friendly.

UNIQUE FEATURE: This Harry Colt course has had few modifications over the years, making this one of those rare courses that retains its historical context.

ACCOMMODATION INFORMATION
Standard hotel: Culloden Hotel (5 star) (Holywood, Belfast), 44 28 90425223

Local hotel/guesthouse/B&B: Ardshane Country Guesthouse (Holywood, Belfast), 44 28 90422044

Restaurant/pub: Culloden Hotel Restaurant (see above), 44 28 90425223

ADDRESS:
Station Road,
Craigavad,
Holywood,
County
Down, Northern
Ireland BT18 0BP

TELEPHONE:
44 28 90428165

FAX: 44 28 90421404

WEB PAGE: NA

E-MAIL: NA

DIRECTIONS TO COURSE:
From Belfast on the A2 (Bangor Road), just beyond a brown sign directing to the Ulster Folk and Transport Museum, turn left onto Station Road. Follow it about ¼ mile to the Royal Belfast Golf Course sign (turn right at the fork).

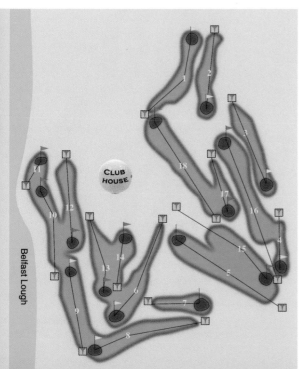

SCORECARD			
HOLE	YDG	PAR	INDEX
1	415	4	7
2	408	4	3
3	370	4	13
4	142	3	15
5	553	5	9
6	351	4	11
7	183	3	17
8	409	4	5
9	408	4	1
OUT	3,239	35	
10	308	4	14
11	174	3	8
12	431	4	4
13	369	4	12
14	186	3	10
15	411	4	2
16	483	5	16
17	195	3	18
18	510	5	6
IN	3,067	35	
TOTAL	6,306	70	

The Royal County Down Golf Club

ADDRESS:
Newcastle, County Down, Northern Ireland BT33 0AN

TELEPHONE:
44 28 43723314

FAX:
44 28 43726281

WEB PAGE: NA

E-MAIL: royal.co.down@virgin.net

DIRECTIONS TO COURSE:
In Newcastle town center, near the ocean, find the looming Slieve Donard Hotel. On the town side of the hotel, take Golf Links Road for about ¼ mile to the course entrance.

The venerable clubhouse is accessible only to members and their guests (jacket and tie required), but restrooms and changing rooms are available for visitors. The pro shop is well stocked. Also on site are a putting green and practice area (the latter for members only). If you need a caddy, reserve one months in advance.

LEVEL OF MAINTENANCE: This course is one of the most spectacular links you will ever play, and maintenance is taken seriously.

COURSE DESCRIPTION: The Royal County Down is a sterling example of man and nature combining to create an extraordinary place. Were it not for the flag sticks, you might never suspect that you are on a golf course. There are towering dunes, abundant heather, unbelievable bunkering, views of the ocean and the Mourne Mountains, and acres of gorse as thick as blackberry bushes and twice as dangerous. We have never seen bunkering of this caliber, and it all looks natural and frightfully difficult. The tees are a joy; the greens are gently rolling but full of subtle breaks. Challenges arise at every turn, including a number of blind tee shots and obscured second shots that draw both criticism and praise. Your game will need to fire on all eight cylinders.

UNIQUE FEATURE: The front 9 holes are possibly the best on the planet.

ACCOMMODATION INFORMATION

Standard hotel: Slieve Donard (4 star; extremely fancy and expensive) (Newcastle), 44 28 43723681

Local hotel/guesthouse/B&B: Burrendale Hotel and Country Club (3 star) (Newcastle), 44 28 43722599

Restaurant/pub: Restaurant at the Burrendale Hotel (see above), 44 28 43722599

GREEN FEES:
High

EQUIPMENT RENTAL
Buggies: no
Trolleys: yes
Caddies: yes
Clubs: yes

DATE FOUNDED: 1889

ARCHITECTS: Old Tom Morris; Harry Vardon (1913); Harry S. Colt (1920s)

TYPE: Links

FACILITIES
Clubhouse at turn: yes
Restrooms on course: no

SCORECARD

HOLE	YDG	PAR	INDEX
1	506	5	13
2	421	4	9
3	474	4	3
4	212	3	15
5	438	4	7
6	396	4	11
7	145	3	17
8	429	4	1
9	486	4	5
OUT	3,507	35	
10	197	3	14
11	438	4	8
12	525	5	10
13	443	4	2
14	213	3	12
15	464	4	4
16	276	4	18
17	427	4	16
18	547	5	6
IN	3,530	36	
TOTAL	**7,037**	**71**	

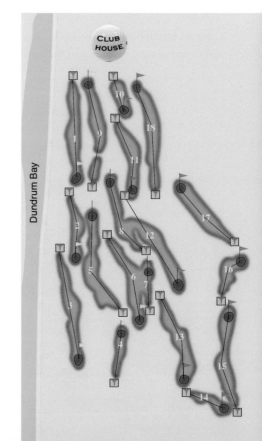

Enniskillen Golf Club

GREEN FEES:
Low

EQUIPMENT RENTAL
Buggies: yes
Trolleys: yes
Caddies: no
Clubs: no

DATE FOUNDED: 1896

ARCHITECT: NA

TYPE: Parkland

FACILITIES
Clubhouse at turn: yes
Restrooms on course: no

Enniskillen offers a modest clubhouse with bar and snacks; there are also changing rooms. The course has a putting green.

LEVEL OF MAINTENANCE: This municipal course is well maintained and is looking to the future with many new plantings. Building facilities are clean and well presented.

COURSE DESCRIPTION: This parkland course, originally 9 holes, was extended to 18, and the change is obvious. The old 9 (the back 9) is claustrophobic and has some crisscrossing holes. The mature trees and meandering stream, coupled with the nearby large lake, make for some lovely scenery. The front 9 is much more spacious, with many new plantings and a number of side-hill fairways. The greens are basically flat, with good turf. You'll find little bunkering. It can be enjoyable and fun, if you keep in mind the fact that it's a municipal course.

UNIQUE FEATURE: Enniskillen is on the former grounds of the Castlecoole Estate.

ACCOMMODATION INFORMATION
Standard hotel: Manor House Country Hotel (3 star) (Enniskillen), 44 28 66621561

Local hotel/guesthouse/B&B: Killyhevlin Hotel (3 star) (Enniskillen), 44 28 66323481

Restaurant/pub: Willie Ramblers Bar and Restaurant (Enniskillen), 44 28 66328584

ADDRESS:
Castlecoole Road,
Enniskillen,
County
Fermanagh,
Northern Ireland
BT74

TELEPHONE:
44 28 66325250

FAX: NA

WEB PAGE: NA

E-MAIL: NA

DIRECTIONS TO COURSE:
From Enniskillen town center, take Castlecoole Road north, about ¾ mile, to the end of the road.

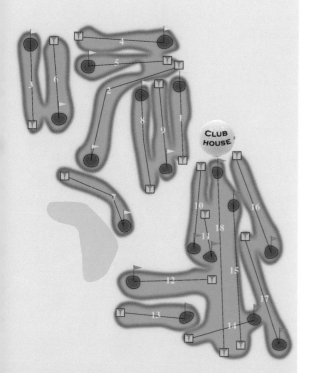

SCORECARD			
HOLE	YDG	PAR	INDEX
1	353	4	5
2	507	5	13
3	178	3	7
4	402	4	1
5	389	4	3
6	161	3	17
7	306	4	15
8	460	5	9
9	380	4	11
OUT	3,136	36	
10	356	4	10
11	127	3	18
12	367	4	6
13	363	4	4
14	183	3	16
15	417	4	2
16	392	4	8
17	340	4	14
18	508	5	12
IN	3,053	35	
TOTAL	**6,189**	**71**	

Estd. 1896

Castlerock Golf Club

ADDRESS: 65 Circular Road, Castlerock, County Londonderry, Northern Ireland BT51

TELEPHONE: 44 28 70848314

FAX: 44 28 70849440

WEB PAGE: NA

E-MAIL: NA

DIRECTIONS TO COURSE: Take the A2 west out of Portstewart, toward Coleraine; stay on the A2 through Coleraine to the B119, and watch for signs to Castlerock town. Once in Castlerock, follow signs to the course, which is just beyond the town center.

Castlerock has a relatively modest clubhouse facility that consists of a restaurant and bar, changing rooms, and a modestly stocked pro shop. It also has a practice area and putting green.

LEVEL OF MAINTENANCE: This is a very well maintained course, with beautiful greens that putt true and that are smoother than those on most links courses. The bunkering, when present, is well tended and well placed. The clubhouse facilities are clean and well presented.

COURSE DESCRIPTION: Castlerock is a fine little links course with great views of Scotland, the North Atlantic, the Inishowen Peninsula of Donegal, and the River Bann estuary. The River Bann is a real bonus in that it affects shots on five different holes. This course has a good, intuitive layout among some high dunes. There are some very strong par 3s, and many of the greens are on elevated plateaus. Wind is a factor on any links course, but it seems to be even more so on this links. This is one of those courses where it feels like you are always going uphill and always hitting into the wind. Opinions about this course differ. Many think that it is underrated; others maintain that it doesn't compare to the better known links courses in the area. If you are in the area, you should definitely stop by and decide for yourself.

UNIQUE FEATURE: The 4th hole is a par 3, called Leg O' Mutton, with out-of-bounds both left and right. Given its 200-yard length, accuracy is at a premium. Don't miss the green.

ACCOMMODATION INFORMATION

Standard hotel: Golf Hotel (Castlerock), 44 28 70848204

Local hotel/guesthouse/B&B: Marine Inn (Castlerock), 44 28 70848456

Restaurant/pub: Clubhouse on site, 44 28 70848314

GREEN FEES: Moderate

EQUIPMENT RENTAL
Buggies: no
Trolleys: yes
Caddies: yes
Clubs: yes

DATE FOUNDED: 1901

ARCHITECT: Ben Sayers

TYPE: Links

FACILITIES
Clubhouse at turn: no
Restrooms on course: no

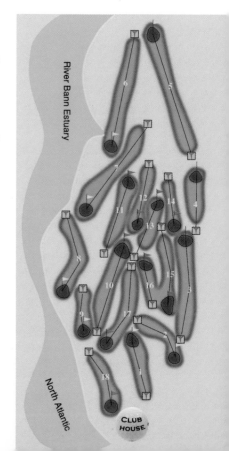

SCORECARD

HOLE	YDG	PAR	INDEX
1	348	4	9
2	375	4	5
3	509	5	13
4	200	3	11
5	477	5	15
6	347	4	7
7	409	4	1
8	411	4	3
9	200	3	17
OUT	3,276	36	
10	391	4	4
11	509	5	16
12	430	4	2
13	379	4	14
14	192	3	8
15	518	5	6
16	157	3	18
17	493	5	12
18	342	4	10
IN	3,411	37	
TOTAL	6,687	73	

City of Derry Golf Club (Prehen Course)

GREEN FEES:
Moderate

EQUIPMENT RENTAL
Buggies: no
Trolleys: yes
Caddies: yes
Clubs: yes

DATE FOUNDED: 1912

ARCHITECTS: First 9 laid out by Willie Park Jr.; revised by Tom Simpson

TYPE: Parkland

FACILITIES
Clubhouse at turn: no
Restrooms on course: no

City of Derry offers a very nice clubhouse with full amenities: bar and large restaurant, locker rooms with showers, and a separate well-stocked pro shop. It also has a practice range and a putting green.

LEVEL OF MAINTENANCE: This is an extremely well maintained municipal course. A high degree of pride obviously goes into the maintenance of all aspects of the course, from the bunkers to the restrooms in the very clean clubhouse.

COURSE DESCRIPTION: City of Derry is a parkland course that now consists of 27 holes; the relatively easy 9-hole course, called Dunhugh, is excellent for developing a neophyte game. The 18-hole Prehen Course is a lovely parkland course that has great greens, excellent tees, and lots of gorse throughout its tract. The greens are gently rolling with many subtle breaks, and the bunkering is relatively small and old-fashioned (but very well kept). There are many side-hill lies, as this course traverses a hillside overlooking the River Foyle. The par 3s are wonderful in that each poses a different test of skill and accuracy. This course is a joy to play and should be visited if you are in the area.

UNIQUE FEATURE: Fred Daly, the only Irishman to win the British Open, was the pro at the City of Derry course from 1939 to 1944, before winning his Open in 1947. Walter Hagen also visited this course and played it in 1937, according to local lore.

ACCOMMODATION INFORMATION

Standard hotel: Everglades Hotel (4 star) (Londonderry), 44 28 71346722

Local hotel/guesthouse/B&B: Waterfoot Hotel and Country Club (3 star) (Londonderry), 44 28 71345500

Restaurant/pub: Restaurants in either of these hotels (see above)

ADDRESS:
49 Victoria Road,
Londonderry,
Northern Ireland
BT47 2PU

TELEPHONE:
44 28 71346369

FAX:
44 28 71310008

WEB PAGE: NA

E-MAIL: NA

DIRECTIONS TO COURSE: Take the A5, 3 miles south of Londonderry town. The course is immediately off the road and well signed.

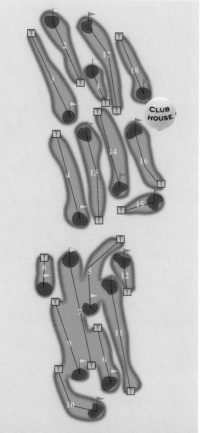

SCORECARD			
HOLE	YDG	PAR	INDEX
1	217	3	14
2	393	4	4
3	534	5	12
4	442	4	2
5	374	4	6
6	344	4	16
7	503	5	8
8	162	3	18
9	381	4	10
OUT	3,350	36	
10	349	4	13
11	504	5	7
12	171	3	11
13	409	4	3
14	439	4	1
15	139	3	15
16	299	4	17
17	402	4	5
18	367	4	9
IN	3,079	35	
TOTAL	6,429	71	

Moyola Park Golf Club

ADDRESS:
Shanemullagh, 15 Curran Road, Castledawson, County Londonderry, Northern Ireland BT45 58DG

TELEPHONE: 44 28 79468468

FAX: 44 28 79468628

WEB PAGE: www.globalgolf.ireland.north

E-MAIL: golf@moyola-park-in-ireland.freeserve.co.uk

DIRECTIONS TO COURSE:
In Castledawson on the A31, go to Curran Road. Turn left and go 1 mile; the course is on the right.

SCORECARD

HOLE	YDG	PAR	INDEX
1	438	4	3
2	418	4	5
3	346	4	13
4	152	3	15
5	521	5	17
6	430	4	7
7	391	4	11
8	421	4	1
9	379	4	9
OUT	3,496	36	
10	348	4	12
11	377	4	4
12	200	3	10
13	494	5	8
14	417	4	2
15	320	4	14
16	177	3	6
17	128	3	16
18	562	5	8
IN	3,023	35	
TOTAL	6,519	71	

Moyola Park is an old estate course, and the clubhouse is the former mansion of the Lord Moyola estate. Facilities include a restaurant, a bar, and recently refurbished changing rooms with lockers and showers. Bar facilities and function rooms are available for private parties, receptions, and conferences. The club has a putting green, practice area, and separate pro shop.

LEVEL OF MAINTENANCE: This is a very well maintained parkland course with excellent greens and well-maintained (though few) bunkers. The clean and inviting building facilities are obviously kept to high standards.

COURSE DESCRIPTION: Moyola Park sits on gently rolling to slightly hilly terrain. The River Moyola and the many mature trees create most of the difficulty on this course. The 8th hole is a difficult, long par 4 of 421 yards. The dogleg left ends with a tough approach shot over the river and through a tree-lined tight fairway to the green. You really need to have "good stuff" to play well here. The 17th hole has a beautiful green that is actually an island in the River Moyola (complete with salmon weir). Heavily bunkered, the 17th is a joy to play. Some recent tree plantings are destined to make this course very difficult in the not-too-distant future.

UNIQUE FEATURE: The course purposefully has few bunkers, as the trees are deemed to be penal enough.

ACCOMMODATION INFORMATION

Standard hotel: Glenavon House Hotel (3 star) (Cookstown), 44 28 86764949

Local hotel/guesthouse/B&B: Tullylagan Country House (Cookstown), 44 28 86765100

Restaurant/pub: Restaurants at either of the hotels listed (see above)

GREEN FEES:
Moderate

EQUIPMENT RENTAL
Buggies: no
Trolleys: yes
Caddies: yes
Clubs: yes

DATE FOUNDED: 1976

ARCHITECT:
Don Patterson

TYPE: Parkland

FACILITIES
Clubhouse at turn: no
Restrooms on course: no

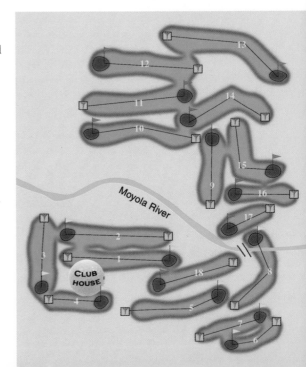

Portstewart Golf Club (Strand Course)

GREEN FEES:
High

EQUIPMENT RENTAL
Buggies: no
Trolleys: yes
Caddies: yes
Clubs: yes

DATE FOUNDED: 1894

ARCHITECTS: Willie Park Jr., A. G. Gow, and Des Giffin

TYPE: Links

FACILITIES
Clubhouse at turn: no
Restrooms on course: no

Portstewart (Strand) provides an immaculate clubhouse with the usual amenities of restaurant, bar, and changing room, as well as separate Ladies and Mixed Lounges. There is a separate, well-stocked pro shop.

LEVEL OF MAINTENANCE: This is a highly maintained links course. Rather than aiming for a "natural" look, Portstewart keeps its fairways and greens closely cropped, and its sand traps crisply cut around the edges; likewise, the tee boxes have specific definition.

COURSE DESCRIPTION: Portstewart's first 9 holes cover some of the most intense, high duneland that you'll find anywhere. The buckthorn thistle, originally introduced to stabilize the dunes, has proliferated into a commanding presence. While not as dramatic, the back 9 offers equally testing golf, with the River Bann very present. Traps are intelligently placed, and the greens conform to the land's contours. If the wind is blowing, hitch up your belt and prepare for survival in the best Irish golf tradition!

UNIQUE FEATURE: The size and stature of the dunes on the front 9 will leave you breathless.

ACCOMMODATION INFORMATION

Standard hotel: Bushmills Inn (3 star, a don't-miss Irish Experience) (Bushmills), 44 28 20732339

Local hotel/guesthouse/B&B: Causeway Hotel (also a don't-miss experience) (Giant's Causeway), 44 28 20731226

Restaurant/pub: Restaurants at either of the hotels listed (see above)

ADDRESS:
117 Strand Road,
Portstewart,
County
Londonderry,
Northern Ireland
BT55 7PG

TELEPHONE:
44 28 70832601

FAX:
44 28 70834097

WEB PAGE: NA

E-MAIL: NA

DIRECTIONS TO COURSE:
Take the A2 through Portstewart town; go to Strand Road, and watch for signage leading to the course.

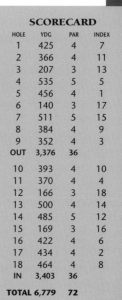

SCORECARD			
HOLE	YDG	PAR	INDEX
1	425	4	7
2	366	4	11
3	207	3	13
4	535	5	5
5	456	4	1
6	140	3	17
7	511	5	15
8	384	4	9
9	352	4	3
OUT	3,376	36	
10	393	4	10
11	370	4	4
12	166	3	18
13	500	4	14
14	485	5	12
15	169	3	16
16	422	4	6
17	434	4	2
18	464	4	8
IN	3,403	36	
TOTAL	6,779	72	

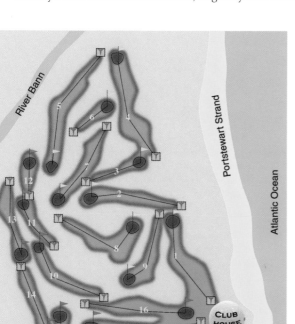

Dungannon Golf Club

ADDRESS: 34 Springfield Lane, Dungannon, County Tyrone, Northern Ireland BT70 1QX

TELEPHONE: 44 28 87727338

FAX: 44 28 87727338

WEB PAGE: NA

E-MAIL: NA

DIRECTIONS TO COURSE: Take the B431 north of Dungannon. The Club is 1 mile out of town, on the right; watch for signs.

SCORECARD

HOLE	YDG	PAR	INDEX
1	477	5	11
2	161	3	15
3	558	5	1
4	341	4	7
5	332	4	13
6	129	3	5
7	488	5	17
8	390	4	3
9	146	3	9
OUT	3,022	36	
10	347	4	12
11	183	3	8
12	492	5	16
13	338	4	2
14	379	4	6
15	283	4	14
16	90	3	18
17	554	5	4
18	358	4	10
IN	3,024	36	
TOTAL	**6,046**	**72**	

Dungannon provides a new clubhouse with bar and grill, changing rooms, and showers. The club has a putting green and small pro shop.

LEVEL OF MAINTENANCE: This is a small, members' course and is maintained to modest standards. There is very little bunkering, but the turf and greens are in good shape.

COURSE DESCRIPTION: Dungannon is a short parkland course with slightly rolling terrain on the front and more hilly terrain on the back 9 holes. Some old trees and many new plantings more often than not are arranged single file and line the fairways. The layout of this course is a little confusing, but excellent strokesaver-variety signage is on the tees. The modest bunkering does not present much of a problem. This would be a good course on which to work on your game.

UNIQUE FEATURE: Dungannon is another fine example of a very old rural course.

ACCOMMODATION INFORMATION

Standard hotel: Inn on the Park (Dungannon), 44 28 87725151

Local hotel/guesthouse/B&B: Cohannon Inn and Auto Lodge (Dungannon), 44 28 87724488

Restaurant/pub: Grange Lodge (gourmet cuisine) (Dungannon), 44 28 87784212

GREEN FEES: Low

EQUIPMENT RENTAL
Buggies: yes
Trolleys: yes
Caddies: no
Clubs: yes

DATE FOUNDED: 1890

ARCHITECTS: Redesigned by Peter Alliss and Dave Thomas

TYPE: Parkland

FACILITIES
Clubhouse at turn: no
Restrooms on course: no

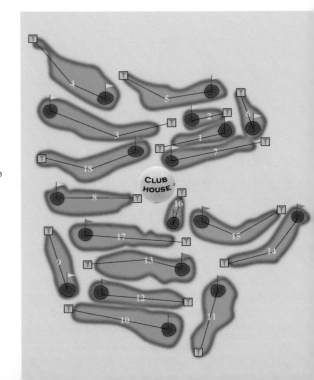

Omagh Golf Club

GREEN FEES:
Low
EQUIPMENT RENTAL
Buggies: no
Trolleys: no
Caddies: no
Clubs: no

DATE FOUNDED: 1891

ARCHITECT: Design of the new 9 by Don Patterson

TYPE: Parkland

FACILITIES
Clubhouse at turn: no
Restrooms on course: no

Omagh offers a small clubhouse with bar and drinks and with snacks on weekends only (no food midweek). There are changing rooms with showers but no pro shop and no equipment for hire.

LEVEL OF MAINTENANCE: This municipal course is maintained to municipal standards, with good greens, adequate fairway turf development, and modest but maintained bunkering.

COURSE DESCRIPTION: This parkland course is divided by the main A5 highway; be careful crossing the road. Four holes contact the River Drumragh, which offers both scenery and difficulty. Like many older courses, Omagh was originally a 9-hole course. The old 9 is crowded and on rolling terrain, with some very interesting side-hill lies; the new 9 is more flat and spacious. The greens, probably the best feature of this course, include some that are gently rolling or undulating, and two that are tiered; all have good putting surfaces. Some mature trees and a great number of new plantings ensure that this course will become more difficult in the future.

UNIQUE FEATURE: The greens are on a 5-year plan of redevelopment. All are to be sand based; thus, the course should improve steadily over time.

ACCOMMODATION INFORMATION
Standard hotel: Silverbirch Hotel (Omagh), 44 28 82242520

Local hotel/guesthouse/B&B: Clanabogan Country House (Omagh), 44 28 82241171

Restaurant/pub: The Mellon Country Inn (Omagh), 44 28 82661224

ADDRESS:
83A Dublin Road,
Omagh, County
Tyrone, Northern
Ireland BT78 1HQ

TELEPHONE:
44 28 82243160

FAX:
44 28 82241442

WEB PAGE: NA

E-MAIL: NA

DIRECTIONS TO COURSE: On the A5 just south of Omagh, the course will be directly off the road, with adequate signage.

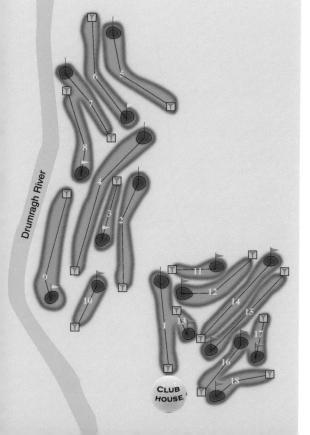

SCORECARD			
HOLE	YDG	PAR	INDEX
1	349	4	5
2	300	4	15
3	216	3	9
4	501	5	13
5	413	4	1
6	545	5	7
7	362	4	6
8	413	4	3
9	335	4	11
OUT	3,441	37	
10	160	3	14
11	283	4	17
12	387	4	4
13	136	3	18
14	424	4	2
15	528	5	10
16	332	4	8
17	178	3	12
18	309	4	16
IN	2,743	34	
TOTAL	6,184	71	

Strabane Golf Club

ADDRESS: 33 Ballycolman Road, Strabane, County Tyrone, Northern Ireland BT82 9PH

TELEPHONE: 44 28 71382271

FAX: 44 28 71382007

WEB PAGE: NA

E-MAIL: NA

DIRECTIONS TO COURSE: Take the A5 to Ballycolman Road, south of Strabane city center, about 1 mile. The course is well signed at Ballycolman Road.

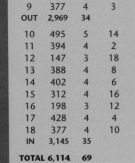

SCORECARD			
HOLE	YDG	PAR	INDEX
1	368	4	7
2	156	3	13
3	461	4	1
4	413	4	5
5	507	5	9
6	327	4	17
7	168	3	15
8	186	3	11
9	377	4	3
OUT	2,969	34	
10	495	5	14
11	394	4	2
12	147	3	18
13	388	4	8
14	402	4	6
15	312	4	16
16	198	3	12
17	428	4	4
18	377	4	10
IN	3,145	35	
TOTAL 6,114		69	

Strabane offers a modest but well-presented clubhouse with a pro shop, two bars, a restaurant, a snooker room, and locker rooms with showers. There is also a putting green.

LEVEL OF MAINTENANCE: This is a very well maintained municipal course that has good turf, greens, and fairways. The building facilities are clean and inviting.

COURSE DESCRIPTION: Strabane is a parkland course with a bit of a strange layout, but it is nonetheless picturesque at the foothills of the Sperrin Mountains and the River Mourne. The river really only affects a few holes but has a particular bearing on the 9th, which requires a specifically placed drive to a 15-yard-wide fairway. This is the course's signature hole and must be played with respect. The course has some nice landscaped areas and is generally fun and visually interesting to play.

UNIQUE FEATURE: The 7th and 8th holes are back-to-back par 3s that require different strategies and different shots; they are interesting by their contrast.

ACCOMMODATION INFORMATION

Standard hotel: Fir Trees Hotel (Strabane), 44 28 71382382

Local hotel/guesthouse/B&B: Mrs. Ballantine's Bed and Breakfast (Strabane), 44 28 71882714

Restaurant/pub: Fir Trees Hotel restaurant (see above), 44 28 71382382

GREEN FEES: Low

EQUIPMENT RENTAL
Buggies: yes
Trolleys: yes
Caddies: not usually
Clubs: yes

DATE FOUNDED: 1908

ARCHITECT: Expanded to 18 holes by Eddie Hackett (1974)

TYPE: Parkland

FACILITIES
Clubhouse at turn: no
Restrooms on course: no

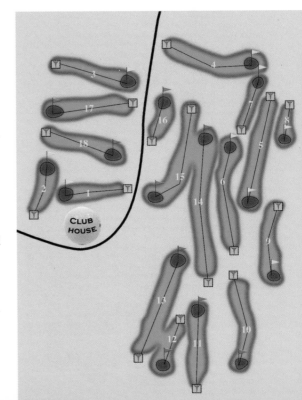

Following is a list of 138 nonfeatured courses, named—again arbitrarily—for Ireland's fast-moving coastal rain showers. For the most part, these are parkland courses; the Trolleys List includes the links courses. Also understand that a Squibs designation is not an implication regarding quality of the course. Rather, these designations have been made for logistical reasons. A course may be on the Squibs List, for example, because we have tried to provide a geographically balanced representation of all the courses throughout Ireland. Thus, of 50 great courses in the Dublin area, we featured only a portion to leave room for courses in the more remote Connemara region. Many of the courses on the Squibs List are as spectacular and extraordinary as some of those on the Trolleys List.

Another thing to keep in mind is that Ireland is undergoing terrific growth in tourism, and golf is one of the big draws. During our 9-month stint, new courses seemed to spring up more frequently than we could track.

Consequently, during your visit, you may encounter courses that appear in neither the Trolleys nor the Squibs List.

The following information is included for each club:

- Golf Club Name
- Town (and, where applicable, postal zone within the town)
- Club telephone number
- Date founded
- Architect(s)
- Hotel
- Hotel telephone number
- Unique feature

In some instances, a club's founding date may be considerably earlier than the architect(s) listed. Many clubs founded in the 19th and early 20th centuries have redesigned their courses or updated them, and thus have a more recent designer or architect. Courses in the Republic of Ireland are listed first, followed by those in Northern Ireland.

The Republic of Ireland

COUNTY CARLOW

See Trolleys List

COUNTY CAVAN

See Trolleys List

COUNTY CLARE

ENNIS GOLF CLUB
Drumbiggle, Ennis
353 65 24074
Founded: 1912
Architect: NA
Hotel: Old Ground Hotel
353 65 6828127
Unique feature: Well-maintained greens

KILRUSH GOLF CLUB
Parknamoney
353 65 1138
Founded: 1934
Architect: Arthur Spring
Hotel: Halpin's Hotel
353 65 9056032
Unique feature: Well-maintained greens

COUNTY CORK

BANDON GOLF CLUB
Killountain
353 23 41111
Founded: 1909
Architect: NA
Hotel: Munster Arms
353 23 41562
Unique feature: Magnificent sylvan setting in the Bandon Valley

CHARLEVILLE GOLF CLUB
Charleville
353 63 81257
Founded: 1909
Architect: Grass Technologies
Hotel: Deer Park Hotel
353 63 81581
Unique feature: Attractive and well-maintained parkland course

DOUGLAS GOLF CLUB
Douglas
353 21 895297
Founded: 1910
Architect: Harry Vardon
Hotel: Dough Cloyne Hotel
353 21 312535
Unique feature: Panoramic views of the Knockmealdown Mountains

EAST CORK GOLF CLUB
Midleton
353 21 631687
Founded: 1969
Architect: Eddie Hackett
Hotel: Commodore Hotel
353 21 811277
Unique feature: One of the first clubs developed from a dairy farm

FERMOY GOLF CLUB
Fermoy
353 25 32694
Founded: 1892
Architect: John Harris

Hotel: Castlehyde Hotel
353 25 31865
Unique feature: Spectacular views of Arondhu countryside

FERNHILL GOLF AND COUNTRY CLUB
Fernhill, Carrigaline
353 21 372226
Founded: 1994
Architect: M. Bowes
Hotel: Fernhill Golf Hotel (on site)
353 21 372226
Unique feature: Unlimited golf from £30; 6 miles from Cork city

HARBOUR POINT GOLF CLUB
Clash, Little Island
353 21 353094
Founded: 1991
Architect: Patrick Merrigan
Hotel: Ambassador Hotel
353 21 551996
Unique feature: Premier championship course; 21-bay all-weather range

KANTURK GOLF CLUB
Fairyhill, Kanturk, Boyle
353 29 50534
Founded: 1972
Architect: R. Berry
Hotel: Assolas Country House
353 29 50015
Unique feature: Views of the Bogeresh Mountains; demands accuracy with its tight fairways and small greens

MAHON GOLF CLUB
Skehard Road, Blackrock
353 21 362480
Founded: 1982
Architect: NA
Hotel: Country Club Hotel
353 21 502922
Unique feature: Municipal course built
on an estuary

MITCHELSTOWN GOLF CLUB
Gurrane, Mitchelstown
353 25 24072
Founded: 1908
Architect: David Jones
Hotel: Fir Grove Hotel
353 25 24111
Unique feature: Plays with backdrop of
the Galtee Mountains

MONKSTOWN GOLF CLUB
Monkstown
353 21 841225
Founded: 1908
Architects: Peter O'Hare and Tom Carey
Hotel: Doughloyne Hotel
353 21 312535
Unique feature: 85 bunkers; several
water hazards; good greens

MUSKERRY GOLF CLUB
Carrigrohane
353 21 385297
Founded: 1895
Architect: NA
Hotel: Blarney Castle Hotel
353 21 385116
Unique feature: Undulating parkland
course; several holes crossing a river

COUNTY DONEGAL

BALLYBOFEY AND STRANORLAR GOLF CLUB
Ballybofey
353 74 31093
Founded: 1958
Architect: Philip Carr
Hotel: Jackson's Hotel
353 74 31021
Unique feature: Stunning views of River
Finn and shores of Lough Alan

DUNFANAGHY GOLF CLUB
Kill, Dunfanaghy
353 74 36335
Founded: 1894
Architect: Harry Vardon
Hotel: Arnold's Hotel
353 74 36208
Unique feature: Commanding views
of Port-na-Blagh on Sheephaven Bay;
designed by legendary Harry Vardon

GREENCASTLE GOLF CLUB
Maghergallon, Derrybeg, Letterkenny
353 75 31140
Founded: 1892
Architect: Eddie Hackett
Hotel: Castle Grove Country House
353 74 51118
Unique feature: Situated along seaside of
Inishowen Peninsula

LETTERKENNY, BARNHILL GOLF CLUB
Letterkenny
353 74 21150
Founded: 1913
Architect: Eddie Hackett
Hotel: Mt. Errigal Hotel

353 74 22700
Unique feature: First 18-hole course
designed by Eddie Hackett

NORTH WEST GOLF CLUB
Lisfannon, Fahan
353 77 61027
Founded: 1892
Architect: Thompson
Hotel: Inishowen Gateway Hotel
353 77 61144
Unique feature: Links course located
near the Mouldy Mountains and Lough
Swilly

COUNTY DUBLIN

BALBRIGGAN GOLF CLUB
Dublin/Belfast Road
353 1 841 2229
Founded: 1945
Architect: Pat Ruddy
Hotel: Ashling Hotel
353 1 677 2324
Unique feature: Challenging parkland
course with fine views of the Mourne
and Cooley Mountains

BALCARRICK GOLF CLUB
Corballis, Donabate
353 1 843 6957
Founded: 1972
Architect: B. Langan
Hotel: Forte Posthouse
353 1 808 0500
Unique feature: Converted to 18 holes
in 1995

BALLINASCORNEY GOLF CLUB
Tallaght, Dublin 24
353 1 451 2775
Founded: 1971
Architect: NA
Hotel: Great Southern Hotel
353 1 844 6000
Unique feature: Overlooks the city of
Dublin and Dublin Bay

BEAVERSTOWN GOLF CLUB
Donabate, Dublin
353 1 843 6439
Founded: 1985
Architect: Eddie Hackett
Hotel: Tir na Nog B&B
353 1 843 6864
Unique feature: Like Augusta National,
this was a fruit orchard; hundreds of
apple trees adorn this course

BEECH PARK GOLF CLUB
Johnstown, Rathcoole
353 1 458 0100
Founded: 1973
Architect: Eddie Hackett
Hotel: Great Southern Hotel
353 1 844 6000
Unique feature: Many mature trees and
water hazards

CASTLE GOLF CLUB
Woodside Drive, Rathfarnham,
Dublin14
353 1 490 4207
Founded: 1913
Architects: Harry S. Colt, Barcroft et al.
Hotel: Bewley's Hotel

353 1 464 0140
Unique feature: 4 miles from Dublin
center; venue for amateur and professional events

CLONTARF GOLF CLUB
Donnycarney House, Malahide Road
353 1 833 1892
Founded: 1912
Architect: Tom Craddock
Hotel: Grand Hotel
353 1 845 0000
Unique feature: original clubhouse
built in 1781; 2½ miles from Dublin
City center

COLD WINTERS GOLF CLUB
Newtownhouse, St. Margarets
353 1 834 1141
Founded: 1994
Architect: NA
Hotel: Clontarf Castle Hotel
353 1 833 2321
Unique feature: 27-hole facility close to
the Dublin Airport

CORRSTOWN GOLF CLUB
Kilsallaghan, County Dublin
353 1 864 0533
Founded: 1933
Architect: Eddie Connaughton
Hotel: Beddington Guesthouse
353 1 497 8047
Unique feature: 18th hole featuring an
island green

DONABATE GOLF CLUB
Balcarrick, Donabate
353 1 843 6346
Founded: 1925
Architect: NA
Hotel: Dunes Hotel
353 1 843 6153
Unique feature: Pleasant course for the
high handicapper

DUBLIN MOUNTAIN GOLF CLUB
Gortlum, Brittas, Dublin
353 1 458 2570
Founded: 1993
Architect: Declan Carroll
Hotel: Tulfarris House Hotel
353 45 867555
Unique feature: New course in close
proximity to Dublin

DUN LAOGHAIRE GOLF CLUB
Tivoli Road, Dun Laoghaire
353 1 280 3916
Founded: 1910
Architect: Harry S. Colt
Hotel: Royal Marine Hotel
353 1 280 1911
Unique feature: One of Ireland's Harry S.
Colt courses

EDMONDSTOWN GOLF CLUB
Edmondstown, Rathfarnham, Dublin 16
353 1 493 2461
Founded: 1944
Architect: McAlister
Hotel: Plaza Hotel
353 1 462 4200
Unique feature: Purported to be one of
the best-appointed clubhouses in Dublin

ELM GREEN GOLF CLUB
Castleknock, Dublin 15
353 1 820 0797
Founded: 1992
Architect: Eddie Hackett
Hotel: Little Chief Hotel
353 1 820 1050
Unique feature: Ireland's largest public golf center; 24-bay all-weather driving range

ELM PARK GOLF CLUB
Elm Park, Nutley House, Donnybrook
353 1 269 3438
Founded: 1925
Architect: NA
Hotel: Abberly Court Hotel
353 1 459 6000
Unique feature: Well-stocked pro shop; stream on 9 holes

FINNSTOWN COUNTRY HOUSE HOTEL AND GOLF
Lucan
353 1 628 0644
Founded: 1990
Architect: Robert Browne
Hotel: Finnstown Country House Hotel
353 1 628 0644
Unique feature: Many trees brought into play on this estate course

GRANGE GOLF CLUB
Whitechurch Road, Rathfarnham, Dublin
353 1 493 2889
Founded: 1910
Architect: NA

Hotel: Adams Trinity Hotel
353 1 670 7100
Unique feature: Near the Dublin Mountains; tree-lined fairways

HERMITAGE GOLF CLUB
Ballydowd, Lucan
353 1 626 8491
Founded: 1905
Architect: NA
Hotel: Finnstown Country House Hotel
353 1 628 0644
Unique feature: Several holes bordered by the River Liffey; good sand-based greens; one of Dublin's most "natural" courses; has hosted several competitons

HOLLYSTOWN GOLF CLUB
Hollystown, Hollywood Rath, Dublin 15
353 1 820 7444
Founded: 1992
Architect: Eddie Hackett
Hotel: Beddington Guesthouse
353 1 497 8047
Unique feature: Many old-growth trees and water hazards

HOLLYWOOD LAKES GOLF CLUB
Ballyboughal, County Dublin
353 1 843 3407
Founded: 1990
Architect: Mel Flanagan
Hotel: Carriage House
353 1 843 8857
Unique feature: Undulating parkland course; 14th hole purported to be the longest in Ireland at 633 yards

KILTERNAN GOLF AND COUNTRY CLUB
Enniskerry Road, Kilternan
353 1 295 5542
Founded: 1987
Architect: Eddie Connaughton
Hotel: Kilternan Club Hotel
353 1 295 5542
Unique feature: Championship course with views over Dublin Bay

LUCAN GOLF CLUB
Cellbridge Road, Lucan
353 1 628 2106
Founded: 1897
Architect: Eddie Hackett
Hotel: Spa Hotel
353 1 628 0494
Unique feature: Challenging course; 18th hole is 587 yards

MALAHIDE GOLF CLUB
Beechwood, The Grange, Malahide
353 1 846 1611
Founded: 1892
Architect: Eddie Hackett
Hotel: Grand Hotel
353 1 845 0000
Unique feature: Championship course with many raised greens bounded by water; gorgeous clubhouse

MILLTOWN GOLF CLUB
Lower Churchtown Road, Dublin 14
353 1 497 6090
Founded: 1907
Architect: Fred Davis
Hotel: Camden Hall Hotel

353 1 475 7906
Unique feature: Convenient location to the suburbs of Dublin

NEWLANDS GOLF CLUB
Clondalkin, Dublin 22
353 1 459 2903
Founded: 1926
Architect: James Braid
Hotel: Clontarf Castle Hotel
353 1 833 2321
Unique feature: Mature parkland designed by one of golf's most renowned designers; a testing course

OPEN GOLF CENTRE
Newtown House, St. Margaret's
353 1 864 0324
Founded: NA
Architect: Martin Hawtree
Hotel: Forte Posthouse
353 1 808 0500
Unique feature: Near the Dublin Airport; driving range; good greens; well-stocked pro shop

RATHFARNHAM GOLF CLUB
Rathfarnham, Dublin
353 1 493 1201
Founded: 1900
Architect: John Jacob
Hotel: Doyle Tara Hotel
353 1 269 4666
Unique feature: Natural-lie greens; mature trees, parkland

SKERRIES GOLF CLUB
Hacketstown, Skerries
353 1 849 1567
Founded: 1905
Architect: NA
Hotel: Redbank House Hotel
353 1 849 1005
Unique feature: Parkland course with undulating terrain

SLADE VALLEY GOLF CLUB
Lynch Park, Brittas
353 1 458 2739
Founded:1970
Architects: P. O'Brien and W. Sullivan
Hotel: Drury Court Hotel
353 1 475 1988
Unique feature: Great views of the Dublin Mountains; suited to all handicaps

STACKSTOWN GOLF CLUB
Kellystown Road, Rathfarnham, Dublin
353 1 494 2338
Founded: 1976
Architect: Shaffreys
Hotel: Grafton Plaza Hotel
353 1 475 0888
Unique feature: Spectacular views of Dublin Mountains and Bay

STEPASIDE PUBLIC GOLF COURSE
Stepaside, County Dublin
353 1 295 2859
Founded: 1980
Architect: Eddie Hackett
Hotel: Rochestown Lodge Hotel
353 1 285 3555
Unique feature: Easily accessible golf course in Dublin

SWORDS OPEN GOLF COURSE
Swords, County Dublin
353 1 840 9819
Founded: 1991
Architect: Tommy Halpin
Hotel: Forte Travelodge
353 1 840 9257
Unique feature: Runs along the banks of the Broadmeadow River

TURVEY GOLF AND COUNTRY CLUB
Turvey Avenue, Donabate
353 1 843 5169
Founded: 1994
Architect: P. McGuirk
Hotel: The Dunes Hotel
353 1 843 6153
Unique feature: Brand-new clubhouse (1999); magnificent old-growth trees on 144-acre parkland course

TYRRELSTOWN, BLANCHARDSTOWN GOLF CENTRE
Tyrrelstown House, Mulhuddart
353 1 821 3206
Founded: NA
Architect: John Young
Hotel: Finnstown Country House Hotel
353 1 628 0644
Unique feature: Floodlit driving range; mature parkland public course

WESTMANSTOWN GOLF CLUB
Clonsilla, Dublin 15
353 1 820 5817
Founded: 1988
Architect: Eddie Hackett

Hotel: Ardagh House
353 1 497 7068
Unique feature: Water hazards featured for 4 holes

COUNTY GALWAY

See Trolleys List

COUNTY KERRY

BEAUFORT GOLF CLUB
Churchtown, Beaufort, Killarney
353 64 44440
Founded: 1993
Architect: Arthur Spring
Hotel: Lake Hotel
353 64·31035
Unique feature: Wonderful setting surrounded by the Kerry Mountains; 13th-century castle dominates back 9

KILLORGLIN GOLF CLUB
Killorglin
353 66 61979
Founded: 1992
Architect: Eddie Hackett
Hotel: Bianconi Inn
353 66 9761146
Unique feature: Located on the Ring of Kerry overlooking Dingle Bay; physically demanding

COUNTY KILDARE

ATHY GOLF CLUB
Geraldine, Athy
353 507 31729
Founded: 1906
Architect: NA

Hotel: Tonlegee House
353 507 31473
Unique feature: River affecting 4 holes; sand-based greens, some 2-tiered

BODENSTOWN GOLF CLUB
Sallins
353 45 897096
Founded: 1973
Architect: Eddie Hackett
Hotel: Annagh Lodge
353 45 433518
Unique feature: Good greens

CASTLEWARDEN GOLF CLUB
Straffan
353 145 89254
Founded: 1990
Architect: NA
Hotel: Kildare Hotel and Country Club
353 160 17200
Unique feature: Great views of the Wicklow Mountains

CRADDOCKSTOWN GOLF CLUB
Bessington Road, Naas
353 45 897610
Founded: 1994
Architect: Arthur Spring
Hotel: Ambassasdor Hotel
353 45 877064
Unique feature: Parkland course spread over 150 acres with 4 lakes

HIGHFIELD GOLF CLUB
Carbury
353 405 31021
Founded: 1992
Architect: Alan Duggan

Hotel: Ballavista B&B
353 405 30179
Unique feature: Family-run, traditional Irish farmhouse hospitality

KILLEEN GOLF CLUB
Kill
353 45 866003
Founded:1986
Architects: Tom Craddock and Pat Ruddy
Hotel: Ambassador Hotel
353 45 877064
Unique feature: Numerous water hazards and good greens

KNOCKANALLY GOLF CLUB
Donadea
353 45 869322
Founded: 1985
Architect: Noel Lyons
Hotel: Glenroyal Hotel
353 1 629 0909
Unique feature: Clubhouse is a grand old mansion; very difficult opening hole

NAAS GOLF CLUB
Kerdiffstown, Nass
353 45 897509
Founded: 1896
Architects: Arthur Spring and Patrick Merrigan
Hotel: Ambassador Hotel
353 45 877064
Unique feature: Parkland course with a good, intuitive layout

NEWBRIDGE GOLF CLUB
Barretstown
353 45 431289
Founded: 1995
Architect: Pat Saltee
Hotel: Anugh Lodge
353 45 433518
Unique feature: Within easy reach of
Dublin

COUNTY KILKENNY

CALLAN GOLF CLUB
Geraldine, Callan
353 56 25136
Founded: 1929
Architect: O. C. M. Associates
Hotel: Headfort Arms Hotel
353 46 40063
Unique feature: 8th hole is a par 3; 155
yards carry over a stream to the green

COUNTY LAOIS

MOUNTRATH GOLF CLUB
Knockinina, Mountrath
353 502 32643
Founded: 1929
Architect: NA
Hotel: Killeshin Hotel
353 502 21663
Unique feature: River flowing through
this lush rolling parkland, coming into
play on 3 holes

PORTARLINGTON GOLF CLUB
Garryhinch, Portarlington
353 502 23044
Founded: 1909

Architect: NA
Hotel: Arlington Tower Hotel
353 502 23225
Unique feature: River and number of
ponds adding challenge and interest

RATHDOWNEY GOLF CLUB
Coulnaboul West, Rathdowney
353 505 46170
Founded: 1930
Architect: Eddie Hackett
Hotel: Leix County Hotel
353 505 41213
Unique feature: Extended to 18 holes in
1997; pleasantly undulating parkland
with a number of very challenging holes

COUNTY LIMERICK

CASTLETROY GOLF CLUB
Castletroy
353 61 335753
Founded: 1937
Architect: Eddie Hackett
Hotel: Castletroy Park Hotel
353 61 335566
Unique feature: 13th tee elevated and
featuring panoramic views; 18th hole a
stern finish

KILLELINE GOLF CLUB
Cork Road, Newcastle West
353 69 61600
Founded: 1950
Architect: John McCoy
Hotel: Devon Inn Hotel
353 69 84122
Unique feature: More than 3,000 mature
trees

LIMERICK GOLF CLUB
Ballyclough, Limerick
353 61 414083
Founded: 1891
Architect: NA
Hotel: South Court Hotel
353 65 6823000
Unique feature: Pleasant, tree-lined
course with no steep hills

COUNTY LONGFORD

See Trolleys List

COUNTY LOUTH

KILLINBEG GOLF AND COUNTRY CLUB
Killin Park, Dundalk
353 42 39303
Founded: 1990
Architect: Eddie Hackett
Hotel: Derryhale Hotel
353 42 9335471
Unique feature: Privately owned course
purported to have excellent drainage

COUNTY MAYO

BALLINA GOLF CLUB
Mossgrove, Shanaghy
353 96 21050
Founded: 1910
Architect: Eddie Hackett
Hotel: Bartra House Hotel
353 96 22200
Unique feature: Abundant wildlife and
birds on parkland course

CLAREMORRIS GOLF CLUB
Castlemagarett, Claremorris
353 94 71527
Founded: 1917
Architect: Tom Craddock
Hotel: Breaffy House Hotel
353 94 22033
Unique feature: Mature parkland course, originally the Castlemagarett estate; several elevated tees and greens

COUNTY MEATH

ASHBOURNE GOLF CLUB
Ashbourne
353 1 835 2005
Founded: 1991
Architect: Des Smyth
Hotel: Ashbourne Hotel
353 1 835 0167
Unique feature: Broadmeadow River and several lakes coming into play on this undulating parkland course

KILCOCK GOLF CLUB
Kilcock
353 1 628 7592
Founded: 1980
Architect: Eddie Hackett
Hotel: Glenroyal Hotel
353 1 629 0909
Unique feature: Two par 4s over 460 yards; just 25 minutes from Dublin

MOORE PARK GOLF CLUB
The Manor, Mooretown, Navan
353 46 27661
Founded: 1993

Architect: Eddie Hackett
Hotel: Ardboyne Hotel
353 46 23119
Unique feature: Near the historic Hill of Tara

COUNTY MONAGHAN

CASTLEBLAYNEY GOLF CLUB
Onomy, Castleblayney
353 42 49485
Founded: 1984
Architect: Robert Browne
Hotel: Glencarn Hotel and Leisure Centre
353 42 9746666
Unique feature: This is a hilly course, with its namesake the Hope Castle

COUNTY OFFALY

CASTLE BARNA GOLF CLUB
Daingean
353 506 53384
Founded: 1994
Architect: Alan Duggan
Hotel: Bridge House Hotel
353 506 21704
Unique feature: Built along the banks of the Grand Canal

COUNTY ROSCOMMON

See Trolleys List

COUNTY SLIGO

See Trolleys List

COUNTY TIPPERARY

CAHIR PARK GOLF CLUB
Kilcommon, Cahir
353 52 41474
Founded: 1968
Architect: Eddie Hackett
Hotel: Kilcoran Lodge Hotel
353 52 41288
Unique feature: The River Suir separating the two halves of the course

CARRICK ON SUIR GOLF CLUB
Carravoone, Carrick on Suir
353 51 640558
Founded: 1939
Architect: Eddie Hackett
Hotel: Carraig Hotel
353 51 641455
Unique feature: Recently redesigned to 18 holes, with the Comeragh Mountains and River Suir Valley surrounding it

CLONMEL GOLF CLUB
Lyneanearla, Mountain Road, Clonmel
353 52 24050
Founded: 1911
Architect: Eddie Hackett
Hotel: Hotel Minella
353 52 22388
Unique feature: Built on the scenic slopes of the Comeragh Mountains

NENAGH GOLF CLUB
Beechwood, Nenagh
353 67 31476
Founded: 1929
Architects: R. Stillwell and J. Paramour

Hotel: Dromineer Bay Hotel
353 67 24114
Unique feature: Playable year-round
because of good drainage; several tiered
greens

TIPPERARY GOLF CLUB
Rathanny
353 62 51119
Founded: 1896
Architect: NA
Hotel: Kilcoran Lodge Hotel
353 52 41288
Unique feature: Beautiful parkland
course situated in the famous Galtee
Mountains

COUNTY WATERFORD

See Trolleys List

COUNTY WESTMEATH

DELVIN CASTLE GOLF CLUB
Clonyn, Delvin
353 44 64315
Founded: 1991
Architect: J. Day
Hotel: Loughcrew House
353 49 41356
Unique feature: Built around Delvin
Castle; an estate course with many old-
growth trees and lakes

MOATE GOLF CLUB
Ballinagarby, Moate
353 902 81271
Founded: 1900
Architect: Robert Browne

Hotel: Grand Hotel
353 902 81104
Unique feature: A narrow course with
good drainage; playable all year

COUNTY WEXFORD

COURTOWN GOLF CLUB
Kiltennel, Gorey
353 55 25166
Founded: 1936
Architects: Harris and Associates
Hotel: Marlfield House Hotel
353 55 21124
Unique feature: A parkland course with
a seaside location and several excellent
par 4s, especially the 18th hole

NEW ROSS GOLF CLUB
Tinneranny, New Ross
353 51 421433
Founded: 1905
Architect: Des Smyth
Hotel: Old Rectory Hotel
353 51 421719
Unique feature: A mature parkland
course with tight fairways

WEXFORD GOLF CLUB
Mulgannon
353 53 42238
Founded: 1961
Architect: H. Stutt
Hotel: Ferrycarrig House
353 53 20999
Unique feature: A mature parkland
course with views of Wexford Harbour,
Blackstairs, and Galtee Mountains

COUNTY WICKLOW

CHARLESLAND GOLF CLUB
Greystones
353 1 287 6764
Founded: 1992
Architect: Eddie Hackett
Hotel: Charlesland Country Hotel
353 1 287 6764
Unique feature: 13th hole, the highest
point on this well-bunkered course;
water hazards on many holes

COOLATTIN GOLF CLUB
Shillelagh, Arklow
353 55 29125
Founded: 1960
Architect: Peter McEvoy
Hotel: Plattenstown House
353 402 37822
Unique feature: Part of an old estate;
recently updated to 18 holes; large old-
growth oak trees featured on the course

DELGANY GOLF CLUB
Delgany
353 1 287 4536
Founded: 1908
Architect: Harry Vardon
Hotel: Glenview Hotel
353 1 287 3399
Unique feature: Designed by Harry
Vardon, one of the most legendary
names in golf

GLENMALURE GOLF CLUB
Greenane, Rathdrum
353 404 46679
Founded: 1993

Architect: P. Suttle
Hotel: Swedish Log Cabins (on site)
353 404 46679
Unique feature: A hilly course with spectacular views of the Wicklow Mountains

GREYSTONES GOLF CLUB
Greystones
353 1 287 6624
Founded: 1895
Architect: NA
Hotel: La Touche Hotel
353 1 287 4401
Unique feature: Wonderful views of the Wicklow coast; view of Wales from the 17th hole on a clear day

ROUNDWOOD GOLF CLUB
Newtownmountkennedy
353 1 281 8488
Founded: 1995
Architects: Smillie, Morgan, and McGuire
Hotel: Bel-Air Hotel
353 404 40109
Unique feature: A heathland course with sand greens built to USPGA standards

TULFARRIS GOLF CLUB
Blessington Lakes
353 45 864574
Founded: 1987
Architect: Patrick Merrigan
Hotel: Tulfarris House Hotel

353 45 867555
Unique feature: Good greens, fairways, and tees; located at the base of the Wicklow Mountains, overlooking Blessington Lakes

WOODENBRIDGE GOLF CLUB
Arklow
353 402 35202
Founded: 1884
Architect: Patrick Merrigan
Hotel: Arklow Bay Hotel
353 402 32309
Unique feature: One of the oldest clubs in Ireland; strategically placed bunkers; meandering rivers throughout

Northern Ireland

COUNTY ANTRIM

ALLEN PARK GOLF CLUB
Allen Park Golf Centre
45 Castle Road, Antrim BT41 4NA
44 28 94429001
Founded: 1996
Architect: Tom MacAuley
Hotel: Dunadry Inn
44 28 94432474
Unique feature: 20-bay floodlit driving range; large leisure facility

BALLYCLARE GOLF CLUB
25 Springvale Road, Ballyclare
44 28 93322696
Founded: 1923

Architect: Tom MacAuley
Hotel: Five Corners Guesthouse
44 28 93322657
Unique feature: Tree-lined fairways; meandering river on several holes

BALLYMENA GOLF CLUB
128 Raceview Road, Ballymena BT42 4HY
44 28 25861487
Founded: 1903
Architect: NA
Hotel: Tullyglass House Hotel
44 28 25652639
Unique feature: A flat moorland course with abundant gorse and heather; St. Patrick's Slemish Mountains to the east

CARRICKFERGUS GOLF CLUB
35 North Road, Carrickfergus BT38 8LP
44 28 93363713
Founded: 1926
Architect: NA
Hotel: Quality Hotel
44 28 93364556
Unique feature: Elevated tee on 1st hole with a shot over a large, intimidating dam; well-maintained but flat course

CUSHENDALL GOLF CLUB
Cushendall
44 28 21771318
Founded: 1937
Architect: D. Delarcy

Hotel: Londonderry Arms
44 28 28885255
Unique feature: The River Dall running through, creating out-of-bounds on 9 holes

DOWN ROYAL GOLF CLUB
Lisburn
44 28 92621339
Founded: 1990
Architect: K. Stewart
Hotel: Silverwood Golf Hotel
44 28 38327722
Unique feature: Playable all year because of naturally draining sandy soil

GREENACRES GOLF CENTRE
153 Ballyrobert Road, Ballyclare
44 28 93354111
Founded: 1996
Architect: NA
Hotel: Templeton Hotel
44 28 92432984
Unique feature: 20-bay floodlit driving range

LAMBEG GOLF CLUB
Aberdelghy, Bells Lane, Lambeg
44 28 92662738
Founded: 1986
Architect: NA
Hotel: Silverwood Golf Hotel
44 28 38327722
Unique feature: Good for medium to high handicappers

LISBURN GOLF CLUB
68 Eglantine Road, Lisburn BT27 5RQ
44 28 92677216
Founded: 1905
Architect: Frederick G. Hawtree
Hotel: White Gables Hotel
44 28 92682755
Unique feature: Many mature trees and water coming into play on this course's undulating terrain

MASSEREENE GOLF CLUB
51 Lough Road, Antrim BT41 4DQ
44 28 94428096
Founded: 1895
Architect: Frederick G. Hawtree
Hotel: Deer Park Hotel
44 28 94462480
Unique feature: Borders Lough Neagh; the front 9 are parkland, and the back 9 resemble a links course

WHITEHEAD GOLF CLUB
McCrea's Brae, Carrickfergus BT38 9
44 28 93353631
Founded: 1904
Architect: NA
Hotel: Quality Hotel
44 28 93364556
Unique feature: Spectacular views of the Mourne Mountains and Ailsa Craig of Scotland

COUNTY ARMAGH

ASHFIELD GOLF CLUB
Freeduff, Cullyhanna BT15
44 28 30868180
Founded: 1990

Architect: Frank Ainsworth
Hotel: Hotel Carlton
44 28 68658282
Unique feature: Many new trees; golf in a rural setting

COUNTY ARMAGH GOLF CLUB
The Demesne, Newry Road, Armagh BT60 1EN
44 28 37525861
Founded: 1893
Architect: NA
Hotel: De Averall Guesthouse
44 28 37511213
Unique feature: The Obelisk, ca.1700s, featured on several holes

EDENMORE GOLF CLUB
Drumnabreeze Road, Craigavon BT67 0RH
44 28 92611310
Founded: 1991
Architect: Frank Ainsworth
Hotel: Ashburn Hotel
44 28 38325711
Unique feature: Old Yard Restaurant on site

LURGAN GOLF CLUB
The Demesne, Lurgan BT67 9BN
44 28 38322087
Founded: 1893
Architect: NA
Hotel: Silverwood Golf Hotel
44 28 38327722
Unique feature: A challenging test for all levels; borders Lurgan Lake; several doglegs and many traps

PORTADOWN GOLF CLUB
192 Guilford Road, Portadown
BT63 5LF
44 28 38355356
Founded: 1900
Architect: Clive Henning
Hotel: Ashburn Hotel
44 28 38325711
Unique feature: A parkland course
incorporating the River Bann

TANDRAGEE GOLF CLUB
Markethill Road, Tandragee BT62 2ER
44 28 38841272
Founded: 1920
Architect: David Jones
Hotel: Drumshill House Hotel
44 28 37522009
Unique feature: The Duke of
Manchester's estate used to develop this
course

CITY OF BELFAST

BALMORAL GOLF CLUB
518 Lisburn Road, Belfast BT9 6GX
44 28 90381514
Founded: 1914
Architect: NA
Hotel: Beechlawn House Hotel
44 28 90612974
Unique feature: A flat parkland course
situated near the Royal Ulster
Agricultural Society; award-winning
clubhouse

DUNMURRY GOLF CLUB
91 Dunmurry Lane BT17 9JS
44 28 90610834
Founded: 1905
Architect: NA
Hotel: Beechlawn House Hotel
44 28 90612974
Unique feature: Offers players of all
handicaps a friendly welcome

FORTWILLIAM GOLF CLUB
Downview Avenue, BT15 4EZ
44 28 90370770
Founded: 1891
Architect: Harry S. Colt
Hotel: Dukes Hotel
44 28 90236666
Unique feature: Significant elevation
changes between front and back 9s;
designed by the legendary Harry S. Colt

KNOCK GOLF CLUB
Summerfield, Dundonald BT16 2QX
44 28 90482249
Founded: 1895
Architects: Colt, Allison, and MacKenzie
Hotel: Stormont Hotel
44 28 90658621
Unique feature: Designed by Alister
MacKenzie, who also designed Augusta
and Royal Melbourne

MOUNT OBER GOLF CLUB
24 Ballymaconaghy Rd, Belfast BT8 4SB
44 28 90401811
Founded: 1969
Architect: NA
Hotel: Dukes Hotel

44 28 90236666
Unique feature: A parkland course overlooking the city of Belfast; driving range
on site

ROCKMOUNT GOLF CLUB
28 Drumalig Road, Carryduff
44 28 90812279
Founded: 1995
Architect: Robert Patterson
Hotel: Pine Lodge
44 28 90814875
Unique feature: A natural drumlin
course with several water features; 10
minutes from Belfast

SHANDON PARK GOLF CLUB
73 Shandon Park BT5 6NY
44 28 90401856
Founded: 1926
Architect: NA
Hotel: Wellington Park Hotel
44 28 90381111
Unique feature: A lush parkland course
in Belfast's eastern suburbs

COUNTY DOWN

BANBRIDGE GOLF CLUB
Huntly Road, Banbridge BT32 34R
44 28 40662211
Founded: 1912
Architect: Frank Ainsworth
Hotel: Downshire Hotel
44 28 40662638
Unique feature: 10th hole, a 221-yard
par 3

BANGOR GOLF CLUB
Bangor BT20 4RH
44 28 91270922
Founded: 1903
Architect: James Braid
Hotel: Clandeboye Lodge Hotel
44 28 91852500
Unique feature: Designed by the renowned James Braid; views of Scotland; hosted the 1993 Irish Amateur Seniors Championships

BRIGHT CASTLE GOLF CLUB
14 Coniamstown Road, Downpatrick
44 28 44841319
Founded: 1970
Architect: A. Ennis Sr.
Hotel: Abbey Lodge Hotel
44 28 44614511
Unique feature: A long course, at 7,143 yards; panoramic views of the Mourne Mountains

CARNALEA GOLF CLUB
Station Road, Bangor BT19 1EZ
44 28 91270368
Founded: 1927
Architect: NA
Hotel: Marine Court Hotel
44 28 91451100
Unique feature: Good views of Scotland; a challenging test; railroad line near 1st hole

DONAGHADEE GOLF CLUB
84 Warren Road, Donaghadee BT21 0PQ
44 28 91883624
Founded: 1899
Architect: NA

Hotel: Clandeboye Lodge Hotel
44 28 91852500
Unique feature: Part links and part parkland; several water hazards; views to Scotland

HOLYWOOD GOLF CLUB
Demesne Road, Holywood BT18 9LE
44 28 90423135
Founded: 1904
Architect: NA
Hotel: Rayanne House
44 28 90425859
Unique feature: Spectacular views across Belfast Lough to Scotland

KILKEEL GOLF CLUB
Mourne Park, Ballyardle, Kilkeel
BT34 4LB
44 28 41765095
Founded:1924
Architects: Lord Babbington and Eddie Hackett
Hotel: Kilmorey Arms Hotel
44 28 41762220
Unique feature: Cohost of British Amateur Championship qualifying rounds in 1999

RINGDUFFERIN GOLF CLUB
Toye, Downpatrick BT30 9PH
44 28 44828812
Founded: 1993
Architect: NA
Hotel: Abbey Lodge Hotel
44 28 44614511
Unique feature: Includes several elevated tees and spectacular views over Strangford Lough

SCRABO GOLF CLUB
233 Scrabo Road, Newtownards
BT23 4SL
44 28 91812355
Founded: 1907
Architect: NA
Hotel: Strangford Arms Hotel
44 28 91814141
Unique feature: Possible to see Scotland, England, and the Isle of Man on a clear day

SPA GOLF CLUB
20 Grove Road, Ballynahinch BT24 8PN
44 28 97562365
Founded: 1907
Architect: Frank Ainsworth
Hotel: Millbrook Lodge Hotel
44 28 97562828
Unique feature: Situated among the famous County Down drumlins, with great views of the Mourne Mountains

WARRENPOINT GOLF CLUB
Lower Dromore Road, Warrenpoint
BT34 3LN
44 28 41753695
Founded: 1893
Architects: Tom Craddock and Pat Ruddy
Hotel: Canal Court Hotel
44 28 30251234
Unique feature: Good variety of holes; not a long course, but demands straight driving; views of Carlingford Mountains

COUNTY FERMANAGH

CASTLEHUME GOLF CLUB
Belleek Road, Enniskillen BT93 7ED
44 28 66327077
Founded: 1991
Architect: Tony Carroll
Hotel: Manor House Country Hotel
44 28 66621561
Unique feature: More than six thousand
trees planted; undulating greens, well-
drained fairways, and large tees

COUNTY LONDONDERRY

FOYLE INTERNATIONAL GOLF CENTRE
12 Alder Road, Londonderry BT48 8DB
44 28 71352222
Founded: 1993
Architect: Frank Ainsworth
Hotel: Beech Hill Country House Hotel
44 28 71349279

Unique feature: A 19-bay, floodlit, covered driving range, and an 18-hole
championship course, along with a 9-
hole par-3 course

ROE PARK GOLF CLUB
Limavaddy, BT49 9LB
44 28 77760105
Founded: 1993
Architect: Frank Ainsworth
Hotel: Radisson Roe Park Hotel
44 28 77722222
Unique feature: Former estate, with
views of Inishowen Peninsula; driving
range on site; the 18th, a stern finish at
423 yards, par 4

COUNTY TYRONE

KILLYMOON GOLF CLUB
200 Killymoon Road, Cookstown
BT80 8TW
44 28 86763762

Founded: 1889
Architect: NA
Hotel: Silverbirch Hotel
44 28 82242520
Unique feature: Woods surrounding
Killymoon Castle

NEWTOWNSTEWART GOLF CLUB
38 Golf Course Road, Omagh BT78 4HU
44 28 82661466
Founded: 1914
Architect: NA
Hotel: Greenmount Lodge Guesthouse
44 28 82841325
Unique feature: Rivers Strule and
Glenelly running through this course,
situated at the base of the Sperrin
Mountains

Itineraries

The following pages are designed to assist you in developing a strategy for scheduling your precious time in Ireland. The best piece of news is that you cannot go wrong, regardless of what you decide. Indeed, if you go to Ireland and just take what fate deals you, you will return home replete with priceless memories.

Most of us, however, like a little more structure, and that is why we have included the following itinerary suggestions. We have tried to keep in mind that we all take different approaches to traveling. For those who appreciate a very tight, rational schedule, we include a number of itineraries that specify each day's destination and where you should be headed by the end of that day. For those who prefer a looser approach, we have included "theme" lists from which you can pick and choose, making your own itinerary. For the most part, this chapter does not include places for overnight accommodation. You will need to consult the information we provide for each club or arrange lodging from your own sources. As with the courses, you must make advance reservations to ensure your first lodging choices. Reservations are essential during the tourist season (May through September), as well as in the off-season, when some places may be closed.

Six day-by-day itineraries suggest daily routes and courses to play, each with a particular focus: Southwest Links,

Northwest Links, Dublin Links, North Links, Old Masters, or Posh. We put these itineraries together based on our experiences and the realities of Irish travel, and we have tried to list venues in reasonable and logical sequences.

In addition to the day-by-day itineraries, we have included four types of course lists:

* Geographical proximity lists suggest possible vacation excursions. These lists can be used to plan golfing trips from 1 to 3 weeks, depending on your inclinations and preferences. The lists are nattily designated as North, East, South, and West.

* Next is a list of courses offering conference/corporate facilities, in case you are planning a golfing holiday that combines work and play.

* We also feature our Famous and Fabulous List. This list includes an assortment of generally agreed-upon Top 20 courses. In compiling this list, we consulted well-respected Irish journalists and golfing professionals. You would not go wrong playing any or all of these courses.

* Finally, we offer an "Irish Experience" List. This is a completely subjective, annotated list of our personal favorites. Some of these courses are unusually "quaint and quirky," and others appear on the more high-profile lists of well-known Irish courses. Each

is wonderfully unique in its own way, and some may be completely unknown to you or your golfing buddies. They await your discovery and fondest memories, just as they did for us.

DAY-BY-DAY ITINERARIES

♣ SOUTHWEST LINKS: 7–10 DAY TRIP

Day 1: Land in Shannon Airport; drive to Lahinch.

Day 2: Play Lahinch Golf Club; drive to Ballybunion.

Day 3: Play Ballybunion Golf Club (both Old and Cashen Courses).

Day 4: Drive to Tralee; play Tralee Golf Club; drive to Dingle.

Day 5; Play Cheann Sibeal Golf Club; sightsee in and around Dingle Peninsula.

Day 6: Drive to Glenbeigh; play Dooks Golf Club; drive to Valencia Island and sightsee.

Day 7: Drive the Ring of Kerry (N70) and sightsee; stop off at Kenmare. If you are desperate to play golf, play the seaside course Ring of Kerry Golf Club near Kenmare.

Day 8: Drive back to Waterville (you will have passed it on your Ring of Kerry drive); play Waterville Golf Links; rest or start your drive back to Lahinch.

Day 9: Drive back to Lahinch or Ballybunion (whichever you prefer); play either again; they are worth it.

Day10: Drive to Shannon; play the Shannon course (parkland) if you have time; fly home.

♣ NORTHWEST LINKS: 14-DAY TRIP

Day 1: Fly into Shannon Airport and drive to Lahinch.

Day 2: Play Lahinch Golf Club (Old Course); drive partway to Ballyconneely.

Day 3: Finish drive to Ballyconneely; play Connemara Golf Club.

Day 4: Drive to Belmullet; play Carne Golf Links.

Day 5: Drive to Enniscrone; play Enniscrone Golf Club.

Day 6: Drive to Sligo; play County Sligo Golf Club.

Day 7: Drive to Donegal; play Donegal Golf Club.

Day 8: Drive to Portnoo: play Narin and Portnoo Golf Club.

Day 9: Drive to Rosapenna; sightsee in this fascinating area.

Day 10: Play Rosapenna Golf Club; drive to Portsalon; play Portsalon Golf Club.

Day 11: Drive back to Donegal; replay Donegal Golf Club.

Day 12: Drive to Sligo; replay County Sligo Golf Club.

Day 13: Drive back to Shannon.

Day 14: Fly home, unless you have time to play the Shannon Golf Club (10 minutes from the airport; not a links, but a good course).

♣ DUBLIN LINKS: 7-DAY TRIP

Day 1: Arrive at Dublin Airport; drive to your accommodations; rest or sightsee.

Day 2: Play Portmarnock Golf Club; play Portmarnock Hotel and Golf Links.

Day 3: Play the Island Golf Club; sightsee.

Day 4: Drive to Brittas Bay; play the European Club.

Day 5: Play the Royal Dublin Golf Club; play St. Anne's Golf Club.

Day 6: Play County Louth Golf Club.

Day 7: If you have time before your flight home, visit some of the many other great courses in and around Dublin. See the County Dublin featured courses for both links and fabulous parkland courses. Fly home.

♣ NORTH LINKS: 10-DAY TRIP

Day 1: Fly into Belfast; rest and sightsee.

Day 2: Drive to Ardglass; play Ardglass Golf Club; drive to Newcastle.

Day 3: Play the Royal County Down Golf Club, twice, or begin your drive to Portrush.

Day 4: Drive to Portrush.

Day 5: Play Royal Portrush (Dunluce Course); play Royal Portrush (Valley Links).

Day 6: Play Portstewart Golf Club; sightsee (don't miss the Giant's Causeway).

Day 7: Play Castlerock Golf Club; drive up to Ballyliffin.

Day 8: Play Ballyliffin Golf Club (Glashedy Links); play Ballyliffin (Old Links).

Day 9: Sightsee in this fascinating area; drive back to Belfast.

Day 10: Slip in one more round before you leave (see either the Trolleys List or Squibs List for the great courses in and around Belfast); fly home.

♣ OLD MASTERS: 14-DAY TRIP

Day 1: Arrive in Dublin Airport; find your hotel; rest or sightsee.

Day 2: Play the Royal Dublin Golf Club, redesigned by Harry S. Colt (1920); drive partway to Newcastle toward Belfast.

Day 3: Complete your drive to Newcastle; play the

Royal County Down Golf Club, designed by Old Tom Morris (1889); drive to Belfast.

Day 4: Play the Royal Belfast Golf Club, designed by Harry S. Colt (1925); drive to and play Belvoir Park Golf Club, also designed by Harry S. Colt (1927).

Day 5: Drive to and play Royal Portrush, Dunluce Course, designed by Harry S. Colt (1929).

Day 6: Play Royal Portrush, Valley Links, designed by Harry S. Colt (1932); drive to Londonderry (aka Derry).

Day 7: Play City of Derry Golf Club, designed by Willie Park Jr. (1911); drive to Rosapenna.

Day 8: Play Rosapenna Golf Club, designed by Old Tom Morris (1893); drive to Bundoran.

Day 9: Play Bundoran Golf Club, designed by Harry Vardon (1894); drive to Sligo.

Day 10: Play County Sligo Golf Club, improved by Harry S. Colt (1920); drive to Galway.

Day 11: Play Galway Golf Club, expanded to 18 holes by Alister MacKenzie (1926); drive to Lahinch.

Day 12: Play Lahinch Golf Club, Old Course, designed by Old Tom Morris (1892), updated by Alister MacKenzie (1927); drive to Mullingar or at least most of the way there.

Day 13: Play Mullingar Golf Club, designed by James Braid (1937); drive to Dublin.

Day 14: If you can, squeeze in one more round (see either the Trolleys List or Squibs List for courses to play in Dublin); fly home.

❧ POSH: 7-DAY TRIP

Day 1: Arrive at Shannon Airport; drive to Adare Manor Hotel for lodging.

Day 2: Play Adare Manor Hotel and Golf Club; drive to Thomastown (south of Kilkenny); stay at Mount Juliet Golf Club Hotel.

Day 3: Play Mount Juliet Golf Club; drive to Tullow; stay at Mount Wolseley Hotel.

Day 4: Play Mount Wolseley Golf Club; drive to Castledermot (just north of Carlow); stay at Kilkea Castle Hotel.

Day 5: Play Kilkea Castle Golf Club; drive to Straffan (just west of Dublin); stay at the Kildare Hotel (The K Club).

Day 6 Play the K Club; drive to Newmarket-on-Fergus (just west of Shannon; this is a long drive); stay at Dromoland Golf and Country Club.

Day 7: Play Dromoland Golf and Country Club; skip over to Shannon Airport; fly home.

FOUR LISTS OF GEOGRAPHICAL PROXIMITY

NORTH

Ballyliffin Golf Club (Glashedy Links)

Belvoir Park Golf Club

Cairndhu Golf Club

Malone Golf Club

Narin and Portnoo Golf Club

Portsalon Golf Club

Portstewart Golf Club

Rosapenna Golf Club

The Royal Belfast Golf Club

The Royal County Down Golf Club

Royal Portrush Golf Club

SOUTH

Cork Golf Club

Dooks Golf Club

Druids Glen Golf Club

The European Club

Fota Island Golf Club

Mount Juliet Golf Club

Old Head Golf Links

Powerscourt Golf Club

Rathsallagh Golf Club

Tralee Golf Club at Barrow

Waterville Golf Links

EAST

Carlow Golf Club

County Louth Golf Club

Druids Glen Golf Club

The European Club

The Island Golf Club

The K Club

Luttrellstown Castle Golf and Country Club

Portmarnock Golf Club

Portmarnock Hotel and Golf Links

The Royal Dublin Golf Club

St. Anne's Golf Club

Slieve Russell Hotel, Golf, and Country Club

WEST

Ballybunion Golf Club (Cashen Course)

Ballybunion Golf Club (Old Course)

Carne (Belmullet) Golf Links

Connemara Golf Club

County Sligo Golf Club

Donegal Golf Club

Enniscrone Golf Club

Killarney Golf and Fishing Club (Killeen Course)

Killarney Golf and Fishing Club (Mahony's Point Course)

Lahinch Golf Club

Westport Golf Club

CONFERENCE/CORPORATE FACILITY LIST

Adare Manor Hotel and Golf Club

Black Bush Golf Club

City West Hotel Conference Centre and Golf Resort

Clandeboye Golf Club

Deer Park Hotel and Golf Courses

Faithlegg Golf Club

Fota Island Golf Club

Galgorm Castle Golf and Country Club

Gold Coast Golf Club

Killarney Golf and Fishing Club

Luttrellstown Castle Golf and Country Club

Mount Wolseley Golf and Country Club

Nuremore Hotel and Country Club

Portmarnock Hotel and Golf Links

Rosapenna Golf Club

St. Helen's Bay Golf and Country Club

St. Margaret's Golf and Country Club

Slieve Russell Hotel, Golf and Country Club

FAMOUS AND FABULOUS LIST

Ballybunion Golf Club (Cashen Course)

Ballybunion Golf Club (Old Course)

Ballyliffin Golf Club (Glashedy Links)

County Louth Golf Club

Donegal Golf Club

Druids Glen Golf Club

The European Club

The Island Golf Club

The K Club

Killarney Golf and Fishing Club (Killeen Course)

Lahinch Golf Club

Mount Juliet Golf Club

Old Head Golf Links

Portmarnock Golf Club

Portstewart Golf Club

The Royal County Down Golf Club

The Royal Dublin Golf Club

Royal Portrush Golf Club (Dunluce Course)

Tralee Golf Club at Barrow

Waterville Golf Links

"IRISH EXPERIENCE" LIST

This list is purely subjective. You may want to pick and choose courses that spark your curiosity. Be sure to consult details for each course as described in this guide.

1. *Lahinch Golf Club* is pure Irish. Very few concessions are made to tourism, even though the course is a tourist attraction. Lahinch Golf Club is proud to be so loved by tourists, but in the end, the best of Lahinch is saved for and savored by the year-round members.

2. *Old Head Golf Links* is the most beautiful venue in which to play golf that anyone could possibly imagine.

Add thousands of years of human history and the fact that it's home to roughly one hundred species of birds, and you have something so spectacular that you may feel like speaking of it only in hushed, reverential tones.

3. **Rosapenna Golf Club** is a working link to the past—and a glorious past indeed. Old Tom Morris laid out the course, James Braid and Harry Vardon worked on it, and that modern master, Pat Ruddy, has left his own indelible stamp. The hotel, before the 1962 fire which destroyed the original structure, was as exclusive and fine as they come. Today, it has dropped the "exclusive" and just concentrates on the "fine," as determined by the classy owner, Frank Casey, son of the last head waiter of the hotel's prefire grandeur.

4. **Cairndhu Golf Club** is simply a fantastic Irish Experience. The staff and members of the club are warm and friendly, the facilities clean and unpretentious, and the golf challenging but fair. Finally, the vista on the 2nd and 3rd holes at Cairndhu would rival that found at any golf course in the world.

5. **Portsalon Golf Club** is yet another reason for flying thousands of miles to get to Ireland. The course, with its great views and challenging holes, is as quirky as anything you will ever play. Keep in mind that the course does not intend to be quirky. It just is, and therefore is completely genuine and totally unforgettable.

Not a lot of tourists visit this venue, so you will probably be lucky enough to run into some of the fine folks who make up the membership.

6. **Gort Golf Club** is one of Ireland's best-kept little secrets. You are not likely to run into hordes of tourists; you might, however, think you've discovered an enchanted forest populated with Ireland's famous fairies and elves. This is a fine, well-designed, modern parkland course.

7. **Ballybunion Golf Club (Cashen Course)** lies in the shadows of the Old Course but is arguably a wonder unto itself. Consider that no less a talent than Robert Trent Jones Sr. designed this course and called it his best work. The locals, for the most part, do not care for the "new course" because it does not permit their bump-and-run game. Given the elevated greens of Jones's design, the locals are right. And if the wind is blowing, heaven help those golfers trying to attack the greens from the air. Cashen is a tough, beautiful course that gives you all you could hope for (or fear) in an Irish links course.

8. **The Island Golf Club** was founded in 1890 by a group of Dublin bachelors, whose original approach to "the island" was by boat, thus ensuring their privacy. Pooling their financial and creative resources, they created a great links golf course. It is challenging, breathtaking in its beauty, and, in places, positively frightening.

9. **The Royal Belfast Golf Club** drips "venerable." It was designed by Harry S. Colt and is truly a gem of a parkland course. The clubhouse is a piece of history unto itself and has the feel of a private museum. Keep your eyes peeled—you may be surprised to see some priceless golfing memorabilia in the ancient clubhouse.

10. **The Royal County Down Golf Club** is a stunning example of Man and Nature putting forth their best in perfect harmony. As you play, you may find yourself looking around, unaware that you are walking a golf course except for the occasional pin and flag. And, oh! Those bunkers! Called "features," they are simply the most beautiful natural bunkering you will ever see, anywhere.

11. **The European Club** is a golf links as wonderful as the owner, Pat Ruddy, is quirky and independent. Both are in a league of their own, and neither should be missed if at all possible. Mr. Ruddy dedicates some of the holes of his course to some of golf's greats, which is fitting, because a few of those holes are the best anywhere in the world.

12. **County Sligo Golf Club** has the best clubhouse-course combination in Ireland. The clubhouse has wooden floors that literally groan and creak as you trod across them. The pictures and memorabilia are presented naturally and without fanfare. You may feel that you are playing "the game" in an atmosphere that has remained unchanged through the ages. The course itself is exhilarating and was designed by the legendary Harry S. Colt. Finally, the staff at this club is wonderful and extremely helpful.

13. **Portmarnock Golf Club** is another old, venerable club with a terrific pedigree. Great tournaments have been played on its fabulous links. Mr. Joe B. Carr, Ireland's greatest amateur, grew up on the course while his parents ran it for many years. This is a tough course, but well worth the time and effort. Because it sits out on a relatively flat promontory, you will always be buffeted by winds. Relax in the clubhouse afterward, and soak in the old leather, wood patina, and gentility of this stately course.

14. **Narin and Portnoo Golf Club** offers up a tremendous plate of absolutely unique golf. It may take you a couple of tries to find the place, and you may need to stop and ask directions, but you will be richly rewarded. You will need to trust your eyes even though you think, at first, they are deceiving you. For example, as you enter the course through the cattle gate, you will notice the practice green surrounded by electrified fencing. The reason for this quickly becomes apparent as you look out over the course to discover that you will be sharing it with a number of four-legged "locals." This is old-world links golf at its best, and this club is truly an Irish Experience.

Glossary

The following words and phrases are unique to the Irish lexicon. Knowing about them ahead of time may be helpful, or at least entertaining.

"Are you OK?": A standard phrase, especially in the area of service, meaning, "Can I help you?"

bap: A small, French bread–style dinner roll often found in little convenience shops and restaurants.

bend: A term describing a curve in the road.

biscuit: A cookie.

blackspot: A term of the highway meaning hidden danger ahead; usually on roadway signs; hardly ever used in daily language.

Bord Fáilte: The Irish Tourist Board; a very active entity, with central offices in Dublin; it operates the Tourist Information Centres (watch for the *"i"* signs in practically every town), where you will find lodging information, along with pamphlets on things to see and do in the area; extremely helpful staff.

buggy: On the Irish golf course, an engine-powered cart; still rather unusual except on the newer courses; a physician's certificate is needed to arrange for one.

bump and run: A type of golf shot played by pitching one's ball into a bank and letting it run up toward the hole.

camogie: The women's form of the sport hurling. *See also* hurling.

caravan park: One of the ubiquitous parking areas for travel trailers found all over Ireland, sometimes in the most scenic spots and around many golf courses; often the home territory of "travelers." *See also* travelers.

Carr, Joe B.: One of Ireland's golfing greats. He is a past captain of the Royal and Ancient Golf Club of St. Andrews and represented Ireland ten times in the Walker Cup; he has won the British Amateur Open three times (1953, 1958, 1960) and the Irish Amateur Open four times (1946, 1950, 1954, 1956).

castor sugar: Granulated sugar.

catering facilities: Same as restaurant facilities; can designate a range of services, from snacks to full meals.

ceili band: One of the traditional Irish music bands, most famous in County Clare.

Celtic: The culture that originated in Ireland and then crossed the Irish Sea over to Scotland; the language is called *Gaelic*. *See also* Gaelic.

chemist: Pharmacist.

chips: French fries.

clamp: A gigantic metal gizmo attached to the front wheel of a car parked in an unauthorized spot or with an unpaid meter. Car driver, be warned!

Colt, Harry S. (1869–1951): Renowned English golf course architect. Notable courses include Eden Course at St. Andrews and Muirfield in Scotland; Pine Valley, New Jersey, in the United States; Rye, Sunningdale, and Wentworth in England; and County Sligo and Rosapenna in Ireland.

competition: A tournament. You will hear, for example, "There will be a competition held here this weekend."

confectionary: A bakery that specializes in "sweets" (cakes and pies); a regular "bakery" deals with breads.

cooker: A stove or range; its "hob" is the top part with the electric plates for cooking pans.

craic (pronounced "crack"): Good, spirited conversation, especially in pubs. Craic is taken seriously in Ireland and is often laced with funny stories, anecdotes, and tales. A "good craic" is not a drug reference.

crawler lane: A term of the road meaning slow lane, usually when three lanes are present.

dear: Expensive.

dual carriageway: A four-lane "highway" with central median; rather unusual in Ireland.

Eire: Ireland

en suite: Any accommodation in which the bathroom is part of the room and is not shared with other guests.

Euro: The new monetary system that Ireland will adopt by 2003; rather than the pound, the Euro will be the unit of exchange, shared by the European Community.

European Community: A group of eleven European countries, including the Republic of Ireland; to date, the United Kingdom has not joined.

Fianna Fail: "Soldiers of Destiny"; one of the Republic of Ireland's political parties, in existence since Irish independence in 1926; established by a famous Irishman, Eamon de Valera (1882–1975). This party, along with Fine Gael and the Labour parties, dominates Irish politics.

filtered coffee: Either coffee brewed using fresh grounds or instant coffee made in a large machine; somewhat confusing.

Fine Gael: "United Ireland"; one of the Republic of Ireland's political parties, formed in 1933. This party, along with Fianna Fail and the Labour parties, dominates Irish politics.

football: Soccer.

fourball: The same as a foursome; a "twoball" would be a twosome, and so on.

full Irish breakfast: Typical fare offered anywhere you stay: eggs prepared any style, often served with fried bread, juice, sautéed tomato and mushrooms, rasher (i.e., bacon) and/or blood or link sausage, and toast and jams.

Gaelic (Gaeltacht): The traditional Irish language, also known as "Irish." Although children in all primary schools learn Gaelic, few adults know it. Irish is spoken as the first language in a number of regions throughout Ireland: throughout the Connemara area in County Galway and in pockets throughout Counties Mayo, Meath, and Kerry. *See also* Irish.

galif (or golf) chumann: Gaelic ("Irish") for "golf course," especially seen on signs in the Connemara area and southeastern and southwestern Ireland.

gammon: Ham.

gazumped: A word meaning something along the lines of "hoodwinked"; most commonly used in reference to a buyer who offers to purchase some item at an agreed-upon cost and then, when the actual time of purchase occurs, finds that the seller has increased the price.

Golfing Union of Ireland (GUI): The major unifying body of all golf clubs throughout both the Republic of Ireland and Northern Ireland. It has been traditionally divided into the following four provinces and their counties: In the Republic, Connacht (Counties Galway, Leitrim, Mayo,

Roscommon, and Sligo), Munster (Counties Clare, Cork, Kerry, Limerick, Tipperary, and Waterford), and Leinster (Counties Carlow, Dublin, Kildare, Kilkenny, Laois, Longford, Louth, Meath, Offaly, Westmeath, Wexford, and Wicklow). The final province, Ulster, has counties in both the Republic and Northern Ireland. In the Republic are the Counties Cavan, Donegal, and Monaghan; in Northern Ireland, Counties Antrim, Armagh, Down, Fermanagh, Londonderry, and Tyrone.

guardai (pronounced "gardee"): Police (state and local) in the Republic of Ireland.

Guinness: A most extraordinary brew that originated in Ireland; a dry stout. The harp is its trademark. Be sure to let the "head" settle before drinking; if you don't, it's considered gauche. Two other well-known Irish stouts are Beamish and Murphy's (both produced in County Cork).

Hackett, Eddie (1910–1996): Ireland's most prolific golf course designer. He is practically a saint in Irish golfing circles. *See also* chapter 4, "Early Golf Architects."

"half nine": A way of stating the time of day. In this case, 9:30 (a.m. or p.m.). "Half eleven" would mean ll:30, and so on.

hire: To rent.

hurling: Ireland's national game; a cross between football, basketball, lacrosse, golf, and sprinting. Wild and woolly, it has to be seen to be believed. *See also* camogie.

icing sugar: Powdered sugar.

Irish: A term for the Gaelic language. The following are some assorted Irish terms you may encounter on some of the golf courses: *achar* (yards), *amach* (out), *inneacs* (index), *iomlan* (total), *isteach* (in), and *poll* (hole). *See also* Gaelic.

Irish Republican Army (IRA): A paramilitary group with some connection to Sinn Fein; espouses pro-Catholic rule and no British governing of Northern Ireland. *See also* Sinn Fein.

jumper: Sweater.

keen: (1) Inexpensive, or "a good value." (2) To be eager.

lazybeds: Pre- and post-Famine cultivation ridges created for potato growing and production. These ridges are often seen running downhill or spanning flat fields. They are also evident on many golf courses, where the terrain has been less cultivated.

to let: To lease (as in "letting a house").

links course: A golf course laid out on naturally occurring sand dunes with a thin topsoil layer; very different from parkland, moorland, or seaside courses. *See also* Chapter 5, "What about Linksland?"

loose chippings: A term referring to loose gravel on a road; often laid down during road repairs.

lorry: Any type of truck, especially one for delivering goods.

Loyalist (Unionist): An individual living in Northern Ireland who prefers ties with Great Britain rather than Republic of Ireland home rule.

margin: A shoulder of a road.

mince: Hamburger.

"Mind the…": Phrase meaning "Be careful of the…" (e.g., "Mind the step [or door]"—Be careful of the step [or door]").

moorland course: A rather vague term, but usually refers to a course built on natural peat or bogs; subject to drainage problems during heavy rain. *See also* chapter 5, "What about Linksland?"

Morris, Old Tom (1821–1908): A great Scottish golfer and architect who won four Open Championships, made sought-after clubs and balls, and was the greenkeeper at Prestwick and St. Andrews; Old Tom designed the original links at Lahinch, along with parts of Ballybunion, Rosapenna, Royal County Down, and Royal Portrush. *See also* chapter 4, "Early Golf Architects."

motorway: A limited-access dual highway.

Nationalist (Republican): A supporter of Northern Ireland being part of the Republic of Ireland rather than under British rule.

Northern Ireland: Part of the island of Ireland under British rule; includes Counties Antrim, Armagh, Down, Fermanagh, Londonderry, and Tyrone. Its prime minister has a seat in the British Parliament. It is a separate country from the Republic of Ireland, with the same monetary system as Britain.

O'Connor, Christy, Jr.: One of Ireland's great golfers. He hit "the shot" in the 1989 Ryder Cup victory over Freddie Couples, which was the final match that beat the United States that year. He has now progressed to become a great golf course designer and plays on the U.S. Senior Tour.

off license: Liquor store.

parkland course: A type of golf course found over most of Ireland, very similar to the inland courses of the United States.

petrol: Gasoline.

pint: A term commonly used for a glass of beer; approximately 20 ounces.

pitch-and-putt golf: A form of golf consisting of a downsized par-3 course, played with only two clubs; has a rather rabid following and even uses its own sanctioned balls, though they are identical to those used for regular golf. These small courses can be found anywhere an enterprising individual decides to set one up.

plaice: A white fish often fried and served with "chips" (French fries).

"play off": A term used to refer to a handicap; thus, "What do you play off?" means "What is your handicap?"

porridge: Oatmeal, often somewhat runny.

Post, the: The postal service.

pram: A baby carriage. Irish mothers are out in any kind of weather with their babies.

rasher: A thick piece of bacon; closest approximation would be Canadian bacon; usually lightly fried and noncrispy; primary ingredient in the full Irish breakfast.

refuse tip: A dumpster.

Republic of Ireland: An independent state, not part of the United Kingdom, with its own parliament; a member of the European Community since 1973.

revetted bunker: A type of bunker often found on classic links courses; characterized by strips of sod, 3–4 inches thick and several feet long, stacked up the steep sides of the bunkers.

roundabout: A road configuration that is circular, used in lieu of stoplights (except for busy roundabouts, which also have stoplights) and designed to feed traffic onto various intersecting roadways. Confusing at first, roundabouts are especially helpful when you are lost, because you can keep circling until you figure out which exit to take. Common in both Great Britain and Ireland.

Royal Ulster Constabulary (RUC): The police force in Northern Ireland.

seaside course: A golf course found on the seaside, but not necessarily a classic links course; often with stunningly spectacular views of the ocean.

session: A vernacular term for a spontaneous musical evening late at night in pubs throughout Ireland.

Sinn Fein: "Ourselves Alone"; a modern-day Republic of Ireland political party central to the "Irish-Ireland" nationalist movement; founded in 1905.

Sláinte (pronounced "Slawnt-yee"): Gaelic ("Irish") toast meaning, "To your health," or "Cheers!"

slan: Gaelic ("Irish") term meaning "good-bye."

secretary: For most golf clubs, the club manager or head administrator.

society: A group of the members of a golf course who meet regularly and often travel to formally scheduled tournaments. Most golf courses have a day set aside for "societies only" tournament play, during which there are no tee times for nonmembers. This is yet another reason to call ahead.

solicitor: An attorney, often one who deals with real estate.

sparkling water: Bottled carbonated water.

squib: A brief, often windy rain shower in a coastal area. Squibs can usually be seen sweeping inland from the ocean and are frequent enough to make you carry your rain gear at all times while in Ireland.

Stableford: A method used to score most Irish competitions, with specific points awarded for eagles (4), birdies (3), pars (2), bogeys (1), and double-bogeys (0).

still water: Noncarbonated bottled water.

surgery: A doctor's or dentist's office (not "surgery" in the American sense).

take-away: Fast food to go.

Taoiseach (pronounced "Teesh-hook"): The Prime Minister of the Republic of Ireland, with an office based in the capital of Dublin. This political role is distinguished from the president of Ireland, a more titular role.

toasty: A common form of lunch sandwich, with grilled or toasted bread, found in most pubs. Fillings can be combinations of ham, cheese, tomato, and onion.

travelers (aka tinkers): A historic group of gypsies who got their name from mending tin products. They live in trailers, or "caravans," often on the side of public roads. Communities are searching for ways to more permanently locate these itinerant groups in what are called "halting sites."

trolley: A pull cart for golf clubs; found on all Irish courses.

troubles: Euphemism for political unrest (often violent) between Irish Catholics and Protestants in Northern Ireland. This issue is definitely not a topic for casual conversation.

tuck shop: A term for a "snack shop," used primarily in Northern Ireland and throughout the rest of the United Kingdom. In the Republic of Ireland, to "tuck" is to sit down and eat a serious meal.

tuition: Golf lessons given by a pro at a golf course.

United Kingdom: The countries governed by England; also called Great Britain. Countries are England, Wales, Scotland, and Northern Ireland.

value-added tax (VAT): A 21 percent tax added onto goods such as books, adult clothing, china, glassware, linens, and other items. It is not added onto children's clothing, food, meals, accommodations, car rental, or personal services.

veg soup: The most common soup served in Ireland, consisting of puréed vegetables in a light broth or cream base.

W/C: A water closet, also known as a toilet or "loo."

Wellies: A ubiquitous type of knee-high rubber boot seen on city folk and farmers alike.

Master List of 291 Courses

This alphabetized list includes all **Trolleys courses** (boldface) and *Squibs courses* (italics).

Index

Notes